Guiding Young Children

Fifth Edition

VERNA HILDEBRAND
Michigan State University

Macmillan College Publishing Company
New York

Maxwell Macmillan Canada
Toronto

Maxwell Macmillan International
New York Oxford Singapore Sydney

Editor: Kevin M. Davis
Production Editor: Christine M. Harrington
Art Coordinator: Ruth A. Kimpel
Text Designer: Marilyn Wilson Phelps
Cover Designer: Thomas Mack
Production Buyer: Jeff Smith
Electronic Text Management: Ben Ko, Marilyn Wilson Phelps

This book was set in Century Schoolbook by Macmillan College Publishing Company and was printed and bound by R. R. Donnelley & Sons Company. The cover was printed by Phoenix Color Corp.

Macmillan College Publishing Company
866 Third Avenue
New York, New York 10022

Macmillan College Publishing Company is part of the
Maxwell Communication Group of Companies.

Maxwell Macmillan Canada, Inc.
1200 Eglinton Avenue East, Suite 200
Don Mills, Ontario M3C 3N1

Library of Congress Cataloging-in-Publication Data
Hildebrand, Verna.
 Guiding young children / Verna Hildebrand.—5th ed.
   p. cm.
 Includes bibliographical references and index.
 ISBN 0-02-354518-6
 1. Education, Preschool. 2. Teacher-student relationships.
 3. Child rearing. I. Title.
 LB1140.2.H52 1994
 372.21—dc20   93-18438
                    CIP

Printing: 1 2 3 4 5 6 7 8 9 Year: 4 5 6 7

To my husband, John; to our children, Carol and Steve; to the many children from whom I have learned so much in the child care centers, nursery schools, and kindergartens with which I have been associated; but, especially to all children of this planet we share as a home. As communicated so beautifully in the following poem by Mamie Gene Cole, the quality of life tomorrow on our planet will be determined by these children.

I Am the Child

I am the child.
All the world waits for my coming.
All the earth watches with interest to see what I shall become.
Civilization hangs in the balance,
For what I am, the world of tomorrow will be.

I am the child.
I have come into your world, about which I know nothing.
Why I came I know not;
How I came I know not.
I am curious; I am interested.

I am the child.
You hold in your hand my destiny.
You determine, largely, whether I shall succeed or fail.
Give me, I pray you, those things that make for happiness.
Train me, I beg you, that I may be a blessing to the world.

—from "Child's Appeal," by Mamie Gene Cole

Preface

Guiding Young Children is designed for use by college students who are learning to communicate with and interact with young children in infant and child care centers, nursery schools, preprimary groups, or at home. Using a developmental approach, *Guiding Young Children* is designed to be a suitable textbook for classroom use in any of the departments of community colleges or universities that offer courses in child care or in early childhood education. The emphasis is on the process of guiding and teaching young children—the interactional communication opportunities of caregivers, teachers, parents, and children themselves to develop the human potential of children.

The fifth edition of *Guiding Young Children* has been extensively revised and updated. A new chapter has been added to help students learn more about promoting children's self-esteem. The chapter on guiding infants and toddlers reflects the growing interest in and demand for care of the youngest children. Observation guides are included in each chapter to serve in courses where some focus is on teaching observational skills. Concepts are listed in the introduction to each chapter to help focus attention on them. The Center Accreditation Project of the National Association for the Education of Young Children (NAEYC) has been highlighted throughout the book along with an emphasis on developmentally appropriate procedures. Methods of evaluating individuals and programs continue to be emphasized to help faculty, students, and others appreciate high-quality standards for early childhood education programs. Many new photos from exemplary programs across the country enliven the pages of the book.

Throughout this country and in other countries, too, there is growing pressure to provide more center care for infants and young children. There is also a pressing need to improve the quality of many of the present programs, making them fulfill social-psychological and educational needs of children. As enrollment of children increases, more and more qualified teachers and caregivers are needed. In addition, there is a need to upgrade a growing cadre of volunteers who give their time and talent in working with young children.

Whether working in small groups of children as in family day care homes or in larger centers, these newcomers to the child care tasks are seeking help. They are asking about ways to handle the ordinary routines, about avoiding or handling behavior problems, and about teaching concepts to young children.

Guiding Young Children offers the student, teacher, assistant, or volunteer basic guidelines to follow in guiding and teaching infants and young children. It offers help in understanding the commonly observed behavior of young children. Suggestions are made for guiding children during all the routines and during the typical learning activities of the school—art, science, literature, language, music, dramatic play, and outdoor play.

The content of the book will be useful for developing the competencies outlined in the Child Development Associate Program (CDA). Also, parents and individuals involved in courses in parenting will find helpful suggestions throughout the book.

Developmental principles and research findings are the basis for guidance suggestions. This book grew out of many years' experience teaching in child care centers, nursery schools, and kindergartens and in guiding college students and Head Start teachers in learning and practicing principles and techniques of interacting with children. It answers questions posed in consultations with child care teachers and directors.

This new edition has been reorganized and rewritten in the hope of perfecting the product. However, I wish explicitly to encourage all instructors using *Guiding Young Children* to apply their ingenuity to adjusting the sequence of topics, to filling gaps, and to clarifying information provided so as to fit best their personal teaching preferences and to offer the best course of study possible for the needs of their particular groups of students.

For additional information, instructors and students may wish to refer to current editions of other books I've authored: *Parenting: Rewards and Responsibilities* (Glencoe/Macmillan/McGraw-Hill, 1994); *Management of Child Development Centers* (third edition, Macmillan, 1993); *Introduction to Early Childhood Education* (fifth edition, Macmillan, 1991); *A Laboratory Workbook for Introduction to Early Childhood Education* (fifth edition, Macmillan, 1991); and *Parenting and Teaching Young Children* (fourth edition, Glencoe/McGraw-Hill Book Company, 1990).

ACKNOWLEDGMENTS

For this fifth edition I renew my debt of gratitude to many individuals. For the insights gained from Leone Kell, Kansas State University, who was my first child guidance instructor; for the inspiration of Catherine Landreth, University of California at Berkeley, who enlivened her classes with anecdotes from lively children in the nursery schools where I was a graduate assistant; and for the support from Virginia Messenger Stapley, Oklahoma State University, who supervised this young instructor in a comfortable fashion that left much room for creativity in developing programs for young children—I am truly grateful.

I am indebted to Helen Hostetter, Kansas State University, who encouraged my early writing of information for the practitioners of the art and science of early child development and education. I wish to thank Estelle Wallace of Texas Tech University and Kenneth Cannon of Brigham Young University and formerly of Texas Tech University; Jessie Bateman Barns and Dora Tyer of Texas Woman's University; and Beatrice Paolucci, Margaret Jacobson Bubolz, Linda Nelson, Eileen Earhart, and Robert Griffore of Michigan State University, who have also encouraged my writing.

To colleagues, professors, students, children, and parents at these various universities, those of the public child care program and kindergarten of Albany, California, and those at Michigan State University and Texas Tech University where I have taught a variety of courses and groups of children in the laboratory nursery schools and kindergartens, I express my thanks for a stimulating environment.

Recognition is due a number of colleagues who have read and reacted to all or portions of the manuscripts of the various editions. They are Rebecca Peña Hines, Texas Southern University; James Walters, University of Georgia; William E. Martin, Purdue University; Sandra Morris, Mississippi State University; Phyllis Lueck, Dearborn Public Schools; Janice Altadonna, Bernice Borgman, Vera Borosage, Margaret Bubolz, Frances Kertesz, Beatrice Paolucci, Lillian Phenice, Marjory Kostelnik and Eric Gentile, Michigan State University; Deanna J. Radeloff, Bowling Green University; Nancy B. Dalrymple, Colorado State University; Mary Gray, University of Missouri—Columbia; Glenda Colton Strange, Dodge City Community College; Elizabeth Jane Rowe, Eastfield Community College; Joan Raven, Cloud County Community College; and Barbara Taylor, Brigham Young University.

For photographs for the various editions I am indebted to directors, teachers, students, parents, and children in many children's groups. I want to thank photographers Ed Breidenbach, Lee Butcher, Donna Creasy, Mary Gray, Roberta Hay, Eddie Hildreth, Rebecca Peña Hines, Joe Kertesz, Connie Lisiecki, Mary Odell, William Mitcham, James Page, Margot Hellerman and Gerald Seelhoff. Also, Flemmie Kittrell's contribution of pictures from a project at Howard University is gratefully acknowledged. Barbara Beebe, Dodge City Community College Child Care Center; Edith Bradford, Everett High School, Lansing, Michigan; Faye Ann Presnal, Kansas State University; Kathryn Madera, Iowa State University; Sister Marie Hopkins, Marygrove College of Detroit; William Mitcham, Vera Borosage, Suzanne Gyeszly, Jo Ann Evers, Michele Kimmel Fors, Carol Austin, Gayle and Lawrence Schiamberg, Michigan State University; Berta Victoria, Oscar Muñoz, Janet Blumenthal, and Rebecca Peña Hines, Parent-Child Development Center, Houston; Bernadette Haschke, Metropolitan State College, Denver; Betty Jane Larson and Joyce Digby, San Antonio College; Margaret Browning, San Diego City College; Theda Connell, Southeast Oakland Vocational Education Center, Royal Oak, Michigan; Norma Gray, Region III Children's Services, Huntington, West Virginia; Pauline Turner, Southwest Texas State University, San Marcos; Barbara Jackson and Diane Hehn, Texas Woman's University; Hannah Lou Benett, University of Hawaii; Queenie Mills, University of Illinois; Janet Allen, University of Minnesota Technical College; Suzanne Strommen, Eleanor Duff, Jeannie James, University of South Carolina; Johanna Hulls, University of Texas-Austin; and Kay Koulouras and Rita Boesky, Perry-Kay Nursery School, Southfield, Michigan.

For the fifth edition, acknowledgment is due Joan Raven Robison, Cloud County Community College; Linda Herring, Beekman School; and Mary Beaubien, Youngstown State University; who have read all or portions of the manuscript. For photographs, acknowledgment is due Beverly Briggs, Kansas State University; Elizabeth Seelhoff Byrum, Calhoun School; Donna Chitwood, Metropolitan State University; Ruth Davis, Oakwood College; Craig Hart, Louisiana State University; Karen Liu, University of Minnesota-Waseca; Debbie Steinberg, University of Illinois; Kevin Swick, University of South Carolina; James Walters, University of Georgia; Karen Winston, Sinclair Community College; Marjory Kostelnik, Laura Stein, Donna Howe, Barbara Rohde, Kitty Payne, Duane Whitbeck, and Grace Martin, Michigan State University; and David Kostelnik, photographer.

For the fifth edition, I am grateful for the additional photos of lively children secured through the cooperation of children's parents and the following early childhood professionals: Sharon Nichols and Sharon Price, The University of Georgia; Martha Childers, Janet Yost, and Rick Haye, Marshall University; Ruth Davis, Oakwood College; Bernadette Haschke, Baylor University; James Moran and Kathy Carlson, The University of Tennessee; Brent McBride, University of Illinois; Carolyn Rafter, Savannah Public Schools; Vicki Spellman and Marge Hopper, Methodist Hospital Child Care Center; and photographers Ishen Li, Susan Russell, and Carol Hildebrand. For this fifth edition, thanks also go to Kevin Davis, editor, and reviewers Deborah A. Jump, Auraria Higher Education Center; Lois Klezmer, Dade Community College; Karen Stephens, Illinois State University; Jill M. Uhlenberg, University of Northern Iowa; and Barbara Gibson Warash, West Virginia University.

Contents

CHAPTER 3

Guiding Young Children Directly Toward Self-Direction   45

CHAPTER 4

Guiding Children Toward Positive Self-Esteem   73

CHAPTER 5
Guiding Infants and Toddlers 91

CHAPTER 6
Introducing a Child to a New Group of Children 115

CHAPTER 7
Scheduling Activities to Meet Children's Needs 129

CHAPTER 8
Guiding Children's Toileting Routine 147

CHAPTER 12
Guiding Children on the Playground   **203**

CHAPTER 13
Guiding Children's Art Activities   **227**

CHAPTER 14
Guiding Children's Science Activities   **245**

CHAPTER 18
Appreciating Positive Behavior   315

CHAPTER 19
Understanding Negative Behavior   327

CHAPTER 20
Mainstreaming Special Needs Children   345

CHAPTER 21
Communicating with Parents of Young Children   359

CHAPTER 22
Being a Professional Early Childhood Educator   375

CHAPTER 23
Developing Human Resources   395

CHAPTER 24
Valuing as a Basis for Actions   409

CHAPTER 25
Evaluating—Who Needs It?   423

PART ONE

Specific Techniques in Child Guidance

CHAPTER 1

Guiding Young Children—A Preview

Key Concepts

◆ Definition of Guidance
◆ Goals of Guidance
◆ Limits
◆ NAEYC Accreditation
◆ CDA Credential

You watch spellbound as a teacher patiently helps four-year-old Jackie learn to skin-the-cat on the horizontal bar. "You can do it, Jackie. That's right, bring your feet through here," directs the teacher, pointing to the space between Jackie's arms. Jackie pulls his legs up and over his head, then manages to get them in the space above his head. The teacher stands nearby and offers encouragement. Jackie laughs, talks, and skins-the-cat over and over again. As an observer, you ask yourself, "Could I be as understanding as that teacher?"

You are visiting a relative whose four-year-old son Stevie comes running indoors with a terrified look on his face. "Mommy," he cries hurling himself into his mother's arms, sobbing so that his whole body shakes. Through the tears you and his mother finally learn that a neighbor's child is hurt. If you were his mother, how would you respond? Who would be your first concern, your relative's child or the neighbor's child? What would be the best way to handle the child's terror? As an interested person, what would you do? What would you say?

You stand in the line at the supermarket. "Please, Daddy, buy me some gum," begs five-year-old Sonia. She picks up two packages of gum from the tempting display and repeats, "Please Daddy, I want some gum." If you were the father, what would you say and do about the purchase of gum? Would you buy it? Why?

Jake Jasper brings his two-and-a-half-year-old son to the child development center early one morning. As he says, "Goodbye, Eli," Eli wails, "Go home. Me go home," and clings to his father. What do you think the teacher does? The father?

GUIDANCE: WHAT IS IT?

What would you do if you were the adult in the four opening episodes? What would you say? How do you act and react to help children learn appropriate behavior and to feel secure? Numerous incidents such as the four described here occur as parents and teachers live with, nurture, and teach young children. As you study, practice, and gain experience interacting with young children, you will learn more about the types of guidance you would use.

Infants come into the world genetically endowed with the potential for growing, developing, and learning. It is interesting to note that the word *potential,* with its root word *potent,* means that there is energy or force for growing, developing, and learning. You will now use your energy or potential to learn how to guide children toward achieving their full physical, social, emotional, and intellectual potential.

Parents, teachers, and others use guidance to help children feel secure and learn desirable habits and ways of behaving. *Guidance* is defined as *everything adults deliberately do and say, either directly or indirectly, to influence a child's behavior.* Even to ignore a child's behavior purposely is an important form of guidance. Ignoring can sometimes be used effectively to influence a child's behavior. Why do you think this is true?

This course can help you learn some effective methods of interacting with children and influencing their behavior. Some effective methods have been discovered by parents and teachers through trial and error. Other methods have been developed and tested by researchers. Through their studies over the years, researchers have also provided information about child development. Knowing how children grow and develop helps you to plan the appropriate type of guidance to use with children of a given age. Chapter 17 provides details about developmental characteristics from infancy through early childhood. You will want to refer to that chapter frequently throughout the course.

Guidance principles from which the helpful techniques are derived will be presented for infants and children through kindergarten age—the ages children are usually enrolled in a child development center. *Child development center* will be used as a shorthand term to mean a pre-primary early childhood education center which may be known in your locality as preschool, nursery school, Head Start, infant and toddler school or center, child care, day care, play school, or kindergarten. These terms have various meanings to depict programs for nurturing and educating young children in groups that may be organized on a part-day or full-day, profit or nonprofit basis. Whatever the centers are called, or however they are organized, the principles of interacting with the children are substantially the same. You will be practicing the methods as a helper in a center and later as a teacher or caregiver. In addition, as a parent or future parent, you may apply the methods and principles of guidance in your own family and neighborhood.

You will be developing your own teaching and parenting style as you study, observe, and gain experience. Because you are a unique person with your own personality, your style can be expected to differ somewhat from other

Early childhood teachers model
play techniques as they interact
with young children.
(University of Minnesota-Waseca
Child Development Laboratory)

people's modes of interacting with young children—even though you and others have similar high standards concerning the understanding, nurturing, and teaching of young children. Your knowledge, your ability to think deeply and well, and your empathetic understanding of children are required. For your part, being humble about what you know and using your best judgment will be helpful. When guiding children and helping parents, few rules apply a hundred percent of the time. The uniqueness of humans and human interaction makes hard and fast rules or prescriptions unwise. What you study here is thus designed to help you become aware of possibilities and of methods that have worked for others. You can be observant and apply the information as creatively as possible. Child development, child guidance, and early childhood education are still young sciences; even the experts have much to learn. Now that you have chosen to study child guidance, you can help with this exciting and forward-looking quest.

Clearly you can be expected to derive personal benefits from your study. Children who have well-qualified teachers and caregivers gain as well. According to the National Day Care Study, education of teachers and caregivers in child-related fields is associated with positive outcomes in the young children enrolled in their groups. The study reported that "Education/training in child-related fields such as developmental psychology, day care, early childhood education or special education is associated with distinctive patterns of caregiver and child behavior and with higher gains in test scores for children." The study further states, "Lead teachers with specialized education or training engage in substantially more social interaction with children (questioning, instructing, responding, praising and comforting) than caregivers without such education or training." It also notes that "Children in classes led by caregivers with specialized preparation show more cooperation and compliance and are less frequently uninvolved in tasks or activities than children in other classes; they also show longer durations of attention to tasks or activities."[1] You will soon be ready to join the ranks of people with special preparation for working with children.

MANY FACTORS INVOLVED IN GUIDANCE

Effective guidance requires that you learn to consider many factors as you decide what to do and what to say to influence children's behavior. Your own upbringing, your experiences, and your knowledge of what is considered best for children will be important factors. You may find that you have some habits that you would like to change. In fact, a frequent comment of early childhood students who have already reared their children is "I wish I'd known these things when my children were growing up." That is, these parents realize—through the opportunity to study, and through opportunities to work and observe under the guidance of an experienced early childhood education teacher—new dimensions of child rearing that were not apparent to them in their earlier years.

The values of the society—goals or principles people cherish and enshrine in institutions and fundamental documents such as the Constitution of the United States—are important to parents and teachers and will influence what you do and say to children. For example, liberty, freedom, human dignity, and equality are basic values for Americans. You translate these values into action for young children by helping them learn to make responsible choices within the framework of those values and to act accordingly without ever-present authority persons—parents, teachers, and the like. And, through practice, children will learn to understand and to respect rights to liberty, freedom, human dignity, and equality for others.

In the first episode, it is obviously important to Jackie and the teacher that Jackie learns to "skin-the-cat." Do you suppose this skill will make Jackie feel more competent and develop a more positive self-concept? Are feelings of competence and confidence important for a child to have? Do other skills demand some of the muscle coordination learned in skinning-the-cat on the jungle gym? Does learning one skill facilitate learning other skills? You'll think about these questions and more as you study child guidance.

In the second instance, how would you respond to a child who cries with terror? Does it make a difference how you feel about crying when you know what caused the crying? How important is it that a child show concern for his or her playmates?

---

[1] Richard Ruopp, Jeffrey Travers, Frederic Flantz, and Craig Coelen, *Children at the Center* (Cambridge, MA: Abt Associates, 1979), pp. 98–100.

In the last two episodes, how do you feel about children who beg for items in the store or children who cry when parents leave them? As a teacher or parent, what criteria would you use to decide your reaction to these behaviors? Stop reading for a moment and think through these questions arising from the four scenes. Think of other situations that pose important questions of guidance and development.

How much difference would children's ages make in what behavior you'd be willing to accept and what behavior you'd decide to stop or redirect? James Hymes, Jr., a famous early childhood educator, once wrote that we accept wetting in infants—we plan for it and adjust to it. However, wetting one's pants is not accepted behavior for a five-year-old, and most people would want to find some guidance technique that would effectively teach a five-year-old wetter to use the bathroom.

The primary focus in this course is on interacting with young children. In other courses you may focus on the curriculum or the administration of a center or primarily on child development. Clearly there is much to learn as you study about and work with children under the leadership of experienced early childhood educators. As you go about your work, you should jot down your confusions, concerns, and questions, and bring them to your instructor's attention. Questioning helps students gain depth in their understanding of children and in the methods teachers use to guide behavior.

STEPS IN YOUR OWN LEARNING

You will be passing through several levels of knowledge about children and the application of that knowledge to early childhood education as you work with young children. The Knowledge Ladder (Figure 1–1) shows those levels as defined by psychologist Benjamin Bloom. The steps shown on the Knowledge Ladder are (1) Knowledge, (2) Comprehension, (3) Application, (4) Analysis, (5) Synthesis, and (6) Evaluation.[2] These steps will be defined and discussed briefly using examples of your learning in your chosen field of study—child development and early childhood education. Later, in Chapter 14, you will apply these steps to children's learning.

Knowledge

In the knowledge step, you already have some facts and perceptions (knowledge) of child development and early education from previous experiences—perhaps as a child, a parent, a relative, or a neighbor of a child, or from other reading and study about children. This course will further extend your knowledge and provide labels for things (abstractions) you have already observed about children, but may or may not have discussed before. With this common framework you can discuss children with your instructors, other students, and

---

[2] Benjamin S. Bloom, ed., *Taxonomy of Educational Objectives, Handbook I: The Cognitive Domain* (New York: David McKay, 1956), pp. 62–168.

Early childhood teachers encourage kindergartners' interest in letters.
(Savannah Public Schools)

people in your profession. Chapter 17 especially focuses on basic information relating to children's development, while other chapters apply the information on development to various components of an early childhood program.

Comprehension

The comprehension step means that, with the knowledge and the labels (abstractions) learned, you can correctly demonstrate use of the knowledge and labels when specifically asked to do so. A list of suggested observations is provided at the end of each chapter to help you begin to see the children as they act in the characteristic ways you are reading about. For example, you can then state the characteristics of a toddler.

Application

The application step means that from your knowledge and comprehension of abstractions regarding child development and early education you can bring those abstractions to mind and use them in your work with and in your discussions about children. For example, given your knowledge and comprehension of toddlers' characteristics, you will be able to pick toddlers out of a group of children from ages one to six and state the basis for your selections. A list of applications is provided at the end of each chapter to help you with this important step.

Analysis

The analysis step means you will be able to break down the material into its constituent parts and detect relationships among the various parts and the ways they are organized. For example, if you are responsible for toddlers who do not seem to be doing what you are expecting, you use the knowledge you will possess about toddlers' physical, social, language, and mental development to help you study the actual situation and to reveal possible reasons for the toddlers' noncompliance.

Synthesis

The synthesis step is one your more experienced teachers and instructors use in solving difficulties. They sift through information gained from observing their children, from talking with children's parents, from professional literature studied, and from previous experiences with children and their parents. Thus, creative solutions to current problems are developed. Early childhood professionals continue to use these logical thought processes throughout their careers. Synthesis ability becomes a long-range development goal for teachers who are starting out in a career program.

Evaluation

The evaluation step involves applying standards of quality to any situation you confront. Here you have formed your own views, know the reasoning of many professionals, and can combine many factors in a professionally responsible

Figure 1-1   *The Knowledge Ladder*

Source: Based on Benjamin S. Bloom, *Taxonomy of Educational Objectives, Handbook I: The Cognitive Domain* (New York: David McKay, 1956).

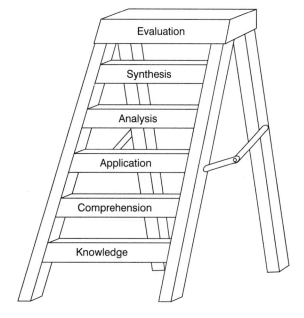

manner whenever called upon to evaluate a situation. For example, you may be involved in helping to write the early childhood education standards for your state or in your profession.

GOALS OF GUIDANCE

Serious thought usually goes into guidance that is effectively carried out by parents, teachers, and caregivers. Even though the adults you observe seem to act spontaneously, they likely have thought about the kind of people they want children to become. They use that background of thinking each time they interact with children. What kind of people do you think you want today's children to become? Discuss this question among your classmates. Remember, these children will become the adults needing to solve the problems of the twenty-first century.

 Talk It Over

What do you think are the primary influences that made you what and who you are today?

What kind of people do you want today's children to become?

What can parents and teachers do to help children reach their fullest potential?

In your discussion concerning the kinds of people you want young children to become, you may get responses such as these:

"I want my child to learn to make responsible decisions about how to behave without me being there all the time."

"I want a child to be a leader."

"I don't want a child to be afraid or whiny," volunteers someone. Often, as in this example, what you *don't* want in a child's behavior is easier to state than what you *do* want. A positive way of expressing the same ideas might be, "I want a child to be courageous and confident, and to speak up with assurance."

There are many possible statements of desirable qualities in children. When you put the statements together you get an idea of the kind of people you want guidance to help produce. Generally, the desire is that children learn the following:

1. To be capable persons who can direct their own behavior without authority figures overseeing them.

2. To be able to make decisions that lead toward a healthy productive life for them individually.
3. To develop all their human abilities—physical, social, emotional, and mental.
4. To develop a caring attitude toward other people.

To Become Self-directed

The first goal to keep in mind when guiding infants, toddlers, and young children is to help them *to become self-directed*.

Parents, teachers, and caregivers must have the expectation that gradually each child will become self-directed. Consequently, as children learn and become self-directed, adults simply ease into the background, allowing children to practice their self-direction. When adults understand human development, they avoid doing for children what the children can do for themselves. Surprisingly, even infants soon learn to help themselves. Throughout life adults must be good observers of children and, upon observing that their guidance has been effective, be ready to let the child take over. Adults then move on to something new that the child needs help in learning.

Early childhood teachers value moments of one-to-one interaction with each child.
(Marshall University Child Development Laboratory)

APPROACHING GUIDANCE DEVELOPMENTALLY

Children, starting at birth, are learning continuously as they develop and mature. Children have an instinctive inclination to become independent, self-directed, and self-sufficient. As they achieve each milestone on the developmental ladder, they use that accomplishment to push themselves toward the next milestone or goal. Thus, as parents, teachers, and caregivers interact with a child, it is important to encourage this natural striving by setting the stage and making it possible for the child to achieve the next developmental milestone safely, and, when ready to do so.

Setting the stage for developmental milestones to occur safely is part of adults' responsibility and part of the guidance each adult will use. An example is the infant's ability to roll over. At about the fourth or fifth month most infants will be able to roll over in bed. However, even before this time, babies become unsafe on an adult bed because they develop the ability to use their toes to move forward and can reach the edge, fall off and get hurt. Responsible adults must always be sure the baby is safely in a crib with sides.

As a student of child guidance, you will learn to guide children through the various stages of their development. Research carried on for many years helps parents and teachers by designating typical stages of development to watch for as children move through various ages. You'll have the benefit of this research without having to discover it all by yourself.

Each child is unique and reaches each developmental stage with some variability. Your task will be to observe the children you work with closely to see just where each one is on the developmental ladder. After you recognize where each child is developmentally, you can use that information when planning your guidance and activities for the child. This is called developmentally appropriate planning.

Developmentally appropriate means *a program is age-appropriate for the children in the group and also individually appropriate, taking into account the developmental characteristics of each specific child in the group.*[3]

For example, to be developmentally appropriate, the room and play yard for toddlers will be arranged and equipped differently from that used by kindergartners. Also, the guidance and curriculum the teachers use will differ widely due to the social, mental, and motor skill differences of the two age groups. As you progress through your early childhood curriculum, you'll become increasingly aware of the stages of children's development and learn how to apply your knowledge of those stages to the guidance and curriculum planning in the school or center.

In a class of college students who were learning to interact with young children, part of the class practiced with the three-year-olds and the other part

---

[3] For helpful descriptions, see Sue Bredekamp (ed.), *Developmentally Appropriate Practice in Early Childhood Programs Serving Children from Birth Through Age 8* (Washington, DC: National Association for the Education of Young Children, 1987).

practiced with the five-year-olds. Those students interacting with the fives lamented that they didn't get to do much. Their classmates working with the threes had held children's hands, cuddled, reassured their charges, and supervised the toileting. Students working with the fives mostly observed as those competent children climbed self-assuredly on the jungle gym, pumped the swings independently, and went to the bathroom without help or reminders. Clearly, the college students would have been poor teachers if they had tried to encourage the fives to become more dependent just so the college students could maintain more interaction with the children. Have you seen parents who helped children more than necessary? How can parents use their energy wisely when their children no longer require continual help?

APPROACHING GUIDANCE POSITIVELY

Recognizing and encouraging healthy positive behavior in a child will be emphasized in this book. You will often find that one episode of negative behavior—say, a fight between two children—gets much attention from observers and teachers while hundreds of positive exchanges go unnoticed. In

Early childhood teachers provide equipment suited to children's motor skills, such as a wide diameter bat.
(University of New Mexico Manzanita Child Care Center)

this book you will approach the study of guidance for young children from a developmental perspective that involves a positive or health viewpoint rather than a negative or sickness viewpoint. The difference is important and will become clearer to you as your knowledge about child development and early childhood education progresses.

Positive guidance means that you'll use your professional know-how to support children's growth and development. Children should always be treated with respect and dignity. A positive approach to guidance makes children and others feel confident, happy, and pleasant. A positive approach does not include shaming, humiliation, ridicule, or pressure to compete; nor is it punitive, impatient, mean, or bossy.

Focusing on problems or sickness rather than on strengths or health is a negative approach that is seldom effective and, consequently, represents a misdirection of adult guidance. The person who focuses entirely on a child's negative or problem behavior, such as hitting, doesn't necessarily correct the problem behavior. In fact, because of the attention resulting from the problem, one may be giving positive reinforcement that causes the negative behavior to persist. On the other hand, recognizing the positive behavior of a child with attention and respect is likely to increase the percentage of positive behavior. Also, as a child begins to think more positively about herself or himself, problem behaviors tend to diminish. Likewise, other people, seeing the child in a better light and responding positively, will contribute toward the child's improved behavior.

It is often through a child's strengths or health aspects that most so-called problems can best be solved. A blind child usually develops, or can develop, sensory acuities in hearing, touching, tasting, and smelling far superior to a sighted child's. A blind child usually has normal physical strength and ability. These are strengths from which the child will learn and develop major perceptions and skills. Although special glasses, braille books, and so on are provided, positive reinforcement for learning through the healthy senses will also contribute significantly toward helping the child learn and, at the same time, help develop a strong, positive self-concept and self-esteem.

Case histories of children with special needs often provide examples of the unfortunate outcome of focusing on sickness rather than on health. For example, parents of an infant blind boy—we'll call him Bert—protected him from responsibility, helping with all the little tasks that children usually learn, instead of teaching him to do them himself. Bert's mother, for instance, always fed him and tied his shoes. Bert could have learned these tasks and many more because his physical dexterity and senses of touch and hearing were excellent. His parents treated him as a sick person, nearly making him into an invalid for life. Years later, after his mother died, the child's strengths were recognized by his stepmother and he was given training in self-help and in an occupation. As an adult, he became self-confident, relatively independent, and financially self-supporting. His stepmother emphasized his strengths, opening up a wide new world for him. This, of course, is the most humane approach, and, in addition, the most socially economical one. Now Bert is a happy taxpayer, not an unhappy tax burden.

Seen from the health viewpoint, a child in this English-speaking country who speaks a foreign language, Spanish, for example, has valuable language skills that can be the basis for learning more Spanish and, also, for learning English. The child can learn names for concepts in both languages, a valuable skill in a world that has not yet agreed on an international language. However, from the sickness approach, a Spanish-speaking child might be deemed to have a problem or deficiency and efforts might be made to eliminate the use of Spanish as quickly as possible. This was the typical procedure in the United States before the more recent bilingual and bicultural approaches were developed and implemented for children using other languages. Bilingualism may not be feasible when the minority language involves only a small number of children—for example, for the few children in a school who speak Vietnamese or Arabic.

Take another example of the health versus sickness approach: a child sucking a thumb or masturbating. Some young children tend to keep their hands on their genitals—for a variety of reasons. Using a health approach, adults accept or deliberately ignore such behavior and concentrate on giving the child interesting activities to do. Thumbsucking or masturbating usually diminishes in the midst of other activities the child finds enjoyable. The sickness approach, however, focuses attention on the thumbsucking or masturbating, analyzing why the child does it and what satisfaction it provides. Often the adult may shame or scold the child for such behavior. The resulting attention may actually encourage the persistence of thumbsucking or masturbating. In the process, parents may become unduly concerned and less effective in dealing with the behavior.

The perspective of focusing on health, competence, and adjustment is called a *developmental perspective* by Dr. Earl S. Schaefer, a well-known psychological researcher. He explains that the *pathological perspective,* which deals with problems or sickness, focuses on screening, diagnosis, treatment, remediation, and prevention of specific pathologies. Schaefer's research clearly indicates the advantages of using the developmental perspective in planning for child care, health care, and other family services. His research, unfortunately, also shows that "many parents believe that children are naturally bad and will be bad unless forced to be good." According to Schaefer, parents holding such negative views have children who exhibit more problem behavior, whereas, on the other hand, parents who view children positively have children who show more strengths, skills, and adaptive behavior.[4]

---

[4] Earl S. Schaefer, "Professional Paradigms in Programs for Parents and Children." Paper presented at a Symposium on Parenting, American Psychological Association, August 1977, pp. 5–8.

Early childhood teachers use eye contact when guiding young children.
(University of Illinois Child Development Laboratory)

LIMITS ON BEHAVIOR

"Peter, you may kick the ball. It hurts Jackie for you to kick him," is guidance limiting a child's behavior. Guidance is presented in a positive way so the child knows what he or she can do. It helps Peter learn that Jackie has feelings. Your study, observation, and practice will help you learn how to develop rules to enforce reasonable limits on children's behavior. Certainly both in homes and in child development centers there will be limits set to help children learn to respect other children's play space or learning environment, to respect their own and other's personal comfort and safety, and to respect furnishings and equipment.

Teaching children to take turns and share may require limits as children learn these important social skills. You can expect to repeat the guidance for many days before it becomes part of children's regular behavior. Rules and limits should be stated and carried out in a spirit of preserving each child's dignity. The atmosphere should be nurturant and supportive rather than harsh or coercive. Many of the lessons children learn from your guidance will be applicable at home, in the community, and in interactions with older children as well.

ADULT PROBLEMS

Some so-called behavior problems of children are frequently adults' problems. That is, the "problems" really don't bother the children. However, adults may feel that the children's behavior must be curtailed, stopped, or redirected. Noise is an example. Most children thrive in noisy settings, but grumpy neighbors, classes down the hall, or unsympathetic principals may require that children learn to "use your quiet voices" or "use your quiet feet." Inhibiting children's natural spontaneity then becomes the goal of some adult guidance. Adults should analyze the behaviors that bother them and that they have the impulse to stop. They should consider whether there are good reasons for stopping the children.

 Talk It Over

Recall something you did as a child that bothered adults around you. What steps did they take to stop or change your behavior? What are things children do or say that bother some adults, yet do not bother the children?

As a student of child guidance you'll develop skill in determining whether the "problem" belongs to the child or the adult, and perhaps find ways of helping children and adults understand the difference. Finding legitimate outlets for children's spontaneity and avoiding placing heavy blame on children for acting like children are significant tasks that you will learn.

PROFESSIONAL CONCERN FOR HIGH-QUALITY GUIDANCE

Various professional groups are concerned with the quality of early childhood education being offered to young children. They have made statements regarding standards, including standards for the interaction processes and guidance techniques used by teachers and caregivers with young children. For example, the Child Development Associate (CDA) competencies include many items related to child guidance. The CDA is a system that trains and provides credentials for persons who work in child care centers. If you are interested in the CDA program or would like to receive the competencies, write to the Council for Early Childhood Professional Recognition, 1341 G Street, Washington, DC 20005–3105, or call 1–800–424–4310.

The National Association for the Education of Young Children (NAEYC) is the largest professional organization concerned with the care and education of young children. In 1982, they published *Guidelines for Early Childhood*

Teacher Education. The published standards are designed to inform colleges with four-year degree programs about the criteria for accrediting their programs with the National Council for Accreditation of Teacher Education (NCATE). The booklet *Guidelines for Early Childhood Education Programs in Associate Degree Granting Institutions* gives standards for community college programs. It is also available from NAEYC. For prices of the publications write NAEYC at 1509 16th Street, N.W., Washington, DC 20036–1436, or call 1–800–424–2460.

Another effort for raising standards of early childhood education is NAEYC's Center Accreditation project. The accreditation criteria were approved in 1984 and many centers have been accredited across the country.

Accreditation is a distinction awarded to early childhood schools and child care centers for having met the standards for high-quality programs and completed the procedures for outside validation of that high quality in a process supervised by the National Academy of Early Childhood Programs, a division of the NAEYC.

The criteria for accreditation of early childhood programs are published in the booklet *Accreditation Criteria and Procedures of the National Academy of Early Childhood Programs.*[5] These standards were agreed on by early childhood professionals and parents from across the nation before they were accepted by the NAEYC board. Accreditation is a voluntary process. Managers, teachers, and policy boards of each school or center, upon deciding to enter into the process, will contact the National Association for the Education of Young Children and proceed at their own pace.

When your center or school decides to work toward the accreditation process, as thousands of centers are now doing, all activities of the center, including the interpersonal interaction and guidance used by teachers, will be under scrutiny. You can inquire of your instructor whether the center where you are participating has been accredited. It is recommended that the accreditation booklet be available to teachers for reference whether or not the center has immediate intentions of entering into the accreditation process. The National Academy of Early Childhood Programs is a unit within NAEYC, the professional association that is responsible for accreditation.

The volunteer nature of the accreditation process, as conceptualized by NAEYC, has helped to define the standards of performance of managers, teachers, caregivers, and others in a manner that will encourage the voluntary efforts of many toward maintaining those high standards.

Licensing is a process operated by your state's government that sets minimum standards for operating a school or center. Government regulations are mandatory, not voluntary, and require consistent and unwavering adherence.

---

[5] Sue Bredekamp (ed.), *Accreditation Criteria and Procedures of the National Academy of Early Childhood Programs* (Washington, DC: NAEYC, 1991).

EVALUATION

The standards listed above are designed to produce an excellent service for children and families and give centers recognition for their hard work. Meeting standards requires knowing the standards and checking up from time to time to see how performance measures up to those standards. Sometimes special effort or strategies need to be devised to achieve the standards and, at times, the standards may need to be adjusted. The higher the standards of a particular center, the more you will learn as you work with the children.

At the end of each chapter of this book, there is a section entitled "Applications." It is suggested that you try your hand at evaluation, because the material discussed in each chapter is similar to the criteria published by NAEYC's Accreditation Project. By giving attention to many details, you will become familiar with standards for high-quality programs. Remember that when you evaluate yourself, you are engaged in a learning process. Always seek ways to improve your performance. When evaluating the center at which you work, you will also want to be positive in your approach—seek to help improve the performance of individuals and programs.

YOUR PERFORMANCE STANDARD

Participation

Your institution has probably arranged a site where you can participate with children in order to learn the principles of guidance more thoroughly; that is, where you can put theory into practice. Participating with children while you are learning is a privilege for you, and you should treat it as such by showing respect for the center staff, children, and parents. They will expect you to be a learner, not a polished teacher; thus, you should freely practice skills and communication techniques, learn from observing others, learn from asking questions, learn from experimenting with various techniques, and learn from your class and reading. Before going to your center, read and study specified pages. See Figure 1–2 for standards to achieve.

Be sure to attend and be prompt as scheduled, just as the teaching staff is required to do. Call in as directed for an excused absence only when a serious illness prevents your attendance. Participate in any planned pre- or post-session conferences. Question the teacher about any instructions you don't understand thoroughly. Volunteer happily for tasks. This shows your interest and your willingness to carry your share of the load. Ask for feedback on your participation, especially on suggestions for improvement. If you were perfect you would not need the course!

When you are in a center, you are part of a team and should be supportive of the other team members. You should carry out your assigned duties as effec-

Student's name _____ Date _____

Group of children _____ Ages _____

Supervising teacher _____

Ratings

5—Highly satisfactory	2—Unsatisfactory
4—Satisfactory	1—Very unsatisfactory
3—Minimum	0—No opportunity

Criteria	Week											
	1	2	3	4	5	6	7	8	9	10	11	12
1. Arrives promptly												
2. Has read specified pages												
3. Checks for area assignment												
4. Attends pre- and post-sessions												
5. Helps prepare and maintain environment												
6. Clarifies directions												
7. Diligent in work and assignment												
8. Practices assigned techniques												
9. Cooperates with staff												
10. Anticipates and responds to children's and teacher's needs												
11. Reports about children												
12. Total performance rating												

Figure 1-2   *Student's Self-Evaluation*

tively as you can. Ask to work in all areas to gain a broad experience. Try to anticipate what your team members need and respond accordingly. Though you may be able to ask for directions, remember that the teachers have to give primary attention to the children. Your own needs may have to be considered later at the end of the day.

If you have a game, song, or poem you'd like to try out with the children, feel free to discuss it ahead of time with the teachers. They may offer suggestions or modifications, but most will be pleased with the interest you are showing.

Every time you attend your center, do a self-evaluation of your participation. Use Figure 1–2, which is a shortened version of the criteria discussed in this section. As you confer with your supervising center teacher and your lecture instructor about your performance, you can gain valuable suggestions for improving your skills for working with young children.

OBSERVATIONS

You will learn many things through carefully observing children, teachers, and parents. Observation means that you look closely, watch for patterns of behavior, and see and hear subtle shades of differences in actions, words, and feel-

Early childhood teachers model play techniques as they interact with toddlers.
(South East Oakland Vocational Technical Child Care Center)

ings of children and adults. As you learn to observe objectively, recording and stating clearly what you see or hear, you can begin the more difficult process of interpreting what the behavior means and deciding what, if anything, to do about it.

Sometimes, on careful observation, adults learn that misbehavior can be eliminated simply by changing the furniture, or serving the snack earlier, rather than doing something to the child. Occasionally, one person is particularly successful with a child while others are not. Some days are better for some children than others. Even the weather affects children. All this and more will become more evident as you gain experience observing.

Often you may need to make observation notes on a small notebook while you are involved in helping with children's activities, such as dressing, toileting, or painting. Thus, you may have to jot down reminders to be filled in more completely when you get back to your desk. Remember to complete your notes at the earliest moment or your memory will fade.

As you progress through the various chapters, suggestions will be made for things to watch for as you observe. It is your privilege to be working with children. Protect that privilege by treating with confidentiality the things you see and hear. If repeated as gossip the center manager may remove your privilege of observing and helping. Discuss your observations only with the instructor of your course and the children's teachers. If you have a question about how to handle a child's behavior your instructor or the child's teacher are the people to ask, too.

Teachers usually appreciate alert students who notice special things about a child or a small group of children. Be able to report this information at the end of the day. Your report may give the teachers a new angle on the children's behavior. Or, it may support other observations the teachers have made. Be sure to check with the teacher as to the appropriateness of reporting to parents. Some teachers feel strongly that it is best for the lead teacher to be the one to report to parents.

CONCLUSION

Infants come into the world genetically endowed with all their human potential for growing, developing, and learning. You, as a parent, teacher, or caregiver, have an exciting opportunity as you become part of a team of adults interacting with young children and stimulating the development of their human potential through careful, thoughtful guidance techniques. A child's natural endowment requires a rich environment and thoughtful nurturing and guidance if the human potential contained in each child is to reach full bloom and contribute fully to improving the quality of human life.

REVIEW AND APPLICATIONS

Twelve Performance Standards for Participators

1. Arrive promptly as scheduled.
2. Read your specified assignment before entering the center. Have all materials needed with you. Wear appropriate clothing.
3. Check immediately for your specific area assignment.
4. Attend planned pre- and post-sessions.
5. Help prepare and maintain the environment.
6. Clarify any confusing directions with the teacher.
7. Carry out your share of the work and your assignment diligently.
8. Practice assigned techniques with children.
9. Cooperate happily with other staff members.
10. Anticipate and respond to the needs of the children or the teacher.
11. Report to the teacher special observations of a child or children.
12. Evaluate your total performance each day using a 1–to–5 scale.

 Observations

Select a child to observe for a special case study. You will keep cumulative records on a single child throughout the course. You will analyze your notes on the basis of questions asked in each chapter. At the end of the course you will complete your case study describing your child. Follow the suggestions for careful observations. Discuss your case study with your teacher at the end of the term.

Applications

1. Make a list of characteristics that you think are most important for young children to develop. List the characteristics in order of priority—the most important one first. Discuss with your classmates your thoughts on how you think you should treat or guide children if you want these characteristics to develop.
2. Talk with at least three different people outside of class, preferably people of different ages. Ask the question, "What kind of people do you want today's young children to become?" Record their answers. Later, in a class discussion, make a complete list of the characteristics collected by various students and determine which characteristics people thought were most important.

3. Discuss the health versus sickness approach to understanding and guiding children. Do you recall children who had problems? How were they treated? What is your conclusion?
4. Study the four examples in the opening pages of this chapter. List some questions you will need to answer before deciding on the appropriate guidance for the children.
5. Write to the Council for Early Childhood Professional Recognition (address in chapter) and ask for the Child Development Associate (CDA) competencies for child care workers. When they arrive, discuss them with your classmates. In the CDA competencies, mark the competencies that relate to guiding children.
6. Use the Twelve Performance Standards for Participators as summarized in Figure 1–2 (Student's Self-Evaluation) as a checksheet to evaluate your performance throughout the entire term. Using a 1-to-5 scale (with 5 as the highest evaluation), rate your performance in each category each week. Discuss your progress and improvements needed with your teacher.

Independent Study

Some colleges have appropriate independent study or community service project courses where capable students can properly receive extra degree credits for providing tutorial help on a scheduled basis to some child (perhaps their case-study child) or to some child care center where help is needed. This can be an important service in a community and a stimulating real-world learning situation for a college student. You might like to investigate this possibility in your college. Keep records showing hours volunteered, duties, and name and address of supervisor and center. This information will be important for your résumé and job search later on.

Resource File

Develop a filing system for categorizing teaching ideas appropriate to use with young children. You will see your lead teacher using many good ideas that you will want to remember for your present and future teaching. Start with several labeled manila folders in a cardboard box. Use 3 by 5 cards. Add any handouts that the teachers provide or that you receive at a conference. The file will become increasingly valuable as you gain experience in other courses.

ADDITIONAL RESOURCES

Suggested Films and Videotapes

The Nurturing Community   VHS 1/2 in.   Color   30 minutes   1988

Thelma Harms and Debby Cryer explore child-rearing choices and the reasons for the choices parents make. Emphasizes that whatever the child care setting, children's lives should be of a high quality. Delmar Publishers, Customer Service, 2 Computer Drive West, Albany, NY 12212, 1–800–347–7707.

What Is Quality Child Care?   VHS 1/2 in.   Color   53 minutes   1988

Bettye M. Caldwell takes a close look at professional care in this thought-provoking address. NAEYC, Media, 1509 16th Street, N.W., Washington, DC 20036–1426.

Using the Early Childhood Classroom Observation   VHS 1/2 in.   Color   26 minutes   1988

How to use the observation scale that is part of the self-study package for NAEYC accreditation. NAEYC, Media, 1509 16th Street, N.W., Washington, DC 20036–1426.

Men in Early Childhood Education   16 mm.   Color   28 minutes   1981

A multiethnic, multiracial, and intergenerational overview of the male's contribution to early childhood education. Davidson's Films, 850 O'Neill Ave, Belmont, CA 94002.

To Teach Young Children   Color   26 minutes   1982

Illustrates the roles a teacher or caregiver assumes when carrying out a short-day early childhood education program for young children. Film designed for training teachers. In 16 mm and in film strip/tape with workbook lessons. Brigham Young University Press, Provo, UT 84602.

FOR FURTHER READING

Alexander, N. P. "School-age child care: Concerns and Challenges," *Young Children,* 42:1, 1986, 3–10.

Brazelton, T. Berry. *Working and Caring.* Reading, MA: Addison-Wesley, 1983.

Caldwell, Bettye M. and Donald J. Steadman, eds. *Infant Education: A Guide to Helping Handicapped Children in the First Three Years.* New York: Walker and Co., 1979.

Caldwell, Bettye M. *Group Care for Young Children: A Supplement to Parental Care.* Lexington, MA: Lexington Books, 1987.

Castle, Kathryn. *The Infant & Toddler Handbook: Invitations for Optimum Development.* Atlanta, GA: Humanics Limited, 1983.

Elkind, David. "Play," *Young Children,* 43:5, July 1988, 2.

Elkind, David. *The Mis-education of the Preschool Child.* Reading, MA: Addison-Wesley, 1987.

Friedman, Dana E. *Encouraging Employer Supports to Working Parents.* New York: Center of Public Advocacy, 1983.

Gartrell, Dan. "Punishment or Guidance?" *Young Children* 42:3, March 1987, 55–61.

Hildebrand, Verna. *Management of Child Development Centers.* New York: Macmillan Publishing Company, 1993.

Hildebrand, Verna. *Introduction to Early Childhood Education.* New York: Macmillan Publishing Company, 1991.

Hildebrand, Verna. *Parenting and Teaching Young Children.* New York: Glencoe/McGraw Hill, 1990.

Honig, Alice Sterling. "Compliance, Control, and Discipline," *Young Children,* 40:2, January 1985, 50–58.

Hymes, James L., Jr. "Public School for 4-Year-Olds," *Young Children,* 42:2, January 1987, 51–52.

McKee, Judy Spitler, ed. *Early Childhood Education 87/88.* Guilford, CT: The Dushkin Publishing Group, Inc., 1988.

Miller, Cheri S. "Building Self Control: Discipline for Young Children," *Young Children,* 40:1, November 1984, 15–25.

Morado, Carolyn. "Prekindergarten Programs for 4-Year-Olds: Some Key Issues," *Young Children,* 41:5, July 1986, 61–63.

NAEYC. "Child Choice—Another Way to Individualize—Another Form of Preventive Discipline," *Young Children,* 43:1, November 1987, 48–54.

Phillips, Deborah and Marcy Whitebook. "Who Are Child Care Workers?" *Young Children,* 41:4, May 1986, 14–20.

Powell, Douglas R. "After-School Child Care," *Young Children,* 42:3, March 1987, 62–70.

Read, Katharine, et al. *Early Childhood Programs: Human Relations and Learning.* New York: Holt, Rinehart & Winston, 1987.

Seefeldt, Carol. *Teaching Young Children.* Englewood Cliffs, NJ: Prentice-Hall, Inc., 1980.

CHAPTER 2

Guiding Young Children Indirectly Toward Self-Direction

Key Concepts

◆ Define Indirect Guidance

◆ Indirect Guidance Techniques

Kimmie came into the playroom and selected a puzzle from the puzzle rack. She put it on the nearby table and began to take it apart.

Kimmie's teacher deliberately stored the puzzles near the table, making it convenient and natural for the children to get out puzzles for use on the table. The arrangement gave them an inviting space to work with minimum interference. The puzzle pieces could be accounted for easily. Kimmie's behavior was being guided indirectly by her teacher who was in the far corner of the room greeting other children. Kimmie is growing in independence and self-control.

Guidance is defined as *everything adults deliberately do and say, either directly or indirectly, to influence a child's behavior*. The *goal* of guidance is to help the child become self-directed and independent, to care about others, and to develop physically, mentally, socially and emotionally.

INDIRECT GUIDANCE

Indirect guidance is the behind-the-scenes work and planning that influences the behavior of the child. Indirect guidance requires the management of the environment—the space, equipment, materials, and people of the center. Indirect guidance does not involve the child directly or specifically. When using indirect guidance, the adults make arrangements, set schedules, or make plans that are easy for children to use, follow safely, healthfully, and happily.

You'll see evidence of indirect guidance, even for adults, if you look around you. For example, in your bank or supermarket you'll find well marked aisles to guide customers indirectly to take turns as they cash checks or check out. In some businesses you are asked to "take a number" in order for people to take turns. Or, in your favorite park or playground you find receptacles for trash that indirectly invite you to "stash your trash."

Although indirect guidance is one of the easiest methods of guidance to use, and probably as successful as many direct methods, it is often overlooked. Indirect guidance is promising because it deals with those elements over which the teacher has major control. Factors outside the child may be affecting the child, being largely responsible for the desirable behavior that the teacher or parent hopes will continue or the undesirable behavior that she or he hopes to eliminate. When searching for a solution to a child's behavior problem, indirect guidance is the first place to turn. Some indirect guidance techniques that you might try will now be discussed.

Adult-Child Ratio

Balance the number of children and the age composition of the group with the number and experience of the teaching staff. There are specific adult-child ratio requirements in the National Association for the Education of Young Children (NAEYC) accreditation guidelines[1] and in most state licensing requirements. Because the NAEYC guidelines are expected to define a "high-quality" program, they usually differ from state licensing guidelines, which are minimum standards. Ask your instructor to show you the licensing standards for your state. Younger children require more adults to care for them. The ratios recommended by NAEYC are listed in the chart below.

Recommended Adult-Child Ratios and Group Size for Each Age

	Adult-Child Ratio	Group Size
Ages Birth to 12 Months	1 to 4	8
Ages 12–24 Months	1 to 5	12
Ages 24–30 Months	1 to 6	12
Ages 30–36 Months	1 to 7	14
Ages 3, 4, 5 Years	1 to 10	20
Ages 6–8	1 to 12	24
Ages 9–12	1 to 14	28

Every group should have at least two teachers to ensure the safety of the children. In an emergency, one teacher may have to attend to a child, and someone else must attend to the remaining children.

The adult-child ratios are directly related to how much personal interaction can occur between the teacher and each child and, also, to how enriching the program can be. When schools and centers try to economize by hiring insufficient staff it is the children who suffer most. It is undesirable to have

---

[1] Sue Bredekamp, *Accreditation Criteria & Procedures of the National Academy of Early Childhood Programs* (Washington, D.C.: NAEYC, 1991, p. 41).

centers look like the "Old Woman in the Shoe" with so many children they don't know what to do.

When students in training are involved in programs they, of course, provide extra hands, laps, and hearts that increase the opportunities for children in the programs. However, the ratio of trained staff should still be maintained because trainees require some staff time as well and are generally not yet ready to assume full responsibility.

Staff Training

All staff members should have training for their teaching and caregiving roles. One of the teachers may have more extensive preparation for the teaching role than others, taking the role of lead teacher; but, aides, assistants, and volunteers should all be given special training to work with young children. In addition, all staff members should expect to participate in various types of in-service education from time to time in order to continue developing their knowledge and skills for working with young children.

If part or all of the teaching staff is inexperienced, then fewer children should be assigned until experience has been gained. Special help in planning and mentoring should be given to inexperienced staff. Planning of all kinds must be done in more detail when staff members are inexperienced, because they have fewer skills for coping with fast-moving events than do experienced teachers.

Group Size

In the chart above, the recommended group size is noted for each age. It has been found that outcomes for children are closely related to group size with more adequate development for each child when groups are smaller.

Schools and centers have various admission and grouping policies. Some managers and teachers prefer a more homogeneous single-age group, like all three- or all four-year-olds. Others decide to have a wider age range, say two to five, so that older children can learn to help younger children, similar to a family situation. This decision must be related to group size and staff-child ratio. Of course, mixed ages will increase the range of individual differences among the children and require curriculum materials and equipment with a greater range of difficulty. Another factor is that some adults work better with one age than another.

 Talk It Over

Name some troublesome behaviors of children, then propose ways that these troublesome behaviors could possibly be averted by parents or teachers using indirect guidance techniques.

Large numbers of children in a single group prove excessively stimulating and fatiguing to each other. The younger the child, the smaller the number of children that each should be required to interact with each day. For infants up to 18 months the groups should be no larger than eight. Three- and four-year-olds' groups should be kept under eighteen to encourage friendships among children and to enable adults to interact with individual children. For toddlers, group size is fourteen. Warehousing children in large masses without adequate adult loving care is a practice to be prohibited.

Person-centered teaching can occur when the teachers deal with a few children and their families on a long-term basis. Mutual trust develops among teachers, parents, and children when the groups are kept small. Keeping children and teacher together as children mature, rather than promoting the children to a new group and teacher, helps avoid the problems accompanying adjustment to a new group. Teachers will also work harder to find solutions to children's problems when they know they will not be able to promote them to some other teacher.

Part-Time Enrollments

To accommodate parents, children are often admitted to a center on a part-time basis. These children often feel that they have missed something when enrolled with many full-time children. Where their numbers are sufficient, the school should assign them all to one group with a sensitive teacher who makes special short-range plans instead of extended week-long plans. If children have an opportunity to complete a project on their day in the center, they'll feel good about coming back. If they feel they have to leave it unfinished, they will be dissatisfied.

Some limits may logically be placed on part-time participation, for example, only mornings, only afternoons, or only a Monday, Wednesday, and Friday sequence. Drop-in-after-school children should likewise be separate from the ongoing groups and should have special plans made especially for them. To get children to participate fully in a regular program, some directors provide a fee-incentive; for example, five days cost parents only a little more than four days. Thus children, parents, and school may all gain needed benefits.

Special-Needs Children

Questions often arise regarding admission of children with special needs. Unless the staff size and expertise are adequate, it is unfair to both the child and the staff to admit such children. Special-needs children often require very complex programs and the support of highly trained technical consultants. This consultation is now becoming more readily available due to recent legislation designed to assist disabled individuals. Parents and teachers are urged to seek the necessary assistance for special-needs children. Some states provide the service beginning at the child's birth, others at age three.

Scheduling

Plan a schedule or sequence of events to suit the pace of the children. A scheduled sequence of events that is followed regularly with only minor changes gives children considerable security and knowledge of what to expect. Knowing what follows will give children clues as to how to behave.

Schedules are typically made up of blocks of time, a block of forty-five minutes to an hour for self-selected activities, thirty minutes for clean-up, snacks, quiet time, and so on. The lengths of these time blocks can be longer or shorter to meet the children's needs.

Special consideration for the schedules the children's families maintain should also be taken into account. Children will be arriving in a child development center at various hours. You may admit certain children within a few minutes of their waking-up time. Others may be hungry, having breakfasted early. Some are not brought to the center until midmorning. Others will be tired, having been up late at night. Some accommodation in the schedule and routine should be possible to allow for individual needs of children. It is very likely that children who are half awake, tired, or hungry will have little interest in normal play activities until personal needs are met. If pressed to participate, they may cry or be difficult to manage.

Planning a schedule with time for one-to-one attention is the basis for individualizing programs for young children.
(Savannah Public Schools)

Playing out of doors meets the needs of many children early in the day. Teachers should consider allowing those who especially need vigorous activity to play outdoors on arrival. When this schedule is used, the parents can be requested to dress children for outdoor play and can readily determine clothing needs themselves, whereas if they expect the teacher to dress children later they may "forget" essentials.

The typical sequence of events or schedule with approximate time of each change should be posted. Some centers use a large chalkboard and write large enough that all workers can see. Parents also can readily see the schedule when they pick up or drop off their children. Children gain security from knowing that snack time follows playtime; they begin guiding their own behavior to meet the typical schedule. This is helpful to the teachers. On days when, for many possible reasons, the schedule has to be altered, the children will require many explanations of what follows what in the new schedule, because they will be accustomed to the routine of the other schedule.

If children seem tired, teachers should examine the schedule to see if there is ample time for quiet, restful activity. If they seem unruly, it could be that the schedule requires too much indoor quiet activity and should be adjusted to allow children to be outdoors sooner or longer. Chapter 5 contains many suggestions regarding the scheduling of events in a child development center.

Organizing Space

Arrange the space so there are clues as to appropriate behavior for that space. As children look around the yard and rooms, they should be able to tell whether a space is for noisy play, for solitary or group play, for active or passive play. Depending on feelings at the moment, a child may choose to play in a certain part of the facility. Clues may be derived from the materials the child sees, pictures that are displayed, or the customary uses made of certain areas. Teachers may tell children, "You may drive the truck in the block room; we keep the trucks out of the art room because their noise bothers us." Because habits take time to develop, there is good reason to keep the space arrangements stable for a while in order for children to learn what activity does take place in certain areas and, therefore, to learn the appropriate behavior for that space. When multiple uses are made of space, such as when naps are taken in the playroom, lowered lights and dividers placed in front of the play materials will give children the clue that it is naptime instead of playtime.

The locker is usually the first space the child is taught to recognize in the school. This is the child's *personal space,* a place for personal belongings. This bit of private territory in public institutions is considered important for one's personal identity. The locker has the child's name carefully lettered in a conspicuous spot and a picture—sometimes of the child. This helps picture-reading children recognize their lockers until they become familiar with their locations and learn to read their names.

Sufficient Play Spaces

Equip the room and yard with sufficient play spaces for the number of children in the group. It is a simple matter to count the number of possible play spaces to see how many children your room or yard can serve. For example, given two tricycles, two swings, and a teeter totter, you have six spaces. Indoors you might have two at the easel, four in the housekeeping corner, and four at the puzzle table, making ten play spaces. There should be about fifty per cent more spaces than children in order to provide freedom of choice and suitable alternatives if one activity isn't working out for some reason. For sixteen children, then, there should be a minimum of twenty-four play spaces. Sufficient well-operating equipment that provides adequate play spaces will help keep harmony.

Setting up learning centers such as these enables children to be monitored as they pursue their own play ideas.
(Marshall University Child Development Laboratory)

Social space refers to an area of space around the child that the child feels belongs to him or her. Social space is also referred to as territoriality. The learning environment in child development centers is set up in activity centers. The number of work or play spaces available to the total group of children determines how close together children will be to each other, that is, how much social space each child has. Johanna Hulls, Director of the University Child Development Laboratory, University of Texas in Austin, says, concerning an individual, "When his social space is violated, he feels discomfort and irritation. The amount of social space needed varies with each person. Thus, one person may feel crowded in a situation while another may not."[3]

As a general rule in early childhood centers, a learning space or environment, such as the seat at the art table or a section of the sandbox, belongs to the child as long as it is being used. Others must respect use of the space until the child leaves. You might say, "Johnny is working there. You can hammer over here." Such guidance defines Johnny's territory or social space.

Crowding violates the individual's social space. You can eliminate many guidance problems by avoiding crowding within various learning centers. If there are frequent behavior problems, teachers should quickly analyze the use of space and the number of children using the space. Reporting on how the amount of space, especially crowding, influenced children's behavior, Professor Hulls observed that the effects of crowding were usually negative, and noted, "One response is to retreat from the group and play alone, establishing psychological distance from other children when it is impossible to establish physical distance. The result is more solitary play, and less social interaction. When this occurs, play becomes less stimulating and there may be more apathy in play."[4]

Some teachers post a number in a learning center. This number helps children learn how many children can play in that area. You often see children counting others to see if they can enter a play space—a good experience in learning about numbers, too.

Balancing Children and Space

Arrange learning centers so that the number of seats available suggests the number of children appropriate at a given time. The best teaching can usually take place with four or five children involved in an activity, so when setting up the space the teacher should place only four or five chairs around the table. Children will generally take the hint and pass by an activity when there is not an empty chair. If not, they can be asked to watch awhile or return when a seat is available. It does not help children to try to squeeze in more children in a given learning center than your working space will accommodate comfortably and the teaching staff can help adequately. For example, a harried teacher trying to keep up with eight or ten fingerpainters surely cannot give the desired

---

[3] Johanna Hulls, "Powerful Space," *The Texas Child Care Quarterly,* 1:1, February 1977, 7.

[4] Ibid., p. 8.

Providing adult support for games that challenge children's memory and talk is desirable.
(Elgin High School Child Care Center)

assistance or reinforcement that is characteristic of effective teaching. More satisfaction comes from keeping the number manageable and repeating the popular activity on ensuing days.

Observing Children

Observe children when other adults can be responsible for them in order to gain basic information about each child's behavior and needs. Observing enables you to collect objective data relative to a child's behavior. When involved with such observations, you may miss significant points if you must also divert attention to other children. From such baseline data provided by observations, you can help develop firmer strategies for guiding the child.

Conferring with Parents

Confer with parents to develop a fuller understanding of the child's total experience and to gain assistance in deciding on guidance strategies. Parents and teachers need to know what the other is doing with the child. By learning from parents more than can be observed at school, and by sharing information with parents, you can often substantially help with a child's behavior. Please refer to Chapter 21 for more details on communicating with parents.

A service orientation is essential for all staff members. Parents and children are the customers who should be pleased. Warmth toward parents helps them in their parenting roles, which in turn helps their children. Reaching out to parents is a hallmark of a high-quality program.

CONCLUSION

Indirect guidance influences children's behavior through management of space, equipment, materials, and the people in the center. Indirect guidance does not deal with the child directly or specifically but is the behind-the-scenes work and planning that pays off in big dividends by helping children become self-directed, self-controlled, and independent. You can become alert to the twelve techniques discussed as you work in a center and consider the ways they are helping or hindering the children's progress. As a helper or an assistant you may be able to make changes that would foster a more responsive environment for children.

These twelve techniques of indirect guidance just discussed will be listed again for your convenience. They are to be carried out, for the most part, when the children are not at school. Time must be set aside when teachers are not responsible for children to enable the staff to do the *thinking* and *preparing* that these techniques require. It is simply not enough to plan on the run, as is the custom in some centers, or to squeeze planning into the time children are napping. There must be planning time, conference time, arranging-the-room time, evaluation time, and seeing-parents time. All early childhood teachers need a chance for feedback from their peers, for sharing ideas and insights, for charting new directions, and simply for knowing each other as people with concerns other than the job. Children generally suffer when planning time is catch-as-catch-can.

Without planning and evaluation, guidance becomes haphazard rather than a consciously determined act based on carefully considered values and goals as is proposed here. Time and thought given to indirect guidance will help insure the success of the direct guidance techniques that follow in Chapter 3.

REVIEW AND APPLICATIONS

Twelve Techniques of Indirect Guidance

1. Balance the number of children and the age composition of the group with the number and experience of the teaching staff.
2. Plan a schedule or sequence of events to suit the pace of the children.

3. Arrange the space so that there are clues as to appropriate behavior for that space.
4. Plan a rich and varied curriculum appropriate to the ages and experience of the children.
5. Arrange activities in an interesting way that invites participation.
6. Arrange materials and equipment so children can use them safely and with minimum help.
7. Store out of sight the materials you'd rather children did not use; materials considered dangerous MUST BE stored outside of children's rooms.
8. Arrange storage for toys and supplies near the area of expected use and near a surface appropriate for their use.
9. Equip the room and yard with sufficient play spaces for the number of children in the group.
10. Arrange learning centers so that the number of seats available suggests the number of children appropriate at a given time.
11. Observe children when other adults can be responsible for them in order to gain basic information about each child's behavior and needs.
12. Confer with parents to develop a fuller understanding of the child's total experience and to gain assistance in deciding on guidance strategies.

 Observations

1. Look for the schedule of activities. Observe children to see which ones seem familiar with the schedule. Write down instances when children let you know what comes next either by word or behavior. Discuss in class.
2. What arrangement of furniture or toys does the teacher prepare before children arrive? If you observe the teacher changing the environment or schedule, ask why this is being done. Describe how the indirect guidance helped children's behavior.
3. Observe children, then tell how the schedule or environmental arrangement tells children:
    a. what to do with their coats and belongings,
    b. what to do with their cup and napkin after a snack,
    c. what to do after using the toilet,
    d. what to do to be safe near the street or on the play yard,
    e. where to paint or draw,
    f. where to be noisy or quiet,
    g. where running is appropriate,
    h. what to do when they first arrive, and
    i. what to do after the snack.

4. Did the schedule or environmental arrangement make it easy or difficult for the child to behave as expected? Discuss.
5. Observe the parent or the teacher guiding your case-study child. Record the child's activities and comments and questions. What indirect guidance seems to be effective? Record examples for your case study report.

Applications

(In all applications at the end of each chapter be sure to identify the ages in years and months of all children discussed.)

1. Observe a young child in a home or school setting. Explain how the arrangement of equipment or supplies makes it hard or easy for the child to behave appropriately.
2. Observe a young child in a home or school setting. In what ways can you discover whether the child is aware of the schedule or sequence of events? Explain.
3. Observe a young child in a home or school setting. Find out all the materials which are kept strictly out of the child's reach. Explain.
4. On a 1-to-5 scale (with 5 highest) evaluate the center's use of indirect guidance using the Twelve Techniques of Indirect Guidance list. Discuss items with your classmates.
5. With the help of your classmates, plan a new arrangement in the classroom or play yard. Ask for permission first, then set up a new arrangement. Observe the children using the new arrangement. Record several responses. Discuss.

ADDITIONAL RESOURCES

Suggested Films and Videotapes

Playing and Learning   VHS 1/2 in.   Color   30 minutes   1988

Explains stages of preschool play as the natural way to learn from infancy through kindergarten. Delmar Publishers, Customer Service, 2 Computer Drive West, Albany, NY 12212, 1-800–347–7707.

Play and Learning   VHS 1/2 in.   Color   18 minutes   1988

A discussion with Dr. Barbara Biber. Why is play important? What do children learn when they play? NAEYC, Media, 1509 16th Street, N.W., Washington, DC 20036–1426.

Environments for Young Children   VHS 1/2 in.   Color   18 minutes   1988

A discussion with Elizabeth Prescott and Elizabeth Jones answering the question, "How do the materials and arrangement of the environment help meet your goals for children?" NAEYC, Media, 1509 16th Street, N.W., Washington, DC 20036–1426.

FOR FURTHER READING

Conger, Flora and Irene Rose. *Child Care Aide Skills.* New York: McGraw-Hill Book Co., 1979.

Fox-Barnett, Marion and Tamar Meyer. "The Teacher's Playing at My House This Week," *Young Children,* 47:5, July 1992, 45–50.

Greenberg, Polly. "How to Institute Some Simple Democratic Practices Pertaining to Respect, Rights, Responsibilities in Any Classroom," *Young Children,* 47:5, July 1992, 10–17.

Hildebrand, Verna. *Management of Child Development Centers.* New York: Macmillan Publishing Company, 1993.

Hildebrand, Verna. *Introduction to Early Childhood Education.* New York: Macmillan Publishing Company, 1991.

Kostelnik, Marjorie, Laura Stein, Alice Whiren, and Anne Soderman. *Guiding Children's Social Development.* Dallas: South-Western Publishing Co., 1988.

CHAPTER 3

Guiding Young Children Directly Toward Self-Direction

Key Concepts

◆ Definition of Direct Guidance
◆ Physical Guidance
◆ Verbal Guidance
◆ Affective Guidance

Cindy is trying to roll out her cookie dough and is rolling it to pieces. The teacher, Olga, says, "Let's roll it soft and slow, like this," as she places her hand on Cindy's hands and demonstrates. "Good," she says with a smile as Cindy begins to respond to the guidance.

Cindy's teacher was using techniques of *direct guidance* as she helped Cindy with the cookie making.

DIRECT GUIDANCE

Direct guidance means the physical, verbal, and affective techniques used to influence a child's behavior. The *goal* is to help the child become self-directed and to become a happy, fully functioning individual who can make decisions. There are three types of direct guidance—physical, verbal, and affective. The example at the beginning of this chapter demonstrates all three types. Direct guidance encompasses all the interpersonal interactional communication processes. The adults' human energy resources—knowledge, skill, empathy, and so forth—are utilized to help children develop skills, knowledge, and self-direction. Direct guidance is expected to be used in conjunction with indirect guidance—the management of the environment—that was discussed in Chapter 2. A discussion of the three types of direct guidance follows.

PHYSICAL GUIDANCE

Physical guidance means all techniques that employ physical contact or physical proximity to influence the child's behavior. Some of these techniques are helping, demonstrating, leading, restraining, removing, and punishing. The physical proximity of an interested adult is significant in helping children follow rules and in their sustained interest in some learning activities. Left to do some activities alone, a child will leave. If an adult is present, then the child is more likely to stay.

Physical guidance is especially effective for children who are just learning to speak and for those whose language is different from the teacher's. By using physical guidance techniques you can help children follow your guidance, even when they don't understand your words. However, even as you physically lead them to do what you want done, keep on talking anyway. Use key words, and they will soon learn the meaning of the words because of their context.

 Talk It Over

Recall attitudes expressed by parents or teachers about disciplining children.

Which of these attitudes shows concern for helping the child grow in self-direction?

Which of these attitudes could be destructive of a child's self-esteem?

Individuality in Guidance

Children's needs vary as to the appropriate amount and type of physical guidance required. Helping in the two-year-old group means giving a hand as a child takes a first voyage up an inclined plane, or climbs the slide, or takes to the swing. As a four- or five-year-old, the same child would feel belittled if the teacher even offered a hand, more so if the teacher insisted. Children will gradually grow in independence and be less in need of help in most of the activities of the school. The challenge to teachers is to know what kind and how much help is needed for each child and to step out of the picture as the child shows ability to do things alone. Research indicates a wide variation in independent behavior among children who are the same age. Also, individuals may backslide even when they've been doing something independently for some time.

Demonstrating

Demonstrating or modeling for children encourages them to imitate the desired behavior. "See, you do it this way" and "Now you try it" are comments the teacher often makes while demonstrating. Perhaps the teacher is showing the children how to flush the toilet, how to use a spoon, how to latch the gate, or

A toddler ventures to new
heights with confidence when an
adult is nearby ensuring safety.
(C. Hildebrand, photographer)

how to step on the scales. Time and time again, if the teacher does it first, then children will quickly follow. They understand actions better than words, although you shouldn't omit words just because this is true.

Children watch other children and imitate them. They learn through this imitation. Watch them at the art table, in the music room, at the lunch table. They may first imitate, then do it their own way. Adults do the same thing when they find themselves in a new situation—they watch others for clues as to the appropriate behavior.

Leading

Leading is a technique that gets children going in the desired direction. Perhaps you realize from various clues that two- or three-year-old Gilbert needs to go to the bathroom. Take his hand and lead him over the most direct route. (Of course, go slowly enough that you don't scare him, but you usually don't have long to ponder!) You can speak quietly to him as you go. If a group is going on a field trip, the children in front especially need someone to take their hands and move toward the goal, to stop at the appropriate corners, streets, or things to see. Children gain comfort and security from holding the hand of a teacher or helper. Wanting to hold hands can be a sign of "I'm feeling lonely," or tired, or scared. Not wanting to hold hands can mean "I feel big enough to go alone."

Restraining

Restrain a child when necessary to protect that child or others. Restraint may be a simple act of putting your hand on a child's arm as a suggestion to go slowly down stairs, or it may be intervention to keep the child from hitting or kicking you or others. Restraint has a legitimate place when the child is out of control. A hand on the arm, however, is not handcuffs. The important thing is to stop the child and then let him or her go on. You have a responsibility to protect the child, others, the learning environment, and property. You can couple restraint with verbal guidance. For example, you can say, "I know you are feeling really angry, but I can't let you hit Jonathan. Let's sit over here (by the art table or puzzle rack) for awhile and rest. You can tell me how you feel if you like." Avoid shaming or moralizing. Don't tell him or her that others won't like him or her; just remain firm, fair, and friendly until the child relaxes, then offer several alternative activities that might be interesting to the child. What you show the child is that you can be counted on to help him or her develop self-control, which isn't a lesson that is learned overnight.

Teachers should not feel that a child "needs" to hit them. The child should not be permitted to do so. Even play therapists do not allow a child to hurt them. Certainly, as therapists do, teachers can offer a Bobo clown to knock down, nails to pound down with a hammer (under supervision, obviously), or clay to punch and bang, things that can be symbolically hurt. If a child repeatedly requires restraint, then an analysis should be made of the behavior exhibited to plan appropriate strategies for helping the child.

Removing

Removing a child from a group sometimes helps one who is having trouble accommodating to group rules. A child may only need to be removed from the center of trouble to a place where he or she can calm down and regain composure. The teacher can sit nearby, providing a loving, nonpunishing support. A frequent cause of aggression is fatigue or hunger, so some effort to rest or feed the child may be called for. At a later time you can take a look at the child's schedule to see if she or he is getting sufficient rest. A child might learn that being removed is more fun than staying with the group, that is, time with the teacher may be positively reinforcing for the child. A conscientious teacher will take a look at expectations for the group if this seems to be the case.

"Time Out"

"Time out" is one means of removing the child from the conflicting situation or giving the child some rest when he or she is simply out of self-control. A "time out" seat can be designated somewhat out of the way along the wall where the child can see and be seen, but not be allowed to play. "Time out" should be explained as time for the child to think things over and decide how to act differently. Avoid giving the child lots of attention during the "Time out." It can become rewarding in itself.

"Time outs" for young children must immediately follow the undesirable behavior in order to help the child realize the connection between the misbehavior and the "Time out." It should last only three or four minutes. "Time out, Jimmy," says the teacher. "You need time to cool off and think about how to play with Salizar."

It is important to use "Time outs" only rarely. If they begin to become common—used for the same children, at the same time of day, or in the same locality—some extra study of the situations should be made, changing the environment in some way perhaps to avoid having habits of misbehavior develop. Always keep in mind the mental reasoning level of children in early childhood programs and do not expect too much of them.

Punishing

Use no guidance or punishment that is meant to hurt or humiliate the young child. Punishment has no place in early childhood education because it produces a child full of resentments, fears, antagonisms, and timidity instead of the healthy, happy child you will hope to rear. In your work with children you must continually seek ways to guide children toward the learning of desirable behavior. In their studies, psychologists have found that punishment is not consistently successful in inhibiting aggression or other undesirable behavior. For a discussion of behavior modification, see the closing topic in this chapter.

Gesturing

Getting down to eye level and using meaningful gestures helps children understand your guidance. Getting down to the children's level helps them know that directions are meant for them. Using gestures helps if they don't quite understand all your words. If you've ever been in a foreign country, you'll recall how much you depend on gestures and the context or immediate setting to give you clues to what is being said. It is well to get in the habit of sitting on a low chair or squatting or kneeling during much of the guidance you give. Remember how you must appear to tower over small children. Good eye-to-eye contact helps children understand your guidance.

Using Body Language

You can give children messages through body language. You can show interest, eagerness, or approval through the use of your body, just as you can show lethargy, reluctance, or disapproval. After being acquainted with you for only a short time, children will know when you are tense, irritable, relaxed, in a hurry, loving, and so on. Your stance, your face, how you hold your hands, and how you walk all tell others how things are going for you. This is one reason it is so important that teachers of young children get sufficient rest. If you're rested you'll find ways to cope, but if you're tired you'll get irritated and it will inevitably affect the children. Young children may indeed be better at reading your nonverbal clues given through body language than in understanding your verbal ones.

Physical proximity of an adult can influence the behavior of a child significantly. If the teacher is close to John and Jerry when they are having an argument, they will know that the teacher knows what has been said and done. If they are unable to solve the problem themselves, the teacher will know how to arbitrate fairly. Even though the rules are not stated, the boys will be reminded of them by a teacher's presence.

If a teacher moves into the vicinity of an argument, the children often calm down. Sometimes it is because just a teacher's presence has a calming effect on them; they do relax when a teacher is there. Or they may be reminded of the rules that they had momentarily forgotten and begin putting them into effect. For example, two children are banging each other's tricycle, each trying to push past. The teacher walks nearby. "Oops," says one, "I'm supposed to go this way." The teacher's presence is a reminder of the direction traffic is supposed to flow on the one-way trike path.

VERBAL GUIDANCE

Verbal guidance means using words to influence the child's behavior. Through talking you expect to communicate with children. You want them to develop standards of taking care of themselves, standards of relating to teachers and children, and standards of using learning materials. Many of these standards will be communicated verbally.

Warm affection is part of appropriate guidance for young children.
(S. Russell, photographer)

Self-directed play and conversation are stimulated when teachers set the stage appropriately. (Baylor University Child Development Laboratory)

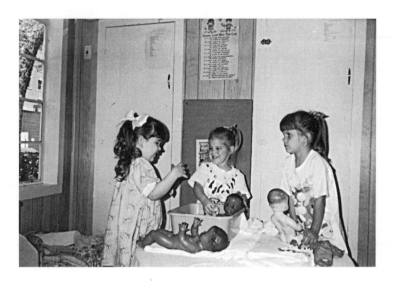

Children's Verbalizations

Children's own verbalizations will be part of the guidance. You must encourage them to talk with you and others about the various requests you are making. Also, suggest that they talk out loud to themselves as they attempt tasks they wish to accomplish. Child psychologist Laura Berk reports that Lev Vygotsky, a Russian psychologist, has recently gained attention with his suggestion that cooperative dialogues between children and the more knowledgeable members of their culture are essential for developmental progress.[1] Thus, if you talk to yourself while attempting a task, your learning is being facilitated, according to Vygotsky.

You must remember that young children's language development is in a primitive state when they are in a child development center. Of course, when infants are admitted to centers you will be privileged to observe their language as it develops almost from the beginning. Young children are just learning to talk and to understand when others talk. They may communicate quite effectively at home. It may come as considerable cultural shock to have to try to understand teachers who have different ways of speaking from their parents and siblings. Following are sixteen guides that you will find helpful in guiding children through verbal means.

Careful Listening

Listen carefully when children communicate their ideas, questions, and feelings. In your contacts with young children try to give them many opportunities to communicate their thoughts and feelings. Children may communicate

---

[1] Laura E. Berk, *Child Development* (Boston: Allyn and Bacon, 1991), p. 30.

verbally and will also communicate with body language, nonverbally. Encourage children to ask questions to get information, and to share their joys and sorrows verbally and nonverbally. Teachers, and parents too, can learn to listen with an ear for the words and with sensitivity for the feelings behind the words as well. To encourage children to talk you first give them your attention by tuning out others, by sitting at the level of the children, and by hearing and observing each child who has something to communicate. Yes, it is generally possible for a teacher to talk alone to one child for a few minutes, if an eye is kept on the rest of the room or yard in order to break away if a big emergency calls.

To encourage the child to talk, sometimes you only need to let the child know you are listening: "Hummmm." "Is that so?" "Yes." or "I'm interested in that." Such nonjudgmental responses encourage a child to go on sharing ideas and feelings.

You may at times use *reflective listening* by putting in words the feeling the child seems to be experiencing. For example, Greg tells you, "My brother hits me." You note the fear in his voice and try to put it in words, saying, "You really are afraid your brother will hurt you." Or, Abby tells you, "My kitty died." Sensing her sadness, you respond, "You feel sad that your kitty has died." Another child tells you, "Sandy told me she likes the birthday present I bought her." Reflecting her apparent happiness, you say, "You're really happy that Sandy liked the present you bought for her." In each instance, state the feeling tentatively enough so that the child could correct you if you are wrong. Reflective listening helps children know you are understanding their feelings as well as their words. By using reflective listening, or *active listening* as some call it, you gain deeper insight into how children think and feel.[2]

Eye Contact

Speak directly to children as you make eye contact with them. Be sure children know you are speaking to them, if you want them to follow your directions. It is never effective to call out directions across the yard or room. Unless you have the voice of a top sergeant, you won't be heard or heeded. Also, children tend to imitate the yelling. It is best to speak to individuals or small groups at their level, using physical closeness and stooping or sitting at their level.

In some cultures eye contact is not a custom or even polite, especially between children and teachers. So children may be taught at home not to look at the adult. Therefore, don't be upset if the child won't look at you and don't try to force the child to look you in the eye. Keep on using your own eyes and talking to the child to gain as much information as you can. Be warmly affectionate to the child and make every effort to reassure the parent that the child

2 For a perceptive article on listening when children talk, see A. Eugene Howard, "When Children Talk Back—LISTEN!" *Early Childhood Education: It's an Art? It's a Science?*, J.D. Andrews (ed.) (Washington, DC: National Association for the Education of Young Children, 1976), pp. 59–72.

is getting along well. When you gain the parent's confidence in you as a teacher the parent is likely to reassure the child at home, which can help you reach the child at school.

Short Sentences

Use short sentences similar to ones the children use until you are sure they will understand more complicated ones. Only the essential words are needed, such as, "Inside now," or "Clean-up time," or "Hold tight."

If you are a teacher working with children from language groups different from your own, listen closely with your eyes on the child's. You can smile, encourage verbal expression, and nod your recognition. Try to learn some words from the child's language. Perhaps you can ask the parent or someone from that cultural group to help you with a minimum set of phrases including yes, no, good, and fantastic. The child will enjoy your effort.

Positive Guidance

Positive guidance requires that adults use an authoritative approach to guidance as opposed to either an authoritarian or a permissive approach. Authoritative, Authoritarian, and Permissive guidance are three types of guidance identified by psychologist Diane Baumrind in relation to the ways parents guide or discipline their children.

Authoritative Guidance is defined by Baumrind as balancing control with granting independence and providing support and nurturing. Children of parents using authoritative guidance are often self-reliant, self-confident, and able to explore their world with enthusiasm and pleasure.

On the other hand, according to Baumrind, parents using *authoritarian guidance* value obedience and are power oriented. Their children often turn out to be withdrawn, unhappy, and distrustful. In contrast, parents using *permissive guidance* give their children as much freedom as possible, with children often ending up more immature and less independent.[3]

It is important that teachers use an authoritative type of guidance with young children in order to have them develop high levels of self-reliance and self-confidence. Your interaction with children should always be supportive of positive growth and development.

Telling Children What to Do

Use positive directions, telling the child what to do instead of what not to do. Even small toddlers can respond to positive directions such as, "Give me the ball," "Eat your cracker," or "Wave bye-bye." These positive directions tell

---

[3] Diane Baumrind, "The Development of Instrumental Competence Through Socialization," in *Minnesota Symposia on Child Psychology,* Vol 7, edited by Ann D. Pick (Minneapolis: University of Minnesota Press, 1973), pp. 3–46.

children what to *do* and suit their level of language development and intellectual understanding. Positive or "do" directions are best for all young children.

You have frequently heard adults say, "I told you not to . . ." (perhaps not to touch the light or flowers, or stove). These are "not to" or negative directions that researchers have found are much harder for children to follow than positive directions. A psychologist at Michigan State University, Ellen Strommen, experimented and found that young children have great difficulty making restraining responses or following "not to" directions. Her study shows that only at around kindergarten and first-grade age does following "not to" directions improve. "But they still make a substantial number of errors of commission," reports Strommen. She also learned that telling young children "not to do something that they have already started seemed to intensify what they are doing, rather than deterring them from it, as though, once they have begun a course of action, they have to complete it before they can shift to something else."[4]

A practical example of this behavior is the child who dashes into the street when the mother yells, "Don't go in the street," or the child who hits another when the teacher calls, "Don't hit Peter." Once children have begun running or hitting they seem to have to complete the behavior before they can shift to something else. Therefore, in such instances, the parents or teachers must use physical guidance (restraint) along with verbal guidance, if they are to succeed in influencing the child's behavior.

 Talk It Over

Recall a number of "Don't" commands you've heard parents use.

Change these into positive commands that tell the child what the adult wants done.

Which commands would you rather have people use with you? Why?

Using "don't" phrases leaves the child suspended and uncomfortable. Remember how you feel if you are driving along a freeway and one of your passengers says, "Don't drive so fast." You probably leave your foot on the accelerator while you look around for the reasons for the advice. Telling children what to do helps them respond quickly, and usually that is what your "don't" commands are designed to do. For example, "Don't spill your milk" or "Don't step on Johnny" or "Don't urinate on the toilet" are often used to get quick results, that is, to stop the behavior for whatever reason you feel it shouldn't go on. Next time such instances occur, try "Hold your milk straight, Janet," "Step over here," or "Raise the seat before you urinate, Jimmy."

The "don't" habit is difficult to break for many adults, but you will find that it is worth the effort, because "do" directions help the child become self-

[4] Ellen Strommen, "Learning Not To: It Takes a Long Time," *Women and Children in Contemporary Society* (Lansing, MI: Michigan Women's Commission, 1976), pp. 55–56.

directed sooner. A calm, positive phrase helps the child correct a behavior and go on. Some adults say that they don't have time to think of the "right" way to phrase guidance, but in practice you usually have more time than you may think before anything really disastrous happens. In fact, taking time to give clear directions is important. Exactly what do you want to happen? Some guidance isn't clear even to an adult listener.

Start Sentence with Action Clause

Place the action part of your guidance statement at the beginning of your statement. "Hold tight" is better than "You might fall out so be sure you are holding the swing tight." The child may lose interest or fall before you get to the most important part. In the earlier example, if you say "Raise the seat" to Jimmy just as he moves to the toilet to urinate, you may catch him before it's too late. If you give a long discussion he may have either urinated in his clothing or on the seat.

Children direct their own exploration with an adult remaining close at hand.

(Oakwood College Child Development Laboratory)

Give Directions One at a Time

Give directions one at a time, if possible, and no more than two at a time. The younger the child, the fewer the number of directions that should be given at a time. If you say "Scrape your boots and take them off, hang up your coat and put your mittens on the register to dry," you should anticipate that you'll be repeating at least the last part if not all of the guidance several times before it is done. The child may forget all of it by being bombarded with so much. Children process directions slowly and need the context to suggest next steps; therefore, try to give directions one at a time, or no more than two at a time.

Select Place and Time for Directions

Give children directions at the time and place you want the behavior to occur. Children don't keep things in mind for very long, so directions that are in context and of current interest are more likely to be heeded. For example, wait until you are outdoors before giving directions about safety on the playground.

Only Necessary Directions

Give only the directions children really need and avoid being overdirective and bossy. Having set the stage for behavior through indirect guidance techniques referred to in Chapter 2, use a little patience and have faith that children will behave acceptably without a steady barrage of "do this," "do that" directions. Stop talking and watch. See if they really need you to tell them what to do. You may be surprised at how self-directed they already are.

Choices

Make it clear whether the children have a choice or not. For example, some adults have a habit of saying, "Would you like to come in?" Now, this question should indicate to children that if they prefer to stay outside the teacher will permit it. If teachers really expect the children to enter the classroom, then a more honest statement is "Come inside now." Watch such statements as "Would you like to take a nap?" or eat lunch, or go home. They usually are not meant as a choice for the child. "Would you like to paint or play with clay?" surely is a reasonable choice, and the child's decision would be acceptable to the teacher in either case. Children should be given opportunities to make choices, but they should not be confused and disappointed by having choices offered and then refused after they're made. When you just want to offer suggestions, then have a take-it-or-leave-it approach, saying, "you could," "you might," "perhaps you would like."[5]

---

[5] For a discussion on how adults' directions and responses to children are often very confusing, see Charles A. Smith and Duane E. Davis, "Teaching Children Non-Sense," *Young Children,* 31:6, September 1976, pp. 438–447.

Logical Reasons

Give logical and accurate reasons for requests. Children need to learn why requests are made of them. It is legitimate to say, "I want you to come to group time because I like to have everyone together" or "Everyone must go outdoors because there is no teacher to stay indoors with the children who want to stay in." In the long run, you want children to be able to reason out new situations with unique elements not in the situation you help them with.

Children who are given reasons for limits or requests are likely to comply. You'll even hear them inform other children as they play. For instance, you might say, "John, drive your trike this way along the trike path. When you go against traffic you'll bump into other children. It could hurt them or damage the trike." Later on John says, "Hey, we go this way."

If at the water table a child splashes water too vigorously, the teacher should give reasons to stop rather than yelling, "Stop that, Jenny." Simply say, "Jenny, pat the water gently. Mary and Ruthie don't want their shirt and jeans to get wet."

It is neither logical nor a good reason to tell a child that "People won't like you if you splash water on them." Such guidance is threatening to a child. One should remember that it is the splashing others don't like rather than the child.

Arbitrary "I told you so" statements are not reasons. If you make rules or set limits that you cannot validly explain to a child, there is serious question whether you are justified in making the rules or setting those limits.

Logical reasons for guidance requests can be presented to children in what Thomas Gordon calls "I-messages." An "I-message" results when, using the first-person pronoun "I," the parent or teacher tells a child how some unacceptable behavior makes that parent or teacher feel. Gordon, a psychologist, has developed the well-known programs for improving parent and teacher communication called P.E.T., Parent Effectiveness Training, and T.E.T., Teacher Effectiveness Training. Gordon contrasts "I-messages" with "you-messages," which tend to put blame or shame on children. For example, "You just want to get some attention," "You are being naughty," "You're acting like a baby," or "Shame on you," are all "you-messages."

Two examples of the more effective, "I-messages" follow:

"When I find water splashed around the bathroom I get my feet wet and I'm afraid I might fall."

"When I find new books with torn pages, I can't read them to the children anymore. It upsets me to have our books damaged."

According to Gordon, such an "I-message" has three parts.

1.   It tells the child in a nonjudgmental statement how a behavior is creating the problem for the teacher. In the examples it is water splashing and book tearing.

2. It tells the child the tangible or concrete effect on the teacher of the specific behavior described in the message's first part. That is, "I can't read torn books," and "I get my feet wet."
3. It states the feelings generated in the teacher because she or he is tangibly affected. That is, "I'm afraid," or "It upsets me."[6]

In *Parent Effectiveness Training* Gordon discusses the value of "I-messages," indicating that they:

1. Let the child know how a behavior is interfering with the parent's enjoyment of life or the parent's rights—that the parent "owns" the problem. For example, "I get my feet wet and I'm afraid I might fall" are the adult's problems.
2. Help the child modify behavior that is unacceptable to the parent without feeling blame or shame, because it is the parent's problem.
3. Provoke less resistance and rebellion from the child.
4. Place responsibility within the child for modifying a behavior.
5. Influence a child to send honest messages about feelings.
6. Produce less struggle—less defending and attacking.
7. Require courage, but the rewards are well worth the risk of exposing inner feelings.[7]

State Limits or Rules Clearly

State limits or rules clearly and positively and follow through on enforcing the limits or rules. Limits or rules protect (1) the child or other children, (2) the learning environment, and (3) the facility and equipment. You can clearly let children know what behavior is desirable and that you won't tolerate unsafe practices, chaos, uncontrolled behavior, or damage to facilities. Limits or rules must be consistently and fairly applied. They should apply equally to girls and boys.

Recall that positive rules are easier for a child to follow than negative rules. You can state limits or rules like the following: "You must stay inside the gate." "Hammers stay at the workbench." "The tricycles go only this direction around the track." Short, logical reasons can follow. Be prepared to follow through on every limit you state to a child—this makes thinking through what you state very important. In the first example, to follow through, lead the child inside the gate and close the gate. In the second, see that the child returns the

---

[6] Thomas Gordon, *T.E.T., Teacher Effectiveness Training* (New York: Peter H. Wyden, Inc., 1974), pp. 142–145.

[7] Thomas Gordon, *P.E.T., Parent Effectiveness Training* (New York: Peter H. Wyden, Inc., 1970), pp. 110–120.

hammer to the workbench. In the third, see that the child turns the tricycle around and pedals with traffic. Some children will need physical guidance. You may need to restate the rule or help or lead these children to follow through on the rule you've stated.

Use your presence, as well as your verbal and physical guidance, to help children remember and follow the rules. For example, simply moving closer to children who appear on the verge of overstepping a rule may help them remember to follow the rule they have previously learned, even without having to restate it. Remember that it takes a number of years for children to develop restraint or inhibiting ability. Even five- and six-year-olds cannot be fully depended on. Consequently, for children to learn the rules and to follow them consistently takes years of practice and patient teaching by the adults in children's lives. Most children do reach the goal of becoming self-directed and self-controlled, fortunately. If you encounter negative behavior, turn to Chapter 19 for some suggestions.

Games requiring matching colors can be child directed and teachers can monitor children's progress in learning the concepts.
(Savannah Public Schools)

Limits and Practicing Student Teachers

Setting limits and following through on limits present a special responsibility for practicing student teachers, such as you. First, confer with the teacher, listening carefully to the explanations to learn about the various stated rules or limits. Ask questions if you do not understand. Then you must try to follow those limits so the children can learn from you just as they do from their full-time teacher. Children will quickly let you know if you state limits that are not typical. When students like you uphold limits consistently—actually tackling and not avoiding situations calling for limits—the children learn to respect student teachers' guidance. Sometimes you'll have to play it by ear, so to speak, as you handle a new situation and then discuss it with your teacher afterward. This occurs when some unforeseen situation comes up, which can be frequent when you work with young children. If college students set limits for children, and then ignore the enforcement of those limits, children soon learn that it isn't necessary to follow guidance given by students. Therefore, for the benefit of children, yourself, and your classmates who follow you, be prepared to set and carry out needed limits with children in a fair, firm, and friendly fashion. With appropriate follow-through each student can be successful in getting children to respond to limits.

Problem-Solving Techniques

Teach children problem-solving techniques. There are times when conflicts arise over rules or limits. It often helps to resolve the conflict through discussion with a child or with several children, especially with four- and five-year-olds. Suppose you have a rule against climbing on the storage shed, yet you frequently find children up there. Meeting with the children involved, you might state the problem, then ask problem-solving questions, waiting patiently for their responses before asking another question. For example, you might say, "We have this problem of climbing on the storage shed. Rough shoes are ruining the shingles on the roof. How could we solve this problem? What do you think, John?" (Wait for his ideas.) Later you can ask, "Is there someplace else we could set aside for climbing?" By involving the children in suggesting solutions to the problem the children may come up with a highly successful solution and readily comply, reminding each other about their decision.

You can help children solve problems by analyzing the problem, its steps, parts, and so on. Try to get them thinking. Help them make personal decisions as to the problem or solution. You may be surprised at the good ideas children often have.

Logical Consequences

Facing the logical consequences of a behavior can help the child learn. Children in the birth-to-age-six group have some difficulty with this theory of discipline proposed by Rudolph Dreikurs.[8] It is discussed here for your information, though it generally applies more effectively to older children because of their more advanced level of mental development. Dreikurs' idea is for the child to feel the consequences of his or her own behavior. For example, if a child dawdles at breakfast and eats very little, the natural consequence is hunger at mid-day. If the child can learn that there is no food until the next regular snack time then the lesson will stimulate less dawdling at mealtime. Such a plan calls for adults with the fortitude to stick to the plan until mealtime. At home many children can help themselves to food from the refrigerator or elsewhere.

The problem with logical consequences is the young child's level of logical thinking. According to Jean Piaget, a psychologist whose work helps teachers understand children's level of thinking, children in early childhood programs are in the earliest stages of logical reasoning. It is difficult for them to see a relationship between two things often very dissimilar—hunger and meals, for example. Adults must remain in control and be responsible in many instances that could bring very harmful consequences to the child, such as running into the street or falling from a high place.

One mother promised her three-year-old that they would go to the airport to watch the planes land "if you settle down quickly and take your nap." He remembered the promise when he awakened. If he slept late they would miss seeing the planes land, a consequence he seemed to understand.

In many situations parents or teachers cannot carry out logical consequences of a child's "forgetting" a rule. For instance, who would back the car over the child's tricycle even though the rule to park the trike out of the driveway had been stated dozens of times?

Avoiding Competition

Keep competition to a minimum by motivating the children through helping them set new personal goals for achievement. You can tell or show children a skill that is logically next in their learning. For example, if Susie can make letters, you can say, "Before long you'll be writing your name." Avoid saying, "Susie, I bet you can make your name as good as Bill does." If Mark can make the swing go with help, you can say, "Before long you'll be pumping the swing all by yourself."

It is not advisable to pit children against friends to motivate them to do the tasks. Deciding to learn something for one's own reasons is growth. A steady increase in skills will help children reach their fullest potential. Adults want children to be happy, not anxious. Competition breeds anxiety. It also thwarts friendships, because people with whom children are highly competitive are seldom their best buddies. The father who came to lunch and cajoled his son to "Eat more like Jimmy across the table" gave the teachers a clue to some of the boy's fears. They envisioned the family dinner table with the young boy

---

[8] Rudolph Dreikurs, *Children: The Challenge* (New York: Hawthorn, 1964).

being pressed to "eat like" the two older brothers. Perhaps here was one reason why he was fearful and shy.

Competition will come soon enough, but let's allow our young children a year or two for them to build their self-images without being challenged to climb higher, run faster, eat more, sing louder, dance faster, or read better than the other children.

Children know when they have succeeded. They are thrilled to zip their own zipper all the way the first time. They call "Teacher!" from the top of the jungle gym when they have conquered their Mount Everest. They take Daddy by the hand to show him how they can do a flip on the monkey bars. These successes are great because children have accomplished skills that yesterday or last month they didn't have. They don't necessarily work hard because they are competing with a peer. They work hard because it is fun to grow in some ability. To be able to share an accomplishment with someone who cares is important.

It is highly desirable for children to become internally self-directed, rather than externally directed by others, and, therefore, not be dependent on receiving praise for every move they make. You can praise in terms of the child's next steps, such as saying at the slide, "Wow! you've made it to the top, Jonathan. Now you are ready to climb up all by yourself, holding on tight."

Using Foresight

Use your foresight in anticipating conditions that might interfere with good relationships among children and suggest or arrange a shift in those conditions. As your experience accumulates, you'll begin to recognize situations that typically interfere with the smooth operation of a group. For example, try guiding a latecomer like Mike into a play group, when you know he isn't skillful at entering groups, by saying, "Mike, we've saved a spot here for you to work." Or, realizing that overcrowding leads to disharmony, when you see numerous children being attracted to a small space you'll quickly adjust equipment to add more play spaces or you may arrange an attractive activity nearby to entice some children from the crowded area. Your foresight combines verbal, physical, and indirect guidance.

Praising

Praise children for jobs well done. Praise and approval should be sincere and given for merit—even if small. When you label desired behaviors as "a good job," the children learn what you like and they will try to repeat that behavior again. You can say, "Phil, you did a good job hanging up your coat." Likewise, you should clearly disapprove of an act you do not want repeated so the children will realize the status of that act, too. For instance, you should say, "Keep food on your plate, not on the table." Focus should be on the tasks rather than on approval or disapproval of the child per se. For example, when the children accomplish taking off boots and putting them in the locker say, "You did a good job of taking off your boots and putting them away," rather than "You are good boys and girls for putting away your boots." Pleasing teachers and parents as shown through social reinforcers such as smiles, hugs, or words of praise, and learning and growing in confidence are the usual rewards. Some special children require special rewards to help them learn. Expert consultation is needed when teachers feel they have children who do not learn by the usual social rewards of a good school experience.

AFFECTIVE GUIDANCE

Affective guidance is interaction between the adult and child wherein the adult expresses emotion or feelings to influence the behavior of the child. The word *affective,* of course, has the same stem as *affection.* Affective guidance particularly helps develop the child's positive self-concept. Affective guidance is part of all the techniques that have been suggested, but because it is important it deserves separate discussion. Affective guidance includes the social rewards of physical affection, smiles, attention, kind words, praise and approval. Praise and approval give a child a good feeling of having pleased the parent or teacher.

Affective guidance is a reflection of genuine feeling. You may give a quick and joyous hug to a child, or you may let a hurt child cry on your shoulder. You can feel free to participate with children in laughter and joy, or to console sad or hurt children without making them feel embarrassed or small.

Positive Feedback

Giving positive feedback on occasions other than when a child follows directions helps keep teachers or parents from just being "the boss." Sometimes when children are "doing okay" a smile or a word helps them know you like them and approve of what they are doing. Recall the discussion of verbal praise in the last section. Praise is positive feedback.

Attention

Giving attention before children demand it helps the children know you know they are there and that you are keeping their needs in mind. Some children who seem to be misbehaving to attract attention can be helped by well-timed doses of attention and positive feedback before they act out to get attention.

Labeling Feelings

Reflecting the feeling the child is expressing and giving it a label helps children understand their feelings. You might say, "You really feel good about climbing way up there, don't you?" or "I know how sad you feel, you really wanted that toy." The ability to reflect a child's true feelings comes with observation and

Climbing is an adventure for children. They feel safe with an adult nearby offering watchful encouragement.
(University of Georgia McPhaul Children's Programs)

practice in being sensitive. Empathy, the ability to feel as others feel, is important. It requires understanding, takes practice, and is essential for needed sensitive relationships at home, school, community, national, and international levels. Recall the discussion of reflective or active listening in the previous section.

Observing

Observing helps you get to know a child better if you find yourself feeling negatively toward the child. This happens occasionally, and you should cope with this feeling as quickly as you can. It usually helps if you understand the child better. For example, what does Sarita do that bothers you? What are her strengths? How can you build on her strengths to improve her relationships with you?

Perhaps a teacher's negative feelings occur when a child exhibits one of the teacher's own weaknesses. For example, if you were whiny and unpopular as a child, then children with these traits may now bother you. Realizing the source of negative feelings can help you plan ways to respond to the child's needs. In every way, try learning more about such children and confer with others to get assistance.

BEHAVIOR MODIFICATION

Psychologists have debated and researched the various methods parents and teachers use to interact with children. Psychological research gives teachers help in selecting guidance techniques and in explaining why some techniques work and others do not.

Behavior modification or operant conditioning is a method developed by psychologist B. F. Skinner of Harvard.[9] It has proved especially useful with behavior disorders, mental retardation, and other problems. In Skinner's system the child is rewarded for the desired response whenever the response occurs. In application with children, small bits of behavior are "shaped" at a time. For example, every time young Merle hangs his coat in the locker he is given praise or *positive reinforcement*. Positive reinforcement is something the child likes and it gives the child the information that he is right. In some experiments positive reinforcers include attention, praise, toys, money, or candy. Of course, normally children discover their own reinforcers. For example, when infants mouth the cup and get a sip of milk their interest in sipping from the cup increases. With positive reinforcement a recurrence of hanging up the coat is more likely to occur than with *negative reinforcement* or no reinforcement. If Merle pricked his finger on a nail in the locker just as he hung up the coat, this might be negatively reinforcing and tend to deter Merle's coat-hanging behavior.

Extinguishing or eliminating negative behavior is one use of behavior modification. Extinguishing behavior is often difficult, because, according to studies, a behavior may persist even when it is rewarded only occasionally. Say a child whines. To extinguish whining requires that on no occasion is the child to be positively reinforced for whining. That is, the child should not get whatever it is he or she is whining for—attention, a drink, or a treat.

Behavior modification theory and research help you understand why it is important that bad habits not be positively reinforced and not be allowed to develop in the first place. Recalling an earlier example of a five-year-old who begged for gum in the supermarket, would you ever reward begging for gum if you did not like begging behavior?

Another finding from this research that helps adults guide children is to learn that the closer to the behavior that positive reinforcement occurs the more quickly the behavior will be learned. For example, immediate praise for hanging up the coat will bring forth more coat-hanging behavior than a compliment at the end of the day.

Behavior modification psychologists have taught teachers to observe children closely and record *baseline data,* i.e., what a child does over a period of time. For example, if Angela bites children, teachers will record the circum-

---

[9] For a helpful reference to understand this approach, see Joel Macht, *Teaching Our Children* (New York: John Wiley & Sons, 1975). Although most of Macht's examples involve older children, the principles are clearly explained.

stances, when and how frequently she bites, and whom she bites. From this record the psychologists or teachers map out a treatment plan using behavior modification techniques to extinguish Angela's biting of others.

Punishment is usually a negative reinforcer, though there might be occasions when a child misbehaves knowing punishment will follow, which makes the punishment positively reinforcing. This is apparently because the child wants to get someone's attention. Physical punishment is not part of a behavior modification program. Although punishment might be effective in suppressing a behavior, a major weakness is that it fails to teach a new positive behavior. Behavior modification plans may call for the use of "time-out boxes," that is, having a child stop everything and just sit in the "time-out box" a few minutes each time after acting out.

Adults at times are quite unaware that they are positively reinforcing a negative behavior, or are failing to reinforce a desired behavior. Sometimes adults give a child a mixed message that confuses the child. By having an observer record a baseline observation or by having a videotape made of the interaction the adult may learn more precisely what he or she is doing when interacting with children. Videotaping is being used in many programs to help in developing parenting and teaching skills. Some parents need extensive practice in giving positive reinforcement, having experienced mostly negative reinforcers during their lives.

Behavior modification has been looked on negatively by many early childhood educators who are concerned that its use might develop a generation of robots. Early childhood educators generally prefer more developmental and humanistic approaches. Some feel the orientation is generally sickness-oriented, focusing on problems rather than on the strengths and health of the child. There are, however, some helpful insights to be gained from the research that aids in explaining why some guidance approaches work and others do not.

CONCLUSION

Guidance is defined as all the adult deliberately does or says, either directly or indirectly, to influence the behavior of the child. Guidance is a consciously determined act which should be based on carefully considered goals and values. The goal of all guidance is to help children to become happy, fully functioning individuals who can make decisions and direct themselves. Direct guidance includes all of the interpersonal communication processes.

Three types of direct guidance have been discussed. Physical guidance includes touching, leading, demonstrating, and the like. Verbal guidance includes techniques for communicating with young children through vocal means. Affective guidance includes techniques in the realm of feeling. The reader will find further elaborations of these techniques throughout the text. These are important techniques to know and to practice. However, knowing techniques is only the beginning. Techniques are no better than the abilities and judgment of people using them. You should try hard to become sensitive to the individual child's needs and to apply the techniques in a humanistic and person-centered way that will really be helpful to the child. With continued study, observation, and practice you can help young children grow in independence and guide them toward their full potential.

REVIEW AND APPLICATIONS

Direct Guidance Techniques

Physical
1. Give help based on the individual child's need.
2. Demonstrate or model the desired behavior or skill.
3. Lead the child by the hand to give direction, reassurance, or assistance.
4. Restrain the child where necessary to protect the child or others.
5. Remove the child from the scene to help the child relax and regain composure.
6. Use no punishment that is meant to hurt or humiliate the child.
7. Get down to eye level and use meaningful gestures.
8. Use your body language to help the child feel competent and comfortable in school.

Verbal
1. Listen carefully when children communicate their ideas, questions, and feelings.
2. Use eye contact when speaking to the child.
3. Use short sentences.
4. Use positive directions, telling the child what to do instead of what not to do.
5. Place the action part of your direction at the beginning of your statement.
6. Give no more than two directions at a time, preferably only one.
7. Give the child directions when it is the time and place you want the behavior to occur.
8. Give only the directions the child really needs and avoid being overdirective and bossy.
9. Make it clear whether the child has a choice or not.
10. Give logical and accurate reasons for requests.
11. State limits or rules clearly and follow through on enforcing them.
12. Use your foresight in anticipating conditions that might interfere with good relationships among children and suggest or arrange a shift in those conditions.

13. Keep competition to a minimum by helping each child set new personal goals for achievement.
14. Praise the child for jobs well done.
15. Use logical consequences and "time outs" when age appropriate.

Affective

1. Give positive feedback for occasions other than when the child follows directions.
2. Give attention before the child demands it.
3. Reflect the feeling the child is expressing and give it a label.
4. Get to know the child better especially if you find yourself feeling negatively toward that child.
5. Show affection and positive regard for children.

 Observations

1. Observe the teacher greeting three children. What does the teacher say? Do? Discuss the effects of the greeting on each child. How do the children respond?
2. Observe and record three examples of physical guidance where the teacher helps, leads, or otherwise physically touches a child to help him or her follow a statement of guidance. Write what was said and done. Discuss the effect of the guidance on the child.
3. Observe, then record three examples of verbal guidance used by the teacher. Write what was said and done. Categorize the guidance according to the examples in the book. Evaluate the effects of the guidance.
4. Observe, then record three examples of affective guidance used by the teacher. What was said and done? Evaluate the effects of the guidance.
5. Observe the parent or the teacher of your case-study child. What direct guidance method seems to be effective? Record examples for your report.

Applications

1. Role play teacher-child interaction by dividing your class into pairs:
    a. A teacher using demonstration, leading, or restraint with a child.
    b. A teacher using gestures to aid communication with a child.
    c. A teacher listening carefully to a child and responding with non-judgmental comments to the child.

       d.   A teacher stating directions positively to a child.

       e.   A teacher using "I-messages" with a child.

       f.   A teacher giving a choice to a child.

       g.   A teacher using affective guidance with a child.

2.   Practice guiding a young child in a home or a school. Give an example of using a form of physical guidance with the child. What was it? How effective was it? Explain.

3.   Practice guiding a young child in a home or a school. Give an example of using a form of verbal guidance with the child. What was it? How effective was it? Explain.

4.   Practice guiding a young child in a home or a school. Give an example of using a form of affective guidance with the child. What was it? How effective was it? Explain.

5.   Write ten verbal guidance statements using "Don't"; then change each one to a positive statement.

6.   Using the list of Direct Guidance Techniques evaluate yourself on a 1-to-5 scale (5 is the highest). On which ones do you need more practice?

ADDITIONAL RESOURCES

Suggested Films and Videotapes

Discipline: Appropriate Guidance of Young Children   VHS 1/2 in.   Color   28 minutes   1988

Illustrates how positive guidance of young children toward healthy development is the foundation of a good early childhood program. It shows ways to handle hitting, tattling, taking turns, temper tantrums. From South Carolina Educational Television. NAEYC, Media, 1509 16th Street, N.W., Washington, DC 20036–1426.

Relating to Others   VHS 1/2 in.   Color   17 minutes   1988

A discussion with Dr. James Hymes, Jr. How do adults help children become self-disciplined? NAEYC, Media, 1509 16th Street, N.W., Washington, DC 20036–1426.

Relating to Others   VHS 1/2 in.   Color   30 minutes   1988

Examines positive ways that adults can help children develop age-appropriate skills such as sharing and empathy. Thelma Harms and Debby Cryer. Delmar Publishers, Customer Service, 2 Computer Drive West, Albany, NY, 12212, 1–800–347–7707.

The Discipline Film: From Awareness to Action   16 mm.   Color   25 minutes   1980

Three dimensions of discipline are examined—Prevention, Action, and Resolution—with a look at teaching behavior required for each. Though elementary teaching is emphasized, the skills presented apply to all levels of instruction. Media Five, 3211 Cahuenga Blvd. West, Hollywood, CA 90068.

Discipline   16 mm.   Color   30 minutes   1981

From the *Look at Me* series on parenting/child development. The film highlights defining the goal of discipline and understanding the processes involved in achieving the goal. Films Incorporated, 733 Green Bay Rd., Wilmette, IL 60091.

FOR FURTHER READING

Cartwright, Sally. "Group Endeavor in Nursery School Can Be Valuable Learning," *Young Children,* 42:5, July 1987, 8–11.

Dinkmeyer, Don. "Teaching Responsibility: Developing Personal Accountability Through Natural and Logical Consequences," Eileen Shiff (ed.), *Experts Advise Parents.* New York: Delacorte Press, 1987, 173–199.

Dinkmeyer, Don and Rudolph Dreikurs. *Encouraging Children to Learn: The Encouragement Process.* Englewood Cliffs, NJ: Prentice-Hall, Inc., 1979.

Dinkmeyer, Don and Gary McKay. *Systematic Training for Effective Parenting Handbook.* New York: Random House, 1984.

Dinkmeyer, Don and Gary McKay. *Systematic Training for Effective Teaching Handbook.* Minneapolis, MN: American Guidance Service, 1980.

Dobson, Fitzhugh. *How to Discipline with Love.* New York: Signet Press, 1981.

Dobson, Fitzhugh. "How to Discipline Effectively," Eileen Shiff (ed.), *Experts Advise Parents.* New York: Delacorte Press, 1987.

Goffin, Stacie G. "Cooperative Behaviors: They Need Our Support," *Young Children,* 42:2, January 1987, 75–81.

Goffin, Stacie G. and Sue Vartuli, eds. *Classroom Management in a New Concept: Teacher as Decision-maker.* Little Rock, AR: Southern Association for Children Under Six, 1987.

Greenberg, Polly. "Promoting Positive Peer Relations," *Young Children,* 47:4, May 1992, 51–55.

Hildebrand, Verna. *Management of Child Development Centers.* New York: Macmillan Publishing Company, 1993.

Hildebrand, Verna. *Introduction to Early Childhood Education.* New York: Macmillan Publishing Company, 1991.

Hitz, Randy and Amy Driscoll. "Praise or Encouragement?" *Young Children,* 43:5, July 1988, 6–13.

Kostelnik, Marjorie, Laura Stein, Alice Whiren, and Anne Soderman. *Guiding Children's Social Development.* Dallas: South-Western Publishing Co., 1988.

Miller, Cheri S. "Building Self Control: Discipline for Young Children," *Young Children,* 40:1, November 1984, 15–25.

NAEYC, "Discipline: Are Tantrums Normal?" *Young Children,* 43:6, September 1988, 35–40.

NAEYC, "Child Choice—Another Way to Individualize—Another Form of Preventive Discipline," *Young Children,* 43:1, November 1987, 48–54.

Rogers, Dwight L. and Dorene D. Ross. "Encouraging Positive Social Interaction Among Young Children," 41:3, March 1986, 12–17.

Weber-Schwartz, Nancy. "Patience or Understanding?" *Young Children,* 42:3, March 1987, 52–54.

CHAPTER 4

Guiding Children Toward Positive Self-Esteem

Key Concepts

◆ Self-efficacy
◆ Self-concept
◆ Self-esteem
◆ Prosocial Behavior

"There! The chinning bar is solid. Who wants to try it?" asks Mr. Clark, the handyman.

"Me," yelled Archie, dashing toward Mr. Clark.

"I do," volunteered Sarah, jumping up and down eagerly and reaching for one end of the bar.

Archie and Sarah were part of Mr. Clark's admiring audience of three- and four-year-old children who watched as the handyman put the new chinning bar in place, positioned the braces to make it hold tight, and finished by firmly tightening two bolts he retrieved from his pocket.

Archie and Sarah were frequently the first volunteers. They had confidence in their abilities. They were curious and adventuresome. Most observers would say that Archie and Sarah each had a positive *self-concept* and a positive *self-esteem*. The one thing they surely possessed was positive *self-efficacy*.

How do children's positive aspects of self develop? Remember to apply both the indirect and direct techniques of guidance studied in Chapters 2 and 3 as you foster children's measures of self. Affective guidance is particularly related to self development. You use affective guidance in words, but also in behavioral cues—a smile, a reassuring glance, or a touch of the hand as you assist the child. As a caregiver or teacher, you can guide children toward a positive self-efficacy, a positive self-concept, and a positive self-esteem. You may be wondering how these three categories of self differ.

"Adventuresome" describes children with high self-efficacy.
(University of Missouri-Columbia Child Development Laboratory)

SELF-EFFICACY

Efficacy is defined as "the power to produce an effect." *Self-efficacy is a personal judgment about one's own ability to produce an effect or to learn a concept or skill.* Self-efficacy has been described in detail by Albert Bandura, a social psychologist, who believes that children learn much from watching others in their environment.[1]

You've seen self-efficacy in operation when you have watched a child copy with confidence a behavior or accomplishment he or she has observed in a parent or others. Often the child copies behaviors without being asked to do so. For instance, Marta takes a pencil and makes curly marks in a notebook as she sees her mother doing. Or Don presses the fork's tine into the piece of meat after seeing an adult do it. Or Linda, the new walker, goes for the stairs every time the gate is left undone, wanting to try the fascinating adventure of stair climbing. Or Randy "plays a tune" on the piano after watching the teacher

[1] Albert Bandura, *Social Foundations of Thought and Action: A Social Cognitive Theory* (Englewood Cliffs, NJ: Prentice-Hall, 1986), pp. 390–431.

play. Or Carla "reads" the picture book, reciting with inflections the story she has just heard her mother read to her. Each is showing self-efficacy, a confidence in themselves and a belief that they can be effective in carrying out an activity.

You've seen self-efficacy among your peers, too. For example, young people often jump on a friend's motorcycle and start the engine without any instruction for driving and stopping safely. Some say the youth is "foolish," while others might say the individual has great confidence in his or her ability to ride just like the friend who came on the motorcycle for a visit. People can be self-efficacious, or very confident of their abilities, even though a skill is new to them.

 Talk It Over

What could we mention that you've never tried, but you think you could handle comfortably? Acting? Computing? Skiing? Skydiving? Quilting? Mountain climbing? White-water rafting? How would you rate your self-efficacy?

CONTRIBUTING TO CHILDREN'S SELF-EFFICACY

What can parents and caregivers do to help children develop self-efficacy? When the environment or surroundings are baby-proofed appropriately, available activities should be safe for the child to investigate. A safe environment means that adults consider the potential hazards and remove them. If a child gets hurt it can curtail an adventuresome spirit and self-efficacy.

Wise parents place covers over electrical outlets, for example, because children can electrocute themselves by inserting metal objects into the socket—perhaps only demonstrating their self-efficacy by inserting an "electric plug" as they have observed others doing. Electric cords are placed out of the way, preventing children from pulling a lamp or appliance over on them while investigating the cord or pulling on it. Breakables, such as vases and figurines, are put up away from small hands. In the baby-proofed room the child is freer to explore without admonitions or danger.

Rooms and playyards of early childhood schools and centers are usually examples of safe environments. The toys are very durable and virtually unbreakable. Equipment is child sized to prevent falls and encourage exploration. Items that will teach the children a skill or a concept are attractively placed to entice them to explore. For instance, paste, paper, and blunt-ended scissors are arranged on a small table inviting practice in cutting, arranging, pasting, and labeling colors and shapes.

Caregivers who have the benefits of training in developmentally appropriate caregiving are encouraged to let the child explore and generally to avoid phrases like "be careful." In reality, most children are quite careful of their own safety. You may recall reading in a child development text about an experiment showing evidence of a child's natural caution. In one experiment the investigator placed the small children on a glass table that appeared through the glass to be a steep cliff. Would the small children risk trying to crawl across the glass even with their mothers on the other side? No. Infants showed fear of the cliff at the 6- to 14-month ages and would not crawl across; they were cautious and protected their own safety.[2]

For self-efficacy or self-confidence to develop, the child needs to explore without pressure. Modeling by others, especially other children, usually encourages children to try a new piece of equipment. When children are successful in using the equipment, that accomplishment is its own reward. They will practice the skill over and over. For example, a father notices that three-year-old Benny hesitates before going down the slide. Rather than tell him, as some parents do, that "Daddy will hold a hand," or "Don't be a baby," the father waits patiently for the child to decide. In only a few days the child's natural curiosity overcomes his fear and he goes to the top of the slide and slides down. Then he shrieks with elation, "I did it!" Benny has conquered his Mt. Everest! The act has its own reward. He goes up and down numerous times during the afternoon.

Self-efficacy shows up in self-care tasks as well. Babies reach for their bottles, or for the spoon when being fed. They reach for the washcloth during their bath. They want to brush their teeth. In every case they have confidence that they, too, can accomplish what they see others doing. Adults should let them try, supporting their beginning efforts in a way that keeps them from hurting themselves. Getting hurt could deter children from trying and cause a setback.

Observing each child and giving close attention to an individual child's needs are hallmarks of a good teacher or caregiver. The need for close attention provides a reason why the number of children per teacher must be low in a high-quality center and also helps explain why parents of young children keep busy in their parenting roles and have trouble getting things other than child care done around the house and yard.

SELF-CONCEPT

A concept is an idea. When does an infant develop a concept or an idea of him- or herself as an entity separate from his or her parents, siblings, or caregivers? Researchers have studied this aspect of human development. Berk, summarizing the studies, describes how infants, watching videotapes of themselves, responded differently than they did to videos showing other infants. Infants clearly knew the difference between self and others among the videos shown to

---

[2] E.J. Gibson & R.D. Walk, "The 'Visual Cliff.'" *Scientific American,* Vol. 202, 1960, pp. 64–71.

"Happy" characterizes children with high self-esteem.
(University of Illinois Child Development Laboratory)

them. By age two the toddler can recognize and give a name to photos of him- or herself. Thus, researchers believe that self-concept develops during the infancy period between 12 and 24 months.[3]

The concept of self continues to develop throughout childhood, adolescence, and into adulthood, all the while changing and growing increasingly complex. All sorts of experiences and people make a difference to the individual's developing self concept.

How do we help children gain a self-concept—the idea that he or she is different from others? Of course, developing a concept of self occurs as children mature enough to learn other concepts. Children are given different names; thus, when you speak to Andy using that name, he gradually begins to know that the word, "Andy," applies only to him. If you record early vocabulary of children you'll see that they learn names of people who are frequently in their environment. If you say to a toddler, "Where's grandma?" the child turns to the grandmother and later learns to say, "Grandma." When referring to his

---

[3] Laura E. Berk, *Child Development* (Boston: Allyn and Bacon, 1991), p. 434.

friend, Ben, Andy learns to say, "Ben." This evidence shows that Andy knows himself and others. At the same time he is also learning words such as milk, kitty, or car from their presence in his surroundings.

As you work with small children you can help them learn the concept of self by saying, as you pat or hug each child, "Billy, you are Billy," or, "You're a boy. Billy is a boy." Children begin learning category words (boy or baby) that relate to themselves as they begin learning other vocabulary words. At first, the vocabulary words consist of nouns, the names of objects in the child's immediate environment.

Categorical Self

Watch infants of 16–20 months learning to understand and use words. They begin to understand that adults are different from children and females different from males. If you say to Lisa, a toddler, "Take the magazine to Uncle Charlie," the child will deliver the magazine across the room to the male. If you say, "Pat the baby, Lisa," she will select the baby from the family circle for her attention. She is learning categories of people as separate from herself. Of course, in a typical family, people identify the infant and toddler as "my baby," or "my little boy," and thus contribute to the learning. Pretty soon the young child says "me" or "I" showing recognition of the category of self.

The language parents and caregivers use with infants and toddlers helps them learn the words for people and objects in their environment. They will be able to understand the words long before they can use them in their own conversation. Thus, it is very important that people speak frequently and warmly to infants and toddlers—using good eye contact whenever possible.

You can see why diapering, a frequently carried out routine, offers parents and caregivers many opportunities for communicating with an infant or toddler. Infants frequently struggle some while being diapered. To get the child's cooperation, you can use your voice, eyes, smiles, and affection along with the gentle physical touching required by the diapering process. Diapering, dressing, and bathing can be a personal time for looking directly into a child's eyes and saying personal things to him or her. These routines do contribute to the child's self-concept, so it is important to carry them out gently and in a pleasant social way.

 Talk It Over

Imagine a child care center where the caregivers, as they change diapers, maintain stoic, impassive expressions without meeting infants' gazes or calling them by name. What do you think would be the long-range impact on those infants?

Gender

Gender is part of one's self. *Gender constancy* is an interesting concept when considering young children. Many are confused about their gender category, and express their confusion in interesting ways, showing that they think they might change from one gender to the other. A boy, Aaron, laughed when asked whether he would like to try on a dress-up dress. "I don't want to be a girl," he said. Julia, a four-year-old-girl, saw her baby pictures where she had short hair and said with amazement, "I used to be a boy!" Such comments give clues to teachers and parents that children do not yet realize the permanency of being a boy or a girl.

There may be some parents who, at their child's birth, wished for a child of the opposite gender and express their disappointment for years, even in front of the child. In some cultures, having a son is very important, especially a first-born son. Girls are often treated as a disappointment throughout life. The parents may need help from professionals in overcoming this disappointment. Teachers can point out to parents the talents and other strengths of their daughters, thus enabling them to appreciate and develop a stronger acceptance of female children.

When a child begins realizing parental preference for the opposite gender it may damage the child's self-esteem. In some instances this non-acceptance also occurs with a disabled child. Wise teachers learn to make every effort to treat children equally within their groups, thereby helping to build positive self-esteem in every child.

Young children often think clothes determine their gender and that of others. For a child learning to identify gender of self and others, hair styles and clothing are important clues. However, today's garments and hair styles for girls and boys are similar and often of little help.

Young children have trouble separating the real world from the pretend world. Teachers can help young children learn that the dress-up hats only help them pretend to be other people, such as firefighters or police officers, and don't turn them into real firefighters or police officers. In one group of threes, the teacher knew that Halloween would be a scary time of year for the children, and for this reason the school did not allow any masks or costumes to be worn to school. On the day of Halloween, the teacher wanted to help prepare the children for the goblins they might face that evening in their neighborhoods. She brought a witch's hat to storytime. First, she just placed it close by her chair where the children could see it. She allowed them to handle the hat and asked them to label it. After several preliminaries she asked them to watch as she put the hat on her head. "Am I still Mrs. Carlson?" she asked.

"No, you're a witch," they said.

She took off the hat. "Who am I now?" she asked.

"Mrs. Carlson," they chorused.

She put on the hat again and asked, "Now, am I still Mrs. Carlson with a witch's hat on?" Many children were confused. One child didn't like the witch at all and moved close to another teacher for reassurance.

Young children's concepts of the world are only just forming and they have difficulty changing from one perspective to another. The rigidness of the young child's thinking is something that psychologist Jean Piaget aptly explained and the example above helps illustrate his point. Often children cannot reverse their thinking, even when the changes are carefully demonstrated to them.

Birth Order

Birth order and space between siblings can also affect a child's self-concept. Research has indicated that only children generally have high levels of self-esteem. Only children and first-born children have common traits, usually including higher mental abilities, largely because enthusiastic new parents generally invest more time in the child's individual development than parents with more children.

Children in a family who are close together in age may develop strong rivalry toward each other. The second child may grow up trying hard to catch up with the older sibling. This tendency can be avoided and competition doesn't develop as readily if the two are of widely differing ages so that each has his or her own place and set of friends. Relationships may also be friendlier and less competitive if the siblings are of different genders.

Teachers should become aware of the family makeup or constellation around each child so they can better understand actions of the child within their groups of children. Teachers may also help children adjust to their home situation if they understand it better. Children who are bossed at home by siblings or parents may tend to be bossy at school. Children who compete at home with a sibling may carry over this competition at school.

"Friendly" describes high self-esteem children.

(University of Georgia McPhaul Children's Programs)

SELF-ESTEEM

What does the child think of herself or himself, the person (self) that he or she comes to understand? *Self-esteem is the judgment a child makes about his or her worth in the eyes of others.* Research indicates that older children who were studied show that their self-esteem is based on two things: (1) social acceptance, and (2) competency, such as mental competency, "I'm smart," or physical competency, "I can run fast." Children who have positive self-esteem, or a positive regard for themselves frequently have parents with the same characteristics. Both parents and children feel competent and accepted.[4]

Prosocial Behavior

Prosocial behavior includes the positive helping actions that children perform for others. Prosocial acts include empathy, sympathy, sharing, taking turns, being helpful, and being generous to others. These behaviors appear to be prominent in children who develop a strong sense of trust during infancy. Children showing prosocial behaviors relate to others in a manner that makes them acceptable playmates to others.[5]

An empathetic child is one who can take the perspective of another child. For instance, Ben, age two, touched Aaron gently under the chin in an apparent consoling action when Aaron cried bitterly after his mother left him at school. Many would believe that a two-year-old is too young to be empathetic; however, Ben's demeanor clearly said, "Your pain, pains me, too."

Prosocial behaviors are characteristic of children with high self-esteem. Prosocial children gain positive responses from others for their helpful behaviors. Other children show their pleasure when the child is helpful and they seek out the child as a playmate. This reinforcement contributes to the child's positive self-esteem. Teachers and caregivers can watch for and positively reinforce prosocial behaviors in efforts to increase the self-esteem of children.

FACILITATING ACCEPTANCE

There are efforts teachers and caregivers can make to help an apparently unliked or unnoticed child find acceptance among peers. When children plaintively beg, "Can I play?" the teacher can offer positive suggestions to the child, sometimes in a whisper, about how to enter a play group. Perhaps the teacher can suggest a role needed in the play theme, by whispering to the child, for example, "Matt, tell the children you're the mail carrier delivering mail."

One girl, Ann, who frequently arrived at the center late, had difficulty entering play groups that were already formed by the time she had arrived.

---

[4] Berk, L. op. cit., pp. 437–444.

[5] Lawrence Steinberg and Jay Belsky, *Infancy, Childhood, & Adolescence* (New York: McGraw Hill, 1991), pp. 288–294.

Children with high self-esteem are often curious and have a desire to learn.
(Parent-Child Development Center, Houston)

The disadvantage of Ann's late arrival was discussed with her parents who appreciated being told of the problem and began carpooling with neighbors. This arrangement brought Ann to school on time and had the added bonus of making her be part of a group of children who arrived together and who often formed a play group together for a time. Ann showed more confidence when arriving with others she knew. This minor adjustment in Ann's arrival helped her become more socially accepted and she showed more positive self-esteem.

To contribute to children's self-esteem, caregivers and teachers must be aware of how children are treating each other, and how adults, including parents, are treating their children. Adults who set appropriate expectations, and convey those expectations to children, can make a positive contribution to children's self-esteem.

Children need pleasurable circumstances and help with handling perceived failure. If you talk to a group of adults about their feelings when in elementary school, you will likely hear some of them recall, often passionately, how dejected they felt at being chosen last for playground teams because they were clumsy or non-athletic. Such experiences have a very negative effect on self-esteem.

Talk It Over

How can adults who organize the sports teams among children at school adjust the way school teams are selected to prevent the process being a threat to children's self-esteem? Where should the emphasis be in games on the playyard? Discuss.

EQUAL TREATMENT

If young children feel they are being unfairly treated, their self-esteem can suffer. Small children are very accepting of children of any racial or ethnic group and they understand nothing about religious differences or discrimination against certain people, until taught.

Allen, a white 3-year-old child, said to a new African-American college student, "You're black." The student, who was participating in the early childhood program as part of her study to be a teacher, was taken aback and questioned her instructor about how she should have responded to the child. To understand the 3-year-old child's point of view, it seemed clear that the child was noticing the new people in the setting—a knowledge skill. The child already knew color names and simply labeled the student "black." Thus, the statement allowed the child to display knowledge of color names—a recently gained ability when you're three. If the student's color had been purple, he would have just as easily said, "You're purple." What was most important was that the child observed others readily accepting the new black student. He soon learned the student's name and interacted with her comfortably. She grew to appreciate the fact that Allen was not already prejudiced at the early age of three.

If you are visiting in a country where children have seldom seen a person like you, you will likely have experiences similar to the one above. For example, when visiting schools and sitting or bending to the children's level to speak or sing to them, many children may crowd around to touch your arm or caress your hair. Their teachers usually apologize for the behavior. However, the children's behavior is simply their natural curiosity and an effort to learn about a person that looks different from those with whom they are familiar.

To paraphrase the United States Constitution, all children are created equal and without prejudice. This is a concept that every early childhood caregiver and teacher, and ideally all parents, should support and help extend throughout their lifetime. In a number of respects each person can be considered a minority person and should be able to identify with the hurt that prejudice can cause. A rural person differs from a city person. A person without grandparents, or without one parent, differs from those with grandparents or with both parents. Those who live in houses differ from persons living in apartments. There are so many ways that any person could be singled out for prejudice, but it isn't kind and should never happen. Children are not born prejudiced. They are taught to dislike those unlike themselves or those living in different circumstances. Children and adults can talk about their likenesses and differences, but the differences do not need to make a difference in our acceptance of each other. When one considers human beings all around the world, there are far more commonalities than differences. Efforts for understanding these commonalities are worthwhile as we all work to knit the world together in global harmony to enhance the quality of life for people everywhere on the planet Earth we all share as a home.

When you meet children, students, parents, or staff members different from yourself, make every effort to reach out to be inclusive and generous with your friendship. You'll be glad you did.

POSITIVE GUIDANCE

The use of positive guidance contributes to positive self-esteem, because the child learns what behavior is expected instead of what behavior to avoid. Positive expectations conveyed to children help them develop positive self-esteem.

Children with high self-esteem tend to share easily with others.
(Marshall University Child Development Laboratory)

Limits conveyed in a positive manner will help the child know what is expected. When limits are expressed clearly and stated directly to the child, he or she is generally willing to comply and will feel good about fulfilling the adult's expectations. Helping children feel successful by pointing out what they are able to do, rather than what they are not able to do, contributes to positive self-esteem.

Psychologist Bruce A. Baldwin states an important idea about self-esteem and winning. He says, "Self-esteem is internally based. The healthy achiever is not emotionally driven to win always, to be number one, or to have the most of everything in order to feel good about himself. Because self-esteem and positive acceptance are based within, that person feels less personal vulnerability when he or she encounters a failure. This quality permits achievement to be an expression of self rather than a way to allay deep insecurity."[6]

SELF CONTROL

Self-control or self-discipline is the major goal of the guidance or discipline you will consider throughout this course. Maintaining and developing strong positive self-esteem should be your goal in every interaction with young children. In the chapters that follow, try to keep self-esteem clearly in the forefront of your thinking as you learn to apply positive guidance procedures.

HANDLING THREATS TO SELF-ESTEEM

Four- and five-year-olds use rather crude and sometimes even cruel measures of acceptance and non-acceptance of their peers. You frequently hear them state clearly who they are inviting and not inviting to their birthday parties, or who they will allow to play in their circle at kindergarten that day. Consistent friendships and overtures from others add to a child's confidence that he or she is regarded highly by others. Consistent rejection can be devastating to a child's self-esteem.

Usually kindergarten children are socialized enough to know they should accept all the other children. Occasionally, as a teacher, you may be concerned about the damage to the self-esteem of a specific child who becomes a target or scapegoat of other children. For instance, in one class of kindergartners, the teacher took the following action when the girls seemed to be rejecting one particular girl for no apparent reason. The girls said such things as, "We won't let Mary come to our party, will we?" or, "She can't play with us." The teacher decided to intervene. The boys were not involved, so she talked to the girls in a separate group.

---

[6] Bruce A. Baldwin, "Building Confidence: Discover Your Child's Natural Motivation." Reprinted in *Annual Editions: Human Development, 1992–93,* edited by Larry Fenson and Judith Fensen (Guilford, CT: The Duskin Publishing Group, Inc.), pp. 72–74.

Highly self-confident children enjoy exploring new ways of doing things.
(University of Tennessee Child Development Laboratory)

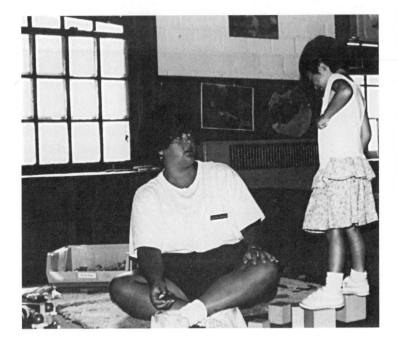

Without referring to Mary specifically, the teacher started by asking "How do you think we should treat people in our class?" and "How do you feel if someone won't let you play?" One girl volunteered that it was wrong not to let people play. Another felt that it wasn't nice not to let someone play with you. Another said that she wouldn't like people who said they didn't like one person or another. In a high moral tone each expressed her idea about appropriate behavior toward others. It was clear they knew the rules of kindness. Yet the discussion was strangely hypothetical, with each girl apparently seeing no relationship to the current problem. The teacher dismissed the group after moralizing a bit about playing with everyone and enjoying the individuality of each friend. Because the discussion appeared to do little good, the teacher continued to work with Mary to help her maintain her self-esteem by giving her extra support through positive feedback and eventually the problem diminished.

PHYSICAL OR SEXUAL ABUSE

Probably no one action by an adult is as harmful to a child's self-esteem as physical or sexual abuse. Young abused children often grow up believing that living with abuse is the norm. Thus, they don't complain. Laws are on the books to protect children from parents or others who are abusive. Teachers and caregivers are required by law to report suspected abuse to the authorities. The major corrective measure is to get the abuse acknowledged and out in the open. Authorities can then deal with the adult and counselors can help the child.

Child care centers have been charged and a few individuals working in those centers found guilty of child sexual abuse. However, a far larger number of abuse cases occur in the homes of children. The seriousness of society's concern about child abuse is evidenced in centers where the doors to all rooms are required to be left open. Toilets have no doors behind which indecent acts could take place. No staff member is allowed to take a child anywhere alone. Visitors and volunteers are carefully screened. Any evidence of indecent conduct within a center should be reported immediately to licensing authorities who will act quickly to protect the children.

HARMFUL ADULT BEHAVIORS

Harmful adult behaviors affecting children's self-efficacy, self-concept, and self-esteem are listed below. Any one or several of these behaviors on the part of significant adults in children's lives can do serious damage to a child's concept of self.

1. Confining the child so he or she cannot explore.
2. Yelling at or punishing a child for natural exploratory behavior.
3. Leaving harmful items in the child's environment, making it possible for the child to get hurt or to harm some cherished object for which the child will feel shame and receive punishment.
4. Being impatient when a child does something that is natural for a child that age to do, such as reach for an item in the environment.
5. Failing to give personal attention to the child.
6. Showing negative non-accepting behavior toward the child.
7. Keeping the child away from other children where new ideas or skills could be learned.
8. Forcing a child to try something that is feared.
9. Failing to recognize and reinforce the positive prosocial behaviors of a child.
10. Stopping the child from verbalizing or explaining an idea or action.
11. Making comparisons among various children.
12. Withholding helpful attention and support from a child who is learning.
13. Paying little attention to a child's verbalizations, thus, not knowing what the child thinks or knows.
14. Failing to appreciate a child due to gender, size, ethnicity, race, or other characteristics.
15. Humiliating or harming the child.
16. Failing to provide adequate nutrition, health protection, or supervision for the child.

17. Stating that the child is too little or too weak to accomplish something the child wants to attempt.
18. Using any form of physical, verbal, or sexual abuse.
19. Failing to acknowledge and really hear both content and feeling expressed when the child speaks.
20. Threatening to abandon the child.

CONCLUSION

Orienting your guidance of young children toward enhancing their self-esteem is the main theme of this chapter. Self-esteem is the judgment a child makes about his or her worth as revealed in the eyes of others. As words or vocabulary become attached to objects and things, the concept of self develops along with other concepts. Self-efficacy is the child's own judgment of being able to do a task or to learn a skill or idea. Gender learning is part of the self-concept. Children are about age four before they are convinced that gender is constant, and does not alter with the change of a name or a garment. Child physical and sexual abuse can be devastating.

REVIEW AND APPLICATIONS

Ten Guides to Developing Positive Self-Esteem

1. Prepare a safe environment with durable toys and equipment so children can explore freely and without pressure.
2. Avoid general use of statements like "Be careful."
3. Point out to children what they can do, rather than what they cannot do.
4. Treat all children equally and avoid comparisons.
5. Recognize the child's elation when accomplishing a task and cheer the child's successes and prosocial behavior.
6. Identify each child by name to aid self-concept learning.
7. Help children form friendships by consciously planning schedules, space use, groupings, and activities to help them learn to form friendships, enjoy others, and cooperate.
8. Assist children in learning that both genders are valued and constant.
9. Study family constellations to understand children's home experiences better.
10. Help parents learn, enjoy and feel competent in their parenting roles.

Observations

1. Observe and listen closely to children at play. Record what each child does and says.
    A. Record two instances of self-efficacy.
    B. Record two statements related to self-concept.
    C. Record two prosocial acts.
    Explain each anecdote. Discuss in terms of self-esteem of children involved.
2. A. Observe and listen closely to your case-study child, recording behavior and conversation samples that show the child's dimensions of self-efficacy, self-concept, and self-esteem. Make a preliminary recording of your assessment of the child's ratings on self-efficacy, self-concept, and self-esteem. For each category, use a scale of 1 to 5 with 5 = high and 1 = low. State your conclusions. Date your notes.
    B. Makes notes on the same aspects of Self during the entire term. Toward the end of the term, using the same scale, rate the child's behavior again on each of the same three dimensions of self based on what you found in later observations of the child. Write a section on aspects of self concerning your case-study child, comparing early and later behavioral examples with your ratings. Discuss changes you've observed, if any.

Applications

1. As you work with children, make notes on two children showing self-efficacy during their play. Give each a positive compliment. Observe and record what happens. Hand in your episode for class discussion.
2. As you work with children, make notes on two children in motor skill play. Listen and record their self-concept statements. State your conclusion regarding the meaning of the children's statements.
3. As you assist with children during group time, record two children's self-concept statements. State your conclusion of the meaning of the statements.
4. As you assist with children, record negative statements you hear any of them make regarding themselves or others. State your conclusion regarding the meaning to the child of each statement.
5. As you work with other adults, record statements of two adults that seemed particularly positive in helping the child develop a high level of self-esteem. State your conclusion regarding the meaning of the statements to each child.

6. Consider cases of child physical or sexual abuse you've heard about. Write an essay on what you think probably happened to the child's self-esteem in these cases.
7. Record a child's prosocial act. Explain what you think the action meant to the child. To others?

ADDITIONAL RESOURCES

Suggested Videotape

A Sense of Self   VHS 1/2 in.   Color   30 minutes   1988

Thelma Harmes and Debby Cryer explore how adults and caregivers can enhance a child's positive self-concept from babyhood on through challenging activities that lead to success. Delmar Publishers, Customer Service, 2 Computer Drive West, Albany, NY 12212, 1–800–347–7707.

FOR FURTHER READING

Baldwin, Bruce A. "Building Confidence: Discover Your Child's Natural Motivation," *Annual Editions: Human Development, 1992–93*. Edited by Larry Fenson and Judith Fensen. Guilford, CT: The Duskin Publishing Group, Inc., 72–74.

Berk, L. E. *Child Development*. Boston: Allyn and Bacon, 1991.

Berne, Patricia H. "Nurturing Success," *Pre-K Today*, August/September 1988, 33–37.

Goffin, Stacie G. "How Well Do We Respect the Children in Our Care?" *Childhood Education*, Winter 1989, 68–74.

Greenberg, Polly. "Promoting Positive Peer Relations," *Young Children*, 47:4, May 1992, 51–55.

Kemple, Kristen M. "Research in Review: Preschool Children's Peer Acceptance and Social Interaction," *Young Children*, Vol. 46, No. 5, 1991, 47–54.

Kostelnik, Marjorie J., Laura C. Stein, and Alice Whiren. "Children's Self-Esteem: The Verbal Environment," *Childhood Education*, Fall 1988, 29–32.

Piaget, Jean. *The Language and Thought of the Child*. London: Routledge & Kegan Paul, 1959.

CHAPTER 5

Guiding Infants and Toddlers

Key Concepts

◆ Infants
◆ Toddlers
◆ Appropriate Guidance
◆ Needs of Parents

Lettie, age 12 months, smiles over her mother's shoulder as she is carried through the door of the infant-toddler center. Her mother plays their usual little game of looking for Cathy, the infant care teacher. "Wh-e-r-e is Cathy? Wh-e-r-e is Cathy?" asks mother in an enthusiastic voice that prompts Lettie to look around with anticipation for her teacher.

"Th-e-r-e she is!" exclaims mother as Cathy sees them and approaches Lettie and her mother with open arms and a big smile.

Lettie is one of thousands of infants who enters an infant center every day to be cared for by competent caregivers while their mothers work outside the home. Lettie is happy as Cathy takes her in her arms, hugs her warmly, and removes her wraps as she tells Lettie about what the day will hold. Lettie's mother is happy, too, as she leaves for work. She feels that Lettie will enjoy the other children at the center and will be well cared for and rested when she picks her up at 5:30 P.M.

There has been a phenomenal growth in the number of infants and toddlers in child care and other early childhood programs in recent years. According to the U.S. Department of Labor, "one half of all women who had a birth in the 12 months preceding the 1984–85 survey were in the labor force. Fourteen percent of the infants of these women were in organized child care facilities with others being cared for in the child's home or another home. These mothers had difficulty in finding child care because organized facilities excluded infants and very young children."[1]

The participation for all women in the labor force has grown steadily from 33 percent in 1950 to 60 percent in 1990. For women with children under

---

[1] *Who's Minding the Kids?* (Washington, DC: U.S. Department of Commerce, Series P–70, No. 9, 1984–85), pp. 3–4.

age six, 12 percent were in the workforce in 1950 as compared to 60 percent in 1990. Predictions indicate that, by the year 2000, women will make up 48 percent of the workforce, according to the Bureau of Labor Statistics.[2]

Labor force statistics such as these help you realize that large numbers of infants and toddlers, along with 3- and 4-year-olds, currently and in the future, will be needing child care. In the last ten years states that previously had no licensing provisions for infant child care have written rules and regulations for centers to follow. The Accreditation Criteria of the National Association for the Education of Young Children includes a substantial portion of criteria devoted to infants and toddlers.[3] In addition, NAEYC has published a booklet of appropriate and inappropriate practices that includes methods of dealing with infants and toddlers.[4] These booklets are useful as part of every teacher's and center manager's library.

 Talk It Over

Assume you are the mother of an infant born today. What conditions would cause you to return to work? Where would you find care for your infant? What quality would it be? How much would it cost? What percentage of your income would that cost be?

INFANT CARE

Infant care outside the baby's own home is essential for babies in many families today. If 50 percent of mothers giving birth in the last year return to the labor force, someone must be caring for their babies. A considerable number of these mothers are single. About 25 percent of working women with children are single, a total of 3.5 million women. Of these, 2.1 million have income under $15,000, 0.9 million have income between $15,000 and $24,999, and 0.5 million have income over $25,000, according to the Bureau of Labor Statistics in 1988. If infant care costs $100 or more weekly you can readily see that a $5,200 yearly child care bill would be pretty devastating to 2.1 million mothers. In 1993 some infant care cost as much as $135 weekly. For this reason, a

---

[2] Bureau of Labor Statistics, November 1991.

[3] See Sue Bredekamp, *Accreditation Criteria and Procedures of the National Academy of Early Childhood Programs* (Washington, DC: NAEYC, 1991).

[4] Sue Bredekamp, *Developmentally Appropriate Practice in Early Childhood Programs Serving Children from Birth Through Age 8* (Washington, DC: NAEYC, 1987). In addition, see Child Development Associate, *Assessment System and Competency Standards for Infant/Toddler Caregivers,* (Washington, DC: Council for Early Childhood Professional Recognition, 1992).

A nursing mother is both wel-
comed and made comfortable in
high-quality centers, thus maintaining and building on the
bonding and attachment the
mother is developing with her
baby.
(C. Hildebrand, photographer)

number of groups and individuals worked for federal support for child care in a
law that was passed in 1990.[5]

Group Size and Staff-Child Ratio

One of the reasons for the high costs of infant care is that groups should be
kept under eight children and the staff-child ratio should be one adult to four
infants. In Chapter 2 you learned about *indirect guidance,* which includes the
ratio of children to caregivers. This discussion of infants will consider infants
before they walk. After walking the infant will be called a toddler.

Small groups are important for safety reasons. Imagine a fire or tornado
emergency where evacuation was required. How many infants could a caregiver carry out and protect safely? Even if you could get four babies in your
arms, could you carry 80 pounds? Licensing regulations usually stipulate that
doors are wide enough that cribs can be pushed through them, enabling a
number of babies to be evacuated via crib.

Group size and staff-infant ratio are important for other reasons, too.
Bonding and attachment are important emotional development processes that
take place in infants. They are becoming bonded to their parents, and must
become bonded to their caregivers. To develop the *sense of trust* that Erik Erikson places as the first stage of development, infants must find a kind, caring,
and responsive environment.[6] Wise managers of centers assign experienced
caregivers to infant care with goals for keeping the staff stable, thus contribut-

[5] "Public Policy Report, '101st Congress: The Children's Congress,'" *Young Children* 46:2, January 1991, pp. 78–81.

[6] Erik Erikson, *Childhood and Society* (New York: Norton, 1963).

ing to the development of bonding, attachment, and a sense of trust in the infants.

 Talk It Over

Assume you are assigned to work with an infant caregiver in your training. How can you keep from interfering with the bonding that is taking place between the caregiver and the infants? Why is the assignment somewhat difficult for you? For the infants? For the caregiver?

Health Protection

One of the areas of greatest concern for parents who send an infant to a center is that of health. Infants are particularly vulnerable to germs, so extra care must be taken to protect their health. Cleanliness, isolation of babies who show symptoms of illness, and particular attention to the health of the caregivers are of vital importance.

Immunizations

One thing parents do before entering the child in the center is to bring the child's immunizations up to date. The American Academy of Pediatrics recommends the following schedule:

2 months:	DTP, Polio
4 months:	DTP, Polio
6 months:	DTP
12 months:	TB Test
15 months:	Measles-Mumps-Rubella
18 months:	DTP, Polio, HIB
4–6 years:	DTP, Polio
14–16 years:	Tetanus-Diphtheria

DTP stands for Diphtheria-Tetanus-Pertussis. Pertussis or whooping cough is particularly dangerous to very young infants, thus the reason it is recommended at such a young age. The vaccines are given in a series with later boosters. HIB is the newest vaccine on the list starting nation-wide in 1987. HIB stands for *Haemophilus influenza type b*. This bacterium causes spinal meningitis, as well as other diseases. HIB is given until the child is 5 years old. Childhood diseases of measles, mumps, and Rubella or German Measles have now been controlled by vaccines. Chicken pox is the next disease officials have hope of eradicating. Polio has come under control in the United States because of the immunization program. UNICEF is spearheading immunizations in the underdeveloped world to help prevent millions of deaths of children each year. With UNICEF's help other diseases may join smallpox as a relic of ages past.

Parents should attend to these immunizations, seeing that they are given on time and that the child gets the needed booster shots. They should maintain a record of immunizations in their files at home, even though their physician will also keep a record. Enrolling a child in a group care program requires up-to-date immunizations for the protection of the child and others. These records must be on file in the center. There is some risk when giving children their immunizations, but these risks are very small compared to the problems that could occur if large numbers of children should contract these diseases. The Vaccine Injury Act of 1986 is expected to compensate the families of children who have adverse reactions to these vaccines.

Illness

Nothing panics parents more than the bad news that their baby has become ill. Not only do parents have concern for the baby, but a working parent also feels responsibility for the job. Centers need some arrangements for taking care of sick babies during the day until the parent gets there. The health team—nurse and doctor—must be contacted. Parents must also be encouraged to have

A three-month-old is bright-eyed and will remain so in infant care if proper steps are taken for her care.
(Ishen Li, photographer)

arrangements made for backup care for a sick child in the home of a relative or friend. Parents will then be able to deal more comfortably with this type of bad news.

The center needs specific policies about when it will care for a child who has what may appear to be a simple cold. Only with proper nursing care can a sick baby be cared for in a center without infecting other children and placing the child's own health in jeopardy.

Parents of sick babies usually feel extremely guilty because often they must continue to work and leave their children with someone else. Caregivers should develop ways of communicating with parents to help them be effective in the parenting hours that remain each day after their babies leave the center.

A recent innovation is a system called sick child care, which has generally been attached to a hospital or health unit. This is a protected place for children who are too ill to attend a regular child care center. These centers are generally in the larger cities and are staffed with nurses and other medical personnel. They are expensive compared to regular child care, but offer families a service that helps avoid the panic felt when a child is sick and some extra important responsibility connected with their employment requires their presence.

President Clinton, early in his term, signed a bill titled The Family Leave and Medical Act that will allow parents to take time off from employment for the birth or adoption of a baby, or the illness of a child, while keeping their jobs and health benefits intact. The law applies to employers of fifty or more people.

Staff Precautions

The first precaution is for all caregivers to meet the health requirements of licensing. Usually this means to be in good health and to have had a negative tuberculosis test. Caregivers should get sufficient nutrients and rest to keep themselves in good health. They also must practice the utmost care in handling items that might transmit germs to the infants or themselves. They should wash their hands frequently to prevent the spread of infection among their charges. After they wipe a nose or after they diaper an infant they should wash their hands very carefully.

Diapering is done only on designated surfaces and the staff uses disinfectant to wipe diapering surfaces. A number of infectious ailments are caused by feces material being spread to the mouths of others, thus the imperative of precautions regarding diapering. Toys that are mouthed are rinsed with disinfectant as recommended by public health agencies. Centers use disposable or diaper-service diapers to ensure sanitary diapers for each child. If you assist in an infant care center it will be essential for you to follow careful hygienic procedures that have been established.

Appropriate clothing is needed to keep children warm in cooler weather and to avoid overheating in warmer climates. Infants need to be dressed so they can comfortably roll over, crawl, and stand, depending on their developmental level. Babies should go barefoot in the warm room.

As a caregiver of infants you will become informed of symptoms of illness in an infant—fever, fretting, or unusual changes in the baby's behavior—and discuss these changes with more experienced caregivers, and the parents.

Safety is of primary concern at all times. Infants are never left unattended. When leaving the room, even for a minute, the staff member alerts another caregiver. Objects that might prove dangerous are picked up, to keep babies from accidentally tumbling over them. All hazardous substances are kept completely out of the infant care center playroom and yard. They should be kept in cupboards that no infant is able to reach.

Low climbing equipment is usually provided to challenge the developing motor skills. Be sure these steps are padded and safe.

While you will want babies to be where you can always see each one, you can let an individual baby play "alone" in a corner for a while. Remember that having many babies together is quite stimulating and tiring, and even a baby may know when some peace and quiet is desirable.

Electrical outlets are kept covered with appropriate covers to prevent babies from sticking objects in them and electrocuting themselves. Babies are often quick in their behaviors. A mother let her baby play with her car keys. The baby turned toward the electric outlet and was about to insert the metal key when the mother, fortunately, turned her attention back to the baby again.

Nutrition

The baby's food is of primary concern to all. The average baby is expected to double its birth weight in six months and triple it in twelve months. When fea-

Sitting safely in a high-chair allows the infant to become involved in his own feeding. Food may cover the face and fingers, but the new skills learned are well worth the cleanup.

(S. Russell, photographer)

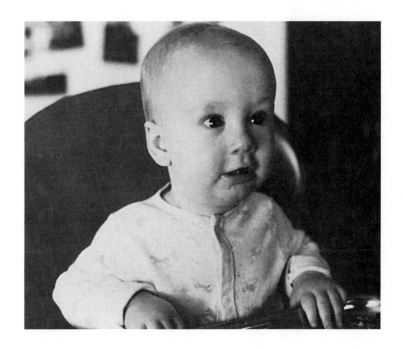

sible, nursing mothers are encouraged to come to the center to nurse their infants. They are provided a quiet comfortable place to nurse and play with their babies. Close proximity to mothers is one advantage of centers that are on the mothers' work site. Or, some nursing mothers express their milk and bring it to the center for their infant's feeding. This milk must be carefully marked with the infant's name, stored in the refrigerator, and warmed in warm water, not a microwave, when the baby needs a feeding. Breast-feeding is considered superior to other feeding forms and should be facilitated by care-givers whenever possible, especially for the youngest infants.

The caregiver's hands are always washed before picking up the bottle. Whether bottles contain mother's milk or formula, caregivers hold the baby warmly cradled in an arm while feeding, talking quietly, and making continuous eye contact. Feeding contributes considerably to the sense of trust and bonding that is taking place for the infant.

Around six months, or when solid food is introduced to the infant, cereal, bananas, applesauce, or other pureed baby food can be fed in a semi-inclined baby seat with you talking to the baby between bites and maintaining eye contact. Use plastic bibs that have a wide pocket to catch the food that falls away. Finger foods such as a toast stick, chunk of banana, or graham cracker are interesting to babies. Their natural inclination to mouth everything gets the reward of a tasty morsel. This is the beginning of self-feeding, a measure of independence that is a goal for the babies.

You may have to feed two or three babies at once, which will challenge you to keep their food and spoons separate. Be sure to refrigerate food immediately after taking a serving out of the jar for the baby. Infants are usually messy eaters when they are learning to take solid foods. You'll find yourself opening your mouth as you wish the babies would. If babies are hungry they will usually be eager to eat, so avoid cajoling them to eat. Just stop when they begin turning their head away or spitting back the food you are spooning in. Also, do not put food back into the jar after it has been stirred and tasted. It is bacteria-laden and will contaminate the food remaining in the jar.

Sleeping

A baby looks so peaceful and trusting when falling asleep. Nothing is more powerful—and evidence of trust—than to have an infant fall asleep in your arms. As a caregiver or parent you will become familiar with each infant's sleeping habits. Like most things about infants, sleeping is very individual. One of the most important things that happens during the third or fourth month is for the infant's sleep habits to become stabilized in a rather regular pattern.

You, as a caregiver, will gain as much information as possible from parents about their infant's sleep habits, in order to make your expectations and services similar to theirs, and to learn what parents think the infant needs.

A bottle feeding is given with warmth and attention while holding each infant.
(University of Missouri-Columbia Child Development Laboratory)

You can learn information in a few moments from them that might take you days to discover on your own. You'll emphasize to parents that the center staff needs to know if the infant had a good night or a sleepless night the night before. This information can alert you to possible needs of the infant each day. Problems with sleep might indicate oncoming illness. Any sort of illness during the evening or night should be reported.

Some parents have cribs similar to those in the center. Another infant's home sleeping arrangements may be quite different and the infant may react restlessly to the center's crib. Safety standards for cribs must be followed. The bars should be close enough together that little heads can't get caught between them, for example. The rollers on the legs should function smoothly, especially when cribs are counted on to be used to evacuate several infants during an emergency. Of course, this use means that the doors have to be large enough for the cribs to roll through. Some cribs have a mirror on one end enabling the baby to watch him- or herself while in the crib. Mirrors are popular with babies and seeing themselves in the mirror is part of learning about oneself.

Your center's sleeping room will be different from the infant's home and it may prove helpful to ask the parents about the infant's sleeping arrangement and routine. Some parents have the infant sleep with them. Some nursing mothers are inclined to spend some time, perhaps nearly all night, with the infant beside them in a combination sleeping-nursing mode. This is a matter of choice for the parents and for discussion with their pediatrician. Upon entering a center, such an infant may feel that the crib is cold and lonely. The infant may need special cuddling or holding close to feel secure before going to sleep. Other infants who are fed and promptly returned to their cribs by parents may readily accept the center's routine.

A pacifier may be used if the infant seems to need additional sucking after feeding. Dentists believe that milk or juice held in the mouth is harmful to the teeth. Thus, it is not recommended to place the infant in a bed with a bottle of milk or juice to help the baby go to sleep or to keep from waking up.

Some parents feel that if the baby is fed "extra" he or she might sleep longer and demand less attention—especially when they wish the infant would sleep through the night. Other parents awaken the baby early to give a feeding before they retire. Nutritionists warn against this overstuffing, believing that it interferes with the child's ability to self-regulate its food intake and may lead to obesity later on.[7]

Self-Quieting at Sleep Time

Many adults, failing to recognize the infant's need to sleep, try to help the baby go to sleep by rocking and so on when they would do infants and themselves a favor if they would just put the baby in the bed and let him or her quiet down alone.

T. Berry Brazelton, noted Harvard pediatrician, has suggested that babies should be allowed to develop their own going-to-sleep routines. He believes that babies, like older children and adults, need some time to get into a resting position and to learn to quiet themselves before falling asleep. Also, they do not always need to eat before going to sleep. Some adults assume the responsibility of quieting the infant when the baby might very well learn to do so without adult help. Psychologist Christophersen advises parents to use several steps to accomplish the sleeptime self-quieting process. He suggests the use of silent touch or massage techniques, as verbalizations can often be too stimulating and disquieting for the infant.[8]

---

[7] Ellyn Satter, "The Feeding Relationship: Implications for Obesity," *Food and Nutrition News,* Vol 59:3, May/June 1987, pp. 1–3.

[8] T. Berry Brazelton, *On Becoming a Family: The Growth of Attachment* (NY: Dell Publishing Co., Inc.), 1981, pp. 148–151. Also, see E. R. Christophersen, *Beyond Discipline: Parenting That Lasts a Lifetime* (Kansas City, MO: Westport Publishers, Inc., 1990), pp. 117–119.

In our Native American and other cultures the swaddling of infants is common. Swaddling means the baby is tightly wrapped in a way that keeps him or her warm, and in the early months prevents the baby from waking due to startle reflexes. If a baby is inclined to awaken itself with startles, you can try swaddling to see if that will help keep the baby asleep.

Your infant center has staff to care for infants and, considering their total caregiving load, probably prefers to have each baby awake at a different time. Thus, caregivers can be relaxed and follow the child's natural rhythms for being awake and asleep. Parents will often lament that they have every night's sleep interrupted. You can empathize and reassure them that most babies eventually develop a pattern of sleeping all night.

Sudden Infant Death Syndrome (SIDS)

Some parents may be worried about Sudden Infant Death Syndrome (SIDS). These deaths occur in sleeping infants who appear healthy when they are put to bed. Some parents have electronic monitors set up at home to help monitor the infant's breathing and sound the alarm if irregularities occur. If a center has a baby that parents are worried about, they should have a discussion with the pediatrician to help understand the problem. Low birth weight and premature infants may be more susceptible to SIDS. The infant center should have sufficient caregivers to help keep an eye on all infants. Some authorities recently suggested that, to prevent SIDS, babies should sleep on their backs or sides and not sleep on their stomachs. However, other authorities were not convinced by this report and feel that most babies prefer to sleep on their stomachs.[9]

Babies Born to Addicted Mothers

Babies whose mothers were drug addicts are presenting increasingly difficult problems for infant care centers. Managers should seek special advice from the medical and drug authorities to gain insight from their experience on how to handle these babies as centers attempt to cope with this increased burden on child care services. If your center enrolls any of these babies whose mothers took the illegal drug cocaine or crack during their prenatal period, then you may find these babies "irritable, tremulous, and difficult to soothe during the first three months," according to researcher Rist. There are increasing numbers of such babies due to the recent increase in the number of cocaine-addicted mothers giving birth. As many as 50 percent of these babies are abandoned in the hospitals by their mothers and may become public wards. The babies have trouble forming attachments. Rist also warns that, since the first

---

[9] Cathy Trost, *Wall Street Journal*, April 16, 1992, B1 and B5.

group of these babies is reaching age three and will soon be school-age, the schools should be thinking ahead and learning about them. These babies may be brain damaged and will always need a special caregiving environment.[10]

Report to Parents

Your center should have a system for reporting to parents when infants sleep, including the time of day and the length of nap. Thus parents may be able to predict what to expect during the evening hours. For example, without a late afternoon nap, the infant will likely fall asleep when riding home in a car. With a recent nap, the baby should be ready to be playful for a period after reaching home. Some working parents prefer to keep their infants awake to be able to enjoy them during the evening hours. In some cases the infant's need for sleep may not be met with this procedure.

Crying

Crying is the means by which infants let you know they need attention. Each will be on an individual schedule of eating and sleeping, thus, rarely will you need to be doing the same thing with all. It is fine this way, because it would be pretty hectic to diaper or feed all three or four of your charges at once. You must be quick to respond to a baby's cry. Each is developing the sense of trust that is so important in these early months. Trust develops as one's needs are met.

You may need to hold the baby to your shoulder or lay it across your knees face down to ease a pain that makes it cry. Sometimes walking helps soothe a restless infant. Laying the baby in the crib on its stomach and patting the back gently may help a baby too. You'll learn to understand the infant's various cries and develop means of coping with them as the two of you get acquainted. Talk to your more experienced co-workers for advice.

It is important that you keep a cool head when babies cry. They need help and have no other way to show or tell you. If they are crying for attention, attention must be given. If they are hungry, they must be fed. If they are tired, they must become relaxed enough to fall asleep. If they are in pain, it could be due to a bubble in their stomach, or the need for a bowel movement, or other more serious problems. You'll learn to observe closely so if you need help in dealing with the infant you can describe what is happening in fine detail to a doctor or a nurse or other person who advises your center.

---

[10] Marilee C. Rist, "The Shadow Children: Preparing for the Arrival of Crack Babies in School," reprinted in *Early Childhood Education 92–93*, edited by Karen M. Paciorek and Joyce H. Munro (Guilford, CT: The Duskin Publishing Group, Inc., 1992), pp. 15–19.

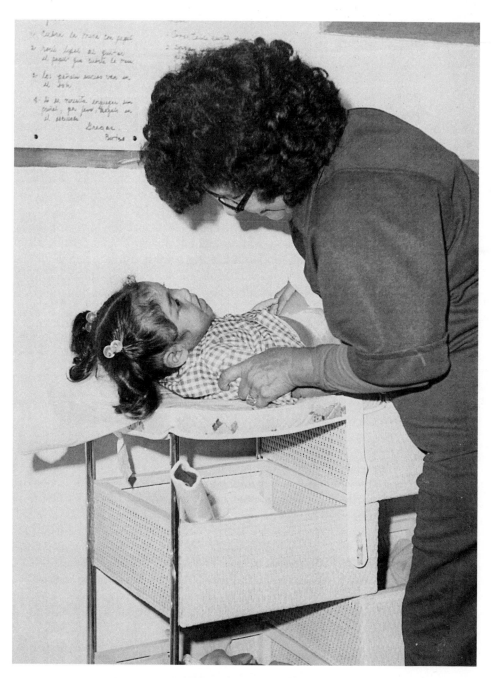

Diapering must be done with special care to prevent the spread of germs and while assuring personal loving attention.
(Parent-Child Development Center, Houston)

Guidance

Use a quiet natural voice when speaking to your babies. Verbal guidance is part of *direct guidance* discussed in Chapter 3. Keep yourself down at the babies' level so you have good eye contact and the baby knows you are speaking to him or her. Make responses to the infants when they say something to you using their babbling or when reaching out to you. They are learning to communicate.

Enjoy entering into baby's play for a few moments, perhaps handing one a toy, patting another, or speaking to another. Respond with quiet enthusiasm to a baby's new accomplishment. Remember, there are several caregivers and neither they nor their babies need to hear everything you say—only the babies you are in charge of. High noise levels are tiring to all.

Babies are learning to socialize with others, so you'll help them offer a toy to another, or accept a toy when one is offered. When a hard toy is in a baby's hand you'll be alert so it isn't accidentally used to clobber a friend. It won't be purposeful, of course; babies are only learning how to say "hello" to their friends. With your alert attention many seemingly antisocial acts can be prevented.

You can engage the babies in little games that you invent or learn from other caregivers. Ask your parents for ideas of things you once enjoyed. Maybe it was the verse

> *Trot Trot to Boston.*
> *Trot Trot to Maine.*
> *Trot Trot to Providence*
> *And back again.*

while you were held on your parent's knee, or the game of hide the sock under the pillow when you were nearing one year of age. Take it easy with the babies and let them entertain themselves for a time unless you feel they are going to interfere with another baby.

Observe for fine details. For example, baby play consists of lots of movement to and fro and up and down. You'll soon quit worrying about most of the falls these little people with a low center of gravity seem to take. Try not to overcaution them about falling. They don't understand your words but may understand your hesitancy and become worriers. Remember their bones are cushioned between cartilage, which helps them to be resilient, and their diapers provide extra padding.

By the time the baby can sit alone, around four to six months, he or she will enjoy a book (made of firm cardboard with one picture to a page) while you turn the pages. As you turn the pages, name an object on a page and wait for the baby to imitate you. The baby will enjoy listening to songs you sing. You can make up short songs to tunes you know and include the baby's name and what the baby is doing. Like, to the tune of *Twinkle, Twinkle Little Star,* sing

John is climbing up so high.
John is climbing down so low.
John is climbing all around
Now he reaches to the ground.

Dr. T. Berry Brazelton encourages parents and caregivers to talk often to their infants. When the baby hears enough it simply turns away for a break, then turns back when it wants to signal that it is ready for more. When you try this with babies you'll soon find them leaning forward, gurgling, and cooing in response.[11] Even during feeding and diapering you can talk about what is happening, the names of items, and what you are going to do next. Of course, you know the baby doesn't understand you yet, but will in time. You are a major source of verbal stimulation when you are the infants' caregiver for eight hours a day, and language is one ability that makes us differ from other animals, so always value these opportunities to talk to your infant. You can also help parents see how important verbalizing is by showing them the games you play with the baby.

Babies enjoy seeing themselves in a mirror, and that is why you frequently find mirrors framed into the wall of infant playrooms. Babies pat the mirror, perhaps saying "Baby." The best toys are colorful and of various weights and textures without sharp, dangerous corners or tiny pieces. Remember that mouthing everything is a universal infant characteristic. It is one way a baby learns about the world at first. Avoid curtailing mouthing; just keep the items that the baby mouths clean and safe.

While you play with the babies they will do new things each day. Your center may have a system for reporting these events to parents. For example, certain records are kept about eating, sleeping, and bowel movements that are given to the parents at the end of the day. You might add a note—Jimmy stood alone, or, Sylvia said, "Da Da." This alerts parents to watch for the same behavior at home and enjoy it with the baby.

Outdoor time is as popular with infants as it is with older children. You may dread the layers of clothing that have to be readied in order to get your charges outside. Learn to move quickly with the preparation so the first infants dressed won't get overheated. Once outside they may enjoy crawling on a padded playpen or pulling up to its sides. The fresh air is good for you as well as the babies, so try ways to make it enjoyable and worth the effort of dressing and undressing that is required.

Sharing with Parents

As a caregiver you are supplementing the care, love, and attention that parents can give their baby. They are the primary caregivers. It is important that you

---

[11] T. Berry Brazelton, *Infants and Mothers* (New York: Dell, 1983).

realize this, and that you help them feel important to and in charge of their baby. Talk with parents as they arrive and depart about routines and little joys and frustrations. Let them know that you value their experience with the child.

Parents also like to share with other parents, comparing their experiences and the things their physician tells them. Thus, you might facilitate two or more parents getting together to talk. You can help parents anticipate the next stage in the infant's development, perhaps by taking time to watch the toddlers in the room next door or talking about getting their house ready (babyproofing) for a moving and climbing toddler. Centers usually have a library of books and pamphlets that parents can borrow to read about child development.

TODDLERS

Life gets more complex with toddlers. Parents soon realize this fact as their sedentary infant becomes a moving dynamo. As you move to participate with toddlers you will recognize parental frustration. Of course, it is exciting when the baby walks. That is a milestone to be recorded in the baby book. However, once upright, there are new vistas for the baby who suddenly has become a *toddler*. Toddlers can get into many things that were safe during infancy. Now, being put in a chair or crib no longer means that the toddler will stay there. They move quickly, often to unsafe places like a driveway, so one never dares let them out of sight. Their knowledge of danger is not at the level of their physical skills for moving, and they need adult protection.

A mother of a sixteen-month-old took her toddler, Randy, to a pediatrician. She called Randy "hyperactive" and wanted a drug to calm him down. While the toddler was in the office he curiously investigated the physician's notebook and pencil, the scales, looked under the table and in the wastebasket. "See," said the mother, "he's never still a minute." Accompanying her was her four-month-old, a quiet and angelic little daughter whom the mother could still happily manage.

 Talk It Over

Referring to Randy in the anecdote mentioned above, discuss what is likely happening in this family. What is normal or abnormal about Randy's behavior? What do you think the doctor did? As a caregiver, what would you advise the mother to do to help Randy have a developmentally appropriate place to play?

Group Size and Adult-Toddler Ratio

The toddler can now move to a group of no more than twelve toddlers with two or three caregivers—a minimum of two for a 1–6 ratio. Recall that group size and adult-child ratio are part of indirect guidance as discussed in Chapter 2.

As with infants, keeping the same people working with the same group of toddlers aids the toddlers' security in the group situation. With a few toddlers and their parents to know well, each staff member can create a more personalized environment, toddlers can become fully acquainted with peers, and staff can learn to predict their needs and reactions. This type of safe environment is contrasted with larger groups in larger spaces where caregivers often do not even know the names of children who seemingly run in circles bumping into each other like loose satellites in orbit. The toddler group could be hectic for all concerned unless organized using indirect guidance to minimize some of the potential problems.

Toddlers need close personal attention from their teachers and caregivers. Observing toddlers one notes considerable *self-efficacy*. Self-efficacy means a commanding confidence that "whatever there is to do, I can do it." Self-efficacy is a concept described by psychologist Albert Bandura.[12] It is a characteristic that is essential in learning many of the things we expect toddlers to learn—eating alone, dressing, moving, climbing, talking, and toileting, for example. A goal of caregivers must be to harness the power and energy of self-efficacy and allow the toddlers to try the things they think they can do.

Personal Greetings and Guidance

When you first see the toddler be sure to give a personal greeting using the child's name and a pleasant smile. This is an example of *Affective Guidance* as discussed in Chapter 3. Such greetings help the child feel warm and accepted by the teachers and others. Avoid focusing on clothing as a major item of discussion. Even as toddlers children can feel left out if their clothing isn't mentioned or isn't especially attractive, as in some cases. Little girls get far more attention for their clothing than little boys, which sets up a gender difference that is unnecessary and unfair to little boys. Also, positive comments on adorable little dresses make children want to wear only dresses when comfortable warm slacks would be much better for them. Expensive dresses are also a drain on many parent's limited resources.

Verbal guidance that you plan and use for each child should be personally given. Each needs to know you are talking especially to him or her. Remember that toddlers are entering what psychologist Erik Erikson called the stage of

---

[12] See Verna Hildebrand, "Young Children's Self-care and Independence Tasks: Applying Self-Efficacy Theory," *Early Child Development and Care,* 30, 1988, pp. 190–204.

autonomy wherein the toddler often exerts choices by saying "no."[13] Parents and others learn to frame questions so "no" isn't so easily answered.

Toddlers aren't yet able to take group directions, so look each one in the eye as you kneel at their level and tell each one what you want done. Often you'll need to follow up with physical guidance of helping or leading the child to do the activity you are suggesting. Use short phrases such as "Hold tight" or "Both hands, Jenny." Reasons given to toddlers usually fall on deaf ears. However, if you give reasons, make them short and be sure you have the toddler's attention. Give directions one at a time and in the place where you expect the behavior to occur.

Health

All the health precautions essential for infants are carried over to the toddler stage. Immunizations should all be up-to-date. Diapering is still needed, so those precautions also carry over into the toddler groups.

Toilet training may begin sometime after about eighteen months, depending on the child's maturity and the parent's wishes. Children usually learn quickly where they see others using the toilet. A routine of toileting may help the children feel like trying to use the toilet even before they have the control to let go and urinate in the toilet. Urinary and bowel control requires a great deal of neurological maturity. It may come earlier in some than in others. You will never shame or punish a child for toilet accidents or wet diapers or panties. Like many things with toddlers, the less fuss made over toileting the sooner it will be learned satisfactorily. Even with daytime success it will likely be a year or more before nighttime dryness results. See Chapter 17 for more details on toilet training.

As you work with toddlers rely on the experienced caregivers for advice about helping individual children. They will likely be conferring with the parents regarding their attitudes and procedures for toilet training, hoping to coordinate the efforts of home and school so as not to confuse the toddler. Once the toddler has the notion of independence at the toilet, the child may totally reject the diaper. Then you should watch closely for the signs of need and guide the child to the toilet quickly. Once the child hears the urine fall into the water of the toilet he or she will be happy over the success. You, too, can show your pleasure in the success by saying, "You did it!" However, always offer praise quietly, for your purpose is to encourage this child, not to make others envious of the verbal praise a single child has received.

Sleeping

Toddlers typically are ready for a good nap after their noon meal is over. Most who have had a busy morning, including some fresh air, will be ready to sleep.

---

[13] Erik Erikson, *Childhood and Society*.

Some may be out of sorts if they do not have a crib to sleep in, wanting to roam from their sleeping cot. Quiet talk, soft music, darkened room, and occasionally a back rub will help the less interested child relax and fall asleep. If a child does not take a nap it is likely that the evening will be a disaster for the parents. Or the child may fall asleep en route home and completely confuse the home routine. Like other things, keep from making a big fuss over napping. The pattern of others sleeping will generally be followed by a toddler.

Safety

Safety is of increasing concern as toddlers move faster and faster on their more confident little legs. They can slip out of sight quickly, so fences and gates and doors with latches out of reach are needed. Self-efficacy is so high that they will follow older children on climbers and slides, sometimes bringing themselves into harmful situations. Thus, careful monitoring by adults is needed, especially when several age groups play together. This role may be assigned to students in training. You should remember that older children may lead toddlers to climb higher than they would climb if they were alone. Your role is to stay close by, even stopping unsafe adventures.

Social Play

Toddlers will touch anything and everything in sight. Thus, the environment should allow for exploration. This is another practical use for the concept of indirect guidance. Each toddler is a little independent world, moving, climbing, and manipulating. Several toys of the same kind encourage a movement from solitary play of infants to parallel play of two- and three-year-olds. *Parallel play* means that children play side by side using similar toys. They seldom integrate their actions in a common theme as they will when they reach age four and beyond when their verbal skills and ideas have developed further.

Toddlers will engage in simple pretend play, like chugging the train, or feeding the bottle to the doll. They may put themselves to bed in the doll bed or want water in the cups at the little table. You can facilitate pretend play by adding appropriate props from time to time and locating additional similar toys when an interest develops in one thing and everyone seems to want to try doing it or using it, for instance, when everyone wants a wheel toy to run up and down a ramp. Waiting is very difficult for toddlers. At times, you can model the pretend play, like drinking pretend coffee from the small cup, to get the action started.

Two toddlers may have difficulty sharing, especially if visiting a friend's house where one believes the toys are all his or hers. Language skills are as yet not developed enough for each child to talk over ideas and wants. Caregivers or parents need to stay close by to help toddlers learn to communicate. They can say, "Give Lisa the truck, Jake." And to Lisa, "Tell Jake, 'Truck, please.'"

Books

When reading books, two or three toddlers make a sufficiently large group. Popular stories are about children their age and must be relatively short to keep the interest of several children. If you mistakenly select a long story and see the interest lag, just skip through the pages, ad-libbing about the pictures. Never nag the children about how to be quiet, sit still, and listen. Just make it so interesting, yet short, that each can have a pleasant reading experience. Practice reading your story to yourself beforehand so you can estimate where children could participate with making sounds or answering a question.

Toddlers are learning to listen to a story with others and it is difficult for some. Their prior experience is on a parent's lap with the book very close at hand. In school the adult's role is to make storytime fun. Let each child select a book to hear. The group should be two or three children. It is better to assign each helper to a few children and have that person read quietly to that group, rather than try to make six to twelve children remain as a group listening to the same story, even if all the caregivers will stay in the group and help. As their story-reading experience grows, toddlers may be able to tolerate larger groups and less individual attention.

Toddlers especially like showing off things they know in a picture book. Hold the book so each can touch "the pretty flowers," or the "red ball." Or, repeat a story line, such as, "And the dog said 'bow wow.'" These techniques keep the toddlers involved and help them learn to speak.

Language Activity

As indicated under guidance the toddler learns to say "no," which may express the autonomy the child is feeling. Early words are often called "telegraphic," because like the telegraph message they are abbreviated sentences. Adults should provide feedback using more elaborate sentences. For example, the child says, "Red shoes," indicating a desire to wear her red shoes. Mother or others can say, "Kim wants to wear her red shoes." Talking about and labeling items is helpful. Between the fifteenth and twentieth month the child typically begins to use longer sentences, much to the surprise of those around him or her.

Encouragement to label items, to talk to you, and to express desires are ways you as a caregiver can help the child learn language. Toddlers' *receptive vocabulary* will be greater than their *productive vocabulary;* therefore, don't hesitate to use words with the child.

It is nice if you can jot down the new words a toddler says each day to inform the parents and encourage them to record words they hear. The early stage of language development is particularly interesting and fun to observe when it occurs before your eyes.

Toddlers begin to have a sense of humor, often enjoying laughter when they fall or are surprised by something. Teachers can get some relief by encouraging some fun times and laughter with the children, perhaps through

CHAPTER 6

Introducing a Child to a New Group of Children

Key Concepts

◆ Parental Considerations
◆ Visiting Centers
◆ Teachers Make Home Visits
◆ Preparing for Opening Day

It was Bradley's turn to have his throat checked. When the nurse started to look at him he tore away from her and cried, "No, no. I want my mamma." His face turned red and his bottom lip puffed out.

Children in new situations frequently resist routines such as the health check carried on in some centers. They cry. It takes a while for a child to become accustomed to the routines of a child development center but the main problem here was that Bradley was not accustomed to having his mother leave him at the school.

In the following pages you will learn some methods for easing children into the early childhood group situation so they will be comfortable and happy. Bradley's mother was one who had time to help with his introduction to the group situation. However, some children are brought to full-day programs "ready or not," as children say in games of hide-and-seek. When a parent is committed to a job, then the child goes to the center "ready or not." Of course, it would be better for the child, the parent, and the center if the child were prepared in advance for the new experience of entering a group. Children who are anxious may not eat or sleep. They may have setbacks of long-standing duration in toilet training and socialization. Some of the following suggestions will help you help the child make a satisfactory entry into a new group.

PARENTS CHOOSE CENTERS

Many parents believe that if a center advertises child care someone has stamped "approved" on that center. This may not be true. There are some reg-

A teacher and mother will confer to help the child adjust to center life.
(University of South Carolina Children's Center)

ulations in nearly every state, but most regulations are minimal; therefore, parents should visit a center to see if it meets their standards. Even after they enroll their child they should be alert to shifts in compliance. One mother placed her child in a center when she began a teaching job. The first day when she returned to pick up the child the entire group was asleep without any supervision. She actually went in and dressed her child, then looked for someone to advise that she was taking the child. She finally found the director in a second-floor room. She told the director that it was the last day her son would be coming to the center for she felt the supervision was not sufficient to keep him safe.

In judging quality the parents who know about accreditation standards will ask for evidence of accreditation of the school or center by the National Association for the Education of Young Children. Accreditation was discussed in Chapter 1. Directors will generally point out their symbol of accreditation framed in their office.

Half Day Visits

Centers should invite prospective customers in for a visit. One or both parents should go with the intention of staying several hours to "just watch." First, the director will likely brief them on program and procedures. The director will be aware of the standards that the center should be meeting and will discuss them with parents in a confident manner, having been through this interview numerous times. After a tour of the facility, parents should ask to sit in the back of the room in which their child will be most of the time. Here they may be able to gain some insights into the type of care and education that children are given. They can note the children's freedom and the interactions among adults and children. Of course, teachers and caregivers may behave differently under observation than they may when visitors are absent, but if the parents stay during several routines they should be able to get a fair idea of the operation.

They can notice if teachers are kind, if children enjoy school, if there is a minimum of crying and aggression. They should also look for cleanliness and for provisions for emergencies such as fire. They should look for children with signs of illness.

 Talk It Over

If a child accompanies the parent to check out a new school or center how could this child's behavior distract the parent who wishes to evaluate the center objectively?

Parents' Visits

The child should not accompany the parents while they are investigating the centers. The presence of the child can be very distracting for parents. Instead of looking at the center discriminatingly, they will be concerned with needs of their own child.

For three- or four-year-olds a premature visit to the center may cause them to be fearful, even rebellious. The children who are enrolled may make what appear to be unfriendly comments to the visitor. The child and even the parents may then conclude that they don't like the center. Once the choice has been narrowed, the center can be introduced as "your school." Then the child may be brought for an introductory visit.

Babies and toddlers, too, should be taken for preliminary visits to their new home-away-from-home before they are left. The steps outlined here can be followed for them as well.

ALTERNATIVES FOR PARENTS AND CENTERS

Parents can agree to introduce their child to an early childhood education program on a trial basis. This is acceptable to many centers. Centers also may exercise some options regarding admission of children.

Sometimes when a new center is opening the staff gets so anxious about numbers that they eagerly take all children—often without regard to age balances, facilities, and staff talents. A few weeks later they may have a waiting list that includes children who would have balanced their classes and operation plans in a far more reasonable manner. There are children who are disabled to various degrees that a particular center definitely should not try to serve because of space, staff, or program limitations. This should be explained to parents frankly.

The center should offer space to a family on a tentative basis. "You try us out, and we'll see if your child likes our school and if we can provide the program your child needs. If either of us feels our school isn't effective for your child, we'll help you locate a more suitable child care service." Such a policy can save many problems and hard feelings for all concerned.

HOME VISITS

When teachers and caregivers make visits to the homes of newly enrolled children, they are setting the stage for a comfortable and happy introduction of the new children into the group. The children will be getting acquainted with one or two new persons on their own ground. The teachers can observe how parents and child interact, how the child rates relative to other children in the family, and how the physical surroundings seem to be influencing each child. Children will feel comfortable with their own toys around and will remember these new people when next they meet them at their "new school." The fact that the teacher knows where children live will give them confidence and security as they become adjusted to the new situation. Home visits have been an integral part of Head Start, the popular Federally funded early childhood program. The work with parents is credited with much of the success of Project Head Start.

Parents, too, will be more at ease in their own home. Appointments are naturally made with indications that the home visit is part of the routine procedure prior to a child's enrollment. The reason for the visit is to become acquainted with the child on his or her home base and to discuss the school program and any concerns the parents may have regarding their child's adjustment. When the visit is made before the child actually enters school, the parents need not worry that their child has been misbehaving or has a problem, as they may later on if an appointment for a home visit is made. At the early date parents are the ones who know the child and have information to give.

Parents of young children are surprisingly easy to talk to once you get acquainted with them. They are happy to find a person with sincere interest in the development of their child. Many are isolated from relatives and friends who are interested in children, so they welcome the teacher who will talk about the child's concerns. Working parents especially have limited time for neighborhood kaffee-klatsches where some commiserating with other parents might take place. Therefore, they welcome the interested teacher who is concerned about their child.

If this sounds like a pep talk to teachers and children's caregivers to make home visits, it is. The benefits will be many, and you will readily discover them by making your first home visit. Visits do take time, but are well worth the effort in the long run. The initial visit need not be long. A half hour will do, and with careful routing you can visit several homes in an afternoon. Children will frequently say, "You came to my house" or "You know where I live, don't you?" indicating increased confidence in teachers whom they have met on their own ground. Of course, subsequent visits besides this initial one are important, and you will note increased rapport with children and parents as a result. As a student you may be included on home visits your lead teacher makes as part of your training. Ask to go on a home visit if it appears they are being omitted.

Goal of Introductory Phase

You will want the new child to feel that school is an interesting and protective place. Consequently, your guidance should support a child making initial adjustments to a new place and people in the absence of parents. All your knowledge of the child, the family, and their needs must be combined to help you decide what course is best during these crucial days.

For children moving from one school to another the teacher helps the new child become acquainted with other children, introducing the child by name and, perhaps, giving a bit of human interest information about the child. For instance, the teacher may say, "Jennifer is our new friend's name. She has a new baby brother named Peter. How many of you have babies at your house?" The teacher can make a special effort to include Jennifer in activities until she seems at ease.

SCHOOL VISIT

A visit to the school facility prior to attending gives the young child a further feeling of confidence in the new situation. The child can explore the playroom and play yard a little at a time with the parents staying as close as needed. It is helpful if the visit can take place when other children are not there, or perhaps while they are outdoors. Thus the new child can survey the physical setting and try out various pieces of equipment without becoming involved with the other children. The child can see the locker which will be a personal space for clothes and treasures brought from home. Each locker and name tag will have the child's name carefully lettered. Using a child's name frequently helps assure each that he or she is personally valued and has a personal identity. The child can even try out the bathroom, a visit that may hold some anxiety, especially if the parents keep stressing that the child must be toilet trained in order to enroll. The sleeping room and cots may also be shown. Plenty of opportunity to explore the play yard and try out the equipment should be allowed. With an unhurried visit the school will usually hold sufficient interest that the child will look forward to attending.

Children learn that their locker or cubby is for their belongings. Teachers may need to help when objects don't quite fit. (Kansas State Early Childhood Laboratory)

 Talk It Over

Discuss the advantages of allowing a child to explore a new school without the presence of other children.

FIRST ATTENDANCE

A first big step toward independence is the child's first introduction to school. The child's first attendance may be with an ongoing group or it may be with a newly forming group. In the ongoing groups, a new child is taken in stride, fitting into the routines. The child may stay for a short time the first few days while the mother or father is usually encouraged to remain to give support where needed.

A Few Children at a Time

In new groups, especially those starting in the fall, the teacher may choose to start only a few children at a time so there will be ample time for the teacher and the assistants to interact with each child individually, showing each one the routines and equipment. Parents may stay if needed or they may tell their child they are leaving and then leave, thus giving their child practice in being self-sufficient for a while. After each group has had its day or two of introduction, the teacher brings the entire group together on a regular basis.

These procedures may sound like idealistic ways to introduce the child to his or her first school experience. Because this is such an important new step, it is well to make it as free of anxiety for as many children as possible. There are families who have time for this casual introduction to the school if the teacher wants to plan it this way.

Employed Mothers and Fathers

There are some employed mothers and fathers who are unable to pay for extra part days at a center or to take time off from their jobs to introduce their children in a gradual supportive manner. Experience with babysitters will facilitate the transition for some children. However, teachers and caregivers can expect to be presented with children who indeed will be left "ready or not." In

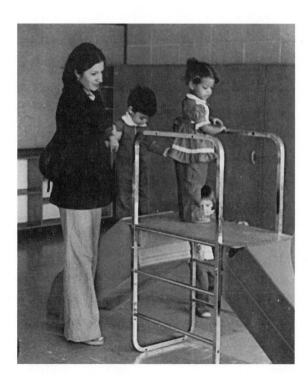

A parent gives her child attention for the first few hours in a new center to help ease the adjustment to the new situation. (Texas Woman's University Child Development Laboratory)

such a case, it seems wise to have the parent simply wave goodbye, so the child knows the parent is really gone, and for the teacher to console the child in whatever way seems appropriate. It is usually unwise to encourage the parent to slip away unnoticed, because the child may become more upset than ever after discovering the parent's absence. The child usually adjusts rather quickly when convinced the parent is really gone. The teacher can volunteer to report to the parents by telephone if desired.

ROLE OF HELPERS

Helping the Child

As a helper you can play a significant role in the introduction of new children to the group, whichever situation applies. For example, one assistant consoled a quietly withdrawn but anxious child while the lead teacher carried through with routines. The assistant sensed the child's need for comfort and responded to that need.

In another example, the new but confident student teacher carried on with a group while the teacher was tied up with a child who cried so loudly that the teacher could not even get away to call the child's mother. The boy was one who had had years of experience with babysitters, so no one had predicted that he would react so violently to being left at school, where he had already visited.

On another occasion a mother entered the parent cooperative nursery school with her own daughter and observed the teacher being overwhelmed by a sobbing child who was unhappy at having been left. The mother's child went happily about her playing and allowed her mother to help the teacher with the sobbing child. After a period of walking and consoling, the child accommodated to the school enough to finish the day playing.

Teachers, as they become acquainted with children on home and school visits, will make estimates of how various ones will adjust. They will take these estimates into account as they plan the learning experiences for the first few days. The estimates will affect the assignment of responsibilities to co-workers. Even so, the helpers will need to be particularly sensitive to children's needs and step in where needed. When the home visits and school visits have been made as suggested, the child who is deeply unhappy will be a rare exception.

As a participating student, be ready to take suggestions quickly and to be helpful to the teacher in any way you can as new children are being introduced. Teachers will be grateful for your help and your interest in assuming responsibility.

Things to Try

There are some things to try when children are unhappy as they enter school. Stay close to the children and console them. Frequently it is necessary to hold

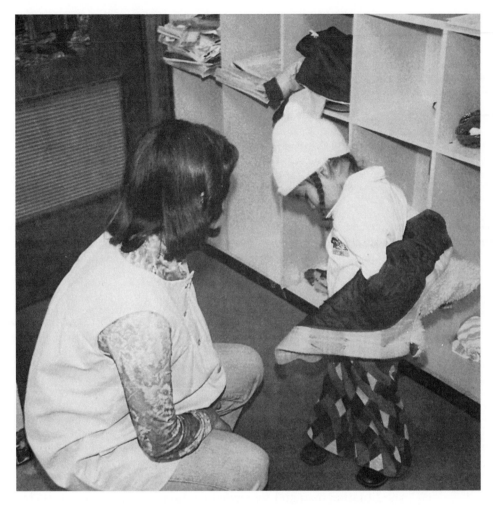

Patience, while the child helps herself, is part of easing the child into a new routine.
(San Antonio College Child Care Center)

a child on your lap. Some monologue-type conversation may alleviate anxiety if you don't press for answers to questions.

The younger children, infants and toddlers, are usually easily distracted by just showing them something new such as a toy or a bus passing by outside. A cracker, a drink, or a walk may be a good diversion for an unhappy child, helping the child think of something else. Occasionally, you can get another child to include the new child in play activity, thereby alleviating the situation. Reminding the child that "Mother will come back" or "Mommies always come back," may be helpful. Reflecting the child's feeling of sadness and reassuring the child that everything will soon be all right may help as well.

Taking the child away from the group to "help" you with some project may work, provided it is possible for you to be away from the group. By helping to clean up the kitchen or bathroom, the child may regain some composure. Some children will relax if they hear a story or record. Others may find painting relaxing. Water play is often good, especially in the kitchen or bathroom setting—this makes the parallel with the home evident.

When a child has been absent for vacations or because of illness, some of the same anxiety about being left may be revived. Generally this anxiety will be overcome far easier than the original anxiety.

It is a rare child who can say to his or her parents, "I'm ready for you to leave." Therefore, it is better not to put the child into a position of making this decision. The teachers and parents should make the decision, anticipating as many of the rough spots as possible, then dealing with the situation decisively when the time comes. Often parents who hesitate or delay departing may upset their child more than necessary. Some gentle guidance for the parents may be called for, the separation being difficult for them, too.

Happy Adjustment

It would be unfair to assume from the time we've spent discussing helping unhappy children that the majority have difficulties entering child development centers. If the preliminary steps have been taken carefully, including choice of school, introduction of the teacher to the child at home, and introduction of the child to the school, then the first days are fairly comfortable for most children. In this aspect, as in all others, there are individual differences among children.

A contrasting type of child bears mentioning, too. This is the fellow who seems to have confidence and moves into play groups with gusto. He, too, may need your help, because if the children are in already-formed play groups, the new child may be rejected by the others. Far wiser is the newcomer who looks the situation over and somewhat cautiously finds a niche little by little. In only a few days the newcomer is likely to be playing with the leader of the group.

The overconfident child is usually a boy, but some girls have a problem, too, especially in late four- and five-year-old groups when girls begin forming "best friend" pairs. A new girl may have some difficulty if she is chosen as a "best friend" of a leader or if a leader decides to reject her. The teacher's role is difficult. A teacher once tried to talk to kindergarten girls about how it felt to be left out. They verbalized about how it was "bad" to leave someone out, that you "shouldn't" do it, and so on. The conversation was very hypothetical, and they never really understood that the situation applied to them.

A parent sometimes apologizes for their child's hesitancy about participating with the other children. Some parents don't like to see a child hold back, perhaps riding a trike alone instead of playing with the group. They may explain it as "unusual" behavior and feel that the child is not happy or is not going to participate as they wish. The teacher's role is to reassure the parents

Warmth indicated in a welcoming smile makes a child feel happy about a new school.
(Marshall University Child Development Laboratory)

that the child knows best, that participation with the larger group will come as the child feels ready. Assuring parents that the teachers will stay close by and be supportive is important.

Helping the Parent

The parent whose child is going through this introductory stage may also need help. A mother or father may have a hard time adjusting to leaving the child regardless of the reasons given for enrolling the child. Parents may interpret their decision as rejecting the child, and they may feel guilty. Through the home visits, conferences, and school visits parents gain confidence in the teacher and in the assistants. Once parents become confident that the school is a good place for their child, leaving their child can be less painful for them.

Sometimes a child can be happily adjusted if the mother brings the child to school, but will be very unhappy if left by the father or a car-pool driver. Fathers may then jump to a conclusion that the child is not enjoying school. The teacher can help parents realize that any change in routine may upset the child, including having a different parent drive to school.

In case of difficult separation, the teacher who has the best rapport with the child should step in to ease the situation and help occupy the child. At this point, a new and strange teacher who tries to help may only compound the problem.

Volunteering to telephone the parent later when the child settles down can help the parent's day go more smoothly. The call can reassure the parent that the child is not ill and is now relaxed and playing happily. It can help alleviate the parent's guilt feelings for having left the child in such a state.

CONCLUSION

The first days of school are of utmost importance for each child. This is often a first experience as an individual separate from the family. Up to this point the child may have been carefully protected from social contacts that would have helped make this new step easier. The teacher's role is to take as many steps as feasible to introduce the child to the center in a gradual way. If this is impossible and the policy of the school is still to admit the child, then the teachers must cope with the child as best they can. Some suggestions have been made. It is important to impress on parents that time should be allowed for this introductory process before they go to work.

Throughout this introductory phase, the child will be accepted and loved by parents and teachers even though there is some difficulty in becoming independent. The child will never be called a baby or be threatened or shamed for his or her behavior. On the contrary, the adults will give love, understanding, and support as each child takes this first important step alone out into the big wide world.

REVIEW AND APPLICATIONS

Ten Guides for Introducing a New Child

1. Invite parents to visit the child development center without the child to observe and to discuss educational and business aspects of the program. Agree on a mutual trial period for the child's enrollment.
2. Arrange to visit the child and parents at home to get acquainted on their grounds.

3. Arrange for the child and parents to visit the school together when no other children are present, allowing the child to explore the lockers, bathroom, and learning centers.
4. Introduce a few children for short periods each day for the first week or so to ease the new child into a group situation.
5. Welcome a parent to stay in school with the child until the teacher and parent feel the child is ready to attend alone for a short time.
6. Label lockers clearly with each child's name and give each child a name tag. Use the child's name frequently to encourage a feeling of personal space and identity.
7. Request that all helpers be prepared to act quickly to comfort a child who has separation anxiety or to relieve the teacher who may then comfort the child.
8. Plan simple activities in which most children can be self-directed during the introductory period, leaving more time for adults to attend to new children.
9. Insist that parents tell their child, "We are leaving and will come back to get you," rather than slip away unnoticed.
10. Assist the parents in separating from the child and, if necessary, reassure them by phone that all is well.

 Observations

1. Observe a new child or a group of children being introduced to a center. Report on the problems encountered, if any. Itemize the suggestions from your text that were being followed. Others?
2. Ask the teacher to point out the child most recently enrolled in the group where you observe. Secure the date of the child's enrollment. Observe, then record that child following routines. Record evidence she or he knows the routines. Observe the child at play. Record the child's social behavior with other children. What evidence have you recorded that indicates the child is new to the group? Discuss.
3. Discuss with the teacher and record how your case-study child was oriented to the new group. If feasible, pay a home visit to your case-study child and write up details of what you see and hear that gives you information on the home environment, and sibling and parental relations with the child.

Applications

1. In class describe the first days of school you remember—your own, your siblings', or those of children in early childhood programs. What feelings are prominent in children during those first days of school?

How do parents feel? What can teachers do to make the initial period easier? Divide your class and role play some of these situations. Discuss the feelings expressed.

2. Discuss with parents of an enrolled child the reasons they have for sending their child to school. Find out what steps they took to decide on the school the child is enrolled in. Write a report of your discussion.

3. Discuss with the teacher the methods used to introduce a new child to the center. Write a brief report of your discussion.

4. Observe a new child or a group of children being introduced to a center and report on the problems encountered, if any. Which suggestions in your text were being followed, if any?

5. Discuss with the teacher and rate your school on the Ten Guides for Introducing a New Child. Use a 1-to-5 scale, with 5 the highest rating.

FOR FURTHER READING

Hildebrand, Verna. *Introduction to Early Childhood Education.* New York: Macmillan Publishing Company, 1991.

Table 7–2 *Continued*

Time Block IV—Preparation for and Eating Lunch

11:25–11:40   Removing outdoor wraps and placing in lockers.
              Toileting and washing.
11:40–11:50   Quiet rest period, singing, story.
11:50–12:20   Lunch.

Time Block V—Naptime

12:20–1:15   When finished eating, each child goes to the bathroom to toilet and wash,
              then goes to nap room that has been prepared and darkened.
1:15–2:30   Sleep.
2:30–3:00   Awakening.
              Toileting.
              Dressing.
              Quiet individual conversation or game.
              Putting on outdoor wraps.

Time Block VI—Self-Selected Activity

3:00–4:00   Outdoor play.
4:00–4:10   Clean up play yard.
4:10–4:25   Snack time.
              Toileting and washing as needed.
4:25–6:00   Quiet time indoors or in yard.
              Story, singing, or records.
              Dressing and dismissing children as parents arrive.
6:00   All children gone!

---

to their lockers. They like this game! "Now," says the teacher, "People wearing red shirts may go," and continues in this manner, achieving an orderly procedure for moving from storytime through the narrow locker passage to outdoor time. Coming back to the circle allows the teachers to help children who need help and to encourage self-help in children. "That's fine," the teacher says to one; "Here, this is the way to start that zipper," to another; and "Let's tie that shoe," to another. An assistant quietly leads those who are dressed outdoors.

These examples of effective transition procedures represent indirect guidance that helps alleviate unnecessary crowding. Crowding often provokes negative behavior in children. The use of planned transitions is indirect guidance and a part of scheduling. That is, the use of interesting and varied transitional techniques helps children proceed to the next event without undue confusion or conflict. However, the transition activity probably consists of verbal and perhaps physical guidance, that is, direct guidance.

Children are more at ease with their familiar routine. Any new activity, new place, or new teacher can interrupt their confidence that they know what to do. Changes in the schedule should be explained to children, such as, "We're playing outdoors first today because a visitor from the band is coming later"; or "We're having snack early because we're going to the museum." Explanations help, but teachers and helpers will of necessity give children more individual directions and more reassurance when changes are made.

Table 7–3 *Sample Daily Plan Sheet*

Time	Class of Activity	Specific Activity	Staff
Time Block I—Self-Selected Activity Indoors			
9:00–10:00	Art	Fingerprint	1. Bob*
	Science	Scrambled eggs	2. Mary
	Table games	Farm lotto	Mary
	Blocks	With telephones	Mary
	Small wheeled objects		Mary
	Books	On breakfast foods	3. Janice
	Language arts		Janice
	Music	Record player	Janice
	Dramatic play	Housekeeping	Janice
	Other		Janice
Time Block II—Teacher-Directed Activity			
10:00–10:15	Clean-up		1. Bob*
	Bathroom		2. Janice
10:15–10:25	Snack	Scrambled eggs, milk	1. Mary*
			2. Janice
			3. Bob
10:25–10:45	Story, music, and talk in small groups	Group 1. *Who's Got the Farmer's Hat?*	Janice
		Group 2. *Farmer Small*	Mary
		Group 3. *A Visit to Grandpa's Farm*	Bob
		Songs: "Farmer in the Dell" and "Old McDonald"	
10:45–10:50	Toileting as needed		Bob
	Dress for outdoor play		Mary
Time Block III—Self-Selected Activity Outdoors			
10:45–11:45	Outdoors	Balance beam	1. Janice*
		Birds and leaves	2. Mary
11:40	Clean-up		3. Bob
11:45	Departure of children		

(*No. 1 sets up activity, gets out equipment, completes clean-up)

Putting on shoes takes time, but promoting independence is worthy of the time allowed.
(Baylor University Child Development Laboratory)

Planning for Transitions

Transitions will occur between the various time blocks in the scheduling plan. Will they be orderly or chaotic? Planning specifically for transitions helps keep them orderly. Children and equipment don't get knocked over and feelings remain less ruffled. Children learn to wait their turns when they know from experience that they'll get a turn. The teacher alternates the selection of children to go first, minimizing competition.

Preparing learning centers ahead of time eases transition times. For example, if the art tables have sufficient supplies laid out, if the music instrument box contains an instrument for each child, if there are plenty of cups for a bean-planting project, then children can proceed to these projects without uncomfortable—and sometimes unruly—waiting.

Recovering from Chaos

When chaos happens occasionally, as it does even with the best-laid plans, teachers need to know a "magic game" that gets children's attention and quiets them down. For example, one teacher, Carla, says quietly to a few children as she takes their hands, "I'm going on a bear hunt—Sh-h-h-h. Come along." They stealthily move to the next group and repeat the invitation. Soon the chaotic group is around her where she tells them a story of a bear hunt in a whispering voice, sings some songs, and leads them in some relaxing exercises. Other teachers read special books or recite poems that can be relied upon to get children's attention. Transitions are excellent places to use the stories, poems, ideas, and so on that are stored in your memory, for you may have no time to prepare before they are needed. If you don't have such a storehouse in your memory, then begin to fill it today.

Teachers must keep their voices calm and movements slow, or else they will further excite children. When a group is having difficulty with transitions it may help for one teacher to observe and record what is happening. Then in a staff discussion plans can be made to iron out the rough spots.

Some teachers use a signal such as a flick of the light switch or a soft chord on the piano to inform children quietly of a shift in plans or to quiet them down. They learn from experience that the teacher wants their attention when the signal is given.

SCHEDULING CHANGES

It should be emphasized that once a schedule is learned by the children any changes can cause mass confusion, unless teachers take pains to guide children confidently. They can tell children several times during the morning, "Remember, we are having a backwards day today" or "Today we are playing outside first, then we are all going to hear a woman play a harp." More verbal guidance will be necessary when routines are interrupted. Children may get in the

Volunteers' time and extra activities must be planned carefully to have an optimal impact for both themselves and the children.
(University of Tennessee Child Development Laboratory)

wrong places at the wrong times, and teachers should realize that this confusion is part of having the regular world jumbled up. However, as soon as the schedule stabilizes, children will again fit into whatever routine the teacher sets up, if it fairly accurately fits their needs for rest and action.

Weather

When it begins to rain or an unexpected learning opportunity arises, changes can be made within the time blocks, thereby confusing the children as little as possible. For example, on a rainy day, Time Block I can be extended a half hour and Time Block III shortened a half hour. Children may play some active games, do calisthenics indoors, or take a walk with umbrellas during the last half hour to give them vigorous exercise within the limits imposed by the total picture. Post a "rainy day plan" to have available anytime it storms. A cupboard stocked with some special activities for rainy days, including suggestions for stories, songs, or poems, is a great help when it rains unexpectedly. Teachers should make such preparations to enable a substitute teacher to take over for them, also.

Special Guests

If an unscheduled special guest arrives offering an unexpected learning opportunity, the teachers might agree to shelve the scheduled plan for the period and listen to the visitor during the minutes the visitor is available. When prior planning includes a special guest, that person's particular activity will dictate the type of activity to eliminate for the day. For example, a visiting twirler who marches children around the yard could be scheduled for outdoor playtime, whereas a guitarist might be scheduled for the time usually reserved for music. Using these considerations when scheduling events ensures that the children's energy level is appropriate for the type of behavior expected—marching with the twirler, or relaxed singing with the guitarist.

Special Events

Field trips, holidays, and local special days such as a Lion's Club parade may make changes in the schedule essential. For example, if a field trip requires walking, then restful activities should be scheduled for the pre- and post-trip period. Or, if children are attending a children's symphony the schedule is rearranged to provide an early period of vigorous outdoor activity to help the children's bodies be ready for restful listening.

When planning a field trip, if most of the events of a regular day can be preserved—even though abbreviated—the children will have fewer questions about "What do we do now?" and "Where do we go?"

Holidays especially can overtire young children unless teachers are especially alert to protecting them from too much stimulation. Children's home schedules are often disrupted with extra shopping trips, late bedtimes, and

The schedule allows plenty of time for a child to savor the experience of creating her own product.
(University of Illinois Child Development Laboratory)

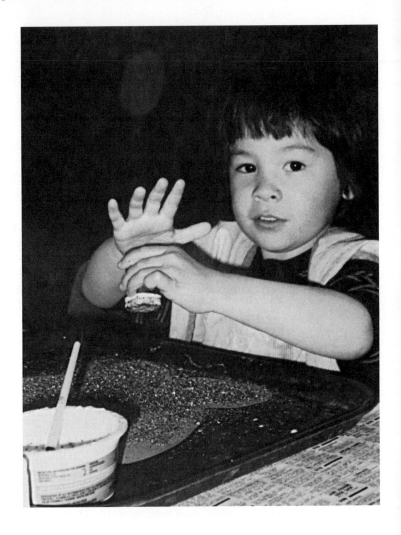

special excitement, making a low-key program at the child development center in order. Some centers receive attention from service clubs in the community who want to do something nice for children. The wise teacher or director, rather than allowing a larger number of interruptions in the children's schedule during the brief holiday season, may find it desirable to encourage service clubs to schedule their events during the January to March period when special events will really brighten children's days. If the teacher explains the situation, most service clubs will readily arrange their event for a later time.

CONCLUSION

Scheduling is the structure that gives freedom to the child development center. The minutes on the clock are used only as approximations. Each group usually evolves a rather unique schedule, giving the school a flexible, easy-going feeling that makes it clear that the schedule is not a straitjacket. It takes careful thought and continuous monitoring to make the schedule meet the needs of everyone concerned.

REVIEW AND APPLICATIONS

Ten Guides for Scheduling

1. Plan and post a schedule or sequence of events to give children and adults the security of knowing what to expect.
2. Make written plans, using more detail if the staff is inexperienced.
3. Consider children's needs for activity and rest when scheduling activities and routines.
4. Plan flexible schedules and adjust them as children's needs indicate.
5. Consider the time of year and weather, taking advantage of nice weather to use the out of doors for more activities.
6. Make specific plans for the transitions between activities.
7. Warn children when a shift in activity is approaching.
8. Alter schedules if staff is frequently heard rushing children.
9. Get staff agreement on individual responsibilities and write them down in order to share the fun and the work equally.
10. Post a rainy day schedule to have available anytime it is needed.

 Observations

1. Observe children arriving or departing. Record evidence—their conversation or action—that tells you that they know, or don't know, what the schedule is. Discuss.
2. Listen closely to children's verbalizations and record any that tell you that a child knows, or does not know, what the usual sequence of events is. Discuss.
3. Describe the schedule that your case-study child seems to find comfortable. Note any rough spots as observed or reported by the teacher or parent.

Applications

1. Copy down the posted schedule of a child development center. Observe to see how closely the teachers follow the schedule. Make notes where they deviate. Do you know why they made the changes? If appropriate, discuss the schedule with them. Summarize your findings.

2. Discuss the home routines a parent follows with a young child. Make a time block plan for the child's day.

3. Assist with a child in a home or a school for several hours. Can you observe that the child understands the schedule? Explain.

4. Rate your center's scheduling procedure using the Ten Guides for Scheduling. Use a 1-to-5 scale with 5 being highest. Discuss your ratings.

FOR FURTHER READING

Christie, James F. and Francis Wardle. "How Much Time Is Needed for Play?" *Young Children,* 47:3, March 1992, 28–32.

Hildebrand, Verna. *Management of Child Development Centers.* New York: Macmillan Publishing Company, 1993.

Hildebrand, Verna. *Introduction to Early Childhood Education.* New York: Macmillan Publishing Company, 1991.

CHAPTER 8

Guiding Children's Toileting Routine

Key Concepts

◆ Toilet training
◆ Parent Cooperation
◆ Sexual Abuse
◆ Routines

Remember
When you were a wee little tot,
When they took you out of your warm warm cot,
And told you to wee-wee whether you could or not?

Thus goes a limerick that tickles the funny bones of the school-aged set. But there is more truth than fiction in the lines. The toileting routine has consumed much of parents' and teachers' time over the years. With infant and toddler centers becoming common, and centers for older children also growing, parents' and teachers' concern for the toileting routine remains. However, with children entering child care programs at earlier ages today, teachers and caregivers do not expect that all children will be toilet trained before they enter the early childhood program, as once was the case. Centers have adjusted their procedures to accommodate children in diapers and those needing help learning how and when to use the toilet.

INFANTS AND TODDLERS

Infants and toddlers were discussed in detail in Chapter 5, including the handling of diapering and toilet training. Toileting for older children builds on the steps taken during the infancy and toddler periods. Most experienced people realize that by far the largest majority of children become trained to manage their elimination processes in a socially satisfactory manner and that it is well to avoid making a big issue of the process. Dr. James Hymes, Jr., a noted early childhood educator, said some years ago, "Everyone of us accepts the fact that

Diapering must follow approved practices to prevent spread of germs to toys, other children, and caregivers.
(Butler Child Care Center, Okinawa)

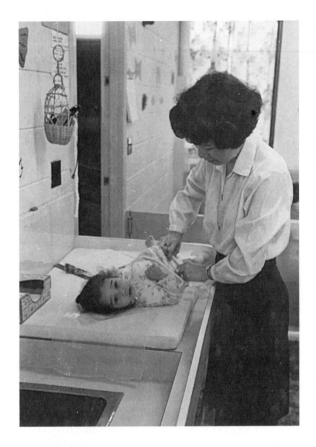

babies wet. We don't let wetting throw us off our stride. We plan for it and arrange our lives accordingly. What do we do with babies? We let them wet."[1] It is well to adopt Hymes' attitude and to adjust our expectations to the baby's and toddler's maturity. Most parents of two children find they are far more relaxed about the second child's toilet training than they were with the first. Teachers and caregivers also view toilet training as a developmental process to start when the child gives some indication of readiness.

YOUNG CHILDREN

Even among the Marks, Bettys, and Jackies whose parents think they are trained, the teacher must be constantly vigilant. Experienced teachers learn the signs of need to eliminate, such as holding the genital area or dancing around. Some children get unusually quiet when they are having a bowel movement; some even hide.

---

[1] James L. Hymes, Jr., *Behavior and Misbehavior* (Englewood Cliffs, NJ: Prentice-Hall, 1955), p. 30.

Each child will be different, but it helps the child and saves the teacher's time and trouble if they can read the signs before the "accident" occurs. Try to teach children to tell you when they need to go or to go on their own to the bathroom. Don't tarry when children tell you they need to go, because the time between when they recognize the signal and when they start urinating may be only a split second. The teacher should check with each parent for the child's word for toileting, because there are some unusual ones used whose meaning might not be guessed until it is too late. Parents may need guidance regarding the type of clothing that is most helpful to training. Play pants with elastic waistbands seem to be the quickest and offer the child the best chance for self-help.

When assistance is needed teachers should sit on a low chair to save fatigue and prevent hovering over children.
(Parent-Child Development Center, Houston)

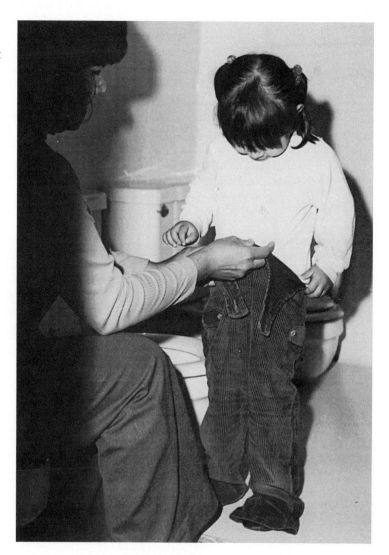

◆ Talk It Over ◆

What are the various names you have heard parents use to teach their children to indicate their need to urinate or defecate?

Why do you think people use these names? Do these names help children learn?

What do you think young children think about these bodily functions?

A routine of toileting reminders is customary in most schools. As noted on the sample schedules in Chapter 7, toileting is scheduled after breakfast, after playtime, after outdoor play, just before lunch, after lunch, after nap, and after being outdoors in the afternoon. These are times when the teacher methodically checks each child to see if he or she needs to eliminate. Food or exercise often stimulates the child's bowels to move. Both indirect guidance and direct guidance—verbal, physical, and affective—are useful in guiding children in toileting routines. These techniques can be reviewed in Chapters 2 and 3.

Because some young children may be in the "negative" stage, it is well to learn to avoid asking them directly if they need to go to the bathroom, for they will surely say, "No." Say instead, "Time to go to the bathroom." You can just accept it if children volunteer, "I don't need to go," but you can still invite them to "wash your hands." The presence of the toilet and other children using it may be suggestion enough if they need to go.

Disposing of tissues and washing hands afterward is mandatory for preventing the spread of colds.
(Butler Child Care Center, Okinawa)

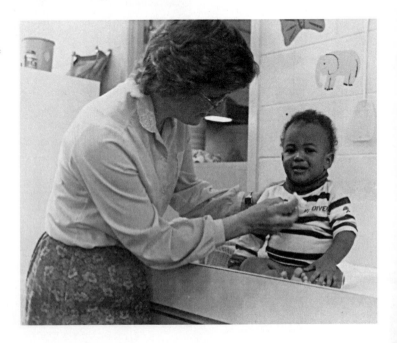

Children, washing independently, must be taught to use
soap to help keep germs from
spreading.
(University of Georgia McPhaul Children's Programs)

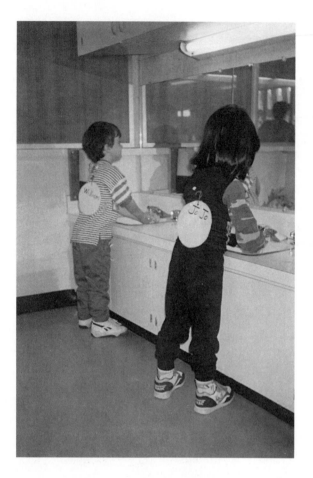

Individual Differences

There are wide individual differences among children as to when conscious control of bowels and urination occurs. Boys are trained more slowly and at an older age than girls, according to studies that have been made, and teachers and parents of boys should keep this in mind. It is simply not fair to expect them to be trained as quickly as girls, and lots of little boys would be happier, more relaxed people today if their parents and caregivers had known this. Pressure to be trained before the muscles are mature enough does not help training and can have detrimental effects on a child's personality.

It is important to allow children to grow in their ability to hold the urine and not contribute to their urinary frequency. Therefore, if a child can go all morning without using the toilet, this is fine. Some parents indicate the child uses the toilet upon arriving home. If a child is afraid of the school toilet, a short time at school may be indicated until the child becomes comfortable at school and ready to use the small school toilet.

Some children are actually fearful of the flushing noise of the toilet, so teachers may need to trip the lever themselves after the child leaves the bathroom. Actually, another child will often oblige, having no hesitancy about the noise. Flushing is not a necessary part of training; therefore, teachers are well advised to keep the emphasis on the important part, the use of the toilet.

Little boys can sit to urinate, and some girls can stand. The convention will eventually be learned, so you need not worry. Because boys have poor aim, they will get the toilet seat wet unless they lift it before urinating. Raising the seat, like flushing, is part of the routine you can help with if it seems too complicated for a given child. Occasionally little boys have erections when they need to urinate, which makes it difficult to aim accurately. They may urinate on the floor, quite by accident. Some teachers care for children without much home training regarding careful use of the toilet. Rather than encourage standing, they require the little boys to sit on the toilet to urinate because of the difficulty the boys have in aiming at the toilet when standing. This proce-

Attention to hair care can be encouraged by teachers and caregivers and is especially important when children are in a full-day program.
(University of Illinois Child Development Laboratory)

dure has greatly improved the cleanliness of their bathrooms and brings no hardship on the boys, they say. Cleaning around the toilet with a disinfectant is essential if the bathroom is to remain a pleasant place. This is a standard practice of good custodial service. Deodorant helps with the odor but should be kept out of the reach of children. See Chapter 17 for more details on toilet training.

Both boys and girls toilet together during the toddler to kindergarten period. They learn valuable facts about sex differences in this casual way. Their questions can be answered matter-of-factly and without embarrassment. Teachers and caregivers should take children's curiosity as a matter of learning, not as premature sex deviance.

Role of Helpers

Helping in the bathroom means lots of buttoning and bending. When there is room, you will be more comfortable if you sit on a low chair near the door. Your presence and counsel may be all that is necessary. Children don't need a tall observer looming over them.

The child having a bowel movement needs to wipe and may require some advice about folding the tissue. Sometimes adults may need to help with wiping. Always encourage the child to wash hands after toileting.

Accidents will happen, so accept them cheerfully and move to remedy the situation as quickly as possible. Parents usually keep a set of dry clothes at school for this and other types of accidents. Each helper should know where the child's clothes are kept, for the child will be much happier wearing his or her own clothes rather than those the school might keep on hand for emergencies. Children who wet should still be encouraged to use the toilet as they may not be finished. The child who defecates may practically need a sponge bath.

 Talk It Over

What are the advantages of the typical open arrangement of toilet rooms in children's centers, that is, where the toilets and lavatories are in the open and there are no individual stalls with doors?

When possible after an accident, it helps avoid embarrassment for children if they are taken to a bathroom where you can clean them up in private. Otherwise you just have to explain to curious friends that "Joe had an accident like some of us do sometimes. I'm helping him get fixed up." Some children make critical comments to the child. Even parents and the child's siblings may not be sympathetic. The teacher may offer them guidance as to a more helpful reaction.

Brushing teeth is considered
essential in full-day programs to
prevent tooth decay.
(Michigan State University Child
Development Laboratory)

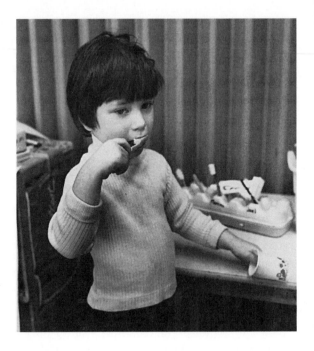

Once the child is dry, the soiled clothes must be wrapped and put in a sack, labeled with the child's name, and placed in his or her locker to be sent home.

Be sure you have carefully washed your hands after assisting each child in the bathroom and with helping them wipe their noses. Many centers are now requiring the use of disposable gloves when there is any danger of handling bodily fluids of any kind.[2]

Kindergartners will be very embarrassed if they have an accident. These usually happen because they do not want to interrupt an activity to take care of toileting. Teachers may simply note the signs and quietly advise them to go before they have an accident.

Children usually enjoy washing with soap and water. They may actually prolong the process, liking the feel of the soap and water. If children repeatedly tarry at the lavatory, some arrangements for water play during a self-selected activity period might be indicated. The crucial times to wash are after toileting and before eating; other occasions may not be worth making an issue of. The temperature of the water heater should be set at warm to avoid burns.

In some schools tooth brushing and hair combing are taught as routines. Little holders for each child's toothbrush and comb are made and carefully labeled. Baths also may be in order for children who do not have such care at

---

[2] For details of useful protections for children see Earline D. Kendall and Virginia E. Moukaddem, "Who's Vulnerable in Infant Care Centers?" *Young Children,* 47:5, July 1992, pp. 72–75.

home. Caregivers are, of course, cautioned never to leave the child alone bathing, for a small amount of water is enough for drowning.

Handling Genitals

Some children handle their genitals more than others. This is called *masturbation*. It gives children a pleasurable sensation and is sometimes comforting. Masturbation is itself a harmless habit, but the punishing or admonishing attitudes of adults may actually make it into a problem for the child.

Handling of genitals may be a symptom of the need to urinate. Some children seem to be literally holding it back, sometimes because they want to finish a game or something they've started. If you promise to "save" their place, they may be willing to go take care of their need. Occasionally children have a rash in the genital area that they are merely rubbing. Teachers should be alert to advise parents or the nurse that the child may need medication. Underwear that is too tight or improperly cut can contribute to the child's pulling at it, which may be interpreted by some as masturbation. This, too, is a problem that is far more easily remedied than tension produced over masturbation.

SEXUAL ABUSE

Sexual abuse is sometimes suspected by teachers and caregivers while helping a child with toileting routines. A child who seems pained when urinating or defecating may have been molested. Or, a child who seems pained as he or she is touched or approached may have been molested. Bleeding may be a result of molesting.

If you notice any of these behaviors or bleeding of any kind, be sure to inform your supervising teachers. Centers are legally obligated to report suspected child abuse of any kind, including sexual abuse. They will take responsibility for making the report to the authorities.

Child care centers have a serious obligation to prevent any staff members from handling a child in any way that could be construed as abusive, including sexually abusive. Your manager will probably make suggestions to individuals to work closely with the other caregivers or teachers to ensure that all staff handle children in healthful ways. Most centers require all doors to be kept open, enabling cross-monitoring of each unit by others. Of course, if you observe any behavior that violates any child's sexuality you should report that behavior to authorities. There have been a few cases involving sexual abuse in child care centers that have prompted most of these precautions by managers and others. Of course, one case is too many, so caring people must be vigilant that it never occurs.

Many teachers are giving children information about "good touches" and "bad touches" to help them know when to tell their parents or teachers if they are being sexually molested.

COMMUNICATING WITH PARENTS

Toilet training, like everything else the child learns, is not all learned at school. The child is at home more than at school. Parents may want a child to become toilet trained far earlier than is feasible because the child's muscle control is not yet present. Helping parents learn about toilet training is often necessary. Communication is essential with each child's parents so that successes, failures, and techniques of training may be shared. Because a change in toilet habits may signal some illness, you should report these to parents. Any emotional crisis—a move to a new house, a new baby at home, or a parent being away on a trip—may be emotionally upsetting to a child and may interfere with training. Parents should advise teachers about any unusual events that might influence behavior at school, especially toileting, eating, or sleeping.

The average child is not dry at night until age three. This statistic means that half are older than three before they are dry at night. The same patience is required in caring for wet sleeping children as for awake ones. They should be loved in spite of their wetting. They should be taken to the toilet just prior to going to bed and immediately upon waking. If children awaken wet, have them try to use the toilet, for they may not be through urinating and would likely wet the diaper before you got them back in bed.

It is better to place extra absorbent diapers and plastic pants on children than to bother them once they are asleep, unless awakening them actually keeps them dry. Very likely the less pressure that is placed on children the sooner they will be trained. Their muscles simply must mature, and usually they want to be trained. The pediatrician should advise parents when other measures should be taken.

CONCLUSION

Guiding children's toilet-training habits should be done in a helpful, supportive way. Teachers and parents who have enough patience to work with and not against the natural maturation of the child will be most successful. Pressure only results in resistance, negativism, unhappiness, and often damage to the child's personality. Children can get the upper hand as they exercise their autonomy, so it is wise to relax when you see indications of resistance. Both the indirect and direct techniques of guidance will be useful in guiding children's toileting.

REVIEW AND APPLICATIONS

Ten Guides to Toileting Routines

1. Wait until the child shows signs of physical maturity and interest before starting toilet training.

2.   Remember that studies show that girls are usually toilet trained earlier than boys of the same age.
3.   Plan a number of times in the schedule for routine toileting; however, remain alert to children's needs that do not fit the schedule.
4.   Accept accidents without blaming or shaming the child.
5.   When children have toilet accidents, encourage them to use the toilet before putting on dry clothes.
6.   Praise children when they have successfully used the toilet.
7.   Encourage children to be independent in adjusting clothing and in washing their hands after toileting and before meals.
8.   Accept and answer matter-of-factly children's natural curiosity about their anatomical differences.
9.   Be alert to a child's behavior or appearance that could indicate sexual abuse and report immediately to your supervising teacher.
10. Communicate with parents about a child's toileting behavior in order to bridge the gap between the child's home and school routines.

 Observations

1.   Observe and record the toileting behavior of two boys and two girls of varied ages. Note the children's ages. Discuss.
2.   Observe and write a report on your case-study child's ability to handle toileting. What is said? What vocabulary is used? How much help is requested? If feasible, learn about the child's toilet training history. Confer with the parents or teacher regarding the child.

Applications

1.   Make notes of a teacher guiding a child in the toileting situation in an early childhood center. Role play the scene in your lecture class. Analyze the effective and ineffective techniques used.
2.   Assist with at least two children in the toilet room either at home or at school. Did they go to the toilet on their own initiative? Were they able to attend to their clothing independently? Were they comfortable and free from anxiety in the situation? Explain your answers. What are the differences between the children?
3.   Discuss toilet training with a parent or teacher. Find out what they think is the best age for initiating toilet training. Find out what procedures they recommend to others. Write a report on your conclusions.

4. Discuss among your friends the various names that have been given the toileting experience. Write them down to share with the class.
5. Rate your center on the Ten Guides to Toileting Routines, using a 1-to-5 scale. Discuss.

FOR FURTHER READING

Kendall, Earline D. and Virginia E. Moukaddem. "Who's Vulnerable in Infant Care Centers?" *Young Children,* 47:5, July 1992, 72–77.

Spock, Benjamin and Michael B. Rothenberg. *Dr. Spock's Baby and Child Care.* New York: Pocket Books, 1992.

CHAPTER 9

Guiding Children's Eating Behavior

Key Concepts

◆ Self-Demand Schedule
◆ Goals for Mealtimes
◆ USDA Minimum Requirements
◆ Nutrition Education

Annette, age three, handled her spoon with ease at the lunch table. She liked the tomato and apple wedges that she ate with her fingers. She poured herself three small glasses of milk. She talked very little during the meal.

Annette was considered a good eater in the child development center's lunchroom. Her meal was small by adult standards, but she was growing and was full of energy for the many activities that kept her busy. Annette's present good eating habits are an outgrowth of the attention that good nutrition and feeding were given during her mother's pregnancy and since her birth. Some of these early feeding concerns are discussed in the following section because infant caregivers today may care for some babies only a few months old and will need an understanding of infant feeding practices beginning with birth.

FEEDING INFANTS

During pregnancy the mother's health and nutrition significantly affect the fetus developing within her. Regular checks of her diet are made. In addition, she plans with her doctor what type of feeding she expects to give her new baby. If she is going to breast feed the baby she will begin to prepare her breasts, toughening them a bit through massage so they won't feel sore when the infant nurses.

The nursing mother will begin nursing the baby a few hours after birth. Babies have an instinctive sucking reflex that permits them to feed during their first days even though they have never had to feed before. They also have a rooting reflex whereby they actively seek the nipple when touched on the lips or cheek. The baby's sucking helps stimulate the milk-flow in the mother's breasts. The closeness and the stimulation contribute to the bonding and attachment of the mother and baby. Bonding is a mutual love affair that develops between infant and parents and is facilitated by closeness at feeding.

For breast-fed babies, the mother's milk supply comes in about the fourth or fifth day, stimulated by several days of sucking and rooting by the baby. The mother's breasts first secrete *colostrum,* a thin yellow liquid. The colostrum contains antibodies that help prevent illnesses during the early months of an infant's life. This colostrum is one of the important advantages that breast-fed infants have over bottle-fed ones. A substitute for colostrum has not been found to supplement formulas that bottle-fed babies receive.

Many hospitals have a "rooming-in" plan allowing mothers to keep their babies in their hospital rooms much of the day. Nurses help them gain knowledge about baby care, nursing and the special needs of their own babies.

If the mother is planning to bottle feed her baby, she is given a hormone drug that keeps her milk supply from coming in. Her baby is given some water and eventually some formula in the hospital nursery. When babies are bottle fed they should be cuddled closely just as if breast fed. Bonding must be facilitated for bottle-fed babies, too.

Self-Demand Schedule

A self-demand schedule is advisable for babies. This means that they are fed when they appear to need it and are not made to wait until some magic time on the clock. This type of schedule allows for the wide differences that exist among babies. At first, one may need to be fed every two hours, whereas another baby in the nursery may not need to nurse for four hours.

At the Center

The close relationship during feeding between the infant and a loving person should be carried over by caregivers when the child enters an infant center. The staff will learn from the parent as much as possible about the usual habits of the baby. Supplementing the care and education the parents give will be an objective of an infant center.

Ages vary as to when an infant enters a center. It usually depends on when the mother must return to work or to school. It is very important that the center staff provide a strong support for the parents and the baby. It may be a difficult time, as some parents feel guilt each day during separation. Support for parental bonding must continue. The center staff should not want the baby to bond to them in the same way that it bonds to its mother or father. Yet a regular caregiver who knows the baby well will be very significant in the baby's adjustment and in the security and trust that is developed.

The center must maintain high standards of hygiene to keep infants healthy. Food offers many opportunities for contamination if it is not handled appropriately. Infant formula should be carefully stored in the refrigerator.

Lunch

Serving lunch is usually more of a group effort than breakfast, because children will be together and the time will be set to complement the other activities of the day. After a busy morning including outdoor play, it helps to gather the children in quiet groups after they have toileted and are washed up for lunch to have them rest before eating. Rested children will eat better and more independently than tired children. The group can listen to a story, sing quiet songs, and stretch out on a carpet if they desire. This quiet time can be more informal than a regular naptime. Calling it "quiet time" or "singing time" may remove the curse that rest time often has for some children.

If children are keyed up from active outdoor play or from other active events and are brought directly to the lunch tables, caregivers will soon discover they are inviting disorder during the lunch period. These children often will not relax in their chairs, but will want to be up moving about. If they are tired, they may also be argumentative or want to be fed by the caregiver.

Seating

Each child should have a designated space for eating. Place cards will help designate the spot as personal space. It is helpful if the child eats with the same teacher or assistant each day. This can provide security for a child at a time when some children may be more susceptible to strain. If the same persons help with the same group each day, they will learn eating habits and be able to help most effectively because they know the children. The seating can be arranged so that compatible children eat together. Occasionally children who you feel would be friends if they knew each other better may be seated together. Experienced good eaters may be seated with less experienced or finicky eaters to serve as models for them. Generally an adult can effectively help five or six children at most. If seated near the middle of a small table the adult can reach each child. Volunteers should be enlisted if there are not enough helpers for this ratio.

Serving

Family-style service is best. The prepared food is placed in serving bowls before the teachers. They serve each child the amount of each food they think each will eat. A few peas or only a teaspoonful of potatoes may be a serving for some children, whereas others may want much more. Some teachers call tiny servings that they hope children will taste the "No thank you" portions. They ask children just to taste one bite. Of course, the children frequently like it well enough to ask for more.

The teacher may serve seconds or allow the children to serve their own seconds. It is convenient to give the children a small dessert spoon when letting them serve seconds. Serving helps a child learn to gauge needs.

The rule "Take what you'll eat and eat what you take" is helpful for children to learn. It usually is far better to serve an amount that the child calls "not enough" and permit seconds than to serve "too much." A clean plate is a worthy goal, but the servers must be careful to do their part in achieving that goal. Obesity is a growing childhood, as well as adulthood, problem that may result from rigid adherence to a clean plate rule.

Other problems may arise from giving children an overly large portion. For example, on one occasion a teacher, Kay, was distracted by a conversation with a child as she filled a plate. She put a "too large" serving of the main dish on Ken's plate, but told Ken "you don't have to eat it all." It would have been better to have removed some of the food before handing it to Ken who, being a very conscientious child, tried to follow the clean plate rule. He ate and ate until he was virtually in pain before giving up.

 Talk It Over

Parents sometimes state arbitrary commands or base their rules regarding their child's eating on the way they, as children, were brought up rather than on the needs of their own child. What are some of these rules? What could be their effect on the child?

Fostering Independence

Milk is best served in small glasses. Seconds can be poured by the child from a small pitcher that doesn't tip easily. Adults should pour into the small pitchers only the amount required by the glass, or the child is likely to run the glass over. Pouring one's own milk increases milk consumption and the child's feeling of independence.

Toast sticks, sandwiches, and vegetable pieces can serve as pushers to help the children maneuver food onto spoons and forks. Say to the child, "Use your pusher to help keep your fingers out of food." Many finger foods are provided in school to aid children in feeding themselves. Carrot sticks, orange or apple slices, green pepper, cabbage, or tomato wedges are examples. Even some meats can be served this way. Others can be cooked soft enough to be easily cut by the side of the fork. Knives are quite difficult for three- and four-year-old children to manage for cutting. They like them for spreading butter, peanut butter, or jelly.

Dessert should be planned to add to the nutritional quality of the meal and should, therefore, be given to all children and never used as a reward for eating all of the main meal. It is customary in many groups for the child to carry the first-course plate to the serving cart to receive dessert. This movement gives the child a little chance to exercise, which some children need.

Children assist with meal preparation by helping set the table. (Denver Parkview Children's Center)

After eating dessert the child then takes the remaining dishes and silverware to the cart before proceeding to the bathroom to wash.

Bibs are important for the younger children who are learning to feed themselves. Napkins will suffice for the older ones. They may need advice about spreading them out on their laps for maximum protection.

When children expect to be fed by an adult, prior training is likely at fault. However, these children might be tired, and an earlier lunchtime or more attention to rest during the morning may be called for. Also, these children might not really be hungry, so they can be encouraged to feed themselves and the amount they eat accepted.

Regardless of the care given to toileting prior to lunch, children may realize a need just at mealtime. There is no alternative but to allow the child to go to the bathroom. A helper should be available to attend to such a child so the teacher at the table does not have to leave the group.

Atmosphere

The atmosphere of mealtime should be quiet and as relaxing as possible. Mealtime should be set (or the amount and timing of the mid-morning snack adjusted) so that children are hungry at lunch time but not starving. Attention should be focused on the eating tasks and less on conversation. Young children have a hard time attending to both at once. Conversation between tables should be highly discouraged, for it has to be loud to be heard and raises the tension within the room. Adults should be attending to children's needs and conversation and not conversing among themselves.

Mealtime is a time children may be lonesome for home. The foods offered may be so like what they eat at home or so different that they become homesick. Tiredness may contribute to this problem, also. A new child may need several weeks to become accustomed to the type of foods and manner of serving it in the center.

Sufficient time should be allowed for children to eat without rushing. If they show indications of merely dawdling or playing with their food, they should be encouraged without admonition to take their plate to the cart, get their dessert, and complete their meal.

Some children may not be accustomed to sitting down for any sustained period during mealtime. Explaining to them that "We get up when we are ready for dessert" may be an appropriate reminder. Then if children get up, tell them, "If you are finished, take your plate to the lady at the cart." If they are indeed not finished but must give up their food, they'll likely remember it on the next day and stay in place. A helper in the lunchroom should firmly direct children who get up too soon back to their table. This help will avoid the distraction for the teacher at the table.

Children assist with cleaning up by placing their dishes on a cart for removal.
(University of Georgia McPhaul Children's Programs)

A helper should be available in the bathroom to receive children who are through with lunch and need to wash their hands. This allows the teacher to remain at the table until the last child finishes. Children usually need to urinate and may need to have a bowel movement after lunch.

Menus

Proper nutrition is a requirement of all high-quality menus. Children need a proper balance of the Basic Four Food Groups:

1.   Milk and milk products;
2.   Meat, fish, poultry, eggs, or dry beans;
3.   Fruits and vegetables; and
4.   Cereal and bread.

Some people recommend a fifth "group"—that is, enough calories to complete the energy requirements of the individual. Calories can come from all of the above groups to round out energy needs.

The U.S. Department of Agriculture has a program of partial support for feeding programs in child care centers and family day care homes. The department stipulates the amount of various foods institutions are required to serve (see Table 9–1). By using these amounts of foods, a well-balanced menu can be served to the children. What each one actually eats is, of course, another matter because some children may not like or even want to try some groups of foods. Short of cajoling children to eat, it is good to encourage them to try a little sample (one teaspoon or a bite) of every food. Since children often hesitate to try new foods, teachers and helpers should set a good example by tasting everything.

Young children can learn to enjoy a wide variety of new foods. However, new foods should be introduced in small quantities along with familiar, well-liked foods. Children like their food "apart," as one child put it. Therefore, separate vegetables are preferred to a mixed salad, and a meat is preferred to stew.

 Talk It Over

What do you remember about the foods you liked or disliked as a child? What guidance were you given?

Children prefer foods of a lukewarm temperature—neither very hot nor very cold. You should allow the soup to cool before serving. Children like ice cream, but you often see them stir it or allow it to warm for a while before eating.

Table 9–1   *Food Requirements for Children Ages 1 to 6**

Type of Food	Ages 1–3	Ages 3–6
Breakfast		
Milk	1/2 cup	3/4 cup
Juice or Fruit or Vegetable	1/4 cup	1/2 cup
Bread or Bread Alternate	1/2 slice	1/2 slice
including cereal, cold	1/4 cup or	1/3 cup or
prepared	1/3 ounce	1/2 ounce
or cereal, hot cooked	1/4 cup	1/4 cup
Snack (Supplement)		
Select two out of the four components		
Milk	1/2 cup	1/2 cup
Juice or Fruit or Vegetable	1/2 cup	1/2 cup
Meat or Meat Alternate	1/2 ounce	1/2 ounce
Bread or Bread Alternate	1/2 slice	1/2 slice
including cereal,	1/4 cup or	1/3 cup or
cold prepared	1/3 ounce	1/2 ounce
or cereal, hot cooked	1/4 cup	1/4 cup
Lunch or Supper		
Milk	1/2 cup	3/4 cup
Meat or Poultry or Fish	1 ounce	1 1/2 ounce
or egg	1	1
or cheese	1 ounce	1 1/2 ounces
or cooked dry beans or peas	1/4 cup	3/8 cup
or peanut butter	2 tablespoons	3 tablespoons
Vegetables and/or Fruits		
two or more	1/4 cup	1/2 cup
Bread or Bread Alternate	1/2 slice	1/2 slice

(*U.S. Department of Agriculture)

Crisp toast and sticks of vegetables are good for children's teeth and are good "pushers" that help them get foods onto the spoon.

Foods high in roughage or highly seasoned are not considered best for young children because they irritate the lining of their immature digestive tracts.

Color, flavor, and textures are important in young children's menus, just as they are in adults'. If you wish to experiment to see how children notice color, as one teacher does, try having everything a single color one day. Even color the milk green!

Children's lunch menus should have a meat or meat substitute, a cooked vegetable, a raw vegetable or fruit, a dessert, and milk. Excessive sweets are avoided in drinks and desserts. Some children tend to fill up on anything sweet and thus miss needed nutrients.

Foods especially enjoyed by various ethnic groups should be worked into the menus. Sometimes these can be main dishes, at other times they can be used for tasting experiences. Parents can be helpful in suggesting favorite foods from their ethnic groups. These foods offer a learning experience for children and staff outside the ethnic group as well as provide a touch of familiarity to the children from each group.

The land-grant colleges in most states have nutrition advisers who can work with child development center lunch programs. They give help with menu planning, nutritional information, and with securing and using surplus commodities.

Accidents

Spilling and even breakage may occur. A helper should have a dustpan, broom, and sponge handy to make quick work of any accident. The child should not be scolded for the accident. With some assessment of the situation, preventive measures might help avoid accidents. For example, in one group the addition of a small side tray made the children's table less crowded, and fewer spills occurred.

Attitudes

Adults' attitudes may interfere with good mealtime guidance. Good food costs money and takes time to prepare and should be appreciated, they think. Thus it is very hard for some adults to see a child refuse food that the adults like. They feel it is wasteful,too, because they know the food will be thrown away. Each teacher has food attitudes, which may be very different from those of co-teachers and children. If you can accept the differences among the adults, then you should be able to accept them between yourself and the children.

You wouldn't tell your co-teacher to eat sweet potatoes just because you like them. Likewise, you wouldn't tell a co-teacher to eat more mashed potatoes or squash, or not to drink more milk, just as you shouldn't tell children. The amount required and the kind of foods liked vary according to personal taste.

The family's culture, life style, education, income, and values will make the meal situation in each home different. As teachers, you must learn to respect these differences, as they are bound to affect the children in your groups.

As adults serving children's food needs, you should be open to trying new foods and never display food aversions to the children. If there is something you can't eat, don't talk about it—just don't serve yourself any or, like you tell the children, "try it—you might like it."

Children will especially enjoy food they have helped make. With a little careful planning and coordination of functions, children can help prepare an item for their lunch. Perhaps it will be a soup that takes two days to make, or a Jello dessert. Whatever it will be, they will surely pronounce it "good."

Mid-morning or Mid-afternoon Snack

A refreshment break helps children in several ways. They get a little fuel for their furnace, and they rest and have good fellowship in the process. A child may be introduced to important concepts through foods such as colors, numbers, and classification of foods as vegetables, fruits, or meat. More important is that children learn basic nutritional information about what is good for them.

Beverages are important snacks for children. They can get thirsty with so much talking and running about. Water might well be served more frequently during the day than it is in many groups. An accessible, easy-to-work water fountain is a "must" for children's centers both indoors and out. Milk is such an important food in children's diets that it often is a preference for snack times. Even children who claim they don't like milk may change their minds when they see their friends and teachers enjoying it. Imitation fruit drinks contain excessive sugar and should not be served.

Service of snacks can be more social and laced with learning experiences than may be possible with meals. Snacks are simpler than meals, as they allow children to consider a few other things while eating them. A casual arrangement with perhaps only a paper cup and a napkin is needed. Place cards are useful to define personal space, to guide children to appropriate seats, and to challenge their reading skills. Name tags that children wear can be color-coded to match place cards at the table. After children finish eating they should be able to take their cups and napkins to a designated tray or wastebasket. Some children may enjoy taking turns being on a committee responsible for setting up the snack, cleaning up after the snack, and helping plan the menus.

To avoid spilled beverage glasses, help children form a habit of setting their glasses toward the center of the table. You can say, "Mary, put your glass at the top of your plate." A child's inclination is to set the glass near the edge of the table nearest the hand used most in eating, thus making it easy to knock over the glass when not looking.

Food Projects for Snacktime

Snacks may be simple or elaborate depending on children's needs, other meals at the school, finances, and the snack planner's creativity. There are numerous opportunities within the curriculum of the school to plan experiences with food that can be used as the snack for the groups. Food experiences offer some children a personal involvement that they may not find in other curriculum materials. They like to work with food—and to eat it!

There is no need for snacks to be humdrum and ordinary. The list of possible food and cooking projects gets longer and longer as creative teachers set their minds to the task. From instant puddings to pancakes, banana bread, applesauce, deviled eggs, or self-squeezed orange juice, the projects that are most successful are those to which the child can contribute "all by myself," by cutting a fruit, by squeezing, by stirring, or by adding an ingredient. Following

A cookie baking project with children can be used for meals, snacks, or special events. (Calhoun School, New York City)

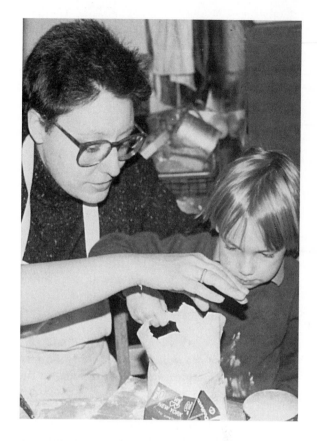

a good learning experience, with a delicious aroma filling the air, and friends trying it, what child could resist the food—even after stating a dislike for it to mother numerous times?[2]

Guiding Table Behavior

Guiding children during meals and at snacktime calls for adults to apply the basic guidance principles discussed in Chapters 2 and 3. Much of this chapter has dealt with setting the stage for children to become self-directed eaters, that is, through indirect guidance. Clearly, many instances of direct verbal, physical, and affective guidance are called for. Positive statements such as "Chew and swallow your food, Cammie, then you may talk" are often helpful. Giving the child a choice when one is feasible such as "Would you like more milk?" often comes in handy. Physical modeling of behavior that you want the child to learn, such as "Cut your meat, like this," accompanied by a quick demonstration, may be helpful. Using short sentences and giving only one direction at a time, such as "Feet under the table, Bob" usually bring results.

---

[2] For further discussion of food projects for children, see Verna Hildebrand, *Introduction to Early Childhood Education* (New York: Macmillan Publishing Company, 1991), Chapter 18.

Table Rules or "Manners"

Guidance techniques are needed to help children learn the eating rules or "manners." These rules or manners help people know the acceptable behavior within a group. Teachers will think of table manners in a broad context. They can decide on some fundamental rules or "manners" that they feel the children are capable of learning and that will make their living together more pleasant. In their decision they will consider the age level of the children and the type of experiences they have had prior to coming to school.

Table manners vary among families, and teachers must be careful not to evaluate those manners as "good" or "bad." It is known that some families rarely eat a meal all sitting down at one time. Some have poorly balanced menus, many including excessive empty-calorie foods such as potato chips and soft drinks. With different food habits and manners learned at home the teachers might expect many children to take days, perhaps weeks, to eat well and accept the rules and manners planned for the mealtime routine at school.

In a group it will help the service if each child waits patiently while the teacher serves the food. This is a school rule or "manner" to be learned. Passing a plate of carrot sticks with each child taking "one" may be a new "manner" for some children.

Chewing with the mouth closed and learning to chew food and swallow before talking are other "manners." Wiping the lips with a napkin, holding the napkin on the lap, and wiping the hands on it are also "manners." Holding a glass without spilling and drinking milk without blowing bubbles are "manners." Swallowing food before drinking may be difficult for some children whose parents may have encouraged them to wash down their food with a beverage. Talking quietly at the table and waiting while others finish are "manners."

Holding tools correctly is a convention that must also be learned, as well as using the appropriate tool for a particular food. Keeping food on the plate instead of laying it around the plate as is allowed on the highchair tray may be a new "manner" to learn.

"Please" and "thank you" will come as children imitate adults who use these phrases. As you see, our manners are the rules we use at mealtime to make the occasion more pleasant for all concerned.

NUTRITION EDUCATION

In child development centers you will be expected to set a good example by serving nutritious, tasty, and colorful meals and snacks. In light of the current low level of nutrition knowledge among both American adults and children, it seems advisable, during all kinds of food experiences, to stress the nutritional aspects of food. During meals, snacks, and cooking experiences you can help children learn nutritional information, such as the following:

Milk builds strong bones and teeth.
Soft drinks and candy often cause cavities in your teeth.
Oranges are good for your gums.
Green beans have vitamins to help you grow.
Meat helps you grow new muscles and skin.

Nutrition is, of course, a complex science. Yet, by talking about nutrition frequently, young children may learn some information to use as a basis for making choices between foods. In the long run, the habits formed early may be the most important factor in the nutritional decisions. That is why work with parents is so essential. They control a major portion of the children's opportunity for food selection and the availability of nutritious or nonnutritious foods. They model food choices numerous times daily.

PARENTAL GUIDANCE

Parents should be given information about their child's participation in mealtimes, snacktimes, and food experiences. They can more effectively plan their home expectations and menus if they are informed. Parents often appreciate recipes of foods that children like. The school should also inform the parents of their effort in nutrition education and enlist their help. They too may wish for help in nutrition education, meal planning, or food purchasing. The teachers can help them get in touch with appropriate resources such as the Cooperative Extension Service where such information is available as a public service.

TEACHERS' MEALTIMES

Teachers' food needs must be met as well while they eat with the children. They too need nutritious food in order to have energy to work and emotional stability to keep them on an even keel with their colleagues and the children. A systematic arrangement of the mealtime allows teachers more of a chance to relax, eat well, and still guide children effectively. A seating plan should be posted and should divide among the adults the difficult children who need closer attention. This will minimize arguments among children and avoid many last-minute changes that are apt to be disruptive. Advance planning can assure more equity for both children and teachers. A teacher feels more effective when no more children are assigned than can be related to comfortably.

Children's food tends to be too bland for most adult tastes. Consequently, salt and pepper should be available. It may be desirable to have coffee available, also. Adults should be sure to eat sufficient food even on those difficult days when frequent interruptions occur.

New teachers and substitutes should be briefed regarding children's eating habits to enable them to carry on as effectively as possible with the plan being followed for each child.

CONCLUSION

From the moment of conception, nutrition plays an important role in the child's development. After birth, infant feeding is regarded as a very serious matter that is critical to life itself. Caregivers who assume the care of an infant will expect to build on the foundations of diet and procedures established by the parents in the early months. The goal is to provide sufficient nourishing foods to fulfill energy and growth needs.

Young children's appetites appear to decrease as their growth rate decreases. Parents and caregivers are cautioned against pressuring children to eat. Children should be allowed to decide when they have had enough. Following the "clean plate" rule may contribute to obesity.

The primary goal of mealtime and snacktime is to provide nutritional foods required for energy and growth needs; however, these periods also afford opportunities for rest, for socialization, and for learning facts about foods and nutrition. Teachers and parents alike must use suitable guidance for establishing good food habits and mealtime behavior.

REVIEW AND APPLICATIONS

Ten Guides to Children's Mealtime

1. Remember that the goal is for children to eat sufficient nourishing food to provide for energy needs and growth, rather than to eat any one particular food.
2. Remember that children have decreased food needs when their rate of growth slows around the age of two and a half to age three.
3. Give the child a rest period just before mealtime.
4. Serve meals before the child gets overly hungry or tired.
5. Serve foods in small servings, making it possible for the child to obtain seconds without help.
6. Serve new foods in small amounts with known and liked foods.
7. Accept the fact that children like lukewarm foods.
8. Allow children to feed themselves finger foods.
9. Teach children about foods that are best for them and about avoiding excessive sweets in drinks, desserts, and snacks.
10. Prepare foods with contrasting colors, flavors, and textures.

Applications

1. Make notes in an early childhood center of a teacher guiding a child in an eating routine. Role play the scene in your lecture class. Analyze the effective and ineffective techniques used.

2. Assist with one or more children eating a meal. Note the indirect guidance utilized. Note what physical, verbal, and affective guidance you utilize. Discuss.
3. Assist with children during snacktime. Note the indirect guidance utilized. Note the physical, verbal, and affective guidance you utilize. Discuss.
4. Assist with children helping prepare a food. Explain how they participate, what they say, and how they seem to be understanding what is taking place.
5. Evaluate your center's mealtimes routines, using the Ten Guides to Children's mealtimes. Use a 1-to-5 scale with 5 highest. Discuss with your classmates.

 Observations

1. Observe one or more children eating a meal. Which children are right-handed? Left-handed? Which children use tools in an adult-like manner? What comments do children make about food? Which children take seconds? Pour their own milk? Discuss.
2. Observe children during snacktime. Which children can eat and talk? Which hand is used to handle food and tools? Are children able to wait their turn to be served? What efforts do children make to clear the table? Discuss.
3. Observe children's reaction to hot and cold foods. Tell what they do. What do you conclude about children's temperature preference for their food?
4. Observe your case-study child's eating behavior. Answer questions 1 and 2 with your case-study child in mind. What food does your child prefer? If feasible, confer with parents and teachers to learn the eating history of the child.

FOR FURTHER READING

Endres, Jeannette B. and Robert Rockwell. *Food, Nutrition and the Young Child.* Columbus, OH: Merrill/Macmillan, 1990.

Reinisch, Edith and Ralph E. Minear, Jr. *Health of the Preschool Child.* New York: John Wiley & Sons, Inc., 1978.

Spock, Benjamin and Michael B. Rothenberg. *Dr. Spock's Baby and Child Care.* New York: Pocket Books, 1992.

CHAPTER 10

Guiding Children's Sleeping Behavior

Key Concepts

◆ Self-Demand Schedule
◆ Sleep for Full-Day Groups
◆ Safe Sleeping Arrangements
◆ Guidance

"Has your baby begun sleeping all night?" "Is the baby still taking two naps a day?" "My baby has given up his daytime naps but he goes to bed early." "What do you do to get your baby to go to bed so early?"

These are some comments you might hear if you spent an afternoon listening to casual conversation among mothers of babies. A baby's sleep is another of the routines that concern parents and caregivers, and they work hard to get a good sleep routine established.

INFANTS AND TODDLERS

There are individual differences in infants' sleep patterns, as indicated by the mothers' questions just quoted. One baby is a regular sleeper from the beginning, perhaps taking a couple of short naps during the morning, one in the afternoon, and sleeping all night starting the third month. Another baby may seem to have a different routine, perhaps sleeping a lot one day and little the next, making it hard to predict a sleep pattern.

In infancy and throughout the early years, the sleeping routine will require the special attention of caregivers, especially when the child is in the center for more than a few hours. The sleeping routine must be handled with loving care whether at home or school. Sleep is indeed "nature's tonic." It restores the body after the physical and psychological activity that the young child typically participates in. Periods of rest and sleep are essential to the individual's growth and total well-being.

Infants' Schedules

Individualized schedules often help caregivers meet the needs of several infants. Fortunately, in a center, babies are seldom all awake and demanding food and changing at the same time. Some sleep while others are awake. Some sleep longer at a given time than others. This is another routine in which the child should be allowed some "self-demand." However, this sleep routine, like other routines, requires caregivers who know the child's needs and who can set the stage for the sleep and rest a child's body requires. Infants need more rest at shorter intervals than toddlers. As children mature they generally require less sleep.

A fussy baby can often be helped by a nap.
(Butler Child Care Center, Okinawa)

The deep sleep of most children shows how much they really need the rest.
(Kansas State University Hoeflin Stone House Child Care Center)

Vigorous and Quiet Activities

All schedules for infants and young children, whether at home or in a center, need to be balanced between active and quiet activities. If there are both types of activities available, then the child can choose the one preferred. Fatigue develops when there is insufficient rest and sleep; it interferes with growth and disturbs the child's social relations. The child may become hyperactive and easily disturbed—crying and overreacting to situations and disturbing the other children and adults.

Overstimulation is frequently a problem in group care situations. Continuous contact with other babies or children, the presence of equipment for vigorous activity, the number of people in the setting, and their voices and actions all combine to make group care highly stimulating and possibly overtiring for children. New children may need a period to adjust to so much stimulus.

Napping

Centers that keep children all day should expect infants and children through the third year to sleep during the day. For four-year-olds and older children, some rest arrangement should be provided but allowances made for those who do not feel like sleeping.

There is general agreement that infants should sleep. Cribs are major equipment in nurseries—and they are costly in terms of dollar outlay and space usage. Most infants will not fight sleep but find comfort in a routine of eating, sleeping, changing, playing, eating, sleeping, changing, playing, and so on.

Considerable loving, cuddling, conversation, even singing, should go into making naptime a pleasant and happily anticipated event. The crib must never become a punishing spot but, instead, a welcome place for rest. Therefore, when a child is having difficulty, is fussy or hungry, nonsleep needs should first be alleviated before the child is placed in the crib.

Even young babies move quite a bit during sleep. That's one reason for padded crib sides, and the reason for never leaving babies unattended on a big bed or table from which they might fall.

Babies like to lie in their cribs and play with their mobiles, rattles, or toes when they are not sleeping. They often practice their vocalizations during this time. As an infant caregiver you can respond to the verbalizing babies with returned bits of conversation, smiles, and momentary games.

Babies also like to be turned over until they are able to perform this feat themselves—it gives them a new perspective, and eases the pressure on certain muscles. A change to a playpen may also be in order to give the child new toys, or new things to look at. Babies should not be placed with other infants for long periods of time because it can be too stimulating and tiring.

Parents of infants will want caregivers to report how their child slept during the day. Some teachers complete a little report form that shows time of naps, feedings, and bowel movements that helps parents plan for the child during the rest of the day and evening.

Some working parents whose infants are in child care develop a family pattern of keeping the baby up quite late in the evening when they are home so they can enjoy playing together. This probably presents little problem while the baby is still not very active. However, in the toddler years, such a pattern is often unfortunate, because most centers offer stimulating morning programs

Safe cribs are equipped with padded bumpers and firm matresses.

(J. Altadona, photographer)

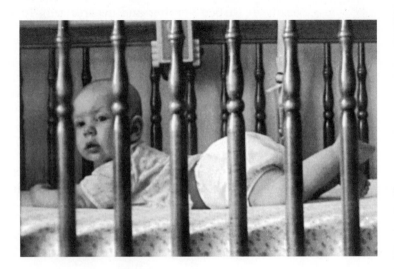

that do not always allow for morning naps. Also, the toddler may begin playing with active peers. Being too tired from a late bedtime the previous night, the toddler can be both frustrating and easily frustrated. Caregivers need to watch for this kind of problem and communicate with parents to work out a solution that benefits all. Some parents need support for being firm about bedtimes; thus, evidence that the child needs more sleep may help convince them to change some home routines to include more sleep for their child.

YOUNG CHILDREN

Space Arrangement

The sleeping room for infants, toddlers, and young children should be located so children can be easily moved out in case of fire. Exits must not be blocked with cribs or other furniture. Fire extinguishers should be readily available, and every nap room supervisor must know how to work them. Fire regulations should also be known, and all workers should see that they are adhered to. Sufficient staff must be on duty to remove children in case of emergency.

If children's cots are adequately separated at naptime, disturbances will be minimized and caregivers will be able to move rapidly among the resting children as needed for emergencies and for normal care.

Children should have their own napping space. Each cot should be labeled with a child's name and placed in a regular place each day to help the child gain a feeling of "personal space," which will give a sense of security. Some licensing regulations do not require cots for napping. If waterproof pads are used, they should be protected with a covering—perhaps like a pillowcase—that can be laundered regularly. Each child should have a pad or mat.

The teacher should plan the sleeping room cot or mat arrangement to facilitate guidance. Two children who are developing a strong friendship may want to talk and thus prevent others from sleeping. They may be widely separated. Dividers in front of toys and between cots or mats may be helpful to reduce stimulation. Dimming the lights and drawing the curtains help set the stage for the resting behavior desired. Distracting entries of either adults or children should be eliminated. The temperature of the room needs to be adjusted to the amount of cover the children have. Drafts must be avoided.

Indirect Guidance

Several indirect guidance techniques are helpful at naptime. The organization of the space has already been mentioned. By establishing a regular sequence of events or schedule, the teacher helps children know when naptime is approaching. Usually it follows lunch, with only toileting, hand washing, removal of shoes, and perhaps removal of play clothes intervening between lunch and nap. The nap room is prepared while children eat and is ready and waiting for them. A quiet period with low-keyed voices and nonhurrying routines helps children get in the mood for resting. A busy morning filled with many interesting activities and including plenty of fresh air and exercise outdoors will cause most children to welcome the opportunity to rest.

Some children seem to go right to sleep once they are in bed, but others may take as long as thirty or forty minutes to relax and go to sleep. Following are a number of direct guidance techniques that teachers find useful in helping children at naptime.

 Talk It Over

What are some rituals you have for relaxing yourself when you want to go to sleep?

How can we help children learn to relax themselves either to go to sleep in the first place or return to sleep if awakened before sleep is finished?

Fatigue comes after a busy morning and can be alleviated by a noontime nap.
(Kansas State Early Childhood Laboratory)

Direct Guidance

A child may be comfortably tucked in only to announce the need to go to the toilet. There seems to be no alternative except to allow it, for one would not want to be responsible for an "accident." Some children's bowels move shortly after eating. Careful attention to post-lunch toileting usually helps alleviate this problem. However, if a child learns that such an announcement is a sure route to delaying bedtime, then teachers may encourage that particular child to use the toilet before entering the nap room. Children should be encouraged to use the toilet immediately upon waking. This is a time when most will need to urinate; however, no pressure should be applied if they do not.

To help children relax you may want to sit on the floor by their cots to massage their backs or talk quietly to them. You may sing to children in a quiet voice. Little songs that mention each child's name may be useful in helping them quiet down and relax. Some children relax better if they lie face down. It helps them avoid being distracted by movement in the room. Children will not relax if afraid, so avoidance of any threat is imperative.

Naptime may be a time when visions of parents and home may be strongest, making the child homesick—even one who has been happy all morning. A toy or blanket from home may be helpful to some; others may suck their thumbs or twist their hair. This is not a time to curb such habits. Adults should be patient and understand that these habits serve comforting functions. It helps sometimes to mention post-nap activity or that they will see mother after snack or after outdoor play—whichever is factual. You may also want to remind children that you will take good care of them while they are asleep.

Four- and five-year-olds may be outgrowing their afternoon naps, especially if they are getting a good night's sleep at home and sufficient opportunities to do restful activity during the day. It seems important for teachers to avoid making an issue over actual sleeping. Children who don't appear to need to sleep may be allowed to read on their cots or to relax on a carpet in another part of the building away from sleeping children. Calling the period "rest" instead of "sleep" may make it more acceptable for many children. Reassuring them that "You only have to stretch out, you don't need to sleep" may help some. Because these older children typically enjoy visiting with each other, it usually helps to separate them widely.

Rest Time in Short-Day Groups

Do we really need "rest time" in short-day groups? This is a question that has bothered teachers, parents, and even children. It has been a custom until recently to require the children to stretch out prone for a given length of time to "rest." Observation showed that these times were quite mislabeled, for in many groups they were anything but "restful." Because of the rest requirements, children have been known to virtually refuse to attend school or to "hate" the rugs that they have to take to school for resting. Teachers found that the rest period was one they did not look forward to and many were led to rethink rest time.

In many groups that meet for only two and a half to three hours, the rest time is a quiet period for snacks, singing, and stories. These organized and interesting periods, which do have other important objectives to fulfill, also provide time for the child's body to become rested and refreshed. Many children will actually lie on the floor to hear a lullaby or two, or to do a quiet finger exercise, or to move their eyes from side to side. They enjoy these times even though they tend to dislike rest.

In short-day groups the children come later in the morning than in full-day groups. Therefore, they usually are able to complete their cycle of sleeping at home. Some children actually arise about 8:30 a.m., eat breakfast, and arrive at school by 9 a.m. If they have had a good night's sleep—eight, ten, even twelve hours for some—they surely aren't in need of much rest by 10 a.m. or 10:30 a.m. Many will go home to a good afternoon of napping if they need it. Afternoon groups often need a more slowly paced program if the children arrive at school without napping.

The point here is for teachers to take a good look at the amount of sleep children are getting at home and to balance the quiet and vigorous activities they are offering at school, then decide if there is a real need for formal resting. Teachers should remember that such activities as sand play, listening to records, painting, or playing with puzzles can be restful. Children can be guided into these quiet activities if they show signs of fatigue.

Each child should have a personal cot, sheet, and blanket.
(University of Missouri-Columbia Child Development Laboratory)

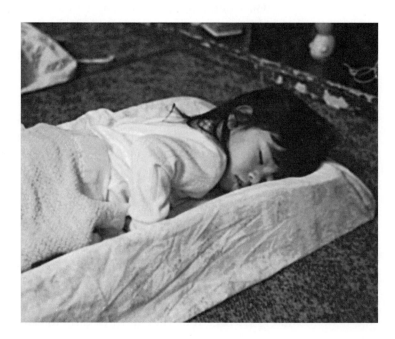

COMMUNICATING WITH PARENTS

Teachers, in consultation with parents, can decide on the amount of napping to encourage in young children at school. In some homes that are crowded and disruptive the child has a hard time getting sufficient sleep, so long nap periods in the center are needed. In others, the parents prefer to have the child take a short nap at the center in order to be ready for a reasonably early bedtime in the evening. Working parents have many other responsibilities in their evening hours, yet this is really the only time they see their children except for weekends. However, most parents agree that it is better for parents and the child if the child goes to bed in the early evening. The school can help by awakening the child from the nap after an hour or so of sleeping. Teachers and caregivers should remember to tell parents how much their children are sleeping and report on any unusual nap problems.

 Talk It Over

What problems and pleasures do parents you know express regarding their child's sleep periods?

What routines do parents you know seem to have for their child's sleep periods?

The going-to-bed routine at home is one that is a problem to some parents. A regular bedtime routine is important at home just as it is at school. For example, about eight o'clock, with a few minutes flexibility either way, the parents can follow a regular sequence of events with their child—such as playing a quiet game, bathing, reading a story, singing a song, toileting, getting a drink, and then tucking the child in bed and saying "Goodnight." This routine can become a habit that will give the child security. The babysitter can follow the same routine.

Roughhousing may overstimulate children and prevent them from relaxing and going to sleep; therefore, bedtime activities should be quiet and low key. Eliminating television, keeping voices low, and making the period intimate with personal attention will help the child relax.

Some children who are tired will rub their eyes, whine, or perhaps cry, whereas others may become hyperactive, even silly. Parents and teachers learn to recognize their child's symptoms of fatigue. Adults must take control and put the child to bed, as going to bed is not a decision that most young children are capable of making independently.

Leaving the light on in the child's room should be accepted by parents if it makes the child happier. Some children do take a while to go to sleep and they may feel more secure when they can see the familiar sights in their room.

The "comfort blanket" or thumb to suck seems to be a need of many children. They all grow out of this need eventually, so there is no reason to admonish them about it when bedtime is approaching.

The average child is dry at night around age three, so for many children extra-absorbent diapers with plastic pants will help keep bedclothes dry. Of course, it is best for parents to take the child to the toilet just before tucking him or her in bed and to restrict fluids in the evening hours. Avoid a battle over bed-wetting; this generally makes the problem worse instead of better. Children eventually stay dry all night when their muscle system is mature enough.

For children who resist napping, the schedule should include a quiet time when they can rest while they look at books.
(South East Oakland Vocational Technical Child Care Center)

CONCLUSION

The sleep and resting routines of the child development center are among the most important points of the day. Children must have ways to alleviate fatigue, as it interferes with growth and good social relations. Communication with parents about nap and rest time can help them coordinate their plans with those of the school. The following ten guides are suggested for teachers who may be asked by parents for help with planning their children's sleep at home.

REVIEW AND APPLICATIONS

Ten Guides to Happy Bedtimes

1. Put the child to bed at a regular bedtime.
2. Consider the kinds of activity and the amount of sleep the child has at school in determining the appropriate bedtime.
3. Establish a regular sequence of events that helps the child know when bedtime is approaching.
4. Plan for the least stimulating of activities during the pre-bedtime period.
5. Allow the child to choose a light, a night light, or total darkness.
6. Accept comforting habits such as thumb sucking, hair twisting, or blanket caressing that help the child relax.
7. Accept the idea that the child may take a half hour or more to fall asleep.
8. Sit near the bed and sing to the child until relaxation comes, rather than permitting the child to leave the bed after being tucked in.
9. Avoid admonitions regarding keeping dry and bed-wetting when putting the child to bed.
10. Reduce environmental noises as much as possible during the child's going-to-sleep period.

 Observations

1. Observe a child at rest or sleep time. What behavior does the child carry out that shows he or she is tired or not tired? What behaviors does the child use to get ready to sleep? What does the adult do to help the child relax?
2. Report sleeping patterns of your case-study child. Learn from parents or teachers what time the child goes to bed at night and how long he or she sleeps. Given the child's level of activity, do you think the child sleeps enough?

Applications

1. Make notes in an early childhood center of a teacher guiding a child in the nap or resting routine. Role play the scene in your lecture class. Analyze the effective and ineffective techniques used.

2. Discuss with a parent the sleep habits of the child. Ask about how long and where the child sleeps, what routines precede bedtime, whether bed-wetting occurs, and what the child's usual behavior is when waking up. Write a report of your findings.

3. Discuss sleeping and resting with a caregiver or teacher. Report whether all children sleep, how long they sleep, where they sleep, where the teachers stay while children sleep, and what techniques teachers find work best for this routine.

4. Assist with a child at rest or sleep time. How is the child behaving? Does the child appear tired? How can you tell? What does the adult do to help? Estimate the child's impression of the situation.

5. Evaluate the center's sleep or rest routine, using the Ten Guides to Happy Bedtimes. Use a 1-to-5 scale. Discuss.

ADDITIONAL RESOURCES

Suggested Videotape

Establishing Healthful Habits VHS 1/2 in. Color 30 minutes 1988

Thelma Harms and Debby Cryer show how to encourage good nutrition, sleep patterns, and other habits that promote wellness, in home and child care. Suggests solutions to health threats for infants in day care settings. Delmar Publishers, Customer Service, 2 Computer Drive West, Albany, NY 12212, 1–800–347–7707.

FOR FURTHER READING

Cuthbertson, Joanne and Susanna Schevill. *Helping Your Child Sleep Through the Night*. Garden City, NY: Doubleday, 1985.

Ferber, Richard. "Sleep, Sleeplessness and Sleep Disturbances in Infants and Young Children," *Annuals of Clinical Research,* 17, 1985, 227–234.

Ferber, Richard. *Solve Your Child's Sleep Problems*. New York: Simon & Schuster, 1985.

Ferber, Richard. "The Child Who Doesn't Sleep: Resolving Common Sleep Problems," Eileen Shiff (ed.), *Experts Advise Parents*. New York: Delacorte Press, 1987, 63–86.

Richman, Naomi and J. Douglas. *My Child Won't Sleep*. London: Penguin, 1984.

CHAPTER 11

Guiding Children's Dressing and Undressing

Key Concepts

- ◆ Independence in Dressing
- ◆ Appropriate Clothing
- ◆ Helpful Guidance

Patrick sat in front of the teacher. He pulled on his boots. He laid his opened ski jacket in front of him on the floor with the collar at his feet. He bent over and slipped his arms into the sleeves. He raised the jacket over his head and it slipped into place. "I did it!" he exclaimed with joy.

Patrick was learning to be independent in his dressing. The teacher was nearby to offer physical and verbal guidance if he needed it. She too felt happy when Patrick was able to get his coat on alone. "You feel good when you can put on your coat," reflected the teacher.

Becoming increasingly independent is a basic goal for the early childhood years, and dressing oneself is part of the independence for which the children, and their parents and teachers strive.

Dressing and undressing children in the child development center can require a great deal of the teachers' and caregivers' time and energy. In cold climates the numbers of garments and complication of the dressing tasks must be experienced to be believed. Dressing in winter especially can be very frustrating and time-consuming for children and adults alike.

INFANTS AND TODDLERS

Each infant and toddler should have a personal space where individual clothing is stored. Dressing infants and young toddlers is largely adults' responsibility. Dressing tables are desirable to help adults avoid back strain. The diaper-changing area was discussed in Chapter 5 and should be separate from the area where other clothing is put on infants and toddlers. Once dressed in warm clothing children should be taken outside to avoid overheating. Thus, a staff member should be dressed to go outdoors as soon as a child is dressed.

Likewise, when children return indoors they should have warm clothing removed quickly. It is easy to see why it takes more caregivers to manage infants and toddlers when one considers the amount of direct help each child requires.

Infants and toddlers respond positively to going outdoors to play, to walk, or to ride in a stroller. The sunshine, fresh air, and exercise are necessary ingredients for good physical and mental health. Caregivers should try to organize the dressing and undressing routines so that the routines do not exhaust either the children or the caregivers.

Infant clothing usually comes with adequate zippers and grippers to aid the caregiver. Infants dislike having things pulled over their heads, so skill and speed are needed when slip-over garments are provided.

Babies are quite easily distracted, and will protest less if you talk to them while dressing them. As they get older and understand the meaning of words and signs, if the caregiver puts on an outdoor hat first and says, "Outside," the infant may then allow outdoor clothing to be put on without so much protest.

Toddlers can help with dressing by handing items to the caregiver. "Bring me your socks" or "Bring me your shoes" helps children learn the names of garments and helps keep their minds on the task, too.

Dressing time is a good time for some one-to-one conversation with the infant or toddler. Use eye contact as you fasten buckles and tie bows.

Children's clothing needs to be easy for children to put on as well as rugged and easily laundered.
(Kansas State University Early Childhood Laboratory)

Adults who are not active sometimes feel that a child wearing only a light wrap must be freezing. Actually, children should have much more to say about how much clothing they wear. Parents may need to be helped to understand this fact.

Tying Shoes

Tying shoes is another problem area. After naps and frequently after outdoor play, the shoes become untied. Sometimes you will want shoes off for music and rhythm experiences. In most groups the teacher simply must retie the

The "trick" of slipping one's coat over the head makes dressing for outdoor play easier for young children.
(South East Oakland Vocational Technical Child Care Center)

shoes. Tying is a motor skill that most children will not be able to learn until kindergarten or first grade. This explains the popularity of Velcro in shoe closings for younger children.

A five-year-old whose coordination is advanced will learn to tie shoes quickly and will enjoy practicing. If the adults sit with the children on their laps or in some way that allows them the same vantage point as the child, they can clearly demonstrate the tying operation. Some people make a loop of each string and then tie the loops into a double knot, and this is satisfactory for some children. One way that has been successful is to label the loops "bunny ears" and demonstrate the tying operation, then encourage the children as they begin to understand the process.

Tying shoes, apron strings, and the like is difficult, and to expect it of the younger two- to four-year-old children is futile and frustrating. Children do not seem to mind having their shoestrings dangle, much to their elders' dismay. For example, a teacher said to a five-year-old, "Dean, your shoe is not tied." He said, "So?" The teacher said, "Can you tie it or shall I?" He quickly said, "I can do it," and proceeded to show his skill. In one sense the adult was interfering with Dean's train of thought for he was busy with something else and unaware of the untied shoestrings. Dean's activity at that point did not require tied shoes for safety; therefore, it would have been better to have ignored the shoelaces and watched to see if Dean would tie them himself without suggestion.

HELPING PARENTS CHOOSE APPROPRIATE CLOTHING

For Children's Independence

Parents frequently need guidance regarding the type of clothing that will make it easy for their child to become independent in dressing. Occasionally a garment simply jeopardizes the child's success in toileting, and parents should be so informed. A one-piece jumpsuit that buttons on the shoulders is such a garment. A competent four-year-old girl wore one of these and cried when she didn't get it unbuttoned in time. On the advice of the teacher, the child quit wearing that garment to school.

Independence is fostered by large zippers that are easily fitted together, large buttons, Velcro fasteners, and elastic waistbands. Items interfering with independence are ties on the shoulders, tiny buttons or zippers, and fancy belts.

For Full Participation in School Activities

Child development center activities require rugged play garments, such as jeans and T-shirts. Rugged clothing will protect a child from the cold weather and from scratches. The clothing should be washable and unharmed by vigorous playground activities or by paints and the like used in art projects. Appropriate clothing for school needs to be described to both parents and children before the wrong garments are purchased. At times, if clothing guidance is lacking, there may be competition—especially among girls—resulting in chil-

In some climates and seasons light clothing is needed, in others children are bundled up in order to enjoy the snow drifts.
(V. Hildebrand, photographer)

dren wearing party clothing that inhibits full participation in school activities. Party dresses are, of course, unsuited to school activities, and dress shoes are actually very dangerous because most of them are slippery.

The staff, participating students, and volunteers may unwittingly positively reinforce the wearing of such inappropriate clothing as frilly short dresses with comments to a girl such as, "My, you look beautiful in your new dress today." With such compliments parents won't stand much of a chance of getting the girl into an appropriate play garment the next day. Positive reinforcement should logically come when children are dressed appropriately, for example, "Those jeans are just right for the climbing we have planned today."

◆   Talk It Over   ◆

Give an example of an adult's comment on a child's clothing that might further the child's self-esteem.

Give an example of a comment on a child's clothing that might further a sex-role stereotype.

Give an example of a comment on a child's clothing that might make old clothes become an embarrassment to another child.

Discuss whether a child's clothing should be the subject of teachers' comments to a child.

Regarding sexist practices, Alleen Nielsen writes, "Most girls are pretty and we encourage them to adorn themselves by complimenting them on their appearance. It would probably be just as effective when we greet children in the morning if we substituted a sincere 'How are you?' or 'What's new?' in place of 'How pretty you look!' or 'You've got a new dress!' Just for fun some-day keep track of how many times you compliment girls on their appearance compared to how many times you compliment boys on their appearance. Girls need to be encouraged to achieve, since about one-third of the families in the United States have a woman as the head of the household, and this is a job that takes more than being pretty."[2]

Parents need the support of the staff when they encourage their child to wear appropriate garments. Wise parents give their child a choice between two appropriate garments—"Do you want to wear your blue or green jeans today?"—rather than allowing the child to choose among all the clothes hanging in the closet. Patched clothing that covers the child adequately should be acceptable to the staff. Children who wear old clothing and hand-me-downs should be as accepted as any other. Care needs to be exercised to be sure you don't routinely comment on new clothing, making children wearing old garments feel uncomfortable and resulting in discrimination based on economic class.

CONCLUSION

The teacher's guidance during dressing should encourage the children to become independent. The children should be helped with tasks they can't perform and aided with those they can almost perform. Allow children to dress voluntarily, giving them minimal directions. Dressing voluntarily is a step toward a more advanced level of independence for children. It is ridiculous to see a five-year-old with an easily handled fat zipper being zipped by a hovering adult. An observant teacher can see when frustration is about to set in and offer a little help or a word of advice and demonstration. Sometimes children do not know an easy way to do a task. It is well to divide the group into small groups of children that an adult can effectively help. Recognition for accomplishments is one of the best guidance techniques.

Independence in dressing is an accomplishment children seem to want to achieve, and the adults in their lives are happy to have them learn. Parents should set the stage for children's learning by purchasing clothing that is easy to manage. You can reward independence in dressing by letting children go outside immediately after they are dressed.

---

[2] Alleen Pace Nielsen, "Alternatives to Sexist Practices in the Classroom," *Young Children*, 32:5, July 1977, p. 58.

REVIEW AND APPLICATIONS

Ten Guides to Children's Dressing

1. Provide children with a locker bearing their name and teach them to put their clothing there.
2. Use verbal and physical guidance to encourage independent dressing and undressing.
3. Encourage children to bring outdoor wraps to a circle some distance from the lockers where teachers, sitting on low chairs, can oversee their dressing.
4. Avoid making discriminatory comments about a child's clothing.
5. Take children outdoors as soon as they are completely dressed as a reward for prompt dressing and to avoid overheating.
6. Explain to children and parents what kind of clothing is best for school activities.
7. Encourage the staff to reinforce positively clothing that is appropriate for school activities, including old garments.
8. Systematize the removal of snowy wraps, the drying of clothing, and the avoidance of puddles.
9. Avoid having children become overheated from wearing too much clothing on warm days.
10. Solicit parental help in removing and in putting on wraps or boots at the beginning and end of the school day.

 Observations

1. Observe a child while dressing or undressing. How independent does the child's clothing allow him or her to be? How does the child feel about his or her clothing?
2. Observe the children going through a toileting or undressing routine. Record the design of clothing and actions of children who finish quickly and those who finish slowly. Does the design of the clothing make a difference between the two groups?
3. Observe your case-study child in a dressing routine for nap, toilet, and outdoor play. Summarize your child's self-efficacy for these self-care tasks.

Applications

1. Make notes in an early childhood center of a teacher guiding a child in a dressing routine. Role play the scene in your lecture class. Analyze the effective and ineffective techniques used.

2. Assist a child with putting on some pieces of clothing in either a home or a school. What is the child old enough to do? What help is asked for? Does the child feel independent? How can you tell that the child feels independent? Summarize.
3. Discuss with a parent or a teacher tips for buying clothing for children that helps them become independent. Summarize your findings.
4. Browse in a children's clothing department and eavesdrop on conversations between parents and clerks. What qualities are parents looking for in children's clothing? If children are present, what part do they play in clothing selections? Write a brief report.
5. Using a 1-to-5 point scale with 5 highest, rate the center on the Ten Guides to Children's Dressing. Discuss.

FOR FURTHER READING

Hildebrand, Verna. "Mothers' Perceptions of Independent and Responsible Behaviors of Their Preschool Children." *Psychological Reports,* 37:3, Fall 1975, 631–641.

Hildebrand, Verna. *Introduction to Early Childhood Education.* New York: Macmillan Publishing Company, 1991.

Hildebrand, Verna. "Young Children's Self-Care and Independence Tasks: Applying Self-Efficacy Theory." *Early Child Development and Care,* March 30, 1988, 199–204.

CHAPTER 12

Guiding Children on the Playground

Key Concepts

◆ Indirect Guidance Outdoors
◆ Direct Guidance Outdoors
◆ Learning vs. Competition
◆ Self-Efficacy, Health, and Outdoor Play

What shall we do when we all go out?
All go out, All go out;
What shall we do when we all go out?
When we all go out to play?

We shall climb on the jungle gym,
Jungle gym, jungle gym;
We shall climb on the jungle gym,
When we all go out to play.

When the teacher began this song, it signaled to the children that singing time was over and that they could proceed to their lockers for their wraps. They chimed in on words as they rose and moved with haste to get their clothing. Going outdoors was indeed a joyous occasion for these children, as it is for most young children.

Play in the out of doors appears to hold a never-ending attraction. Children need this period in the day whether at home or at school. Adults who work with children can use the period to teach many worthwhile concepts relating to every aspect of the child's development. Outdoor play gives you many opportunities to use all of the guidance techniques and to make a significant contribution to the child's learning.

TEACHING VERSUS SUPERVISING

You can be a far more important person to the children on the playground than a mere supervisor. Usually supervisors just stand around, waiting until something unpleasant happens, then try to do something about it. Teachers, on the other hand, interact with the children, stay close to them, and listen to what they say, what they ask, and what they need. Teachers are quick to give the appropriate guidance that encourages children to grow in knowledge, independence, skill, and personal relationships. Being alert and involved, teachers adjust the situation to avoid having unproductive situations take place.

Beginning assistants are frequently given lots of time on outdoor duty. For example, one student, Paula, said, "Somehow I always get out there with the children. I wonder if the other teachers are afraid they might get cold." The student went on to relate what a marvelous time she had playing with the children in the snowy yard. She had helped them examine snowflakes under the magnifying glass, knocked snow from branches, and made snow angels "just like Peter in *The Snowy Day*." Those "other teachers" may have thought that playground duty was being done by the "low persons on the totem pole," but this intelligent young woman hadn't allowed herself to treat the children as though it were. Directors and head teachers should set an example by demonstrating their appreciation for and utilization of this outdoor learning environment by participating in outdoor play.

Actually, teachers often find vigorous outdoor activity as enjoyable and tension-releasing for them as it is for the children. Playing follow the leader, walking in the "giant's tracks," flying like a bird or an airplane, or playing ball or some version of shadow tag can be as much fun for the teacher as for the children. Teachers serve as models for children, and enjoying the outdoors helps children develop an appreciation for nature and for body skills that can help them throughout life. Some children need to be taught how to relate to the out of doors. It is unfortunate for children to have teachers who find excuses to keep children indoors—ignoring the resources of the playground and of nature. Male teachers should protest if they are always expected to be the "outdoors teacher," allowing the women to toast their toes by the fire. Both should share all aspects of the school programs.

DRESSED FOR THE JOB

One important way for teachers to enjoy the out of doors is to dress for it— warm clothes in the winter and cool clothes in the summer. Early childhood teachers are among the professionals who can appropriately enjoy wearing pant suits and slacks to work. Nothing else is as practical for working with young children. Gone are the days when you need to freeze on the playground to please "dame fashion." Comfortable shoes with wide toes and heels are musts, as far as women early childhood teachers are concerned, for they give you firm footing on walks, in the yard, on stairs, and when carrying equipment and children. Warm scarves, mittens, boots, and a coat that can take the rugged use it will get are important in winter climates. Attached hoods on coats help teachers always to have their hats handy.

Summer and warmer climates should leave all teachers just as free to dress in shorts or slacks with cool blouses or shirts as preferred. Teachers will meet the outdoor period with the same enthusiasm as the children if they are properly dressed and if they also use the time to get refreshed.

Children also should be comfortably and adequately clothed for the weather. Details regarding dressing were given in Chapter 11.

Your guidance on the playground will serve to enhance the child's development. It should promote physical-motor development, intellectual development, social development, emotional development, and creative development. You can utilize both indirect and direct methods of guidance, as indicated in Chapters 2 and 3. You'll use indirect guidance when you make plans, arrange the environment, set the schedule, or assign the helpers. You'll be using direct physical, verbal, or affective guidance as you interact with the children face-to-face.

SELF-EFFICACY IN MOTOR SKILLS

Self-efficacy means *the child's judgment of what he or she can do with whatever skill possessed.* Self-efficacy is a concept described by social psychologist Albert Bandura that was introduced in Chapter 4.[1] Self-efficacy, especially in motor skills, can be readily observed on the playground. You'll see children who feel confident they can ride a tricycle, climb the jungle gym, or swing on the trapeze rings. As children are free to explore, observe, and imitate, they go where they feel confident and motivated to go. A child with high self-efficacy may climb on the highest slide or persevere in an attempt to make a large tricycle go. The child may be successful after trying various forms of behavior and strategies. Children who doubt their abilities are not self-efficacious and quit trying easily. You may recognize self-efficacy in yourself or friends who tackle learning to operate a computer, to execute a complex sports skill, or to handle the intricacies of becoming a teacher.

Self-efficacy is a personal characteristic of self-judgment that parents and educators should plan to recognize, preserve, and support in young children. We can avoid damaging children's self-efficacy by allowing them to try things that interest them and seeing that they do not get hurt, rather than limiting their opportunities to explore by being overly cautious or expressing worry over their safety. We should give them the gift of time to explore and to stick to a task or skill until they master it, rather than hurrying them to something adults consider safer.

Playyards should be set up to be reasonably safe for the ages of the children using them. Responsible adults should have the time and interest to stay nearby while children try their skills. Of course, small children may not be

---

[1] See Albert Bandura, "Self-Efficacy," *Social Foundations of Thought and Action: A Social Cognitive Theory* (Englewood Cliffs, NJ: Prentice-Hall, 1986), pp. 390–431.

Toddlers will hold tight as they venture to the top of the jungle gym, as long as they are not crowded or pushed by others.
(C. Hildebrand, photographer)

able to reason adequately about all the perils that may await them. However, having sufficient adults present and interacting with children on the playground makes it possible for children to explore. Adults should stop a behavior only when it is potentially dangerous to the child or others. As a student in your professional preparation, you can play a significant role in children's practice of motor skills and other learning on the playground.

 Talk It Over

What are some things a child might say or do to give you clues that he or she feels self-efficacious, or judges him- or herself capable of motor skill tasks on the playground?

PLANNING AND SETTING UP THE YARD

Outdoor play should be given attention during the teacher's regular planning sessions each week. The indoor activities and the outdoor activities should be varied and challenging. They should never offer a "Ho-hum, I've done this all before" appearance. Equipment should be rearranged frequently to challenge the children's motivation to use it.

In some climates, and in fall and spring in others, virtually the whole program can be moved outdoors. Children enjoy having art, music, and literature outdoors. These activities allow children quiet interludes that keep them from becoming overfatigued. A balance of quiet and active activities should be planned.

In planning, each child's motor needs should be considered and equipment arranged to challenge and test skills. Many scientific concepts can be learned outdoors, and these should be planned on a regular basis. Spontaneous interests may supersede the plan, but plans must be made or a program will surely stagnate.

One teacher should take the responsibility for setting up the outdoor learning environment each day. This teacher may also be the one to go out with the first children to get dressed for their outdoor period. Nothing rewards fast dressing like a chance to be first at the equipment.

This chapter will help you meet the playground criteria for accreditation of schools and centers as published by the National Association for the Education of Young Children as well as objectives developed by Head Start and the Child Development Associate programs. Professional early childhood educators responsible for these documents are firmly convinced of the importance of children's development that is fostered by a well-designed program on the playground.[2]

It is important to remember that both boys and girls have a need and the ability to develop physically and to benefit equally from full participation in all physical-motor activities. Therefore, forget any gender stereotypes you have. Boys and girls this age are capable of doing the same things.

Physical-Motor Objectives

To provide fresh air, sunlight, and exercise, which promote good health.

Nature provides vitamin D through sunlight's activation of a substance on the skin. Vitamin D is essential for the growth of strong bones and teeth. Because infants and young children have important growth to achieve in bones and teeth, they need regular doses of vitamin D. By spending some time outdoors in the sunshine each day the child can receive this health-giving vitamin.

Oxygen, which is of course found in fresh air, is essential for life. Oxygen is essential for the brain to function, and deficiency of oxygen will cause brain

---

[2] Sue Bredekamp (ed.), *Accreditation Criteria and Procedures of the National Academy of Early Childhood Programs* (Washington DC: NAEYC, 1991).

Also see, *Head Start Program Performance Standards* (Washington, DC: Head Start Bureau, Department of Health and Human Services, November 1984).

In addition see, Child Development Associate, *Assessment System and Competency Standards for Preschool Caregivers* and *Assessment System and Competency Standards for Infant/Toddler Caregivers* (Washington, DC: Council for Early Childhood Professional Recognition, 1992).

A climber located under a shade tree makes a pleasant play-space on a warm day.
(Baylor University Child Development Laboratory)

injury. Young children use much more oxygen for a given volume of brain tissue than adults. Exercise fosters deep breathing and oxygen intake.

Exercise is essential to aid all the body's inner systems to grow, develop, and function as they should. Respiratory, circulatory, digestive, and elimination systems all function more fully when the child has adequate exercise. Fortunately, children are happiest when they are allowed to move and be active; exercise comes quite naturally to most children. Parents and caregivers must understand how essential exercise is so they will encourage and plan for it rather than try to quiet children down to keep them from becoming so active. Exercise and fresh air will create the need for eating, and good nutrition is essential to overall good health.

To provide a setting and equipment that motivate the child to practice motor skills and develop independence.

Free, open space is important for practicing many skills. Room to move quickly without interfering with other children is essential. Another requirement is a sufficient number of play spaces and pieces of equipment that allow the child a choice in exercising muscles and developing skills of particular interest at the moment.

As the small toddler begins using the play yard independently, the adult will stay close by to lend a supporting hand when necessary. Some tumbles that might discourage further adventures can be prevented. The adult can also prevent one child from inadvertently interfering with another. That is, one toddler may tumble or push, causing another child to fall unless an alert adult guides the play, foresees points where interference might occur, and diverts the movement of the child. Young toddlers have a low center of gravity, but may tumble easily. Children are also well padded, so the falls are usually not hurtful, and the adult need not say much more than "Oops! That must have hurt. Hop up and brush off the dirt," and the child will be on the go again.

Three-year-olds are typically somewhat cautious as they practice new motor skills. They watch older children and follow their lead. Four- and five-year-olds love to run fast and climb high. It is a wonderful school that provides open spaces for their expansive cooperative games that involve quick movements.

Skills in using the body and holding the body erect are promoted during the outdoor play. The gross or large motor skills such as walking, running, climbing, pedaling, pushing, and pulling develop first in the child's repertoire of skills. The child with the best-developed motor skills is frequently a leader in the group.

Two physical education researchers, John Haubenstricker and Vern Seefeldt, are learning from studies of children carried on for a number of years that when children's large motor skills are poorly developed at age five they may never really become skilled, even with remedial help. For this reason they advocate that teachers of young children help children learn and practice certain motor skills.

These researchers studied three types of skills: (1) body management skills, (2) locomotor skills, and (3) projection and reception skills.[3] Suggestions for activities encouraging children to practice these three types of motor skills are given below.

Body Management Skills

Body management skills include such things as bouncing on a trampoline, jumping board, or mattress. Hopping exercises with eyes opened and closed and walking a balance beam forward and backward are body management skills. Climbing and descending various ladders and stairs and hanging from climbing structures are helpful exercises. Stunts, such as pretending to be

---

[3] Vern Seefeldt, "The Role of Motor Skills in the Lives of Children with Learning Disabilities," paper presented to the Conference on Children with Learning Disabilities, Detroit, Michigan, March 1973. Also, pictures from the Seefeldt-Haubenstricker study are found in Verna Hildebrand, *Introduction to Early Childhood Education* (New York: Macmillan Publishing Company, 1991), pp. 165–173.

A slide down the "fireman's pole" is an adventure for this five-year-old.
(V. Hildebrand, photographer)

snakes, frogs, kangaroos, or ducks, give experience in handling the body. Sitting and rolling forward, backward, and around are interesting to children and useful for body control. Make a little list of these activities, take it to the play yard, and try out the ideas with the children.

Locomotor Skills

Locomotor skills include walking backward and forward, running toward a goal, running with a stop-and-go signal, or running on tiptoes. Jumping, galloping, and hopping can be encouraged through various games either indoors or out. A bamboo pole, placed with one end on the ground and the other end propped up on a sawhorse, encourages practice in hurdle jumping, with each child selecting the appropriate height to jump.

Projection and Reception Skills

Projection and reception skills are those of throwing and receiving a ball, or kicking or batting a ball. Big balls and beanbags are useful for beginning games with large targets such as wastebaskets to receive the balls. Plastic bats and balls used by the child with an adult make batting practice a successful and fun activity. Also, an adult should play throwing and catching games with the young child because at that age skills are poorly developed and games between children are frustrating. That is, a child who can't throw straight isn't a good partner for one who has minimum catching skills.

Observing how skilled players follow through with the total body makes one realize how much a young child has to develop to become skilled. It is important that the child be encouraged to practice these projection and reception skills.

Pedaling and Other Skills

Wheel toys need to be sized appropriately for the children using the yard. Toddlers can't feel successful trying to reach the pedals of the four-year-old's tricycle and the four-year-old won't be able to enjoy the toddler's toy either. Each yard should afford some equipment that offers a challenge to the children in the group. A desirable arrangement for wheel-toy use is a ribbon of paving that circles the yard. Then rules of guidance about the appropriate direction of the traffic to flow are easily maintained.

Swings that two children can push and pull to make themselves swing are a challenge to the pumping skills of threes and fours.

Independence in swinging on a traditional swing can be promoted by building a ramp under the swing. This can be either a permanent construction or a temporary inclined plane built with a board and a sawhorse. Children hold tight to the swing chains and with the swing behind them walk backward up the inclined plane. They walk as far as the swing reaches and sit down in the swing. Gravity carries them forward, and their bodies achieve the posture required to keep the swing moving. Children feel a new-found independence as they make the swing go "all by myself!"

To further encourage pumping skills, the adult should stand in front of the children, urging them to reach out with their feet. This will enable the adult to push the children's feet. A front position has the advantage of eye contact and personal interaction with the child compared to pushing from the back. As the children stretch for your hand they'll get the feel of pumping the swing.

Adult Guidance

The urge for independence and achievement can be a highly motivating drive for a child. When children challenge themselves, they usually will go only as high as they feel safe. Wise teachers stay close by when one child is encouraging another child to go beyond where that child feels safe, because this is a situation that often creates fear, and the child may let go if scared. Adults should avoid motivating one child to achieve heights or speed just because another has. If a child is prone to show off to other children or to adults, this, too, is a potentially dangerous situation. Once a child learns a skill, help find a new feat that is now appropriate. For example, saying, "Since you can climb this ladder, Jim, you might try the tree house tomorrow" encourages a child to continue developing his or her climbing skills.

Being close to children and talking with them occur easily in the outdoor environment.
(University of Wisconsin-Madison Child Development Laboratory)

The guidance of the teacher should be very personal—given directly to the child in quiet, reassuring tones. Shouts across the play yard are usually totally ineffective. Children don't know that the shouts are meant for them, and they may actually not hear what is said.

 Talk It Over

What are some ways adults guided you as a child that fostered or inhibited your motor skill development?

Imitating Peers

To provide an opportunity for a child to imitate peers and to compare motor skills with theirs on an informal noncompetitive basis.

Sharon watched Pam climb a tree and decided to try it herself. She tried several times and finally succeeded in getting into the tree. When she had firm, secure footing she smiled, then laughed, then yelled, "Look at me! I'm up here!" She took time deciding to jump down; when she did, she laughed, skipped around, and climbed into the tree again. Sharon was a quiet child who knew when she was ready to try something new. Watching Pam had helped her decide.

Children learn many things by watching their friends. Modeling or imitation is an important method of learning. If something looks like fun, they will want to try it and won't need any encouragement from adults. The adults can help by having several pieces of equipment available so that one child does not have to give up a place to allow a novice to try. For example, at the carpentry bench an experienced hammerer can show the newcomer some tricks of the trade. With tricycles, the skillful driver may lead the less skillful, teaching them skills in the process. The child dangling by the knees on the jungle gym usually encourages friends to try the "trick."

The adult may need to protect the less skillful children from the ridicule of the more skillful by comments such as "After Carlos practices a while he'll be able to do it like you," or "Don't you remember only a short time ago when you were learning?" "Yes, Joan is taking longer, but that's all right. She's learning." This helps the beginner to know that a friend was once a beginner too.

As mentioned earlier, it is poor procedure to motivate children by comparing them to their friends. Avoid statements like "Jimmy climbed up here, you try it" or "See if you can beat Jimmy to the top of the climber." The child might be secretly admiring Jimmy, but this places them in open competition, which may leave both children quite uncomfortable.

Children may want to wrestle, and a good rule is that "wrestling is for outdoors." Then allow only two children at a time and have the understanding that the goal is "to have fun." They should also agree to stop if one partner says "Up." A teacher should stay nearby.

Intellectual Objectives

To provide opportunities for the child to develop concepts of the order and beauty of nature.

Children have to learn that spring follows winter and summer follows spring. In their short life spans they will not know this from experience. By having it drawn to their attention, they will begin to have some appreciation of the order of nature. They will also learn to see as beautiful the wonders of nature that unfold around them each season, if adults will look for, show, and talk about these natural wonders.

Children need to know the names of all the things in their small world, because these, too, are new to them. Names should be accurate. Adults should develop curiosity and interest in nature and learn correct facts to relate to the small children in their care. From the puddle that freezes over on the first cold night of fall to the bloom on the crocus in spring, the teacher has untold opportunities to teach children about nature. Be sure to control any squeamishness you feel toward worms and insects, or you are likely to pass on those feelings to the children. Learn what these animals will do. Most are harmless. If they sting—as do bees or hornets—then you should teach children to give them high respect and keep a safe distance.

An Environmental Laboratory

To provide an environmental laboratory for learning about nature, weather, plants, animals, and insects and about such concepts as number, speed, gravity, height, weight, and balance.

A laboratory is a place where you try things out. It is action-packed, not quiet like a library. The play yard can be full of experimental situations.

In guiding children in their experiments, the teacher should happily encourage children's curiosity. "What would happen if we . . ." can be a question the teacher often asks children. "How did you make it do that?" is another. "Tell me what happened. What do you think the (worm, bird, squirrel, and so on) is trying to do?" can encourage children to relate what they have observed. The important thing is that the teacher be alert to the child's activity. Commenting on something a child sees, picks up, or even what is feared provides excellent learning situations. Sometimes the episode is meaningful for one child, and sometimes it can be developed or repeated so that the total group benefits from it. Teachers should feel that stimulation of one child's sense of inquiry is significant and probably of far more worth to the child personally than numerous group experiences that might be planned. This type of spontaneous experience grows out of the child's own interest.

Children make a counting experience out of a delightful time on the large wooden rocking boat. They chant

Teeter totter, Full—
Teeter totter, Full—
Teeter totter, One More, (One child rolled off.)
Teeter totter, Two More, (Another rolled off.)
Teeter totter, Three More. (Another rolled off, then they climbed on and
        began the chant over.)

Science experiments should be planned frequently for the outdoors to supplement the experiments that may be going on indoors with somewhat different equipment. Observations done indoors can be checked outdoors and vice versa. Gravity, the properties of inclined planes and teeter boards, and balance are examples. Labeling these concepts indoors and again outdoors helps children learn that knowledge carries over and is applicable to other situations. Planting seeds and bulbs in a garden or flowerbed makes a challenging learning experience. Children realize the time lag between planting and sprouting and the "long time" to wait before blooming or harvesting.

A playscape with a variety of levels, stairs, and textures attracts young climbers.
(University of New Mexico Manzanita Child Care Center)

Caring for the Environment

To learn the rules of using and caring for the outdoor environment, property, and equipment.

Rules or limits related to safe usage of equipment must be repeated numerous times before they become effective in children's actions. Memory is required, and the rules must be recalled at the right time. Use verbal guidance such as "Both hands on the jungle gym," "Drive the tricycle this way around the circle," and "Play inside the fence." These are samples of rules you may be stating to children to help them remain safe and sound on the playground. Rules stated in positive form, in short direct sentences, help the child know the behavior that you want. Because the children might not understand all the words you say—"inside," "behind," "around"—you will also lead or gesture to give them further clues about what you'd like them to do.

Rules will also be made to protect the child, the learning environment, equipment, and other children. These rules are important to protect children, to facilitate individual learning, and to preserve what you have for tomorrow and for future classes. Tricycles won't last long if they are abused by running them together. Wooden blocks will split if dropped from heights. Paint will chip off wood fences if hammered. The carpentry bench, rather than a fence or a part of the building, is the place for hammering.

Guidance, rules, and reasons for all rules can be short and factual, given in a positive tone that anticipates that the child will follow your guidance. Even young children must learn that there are limits to their behavior, so you needn't apologize for setting limits or for refusing to allow a child to do something. However, be sure to follow through on enforcement as discussed in Chapter 3.

The point is to use guidance in a fair manner with a suggestion for an acceptable alternative that fits in with the mood or need of the child. The child who wants to drop something from the top of the treehouse can make paper airplanes and fly them from there. The child who wants to paint the building can paint with water. The child who wants to climb high must do it on the jungle gym instead of on the storage shed. Children will follow a confident teacher who has an honest explanation and a helping hand and thus be moved into the right course.

Social-Emotional Objectives

To grow from an egocentric infant to a cooperative kindergartner.

When infants go outdoors, they enjoy the change of scene as much as other children. They are self-centered, playing in their own places with their own toys without much regard for others unless their familiar caregiver gets out of sight—then they may be unhappy. This is called the *solitary stage* of play, which is typical of the infant to two-year-old child.

Following solitary play, or from about two to three years of age, the children are in a *parallel play stage* where they enjoy the presence of other children. They like to be near them but still play by themselves. Interactions, when they occur, may be rather rough—perhaps one grabs a shovel or pushes another child—almost as a way of getting attention. Each likes to push a little car, paint side by side at the easel, ride a kiddie car side by side, or spoon sand into cups as they sit together in the sand pile. The kiddie car, the little wagon, and the swing are popular toys at this age. As language develops, interaction becomes more friendly.

Four-year-olds become able to express their needs and ideas through words. They plan their play—or, perhaps more accurately, they evolve a theme as they play. Their play lasts for longer periods of time than it did during earlier stages. Their group is larger. This is the *cooperative play stage.*

Cooperative play of fours and fives can become quite complex, involving plots and counterplots. Language is used extensively. Your role is to observe, help where needed, and to teach some problem-solving skills. Problem-solving skills help with settling conflicts, and they also help when one is trying to work out a problem, such as how to get a kite out of the tree, or how to move a large wooden box.

Five-year-old boys typically enjoy playing in a large group. Girls that age start having "best friends" and may exclude a child from their circle in a rude manner that can be disrupting to the social harmony in a group.

Holding nonsexist expectations may help prevent some of these divisions. Boys and girls should not be encouraged to engage in different types of play.

That is, you should not say, "Girls don't jump the high jump," but should say, "Of course, girls jump the high jump and all other types of track events." Five-year-olds may play alone, too, because they now have a sustained interest in some project—usually not because they lack social skills.

These stages should be kept in mind as you guide children's play. Adults often are anxious when a child plays alone, although playing alone may be very normal for that age.

A new child may play alone until familiarity sets in. It is wise to allow new children some time to decide when they want to join in. You can stay in the new child's vicinity to help in the get-acquainted process with the other children and to provide reassurance if needed.

Getting Along with Others

To learn and practice social skills that enable children to get along with their peers and with adults.

Social objectives are of equal importance to other objectives. Children simply must learn to get along with others. Living in harmony with other human beings may be one of the outstanding challenges for the whole human race. Infants are very self-centered or egocentric, concerned with their own interests and needs. As children mature they learn social skills. Language facility helps the social give-and-take and aids problem-solving in the social situation.

You can help with social learning by guiding children to work together. For instance, you can encourage one to ride sitting in the trailer while another child pedals the tricycle. Or, you can encourage two children to pool their blocks to make a bigger structure than either could make alone. After they accomplish this you may be able to help them evolve a theme for their block play and practice some social give and take.

Sharing

Sharing is a spontaneous act of generosity with play materials, play space, and the like. To be considered genuine sharing, the child must show generous feelings. If adults force children to divide something, it is really not sharing. You may hear people say, "You have to share." Sharing is a social skill that is fostered in outdoor play and in numerous other segments of the early childhood program. It is an attribute that parents and teachers alike wish that children would learn early. Geri shares in the following example.

Sherry joined the children at the sand pile after the sand shovels had been divided by the three children present. Sherry said nothing for a while, just watched as the three children scooped and filled their containers. Geri looked at her and said, "Oh, you don't have a shovel. You can have one of mine." Ben said, "She can't have none of mine." Mary, the third child, said nothing. Sherry played happily with the shovel Geri gave her.

Such examples of generous behavior will be noted frequently as you observe. If an adult had said, "Geri, it was nice that you shared your shovel," it would have helped the children learn the concept of sharing by labeling the behavior. Praise would indicate to the children that sharing is desirable.

Children are first self-centered or egocentric. They have to mature before they can take the perspective of another child. Or, they may simply have to feel that they have had "enough."

Ben and Mary probably had their reasons for not feeling generous. All of us have to feel we've had "enough" of something before we feel like sharing some of what we have. "Enough" is very individually defined. Empathy and sympathy are not common traits in young children.

Spontaneous generosity is the desired behavior, although dividing up may be called for at times. The often-heard phrase "You gotta share" is quite ineffective in promoting the desired behavior and accompanying feeling, because forced sharing only makes a child feel that adults are on the other child's side. Children who have difficulty sharing should be helped to have long, sustained experiences with equipment and supplies that no one forces them to relinquish, so they can finally feel that they have "enough."

Sharing need not be related to material goods. It can be verbal, like sharing a joke, a song, or a story. The following conversation was heard as two children played in the improvised housekeeping area in the play yard.

Doug: I am going to iron.
Mary: I'm the mother around this house. Doug, you're the father.
Doug: No, I'm the maid.
Mary: Oh, let's eat breakfast. (She laughed as though she had a hidden secret.) Did you see Sesame Street? It was so funny.
Doug: No. Did you see The Wizard of Oz?
Mary: (giggling and waiving her hand in a sophisticated manner) Yes, that silly ole lion.
(Both of the children laughed.)

Taking Turns

Taking turns is another type of behavior you'd like children to be born with but that unfortunately must be learned. It is seen more often in fours and fives, who have language to express their needs and can respond to verbal guidance, as the following example indicates.

The teacher brought water to the yard in a pitcher. Pam grabbed a cup and held it to the teacher, pushing in front of Diane, who was already there. "Pam, Diane was here first. First come, first served, you know," said the teacher, helping children learn a rule for taking turns the next time.

The rule in most centers is that a child has a right to a piece of equipment as long as it is being used by that child. Occasionally a very popular item requires some adult help in monitoring turntaking until the novelty wears off. For example, when a conflict arises over who is in charge of a tricycle as it sometimes does when a child gets off to attend to something else, you will first want to encourage the two to help solve the problem themselves by each offering a possible solution. Then, you may summarize, "Alright, how about letting John drive one turn around the cement circle, then get off the tricycle and watch while Mike takes his turn driving around the circle? How does that sound, John? Mike? Good for you both. We have thought about and figured out how to solve our problem."

Leadership

To practice being a leader as well as a follower.

Leadership, another social behavior, develops as the child matures and learns language to communicate ideas. Children must take turns leading and being led in the group situation. In mixed age groups the leadership almost always goes to the older children. The cooperative play of four- and five-year-olds, observed with regard to leadership—who, and how, and in what situation a child leads—is extremely interesting to note.

The concepts of sharing, taking turns, being leader, and being led can all be interlaced with rules of safety and fair play. Learning to get along with others is fostered in the free activity of the outdoor play yard.

The teacher stays nearby, offering indirect guidance and direct verbal, physical, and affective guidance as needed. The teacher's presence seems to help remind children to follow the rules that they know.

Handling Feelings

To learn to handle their feelings of joy and satisfaction, or of anger and hostility.

Happiness, smiles, satisfactions: if life could be all of these who would complain? As a teacher, you indeed work to achieve more of these pleasant feelings and try to avoid unpleasant ones. You help children express their feelings through various media. In the out of doors you sense a feeling of freedom that often does not exist indoors. Perhaps it is the chance to be alone more, or, to test oneself instead of always being part of a group, that makes the outdoor period refreshing.

Inevitably there will be moments of frustration, anger, and hostility that adults and children must learn to cope with. Encouraging children to develop problem-solving skills helps here. Say, "Let's look at this problem. What can we do?" Then wait for their suggestions. Children should not be blamed or admonished for these feelings. They should be helped so that this form of reacting to a situation does not become a habit. The teacher can simply say, "I know you feel angry, but I can't let you hit Jimmy." When a child complains that something is too hard, you can say, "It is hard, but I think you can do it."

Expressing Feelings

To allow children to express their feelings, to let off steam, to shout, to run vigorously, or to rest as desired.

Children must often experience a cooped-up feeling, for when they flock out of a schoolhouse or car into a play yard, they exhibit a happy abandon. They need to be free to shout and run. In guiding their behavior you should keep these needs in mind. The rules you state and the behavior you stop must be important. The time spent outdoors should be simpler and less confining than indoors. There are usually few reasons for limiting children's noise—compared to usual city noises, these are quiet sounds. The outdoor period should not be organized so tightly that children have no time to do what they want, or resistance will surely arise. If a child does not want to socialize, permit playing alone. If a child prefers climbing to carpentry, then allow that decision. There should, however, be quiet places outdoors. The swing can be such a place to escape. The sandbox can be a restful area. An autoharp under a tree or storybooks to look at and to read should meet the needs of children who like things less active or who become tired from vigorous activity.

Creative Objectives

To use ingenuity and creativity in devising new ways to use one's body, the equipment, and space, and in creating games and dramatic play of one's own choosing.

These objectives in a sense combine all the others. However, creativity is important to emphasize, and it occurs every moment on the playground. Teachers should be open to learning new ways that children play, for each group will surely teach you something new.

You can note the integration of all of the areas of development in the following instance of dramatic play.

The large wooden packing boxes in the yard were lined up somewhat like a train, but in the middle there was a blank space. Only two boxes were not already in the line, a very large green box and a smaller blue one. David and Mark tried to put the green box into the space. It was too heavy. David said, "Hey teacher, get these hooked up better and turn it over, upside down." The teacher went over to the boxes and David said, "Turn it upside down and put that [there]—you're doing a good job!" The teacher stopped because it wouldn't fit, and David said, "Hot dog, help me! Hook this one on—Hook it on, teacher! Get that end and put it up there." The teacher said, "Both ends of the box won't fit. Do you want to use the blue one here?" The boys were disappointed and wandered off, seeming to abandon their idea. Then Mark came back, stood the big green box on end at one outside edge of the open space and the blue box at the other side. The problem of fit had been solved creatively. David put a ladder down into the enclosure they had made, and Mark shouted, "Come see the monkey house!" Aided minimally by the teacher, the boys had

Either indoors or outdoors, a "hideout" is a popular place for four-year-olds.
(University of Missouri-Columbia Child Development Laboratory)

spent almost the entire play period making their "monkey house." On Monday when they returned they rebuilt it in less than five minutes and played inside it the entire period.

The teacher was supportive but never overdirected the boys. Their idea was their own, and they were allowed to pursue it. They used language and gross motor skills. They applied what they knew about monkey cages—ladder and all. They were accepting of each other's ideas, and they worked together in a harmonious, mature manner. The children used themselves, the space, the equipment, and time in a creative manner.

EMERGENCIES

A plan for emergencies should be made in policy-making sessions prior to the admission of children. Names of parents and their telephone numbers at home and at work should be kept at each telephone of the school and in the teacher's pocket for use on field trips. The child's doctor's name and phone number should also be on the list. Written permissions are needed on file for the school to contact emergency medical service if parents cannot be reached. The staff should know general procedures to use in case of emergency. They should also be aware of the reporting procedures required.

Emergencies can occur both indoors and outdoors. There should be few serious emergencies if there are sufficient adults for the number and ages of the children and if adults are spaced well throughout the classroom and play yard so they are indeed interacting with children as discussed in this chapter. Safety will remain a prime concern of all adults.

Adults will never leave children unattended. If someone feels an activity is dangerous, then it should be stopped until the staff can decide whether it should be permitted. Of course, children should not be smothered by adults to keep them safe, but being on the safe side is the best rule.

When you are a new teacher, you may occasionally wonder if the children should be permitted to do something. The best procedure is to take the child by the hand and say, "Let's ask Miss X if it is all right for you to do this." This way your guidance and standards fit in with ongoing rules.

If a child falls or appears hurt, a teacher's calm behavior is a first requirement. If you get hysterical, the child—and probably the whole group—will get hysterical, too. Have the child stay quiet, and do not jerk the child to standing or into your arms. Reassure the hurt child and advise helpers how they can help. Perhaps they can call the parent or doctor or both. Tell them what to say and do. The person whom the child knows best should provide comfort and reassurance until the parent arrives. Situations like this call for the utmost professional behavior of adults. You must remain calm, or you will disturb all around you.

Someone must be delegated to continue guiding the rest of the children, and they will likely need a calm explanation of what has happened and how the hurt child is feeling. A quiet time for talking about the times when they have been hurt may be called for. The incident will be meaningful, as some may have experienced such accidents before. They may be extremely fearful and need reassurance.

ADDITIONAL CONSIDERATIONS

Equipment

The amount, type, storage, and maintenance of outdoor equipment should have top priority with the planning team. If children are having an unusual number of disagreements on the playground, then the number of play spaces may not be sufficient—perhaps there are fifteen places and twenty-five children are using the yard. Or, perhaps there is the wrong kind of equipment. If the sandbox is overcrowded, perhaps the group needs two. If the swings have too many customers, perhaps the group needs more swings or needs the type where two children can work one swing together. Tricycles may need a trailer to enable two children to cooperate, and so on.

Storage

Storage of outdoor equipment must be arranged to protect the equipment from the elements and from damage from stacking. Inadequate storage for equipment can also be a factor if teachers dislike the outdoor period. Storage should be arranged so that getting equipment in and out is easy. Children should be able to help put nearly everything away. If teachers must lift items into inconvenient storage, then it is natural for them to dislike the task.

Understanding must be arrived at among staff as to who will put equipment away—many harmonious relationships can be disrupted if staff members slip away just when this hard part of the day arrives.

Maintenance

Maintenance of outdoor equipment is of utmost importance. Nothing frustrates a child more than having a tricycle or other toy that doesn't work. Wheel toys should be oiled regularly. Broken parts should be fixed. These kinds of costly items are worth maintaining well. Nonworking toys should be removed from the playground until repaired. The teacher should watch for such items and call them to the maintenance person's attention. A teacher can learn to use pliers to make minor repairs. Children like to help.

Beauty of Play Yard

The beauty of the playground should be given some attention in planning. Keeping litter off the grounds and placing equipment in an orderly arrangement will help children to learn about aesthetics and to care for their own living space.

CONCLUSION

Self-efficacy is each child's judgment of what he or she can do with whatever skills each possesses. Evidence of children's self-efficacy is demonstrated during activities on the playground.

To meet the objectives for outdoor play, teachers should give special thought to the opportunity and responsibility they have in guiding children's activity there each day. They should use all of the guidance principles discussed in Chapters 2 and 3 and apply each one in a creative way with each child. Children are individuals with differences in development, as discussed under each objective. The teacher's challenge is to determine where children are on the development ladder and to help them reach a higher rung each day.

REVIEW AND APPLICATIONS

Twelve Guides to Outdoor Play

1. Plan at least one outdoor activity period for both boys and girls every day.
2. Vary the outdoor activities and arrange to challenge and test motor skills.

3. Seek natural environments to give children an opportunity to know nature and help them to learn to protect the environment.
4. Participate actively in children's learning and in their vigorous activity as a teacher, not just as a supervisor, while remaining aware of the whole group.
5. Be sure that you, as well as the children, are dressed appropriately for enjoying and participating in the outdoors in every season.
6. Encourage independence, creativity, and socialization in children's outdoor activity.
7. Introduce games that will build children's body management, loco-motor, projection, and reception skills.
8. Motivate children by identifying the next skill in the sequence that they appear ready to learn.
9. Avoid motivating children through competition with others.
10. Encourage the tension-releasing behavior and appreciate the generous sharing behavior exhibited by children.
11. Encourage investigating, questioning, and generalizing of information observed out of doors.
12. Teach and follow rules of safety for protection of individuals and property.

 Observations

1. Observe children playing on the playground. Record a child's age, then describe what the child does and says. Looking over your notes place the child in one of the stages of play as noted in the text. Discuss.
2. Take an inventory of each child on the playground about a half hour after the children have begun playing. Where, with whom, and with what is each child playing? Discuss.
3. Using the inventory completed in No. 2, discuss the gender and age of each child related to each activity observed. State points from the text that your observation shows.
4. Observe and record the teacher helping a child learn a skill. Tell what was said and done and what the child eventually did. Discuss.
5. Observe your case-study child on the playground. What is the child's judgment of his or her motor capabilities (self-efficacy)? State your evidence for your decision. What motor skills, social skills, and language skills did the child practice?

Applications

1. Assist children playing on a playground. What are they doing? Are they playing in groups or alone? Would their play be classified as

active or quiet? How much help do they need? How are conflicts settled? Summarize your findings.

2. Note two instances of physical guidance used on an outdoor playground. Note two instances of verbal guidance used. Were these
instances effective in getting the child to do the desired thing?
Explain.

3. Count the number of play spaces available on the playground. How
many are there? Evaluate the number in terms of the number of children using the yard at any one time. Is there enough equipment?
Summarize.

4. On a 1-to-5 scale rate the center's play yard provision on the Twelve
Guides to Outdoor Play. Discuss.

ADDITIONAL RESOURCES

Suggested Videotapes

Fundamental Object Control Skills   VHS   1/2 in.   Color   60 Minutes   1994

Developmental Patterns for throwing, catching, kicking, punting and
striking skills. Vern Seefeldt and John Haubenstricker, Michigan State
University Motor Performance Study, IMC 134, East Lansing, Michigan
48824–1030, Phone: 517–355–4741.

Fundamental Locomotor Skills   VHS   1/2 in.   Color   60 minutes   1994

Developmental Patterns for running, galloping, hopping, skipping, and
jumping skills. John Haubenstricker and Vern Seefeldt, Michigan State
University, IMC 134, East Lansing, Michigan 48824–1030, Phone:
517–355–4741.

FOR FURTHER READING

Branta, Crystal F. "Motoric and Fitness Assessment of Young Children," in
Charlotte M. Hendricks (ed.). *Young Children on the Grow: Health, Activity, and Education in the Preschool Setting*. Washington, DC: ERIC Clear-
inghouse on Teacher Education, 1992, 89–107.

Castle, Kathryn. *The Infant and Toddler Handbook—Invitations for Optimum
Early Development*. Atlanta, GA: Humanics Limited, 1983.

Cratty, Bryant J. *Perceptual and Motor Development in Infants and Young
Children*. Englewood Cliffs, NJ: Prentice Hall, 1986.

Frost, Joe L. and Michael Henniger. "Making Playgrounds Safe for Children
and Children Safe for Playgrounds," *Young Children,* 34:5, July 1979,
23–30.

Frost, Joe L. and Barry L. Klein. *Children's Play and Playgrounds.* Boston: Allyn & Bacon, Inc., 1979.

Frost, Joe L. and Sue C. Wortham. "The Evolution of American Playgrounds," *Young Children,* 43:5, July 1988, 19–28.

Hildebrand, Verna. *Introduction to Early Childhood Education.* New York: Macmillan Publishing Company, 1991.

Kamii, Constance and Rheta De Vries. *Group Games in Early Education.* Washington, DC: National Association for the Education of Young Children, 1980.

Kritchevsky, Sybil and Elizabeth Prescott. *Planning Environments for Young Children.* Washington, D.C.: National Association for the Education of Young Children, 1977.

Lueck, Phyllis. "Planning an Outdoor Learning Environment." *Theory into Practice,* 12:2, April 1973, 121–127.

CHAPTER 13

Guiding Children's Art Activities

Key Concepts

◆ Creative Expression
◆ Stages of Representation
◆ Learning Center Arrangement
◆ Indirect Guidance for Art
◆ Direct Guidance During Art Activity
◆ Pre-writing and Pre-reading in Art Activity

Clair was painting at the easel. She drew lines and splashed paint in the square shape. Libby asked, "What are you painting?" Clair answered, "I don't know." Using orange and green, she painted in the squares she had outlined. The colors mixed, "Look, it's brown!" she exclaimed. Libby said, "Well, I'm going to make a rainbow with every color."

The guidance for Clair and Libby was indirect, because the easels had been set up side by side with large, clean sheets of paper, long-handled brushes, and glasses of paints. Libby and Clair were free to go to the easel during their self-selected activity period. During this one activity, these two four-year-olds were having an experience that was meeting objectives for motor coordination, intellectual development, social exchange, and creative and emotional expression.

A high-quality early childhood program includes many opportunities for children's creative or aesthetic expression and gives them opportunities to appreciate the arts, according to the accreditation criteria of the National Association for the Education of Young Children (NAEYC).[1] Skills practiced and attitudes developed during art activities carry over into other areas of learning. According to Lowenfeld, a noted art educator, "The goal of art education is to use the creative process to make people more creative regardless of

---

[1] Sue Bredekamp (ed.), *Accreditation Criteria and Procedures of the National Academy of Early Childhood Programs* (Washington, DC: NAEYC, 1991), pp. 23 and 66.

where their creativeness will be applied."[2] With new issues requiring creative solutions arising daily in all fields of endeavor, including the home, industry, agriculture, medicine, and even politics, it is imperative that children's creativity be given many avenues of expression.

OBJECTIVES

If you have been participating with young children for a period of time now you may have noted how the teachers have set up art activities in the learning centers. The *learning center* is a small area of the room or yard where an activity is set up. Generally the room has several learning centers available for children to use throughout a period of an hour or two. Some teachers call this period the *self-selected activity period* or *free play*, because the children make choices among the learning centers as the period progresses. Children generally are not rotated through activities, but are allowed to choose what activity they desire, moving freely among the learning centers. Because all activities are considered of educational worth, the teachers feel free to allow the children to choose. One activity fulfills many objectives. Consider the following objectives that guide the teacher as art activities are planned:

To Develop the Child's Creativity. The opportunity to create something original is one of the most important objectives. Children can decide independently what type of art activity they wish to do, what designs to use, how long to stay, what to do with the product (if any) when finished, and so on. The emphasis is on the *process* of creating rather than on any *product* per se. Materials are children's to control. This important objective influences your indirect guidance—how you set up the situation—and your direct guidance—your physical, verbal, and affective interaction designed to influence the child's behavior.

Creative expression, which some may call aesthetic expression, is fostered by providing children opportunities to use materials in their own personal and unique way. Both words—creative and expression—are important to children. To be *creative* means to express a thought, or execute a design, or make something entirely new, unique, or original. *Expression* means that the child is communicating through personal ideas and feelings, and through work expended on physical objects and materials.

Rooms and playyards, as well as materials, can be arranged artistically or aesthetically, which means pleasing to the eye. Children need beauty in their lives and for some children who may live in less than beautiful surroundings teachers must make extra efforts to see that the children experience beautiful things—perhaps a painting, a sculpture, a vase, or a fabric, as well as experience an aesthetically pleasing school environment. Part of this requirement is that things should be orderly and clean. You can help arrange and maintain an

[2] Viktor Lowenfeld, *Creative and Mental Growth* (New York: Macmillan Publishing Company, 1957), p. 5. See also, Elaine Pear Cohen, "Does Art Matter in the Education of the Black Ghetto Child?" *Young Children,* 29:3, March 1974, pp. 170–181.

Playdough lends itself to children's creative uses as they pound, twist, cut, and roll the colorful pieces.
(Marshall University Child Development Laboratory)

aesthetic environment and help establish a creative atmosphere in the early childhood school.

◆ **Talk It Over** ◆

In what aspects of your life do you feel really creative or original?
Name some instances when you'd like to be more creative in your behavior, yet hold back?
To what do you attribute your reserve?

To Foster Cognitive Development. Cognitive or intellectual concepts are learned during every art project. For example, in the opening anecdote, Clair and Libby were learning the names of colors—"Look, it's brown"—as well as the concept that orange and green mixed make brown. Libby was remembering that "every color" made up the rainbow. Clair and Libby are moving to an advanced stage in which they attempt to represent things they observe and to paint from memory objects seen previously.

To Practice Coordinating Eyes and Hands. Eye-hand coordination or small muscle or motor skill development is an important outcome of experiences with art materials.

Art activities offer the children many pre-writing and pre-reading experiences. The children are developing skill with writing tools—crayons, brushes, and chalk. They are training the small muscles of the hand and the eyes as they paint and draw, cut and paste, or pinch and mold their many materials. The drawing of squares and circles and differentiating between them help in later reading skills, where children must note the differences among squiggles on a page.

The teacher will label the child's products with the child's name using manuscript printing with upper- and lower-case letters. This is the first writing that the kindergarten or first grade teacher will teach, so it is less confus-

A child who is nearly three begins writing with various tools she finds available, modeling behavior observed among family members.

Ellen
age 2-11   1988

ing if manuscript printing is used on products whether the child or the teacher does the writing.

The teacher should start names in the upper left-hand corner to help the child learn that writing and reading are done from left to right. Encourage the children to start at the left, too, when they attempt to write their name. Say, "Always start your name up here," and mark lightly where you mean the top and left, for example. By starting at the left the child has the entire width of the paper for writing the name. If the children start writing near the right-hand side, they are likely to run out of space. Then they will often place their last few letters in front of the first ones, creating what may look to parents like the beginnings of "mirror writing." Parents may get worried and tell children how wrong it is, and discourage them, thus, informing parents about your reasoning becomes important. Both the teacher's writing and that of the children provide pre-writing and pre-reading experiences and contribute to emerging literacy.

To Communicate with Others Through Art Media and During the Art Activity. Most art projects are social in nature in that children share materials around a common table and take turns with various items of equipment. They frequently have delightful conversations such as the one Libby and Clair had in the anecdote that opened this chapter. Therefore, social and language development are enhanced. Psychologists find this social conversation is basic to learning.

To Provide an Opportunity for Emotional Expression. Art activities offer emotional release. Watch children pound the mud clay or playdough. See how they draw figures in their fingerpaint, then with one swoosh erase them. Observe how they laugh when they draw something that pleases them. Many very personal feelings will be expressed that only the most sensitive observer and one who knows the child well will be able to interpret.

PLANNING

Good guidance begins with planning. The art activities should be planned during the regular planning sessions, with the needs, interests, and skills of the children in mind. There should be an interesting variety of projects offered to the children. Materials are arranged in the learning center before children arrive.

Easel painting, drawing paper, and crayons are usually available daily. Materials such as staplers, masking tape, glue, and scissors are openly available to encourage children to make props for their dramatic play. For example, besides making pictures they might make tickets or paper money for a plane ride.

Other projects are rotated on a regular basis, with interesting variations added to encourage children to experiment with the materials. The teacher who wishes detailed explanations of suitable art materials and interesting variations is referred to Chapter 8 of the author's book, *Introduction to Early Childhood Education*, which is included in the reading list at the end of this chapter.

Only nonstructured materials that leave the child wide latitude for using them are appropriate for young children. That is, plain paper is superior to coloring books and the related dittoed pictures that are sometimes prepared for children to "color." The latter fail on all counts to meet objectives for creative art activities. These emphasize a product—a very stilted and unimaginative one at that. Any observer will quickly note that children fill in the spaces they draw, too, such as Clair did with the orange and green paint in the opening example. Thus Clair was learning not just to fill in spaces as provided in a coloring book but was actually making her own spaces in a planned way as well.

Materials must be prepared for the activities of the day. These may be prepared in the afternoon for the following day's classes in order to have them ready when the children arrive in the morning. Good guidance of art projects begins by having materials neatly organized in the learning centers when children begin arriving.

In organizing the center you must think through the entire project to foresee possible problems. Do the children need aprons? Do they need a place to wash after the project? Do you need a sponge at the art table? Do you need a place to dry the products? Will newspapers on the tables make clean-up easier? How many children can one adult comfortably interact with? This planning and organizing are now familiar to you as indirect guidance.

Group Size

A group of four or five three- to five-year-olds is the largest that one adult should try to interact with at a time during creative arts and crafts projects. In this size group or smaller, the adult can help the children as needed. In small groups the intimate conversation and answering of questions that are so important to the child's satisfaction and learning can take place. A small table with only five chairs (or fewer) helps children know that only five can do the project and that if the chairs are filled they can have their turn later. Or, they can just watch another child until a space opens up. When there is big demand for the activity, it can be repeated on ensuing days until all children are satisfied. If the teacher must be responsible for more than five children, a second table with an activity that is more self-directed should be planned. This will leave the teacher freer to attend to the more complex project—say fingerpainting—at the first table.

Stages of Representation

The stages of artistic representation are an important factor in the teacher's planning. It is desirable to have activities planned that fit the stage of art representation of the children. Activities should be neither too easy nor too hard. There will be a range of abilities within any group. Therefore, the teacher will plan activities that can be used in many ways and developed to the level of difficulty that the child is able to achieve. The following stage descriptions should

Easel painting on large sheets of paper is a favorite among young children.
(University of Idaho Child Development Laboratory)

become very familiar to you and guide your planning and interaction with children.

The toddlers who first enter a group will use a crayon to make random, uncontrolled marks in what Lowenfeld and Brittain[3] call the *scribble stage.* Later, children enter the *named scribble* stage. They may say it's a "dog." Even five-year-olds might be in the scribble stage if they have had only a few art experiences.

At about three years of age, the child makes scribbles go in whatever direction desired, such as diagonally or in a circle. These are *controlled scribbles.*

---

[3] Viktor Lowenfeld and W. Lambert Brittain, *Creative and Mental Growth,* 7th ed. (New York: Macmillan Publishing Company, 1982), Chapters 4 and 5. And see W. Lambert Brittain, *Creativity, Art, and the Young Child* (New York: Macmillan Publishing Company, 1979), Chapter 2.

The *preschematic stage* occurs between four and seven years when children make their first representation of observed objects. Usually they make a head first by joining up circular scribbles. They try putting in the eyes, nose, and mouth. Don't be surprised if these are not where you would put them. They also make rectangles and fill them in. The next stage observed in five-year-olds is the *schematic stage* where the children focus on drawing the human figure—usually themselves or someone in their family.

Teachers can make use of these stages by not expecting too much of the young children they teach and by helping parents understand that their children are "normal" when they only make scribbles on paintings and drawings. The same stages also are useful when looking at clay products.

Pre-writing and Pre-reading

Pre-writing and pre-reading naturally become part of the drawing and painting experiences of young children. First, they are practicing using a writing tool when they use a crayon, marker, or paintbrush. They eventually outgrow the fist grasp typical of infants and begin to use the pincer grasp typical of

Making prints using various forms offers children an opportunity to experiment with form and color.
(Metropolitan State College Child Development Laboratory)

Miranda, a kindergartner, draws "the whole class." The "grass" at the bottom is character-
istic of kindergartners who usually begin including such a base on their drawings.
(Source: Savannah Public Schools)

adults. Physical maturity and opportunity to practice work together to help children learn the motor skills for holding and using a writing tool.

Second, with practice, the tool becomes more controlled—going where the child wants it to go in what is often called *controlled scribbling*. Later the child will scribble and call the drawing something like "my house."

Third, representation follows scribbling, as the child makes a circle or a rectangle. Symbolic representation, or making pictures, is a form of language expression. The child may draw a circle and label it "a boy," or a rectangle and label it "a house." By combining forms the child is able to represent many ideas. With lots of time to explore materials, the child's thoughts will flow from his or her mind to the paper, representing the child's thinking.

The child, let's call him Mark, will request that his name be placed on his picture. Of course, the teacher wants to label the pictures anyway in order to sort them out to send home. The name should be hand printed carefully in upper- and lowercase letters starting in the left-hand corner of the paper. Consistently starting at the left helps children learn the appropriate left to right progression necessary for reading and writing skills. It also gives children with long names room to write them. According to studies, about half the children start writing from the right-hand side of the paper; thus, adults have to guide them toward shifting to the left side. Routinely writing in the same style letters helps the child learn to read his or her name quickly. You'll see evidence of children's reading when they sort out name tags or drawings with names carefully printed on them.

Later on you can encourage the child to write the first letter of his or her name until gradually the whole name is accomplished. The child can sound the letters as they are written, thereby gaining some phonics practice and a start toward writing and reading.[4]

The teacher can volunteer to write a sentence describing what the child says a drawing is about, such as, "This is me ice skating," or "This is my sister." (Even when it is a scribble.) This sentence provides an early reading experience. A little later the child may want to label parts of a picture he or she is drawing, such as printing *Daddy* under the daddy figure. The child may ask how to write Daddy, or, the child may try to write the word phonetically, such as *Dadi*. Avoid the temptation to correct the child's spelling. These invented spellings are exciting developments in a child's growing literacy. They usually occur in the late fourth and fifth year as the child approaches kindergarten age. Kindergarten and early elementary teachers are encouraging children to write using invented spelling. They find that children thus encouraged become fluent writers earlier than if they are held to spelling correctly at first.[5]

Such activities are part of the young child's emerging literacy that occurs during these early childhood years. In a study of three-, four-, and five-year-olds in early childhood programs, it was learned that many of the late fours and fives could already write all or part of their name. Some could write a number of the ABCs. It was clear that these children were learning literacy skills well before they entered kindergarten.[6]

TEACHER'S GUIDANCE

As the teacher you will stress to children that they can decide what art projects to do and how to do them. It is the child's ideas that are important, not your

[4] Sally Hruska, "Namewriting: A Step Toward Reading and Writing," *Day Care and Early Education,* 12:2, Winter 1984, pp. 36–38.

[5] Moira Juliebö and Joyce Edwards, "Encouraging Meaning Making in Young Writers," *Young Children,* 44:2, January 1989, pp. 22–27. For more on this view of early writing, see Donald Graves and Virginia Stuart, *Write from the Start: Tapping Your Child's Natural Writing Abilities,* New York: E.P. Dutton, 1985.

[6] Lois Bader and Verna Hildebrand, "An Exploratory Study of Three to Five Year Olds' Responses on the Bader Reading and Language Inventory to Determine Developmental Stages of Emerging Literacy," *Early Child Development and Care,* Vol. 77, August 1992, pp. 83–95.

preconceived notion. "Let me see what colors you like" or "You can decide. Do you like long strips or shiny pieces?" you might ask. Each child will use materials differently and come up with different products.

Children may wait for you to give them ideas. Adults without a creative orientation usually tell children what to make or draw. However, you can be different. Do not shower children with your ideas, but respond as a professional by encouraging them to explore the materials and see what they come up with. Praise their effort by saying, "You worked hard to choose which materials to use, didn't you?" or "You did a good job in deciding on your colors." Encourage children to discuss among themselves various ideas for painting, drawing, or sculpting.

 Talk It Over

How would you feel if you were painting and another adult said, "Be sure to fill up the page," or "You messed up your colors," or "Who ever saw a purple house?" Would you be proud of your picture, feel good about your effort, or even want to paint again?

Make No Models

Because the creative process within the child is what is important, you won't care how the product (painting, drawing, or clay object) looks. You will not make a model for the child to copy, because it is the child's own ideas you want to bring out.

Even if a child begs you to "draw something for me," be steadfast in encouraging the child to experiment. Say for example, "What happens if you pound your clay or roll it?" Or, "Show me what happens if you roll it out fast with one hand or curl it around." After the child experiments for a time, say, "See, you can find lots of things you can do." If you keep your focus on the goals for the child, you'll realize why this approach is more helpful than one in which the adult ends up entertaining the children by drawing funny faces for the period. Once you have experience with large numbers of children and see how creative and confident in their own abilities and ideas they become, you'll become convinced that avoiding models and patterns is the best approach. This tack may be very different than the one the child experiences at home and will, therefore, take time for the child, and perhaps the parents, to learn to accept.

Actually, adults who are tempted to make models for the children should work with the materials in a staff meeting and take turns telling other adults how to make their product. You will quickly understand why making models hurts motivation and hinders creative expression.

Downplay Products

Avoid praising the children's products—to be consistent with the principle that the process is the important aspect of the art activity. Some teachers "ooh!" and "ah!" over finished products, leading the children to believe that's what's important, even though they say, "You do it your way." Praise such as "You did a good job" should be given to an individual child in a quiet, personal way so the other children won't look at the product of the complimented child and try to imitate it.

Listen to what children say as they create. They often tell what they are making. Avoid asking them "What's this?" Since they are free just to experiment with materials, this question places too much emphasis on a recognizable product. Also, they frequently don't name their products until they are finished.

Allow Messes

Many activities suitable for young children are messy. In fact, that is one reason they are planned for the children. Children today are kept so clean that many don't know the joy of working with messy material such as mud, clay, and fingerpaint. Try to be accepting of these materials and learn to enjoy them as children do. Cover the tables with newspaper to make clean-up easy. Cover the children with wide aprons to make them easily cleaned up. Then watch them enjoy some of these messy activities. You'll see how much emotional release they receive. Watch them become relaxed. Listen to their conversation. If some children seem very concerned about getting messy, don't press them. You can sit with the children and manipulate the material in the same way they might just to show that you like it and don't mind getting your hands messy. You need not talk much about what you're doing; just relax and learn from the children.

Give Plenty of Time

Give children plenty of time to do a project. The process of creating often takes lots of time and thought and sometimes some rearranging. Try to plan enough play activities in the room so that children will have other things to do while they wait for a place at the art table or easel. This way the children who are there painting can savor the experience, really learn from it, and take all the time needed.

Clean, Dry, Display

Allow children to help with the art clean-up. They learn from cleaning up and they enjoy it. Washing paint brushes or sponging the easels will be a special privilege if you set it up right. Many like to be known as "helpers." In some groups clean-up jobs are rotated each week, and children go to their assigned

Blocks of various materials and sizes encourage creativity in a three-dimensional medium. Children learn to match sizes, figure equivalents, and develop balance.
(Baylor University Child Development Laboratory)

area and clean up regardless of whether they have used the material. Willy, a four-year-old, was one who really enjoyed the task of washing the paint brushes. For several days when he came home from school his hands held the evidence of his clean-up responsibility. On Friday his mother told him, "You have a dental appointment after school. Could you maybe let someone else wash the brushes so you'll be clean enough to go see the dentist?" "Mother," said Willy, "It's my job. I've got to do a good job of washing the brushes."

A suitable place for drying must be planned. Some projects may need to be kept overnight. Fingerpaints, for example, may require a great deal of drying time if children are allowed to use as much paint as *they* desire. Because children and teachers are primarily interested in the process, the use of a plastic tablecloth with fingerpainting done directly on the plastic may be desirable at times. Or serving trays can be used to paint on; then the paint can be washed off in the sink when the painting is finished. Children usually care very little about a painting when it is held over to another day to dry. They may even forget which one is theirs.

Children's art products can add nice color and design to the child development center. The displays can be artistically arranged with colorful mats behind drawings and paintings. They are more interesting to children if changed frequently. Every child's work must be displayed from time to time. The teacher customarily asks children if their product can be displayed, for

Drawing tools offer an opportunity for children to experiment with writing as literacy emerges. (V. Hildebrand, photographer)

some feel strongly about taking the product home. They may be competing with an older sibling who brings home seatwork for parents to see, and therefore want to have something to show too.

HELP PARENTS APPRECIATE ART

The guidance of parents and their reactions to the child's art is important. They often need help in understanding their child's level of representation. Some overemphasize a product until a child may dab a glob of paint on a paper just to have something to take home. A child who uses the blocks creatively may need some help in explaining to parents why there is no art product to bring home. Siblings, too, can create problems. They may criticize a younger child's painting or press the child into competition with them. Parents may need help from teachers in alleviating this problem.

CONCLUSION

Art activities are an important part of the early childhood program, providing many opportunities for appropriate teacher guidance. From adequate indirect guidance through planning and placement of the materials, to direct, verbal, physical, and affective guidance as the children use the materials, the teacher has many opportunities to help children fulfill objectives for growth and development that can be achieved through use of art materials. An understanding of the stages of artistic expression helps the teacher plan appropriate guidance for each child. By listening to each child personally during art activities, you will learn much about that child's inner thoughts and feelings.

REVIEW AND APPLICATIONS

Ten Guides to Art Activities

1. Place emphasis on the *process,* not the product, when presenting or commenting on children's art experiences.
2. Encourage the unique creative expression of each child by avoiding models for children to copy or coloring-book type drawings, both of which interfere with creativity.
3. Appreciate the various stages through which children progress in their ability to represent "reality."
4. Plan and prepare activities in detail ahead of time to leave time to appreciate the individual responses of each child using a material.
5. Provide nonstructured materials to which the children can add their personal touch.
6. Avoid asking children "What are you making?" or guessing what they have made. Listen, because they'll tell you.
7. Use physical, verbal, and affective guidance as appropriate for the age and stage of the child.
8. Think of art activities as pre-writing and pre-reading experiences.
9. Teach intellectual concepts, like colors, sizes, and shapes, through art activities.
10. Interpret to parents the goals and procedures of creative art education for children.

 Observations

1. Observe three children using art materials. Carefully write down details of what each does and says. Classify each child's work into stages of representations discussed in your text. Discuss your conclusions.
2. Observe and make notes on a child using paints or crayons. Analyze your notes for information the child has on color. Discuss.
3. Analyze your notes for question No. 1 for language expression of children while they are involved with art materials. Discuss.
4. Analyze your notes for children's expression of creativity. Write your conclusions.

5. Summarize your observations of your case-study child using art materials. Collect a sample of the child's work from time to time over the period of your observation. (Be sure to ask the child for permission to keep a drawing.) Date the product and give the child's age.

Applications

1. Make notes in an early childhood center of a teacher guiding a child in an art activity. Role play the scene in your lecture class. Analyze the effective and ineffective techniques used.
2. Assist a child using art materials at home or at school. Give an example of your verbal guidance. Was the guidance understood? Did it help the child? Did it interfere with the child's work? Explain.
3. Assist a child using art materials at home or at school. Give an example of your physical guidance. Was the guidance helpful? Explain.
4. Talk to a teacher or a parent about children's art projects. What types of projects do they provide? What objectives do they appear to be working toward? Explain.
5. Using the Ten Guides to Art Activities, rate on a 1-to-5 scale the center's art activities and guidance. Discuss.

ADDITIONAL RESOURCES

Suggested Videotape

Thinking and Creativity   VHS 1/2 in.   Color   30 minutes   1988

Thelma Harms and Debby Cryer explore the differences between adults' and children's thinking and describe the function of creative experiences as a unique way of learning through discovery. Explores the concept of giftedness. Delmar Publishers, Customer Service, 2 Computer Drive West, Albany, NY 12212, 1–800–347–7707.

FOR FURTHER READING

Brittain, W. Lambert. *Creativity, Art, and the Young Child*. New York: Macmillan Publishing Company, 1979.

Dyson, Anne Haas. "Appreciate the Drawing and Dictating of Young Children," *Young Children,* 43:3, March 1988, 25–32.

Goodnow, Jacqueline. *Children's Drawing*. Cambridge, MA: Harvard University Press, 1977.

Kellogg, Rhoda. *Analyzing Children's Art*. Palo Alto, CA: National Press, 1969.

LeeKeenan, Debbie and Carolyn P. Edwards. "Using the Project Approach with Toddlers," *Young Children,* 47:4, May 1992, 31–35.

Lowenfeld, Viktor and W. Lambert Brittain. *Creative and Mental Growth.* New York: Macmillan Publishing Company, 1982.

Schirrmacher, Robert. "Talking with Young Children About Their Art," *Young Children,* 41:5, July 1986, 3–7.

Tegano, Deborah, James D. Moran, III, and Janet K. Sawyers. *Creativity in Early Childhood Classrooms.* Washington, DC: National Education Association, 1991.

Thompson, C. "I Make a Mark: The Significance of Talk in Young Children's Artistic Development," *Early Childhood Research Quarterly,* 5:2, 1990, 215–232.

CHAPTER 14

Guiding Children's Science Activities

Key Concepts

◆ Goals for Cognitive Development
◆ Stages of Cognitive Development
◆ Appropriate Guidance

Kevin was sawing a piece of wood with much vigor. He pulled out the saw and touched it. He drew back his finger and exclaimed, "Ouch!" He asked the teacher, "Why is it so hot?" The teacher explained, "You rubbed the saw and wood together when you were sawing so fast. You made a lot of friction. That made the saw hot."

Learning about friction may not be a scientific concept that is high on early childhood priority lists, but Kevin discovered it that morning at the carpentry bench. He perceived a stimulus through his sense of touch. He reacted, asked a question, and received a knowledgeable answer from his teacher. This is the most effective order for young children's scientific education to follow. Play is young children's work. Children will learn many things in the context of playing with other children as together they use appropriately selected materials and equipment. The playyard and playroom are children's scientific laboratory. These environments are set up to invite children to explore spontaneously the equipment and learning materials they find in each learning center. When each learning center is related to the needs and interests of the children using the room one observes children busily going about their exploration.

Helping children learn to think, reason, question, and experiment is a broad and inclusive goal stated as part of the curriculum requirements for high-quality early childhood programs, as defined by the National Association for the Education of Young Children (NAEYC).[1] Of course, this is part of cognitive learning that develops significantly during the early years.

---

[1] Sue Bredekamp (ed.), *Accreditation Criteria and Procedures of the National Academy of Early Childhood Programs* (Washington, DC: NAEYC, 1991), pp. 20–25.

Parents as well as teachers are thrilled to see children develop cognitive skills. There is a tendency for some adults to become overly anxious about this development and push children into activities before they are developmentally ready. We see this often when four-year-olds are pressed to learn what six- and seven-year-olds once were expected to learn. To define these thresholds of readiness, NAEYC has published a helpful booklet called *Developmentally Appropriate Practice in Early Childhood Programs Serving Children from Birth Through Age 8.*[2] In this booklet you are given examples of both appropriate and inappropriate practice.

Your study and work with young children in this course will help you understand the importance of a rich environment if children are going to develop cognitively while exploring it. You can utilize your developing skills for indirect and direct guidance to foster children's thinking, reasoning, questioning, and experimenting.

COGNITIVE DEVELOPMENT

Developing an understanding of the world around you is a lifetime process that begins at birth. Knowing about the regularity and predictability of the universe is important information to have. This knowledge is learned through mental processes and sensory perceptions. It is called cognitive development, which means the development of knowledge. The ability to use all five of the sensory modes—seeing, hearing, touching, tasting, and smelling—is required for maximum development of the mental or cognitive processes.

High-quality child development centers have always placed priority on children's intellectual learning. Today the emphasis is greater than ever because new research is being reported that helps teachers better understand the mental or cognitive processes that are at work in the child.

Jean Piaget,[3] the Swiss psychologist, is probably the most noted of the researchers who have investigated children's learning. He explained that infants are in the *sensorimotor stage* of intellectual development. They make sense out of the world by interacting through reflexes and perceptual-motor activities. They are learning through tasting, grasping, and manipulating the objects with which they come in contact.

Object Permanence

During the first eighteen months babies come to realize that objects exist even when they are not able to see or hear (perceive) them. You know, for example, that your bedroom door exists even if you cannot see it. You would have confi-

[2] Sue Bredekamp (ed.), *Developmentally Appropriate Practice in Early Childhood Programs Serving Children from Birth Through Age 8* (Washington, DC: NAEYC, 1987).

[3] John L. Phillips, Jr., *The Origins of Intellect: Piaget's Theory* (San Francisco: W. H. Freeman, 1969), pp. 15–66.

A "great big" steam engine is a favorite stop on a visit to the park. Toddlers are learning many things.
(C. Hildebrand, photographer)

dence the door is there if you needed to get out of your bedroom in the dark. Or you know that your brother away at college exists even though you cannot see him. Piaget has labeled this concept *object permanence* and has indicated that it is a concept that babies learn little by little in their early months.

Achieving a sense of object permanence is basic to infants developing a sense of trust. In Chapter 17 you'll learn how infants may react with relief— sometimes crying—as they see their mothers return to the infant center to pick them up. Such infants are developing a sense of object permanence, in this case realizing that their mothers exist even when they have not been able to see them. Along with this learning infants develop what psychologist Erik Erikson called a *sense of trust*—a belief in people around them and a good feeling about themselves and the regularity and order of the world.[4]

Understanding Piaget's sensorimotor stage and its related concept of object permanence and Erikson's concept of sense of trust is important for you as a parent or caregiver. The concepts include intellectual, emotional, and social learning. You will endeavor to give consistently warm physical care as you are feeding, bathing, changing, and rocking the baby. You will give love and very personalized attention and conversation as well. Games, such as hid-

---

[4] Lawrence B. Schiamberg, *Child and Adolescent Development* (New York: Macmillan Publishing Company, 1988), pp. 239–245 and 371–380.

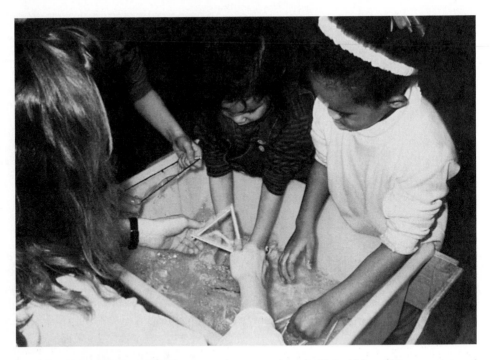

Children use colored water and soap suds to experiment with bubble-making.
(University of Illinois Child Development Laboratory)

ing and helping baby find a favorite toy or milk bottle under a towel, or playing peek-a-boo through the crib or playpen slats, help the infant realize that objects that disappear return again. Fun and good feelings are the result.

From age two toddlers and young children are in what Piaget called the *Preoperational stage,* which lasts until about the seventh year. The two- to seven-year-olds focus on one variable at a time. They are confused, for example, if you try to teach them brown and round, but they can concentrate on color and shape as separate variables.

One of the important things that can be learned from Piaget is that children learn as they interact with forces and things in their environment. Learning cannot be imposed from the outside. The children must interact with their world. Learning follows a definite sequence that cannot be hurried by any adult.

During the preoperational stage you will notice that children are what Piaget called "centered" on one aspect of a problem, disregarding other aspects. For example, they can sort beads or cards according to color, but if asked to then sort the same beads or cards according to shape the two- to five-year-old will have trouble "decentering" from color and refocusing on shape. Children's thinking has a certain rigidity that you will observe as you work with them. You may note this characteristic if a child forgets to bring some item to school that he or she had intended bringing. It becomes quite difficult

In a center connected to a hospital, the dramatic play turns to
medical roles.
(Methodist Hospital Child Care Center, Lubbock, Texas)

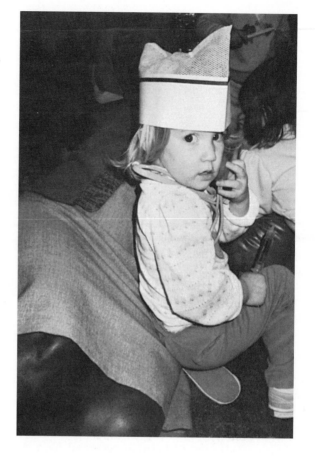

They formed a fast friendship that lasted into their elementary years, until one
of them moved away.

Children should be free to move from one area of the room to another
and to combine toys from one area with those of another. For example, they
sometimes move the housekeeping equipment to furnish a house that they
have built in the block corner. They can move the doll bed to the hospital they
have constructed. They freely use paper supplies to supplement their dramatic
play by making items such as tickets, labels, signs, and airplanes.

 Talk It Over

What themes have you seen children develop during their dramatic play?

What do you think they were learning?

How would you explain children's learning through dramatic play to their
parents?

Playing "beauty shop" is a
perennial favorite.
(Metropolitan College Child Development Center)

DIRECT GUIDANCE FOR DRAMATIC PLAY

Spontaneity is the most important characteristic of dramatic play. The teacher's guidance is primarily directed toward maintaining harmony among the children, interpreting feelings, and adding props that appear to be needed to expand the play.

When children have immature social skills, they sometimes need to learn how to become accepted by a group. They may keep asking, "Can I play?" which nearly always guarantees a "No." Jennifer was a three-year-old who needed this type of help. She was having difficulty being accepted in the house-keeping area. On observing Jennifer approaching the group again, the teacher said quietly, "Jennifer, let's knock here on the door and see if anyone is at home." The teacher stood by Jennifer as the "mother" arrived to answer the door. "Mrs. Susan, we have come for a visit," the teacher said. The children admitted them, and the teacher helped interest the children in the suitcase that Jennifer was carrying. Then the teacher quietly slipped out of the scene. Another day Jennifer was observed knocking before she entered.

By bringing in a new piece of equipment, the teacher can help extend the play to a child who is being rejected by a group. For example, Ron and Brad were building a space ship out of the wooden blocks. Dean was also building a space ship from the same supply of blocks. Dean made several overtures to Ron and Brad, hoping to be included in their play, but they were in a "You can't play with us" mood. The teacher, sensing how much Dean wanted to be included, said, "Dean, would you like to help me get something from the store-room?" Dean was curious and followed. They returned with a steering wheel, which Dean placed in his space ship. Rod and Brad were now a little envious.

Brad said, "Dean, could we hook our space ship on to yours?" Dean, now in the driver's seat, said "Okay," and the three boys played for the remainder of the hour.

Children can learn and practice some problem-solving skills. If something doesn't work they can seek the source of the difficulty. If they are short of a prop they can decide what might substitute for it. Problems of sharing and taking turns are settled.

The teacher helps children who are grabbing or hitting to use words to get what they want. She says, "Tell John that you would like to use the truck," or "Ask Mary to move instead of hitting her. She doesn't know you were using the telephone."

The teacher may protect one group from intrusion by others. Two bigger boys were involved in a cooking project. Meanwhile, other children had set up the blocks, making a railroad for their train. The bigger boys, finished with their cooking, started to enter the block area with the intention of taking over—it being their usual domain. The teacher, foreseeing trouble, approached the two bigger boys, saying, "You fellows might play in the housekeeping area, or you could paint, but right now these children are using the blocks." After a moment of discussion, the boys selected painting and left the scene.

The teachers may sometimes see children who spank the dolls and shout at others during the "dinner." Realizing that the children are playing a role that may have deep meaning for them personally, the teacher allows them to express these strong feelings unless they harm another child. On the strength of only one observation, however, the teacher should not conclude that children are spanked at home.

The teacher may help children control their anger to avoid hurting others. Jay and Delbert were building roads in the sandbox. They stood a four-foot

Blocks are used to develop a background for dramatic play. (Baylor University Child Development Center)

cardboard tube in a large juice can and filled it with water at the hydrant. With one boy at each end they carried it precariously back to the sandbox. Jay's end slipped, and down fell the tube, spilling water on his pants. He grabbed sand toys and started to throw them at Delbert, blaming him for the accident. The teacher stepped in quickly, putting her hands on Jay's shoulders, saying, "Jay, it was your end that slipped. Your pants will dry, why don't you go ahead with your road?" Her calm manner and the fact that Delbert was already working in the sand helped Jay return to his digging.

Guiding dramatic play calls for unobtrusive observation until the moment assistance is called for. Through observation, the teacher can receive many clues that help in understanding the inner thoughts and feelings of children. Insights are gained into children's level of concepts and their misconceptions. For instance, when Jim was building a space station, the teacher asked him if he knew how big a space ship was. Jim said, "No." The teacher said, "It is taller than the tallest buildings downtown." Jim said, "Oh, I bet they are bigger than God."

Language develops well in the relaxed setting of dramatic play. Children practice words they know, learn new words, and combine words creatively as they play cooperatively. By listening to conversation during dramatic play, the teacher may get ideas of things children are interested in that would make worthwhile field trips or class experiences for the future. The teacher also learns something of the life situation for the children at home with parents and siblings; from this may come clues as to how the children could be helped.

In their spontaneous dramatic play, children often welcome one more child to their small space.
(University of Illinois Child Development Laboratory)

If children dominate at school, they may be gaining strength to cope with their home situation, where they are dominated. Releasing negative feelings during dramatic play may help children. They should not be told they are "naughty" when they express strong feelings. Rather, you can reflect the feeling, "You get angry when . . . ," and see how they respond.

 Talk It Over

What are some problems and pleasures you experience when you are responsible for children during their dramatic play?

VARIETIES OF DRAMATIC PLAY

The variety of dramatic play can range from A to Z—from the art table, where children pat out "biscuits" and "rockets," to the sandbox where "pies and cakes" are made alongside "tunnels and rivers," to the carpentry bench where two slender sticks become "airplanes," or in the play yard among the packing boxes which at times are a "zoo" with "wild animals" scurrying among the boxes and climbing on the play equipment. Opportunities abound for imaginative dramatic play. Children generally will suggest their own themes based on experiences they are having at home or in the community at the time. The teacher can provide props for some of the following types of play in one or several of these locations. In Chapter 14 of the author's book, *Introduction to Early Childhood Education,* the following suggestions are described in more detail: housekeeping, shoe store, grocery store, pet store, office, school, post office, farming, flower shop, gardening, hospital, restaurant, church, beauty and barber shop, fire house, gas station, car wash, camping, fishing, cowboys, road-building, airplane, boat, train, and outer space.

CONCLUSION

Teachers have many opportunities to contribute to children's total development as they plan and guide dramatic play, the spontaneous role playing so popular with children in the child development center. Teachers set the stage through indirect guidance, having everything set up invitingly as the children arrive. Teachers help where needed, using direct guidance, and value the time for observing the child-child interaction taking place. They get to know children better through studying this interaction.

REVIEW AND APPLICATIONS

Ten Guides to Dramatic Play

1. Provide props and dress-up clothing to stimulate spontaneous role playing of familiar persons.
2. Introduce children to new workers' roles and ideas that might suggest roles for dramatic play.
3. Provide a full-length mirror to enable children to see how they look in their dress-up clothing.
4. Allow sufficient time in the schedule for children to develop dramatic play roles and themes.
5. Guide children unobtrusively, allowing them to solve social problems as much as possible.
6. Suggest a relevant supporting role for a child who is having difficulty entering a dramatic play situation.
7. Listen to conversations to learn what children's interests, feelings, experiences, and concerns are.
8. Set up areas and provide equipment on the playground for dramatic play.
9. Encourage language development by supplying labels for equipment, roles, and ideas children are dramatizing.
10. Allow children to make props and to use them for dramatic play.

  ## Observations

1. Observe two or three children playing in a dramatic play area such as the housekeeping corner or the block corner. Record what children do and say.
2. Analyze your notes from question No. 1. Categorize the stages of play the children are engaged in. State your evidence for your decisions. Discuss.
3. Analyze your notes from question No. 1. List the sentences spoken by the children. What was the average sentence length? What percent had adjectives? Adverbs? How many questions asked by one child were directly answered by another? Discuss your conclusion regarding dramatic play and language.
4. Observe your case-study child in dramatic play. Note with whom the child played, what the themes were, how roles were decided upon, and how much language played a part.

Applications

1. Assist children at home or in a school as they carry out spontaneous dramatic play. What roles are they playing? How authentic are the roles? Where do you think they learned the roles? Were children playing roles similar to or different from their usual roles? Explain.
2. Assist in the dramatic play area of your center. Note what guidance opportunities arise. What guidance did you use? Give details of two situations. Did you achieve your objective? Explain.
3. Recall your own childhood. What imaginative roles did you play? What props did you use? Do you think the play served a purpose for you? Explain.
4. On a 1-to-5 scale rate your center on the Ten Guides to Dramatic Play. Discuss.

ADDITIONAL RESOURCES

Suggested Videotapes

Curriculum for Preschool and Kindergarten   VHS   1/2 in.   Color   16 minutes   1988

Dr. Lillian Katz discusses appropriate curriculum for four- and five-year-olds. NAEYC, Media, 1509 16th Street, N.W., Washington, DC 20036-1426.

Culture and Education of Young Children   VHS   1/2 in.   Color   16 minutes   1988

A discussion with Carol Phillips on how programs can show respect for our cultural diversity and use this richness to enhance children's learning. NAEYC, Media, 1509 16th Street, N.W., Washington, DC 20036-1426.

FOR FURTHER READING

Christie, James F. and Francis Wardle. "How Much Time Is Needed for Play?" *Young Children,* 47:3, March 1992, 28–32.

Hildebrand, Verna. *Introduction to Early Childhood Education.* New York: Macmillan Publishing Company, 1991.

Kostelnik, Marjorie (ed.). *Teaching Young Children Using Themes.* Chicago: Scott Foresman Publishing Co., 1991.

Kostelnik, Marjorie, Alice Whiren, and Laura Stein. "Living with He-Man: Managing Superhero Fantasy Play," *Young Children,* 41:4, May 1986, 3–9.

Trawick-Smith, Jeffrey. "Play Leadership and Following Behavior of Young Children," *Young Children,* 43:5, July 1988, 51–59.

CHAPTER 16

Guiding Children's Literature, Language and Music Activities

Key Concepts

◆ Values of Literature, Language, and Music Activities
◆ Guidance for Literature, Language, and Music Activities

Deanna and Peggy were looking at one book. Steve and Mark were looking at another book next to Deanna. Steve laughed and pointed, "Look at the monkeys!" The others looked and laughed with him.

Books are for reading. Books are for sharing. Books are for enjoying. Books are for communicating ideas. The children's teacher had these objectives in mind when arranging books for informal "reading" by the children before the official storytime began.

Literature experiences in the child development center offer the children important pre-reading experiences. When a child is given time to enjoy and savor good literature early in life, the problem of being a nonreader rarely occurs.

Many pre-writing and pre-reading activities are part of the young child's emerging literacy that occurs during the early childhood years. In a study of three-, four-, and five-year-olds in early childhood programs, it was discovered that even some of the youngest had well-developed print recognition skills. They knew the front from the back of the book, knew when the book was upright, and could point to a word. When queried, the parents whose children showed the most literacy skills indicated that they read to their children, used ABC blocks and books, and checked out books from the library. To find children in early childhood centers without any literacy skills the researchers concluded that the sample would have had to include children younger than three.[1]

---

[1] Lois Bader and Verna Hildebrand. "An Exploratory Study of Three to Five Year Old's Responses on the Bader Reading and Language Inventory to Determine Developmental Stages of Emerging Literacy," *Early Child Development and Care*, Vol. 77, August 1992, pp. 83–95.

VALUES OF LITERATURE, LANGUAGE, AND MUSIC ACTIVITIES

The cultural aspects of any nation's life are expressed through literature, language, and music. Thus, it is not surprising to find that all high-quality early childhood schools and centers reserve time for emphasizing these activities. As you think about it, you'll agree that language is at the heart of literature and music activities. The encouragement of language development is one of the major goals of the accreditation process of the National Association for the Education of Young Children (NAEYC).[2] Of course, oral and aural language (speaking and understanding others speaking) are the basis for later learning to write and read printed language.

Literature, language, and music activities all give children opportunities to increase their vocabularies and to practice their verbal expressions. They learn *receptive discipline*, an ability to listen to others' communications. Receptive discipline has been discussed by Dr. David Elkind as an important ingredient of learning to read. In early childhood story- and singing-time groups children learn to pay attention to a leader and share attention with a number of other children. Children are not born with these abilities, of course. Children's receptive discipline must be developed over time. For a small child, it is a giant leap from having parents read while seated on their comfortable lap to sitting with other children while a book is held several feet away. It is of particular importance that those planning and carrying out these experiences take the ages and experiences of the children into consideration. You, as a student helper, can be particularly helpful in these experiences, either by assisting the teacher or by reading to a child alone.

"Developmentally appropriate" is a concept related to every part of the early childhood school, including literature, language, and music. NAEYC's publication *Developmentally Appropriate Practice in Early Childhood Programs Serving Children from Birth Through Age 8* offers guidelines similar to those you will find in this chapter.[3] All high-quality programs plan these experiences for small groups of children, rather than whole-group activities that tend to obscure the needs, spontaneity, and interests of individual children. The younger the children the smaller and more intimate the group needs to be. Language development is, after all, an individual accomplishment and language itself must be uttered and responded to on an individual basis.

While literature, language, and music may hold center stage only a brief time during a short-day program, they are typically introduced numerous times during full-day child care programs, for example, in the morning, during quiet time just before lunch, after naptime, and while waiting for parents at the end of the day. In addition, the self-selected activity period allows individ-

---

[2] Sue Bredekamp (ed.). *Accreditation Criteria and Procedures of the National Academy of Early Childhood Programs* (Washington, DC: NAEYC, 1991), pp. 20–25.

[3] Sue Bredekamp (ed.). *Developmentally Appropriate Practice in Early Childhood Programs Serving Children from Birth Through Age 8* (Washington, DC: NAEYC, 1987).

The value placed on reading is shown when the teacher takes time to read to an individual child.
(University of Illinois Child Development Laboratory)

ual children time to hear a story, listen to a record, or use language through dramatic play.

These activities are fun for children when they are appropriate for the children—not too hard, not too easy. The parent of a two-year-old was surprised at the new things his son was saying and asked, "Where did you learn that?" Without hesitation the child responded, "My teacher told me." Activities were obviously being offered to him in thoroughly enjoyable ways.

As a student preparing for teaching, you can gain valuable experience during the literature, language, and music activities. You can have opportunities for one-to-one interaction with a child or be a support person while another teacher remains in charge. Take some time to become familiar with the materials, books, and songs being used and the techniques the adults are using so you can take charge with confidence whenever the opportunity arises. Feel free to offer your assistance when you are ready to do so.

PLANNING LITERATURE ACTIVITIES

Careful planning went into the literature and language activities of Peggy's and Deanna's class mentioned in the introductory quote. The teacher kept in touch with new books that were appropriate for the children's interests and level of understanding.

Talk It Over

What are your earliest memories of books or stories? Who played a significant role in your early literary experiences?

Selecting Appropriate Books

For the infants and youngest toddlers, books may contain single items on a page for them to point out and name. "Ball," "Cup," "Shoe," says the child as you turn the pages of the heavy cardboard book and listen as the child names the items. The next books are those with one idea on a page, like Eloise Wilkins' *Busy Timmy* who "puts on his outdoor clothes and walks down the steps with no help at all." Books of this level typically depict action familiar to the child who is not yet worldly enough to have many experiences that relate to reading matter.

Through the third year the books should be short and personally oriented for the child. In a group situation it is better to read several short books to three-year-olds than to try a longer one and realize in the middle that the children are not understanding the book. On an individual basis an adult can digress and explain a point, but that is often difficult when reading to a group of children because their interest wanders.

Four-year-olds will enjoy longer books if they have had solid earlier experiences. The subject matter still needs to be quite factual and true to life. Toward the end of their fourth year, children will begin to understand fanciful stories. They'll know that animals don't really talk and trains don't say "I think I can."

It is extremely important that the books chosen for reading to a group be appropriate for the age level of the children. Some books that are not suitable for the group might be read to individual children; when reading to one child you can elaborate and allow the child to question and discuss in more detail than you usually are able to in a group situation. If you are having trouble keeping children's attention at storytime, be sure you are selecting appropriate books and, if anything, err on the simple side. Once you have established a pattern of attentiveness, you may then be able to move on to more difficult books. Good storytime guidance begins with selecting the right books.

Organizing Story Groups

Story groups should be small, containing no more than two infants or toddlers or four three- or four-year-old children, especially when children are first learning to function as a group. Young children come to school with the experience of one-to-one storytime—sitting on the parent's lap while a story is read. If they are from homes where there are no books and they have never been

The youngest children are provided appropriate books with single ideas per heavy cardboard pages. They can turn the heavy pages without tearing them.
(University of Georgia McPhail Children's Programs)

read to, then they need the same experience as a toddler for a time. That is, they need to have one adult share a book with them and allow them to react to the pictures they see. After a period of experience, they can graduate to listening with a few children.

The group can be divided so that compatible children are in a small group. Logically, they are the children with interests in the same type of stories. A regular teacher for each group will help maintain continuity for the children. The teacher will be able to build a logical sequence of experiences for the group once he or she is familiar with it.

A literature experience with a group of fifteen or twenty children does not do justice to the interests and needs of individual children. One has only to observe storytime in a large group to note that children do not get involved with a story in the way they do when the story is read in a smaller group. Much of the time is usually spent keeping order. "Experience in a large group" is often the stated objective or rationalization for organizing one story group instead of several. Teachers who read to large groups should realize that when coercion is required to keep order, it detracts from the enjoyment of the literature experience.

Because early childhood groups typically have several teachers as well as volunteers, it is usually possible to organize small story groups. You can gain some valuable experience preparing for and reading to a few children. If the group must be kept together, then the assistants should sit among the children to help with problems that arise. Storytime guidance is helped by organizing the groups to facilitate good listening for each child.

Judith Schickedanz's work supports small story groups. She states that to promote cognitive learning from story reading experiences, "a closeness between the adult reader and the child is required. In other words, a story reading situation that is loaded with positive affect (e.g., individual attention, physical contact, verbal praise, etc.) is the same situation that is loaded with information for the child. Part of the 'loading' no doubt results because the adult is in a situation where he or she can be *responsive* to an individual child's behavior. The adult can be directed by the child to back up or to go forward, to repeat, to answer questions, and so on."[4]

Preparing for Storytime

The teacher who has an inspirational storytime and meets the objectives that can be achieved by it does so by design, not by chance. It is a great loss when the teacher grabs a stack of ragged books on the way to storytime and expects to muddle through the next few minutes without preparation. Storytime needs planning. The teacher must know the book well and have some idea of how it will affect the children. Often some teaching aids, such as puppets, flannel board figures, or pictures, will be prepared to use with books to help the children understand better.

Part of the preparation includes guidance that has a quieting effect to help the children get ready for the listening behavior expected. You could use finger-plays and little songs that interest the children and help them to fidget less. After a few of these transitional techniques, the teacher will open a book and read.

Of course, each day the teacher does different things with the story period, keeping it varied so that children will look forward to what surprises have been planned. Variety will indeed make storytime more interesting.

Reading or Telling the Story

When you know the story well, you'll feel free to allow children to respond, for you'll have confidence that you can resume the story, maintain interest, and keep the group together. By seating children with their backs to the window, you can prevent glare from interfering with their seeing the pictures. You can use voice techniques to speak for the various characters but should avoid making them sound too harsh or scary. Young children are seldom interested in the author of a picture book, so once your quieting efforts are successful, open the book and begin reading at once.

Your storytime groups should be situated away from distracting toys. A portable screen may come in handy to shield toys from view. Once again, make use of your now familiar indirect guidance to help children by shielding distractions from them.

If there is a child who simply will not sit still for a group storytime even when given a special place by the teacher, a volunteer should be engaged to

---

[4] Judith A. Schickedanz, "Please Read That Story Again! Exploring Relationships Between Story Reading and Learning to Read," *Young Children,* 33:5, July 1978, p. 54.

Taped stories listened to through headsets give children an individual literature experience amidst a busy kindergarten classroom.
(Savannah Public Schools)

read to that child individually. This assignment may fall to you, as a student. Let the child select the books to read. Sometimes another available adult can help supervise while such a child listens to a recorded story. This is a special plan for a special child and should be explained as such.

Because literature experiences are so important for learning to read later, teachers should do everything in their power to make books interesting for children. Some effort to help a child develop receptive discipline can take place during regular self-selected activity time where a storybook corner is set up for individual browsing. The flannel board may be used there, too. Children can take turns at telling their own stories with the figures. Teachers often tape record stories for individual listening. Videotapes are now available with children's stories and movies that may be useful in a center that has the appropriate equipment available.

In one child development center, a volunteer "storylady" handles much of the storytime for the center. She maintains a little library with loungers, easy chairs, and rugs where the children can browse through books. She reads to small groups as they are interested. She thus relieves some of the other teachers at various points in the day, although they all keep a story corner in their classrooms and prepare a story of their own each day. The "storylady" acts as a book reviewer for new books, giving the director a list of books to buy from time to time. She also procures books from a local library to supplement the supply of the center. Children take turns going to the city library to help with book selection.

PLANNING LANGUAGE ACTIVITIES

The literature experiences are also language experiences. In fact, language is an important part of all school experiences and should be placed in high priority. Language is learned through talking, listening, and responding to conversation. A room full of meaningful conversations is far more desirable than a quiet room.

Puppets help children express their ideas and feelings.
(Michigan State University Child Development Laboratory)

As teachers, you must be sure to allow children to do some of the talking. Sometimes teachers simply do not notice how they are dominating the conversation, and that children may be only saying "yes" or "no" or even shaking their heads. Many television shows which purport to stimulate children's language development have been found to have a very high percentage of adult conversation. Most television is a passive experience for children.

With each planned experience—art, science, dramatic play, field trip, visitor, or the like—the teacher emphasizes the new vocabulary that naturally flows from it. As experiences are repeated throughout the year, the words will gradually find their way into a child's usage and understanding.

The free self-selected activity organization that is common in most schools encourages children to practice the language that they know and to learn to respond to the language of their peers and the teacher. Dramatic play and outdoor play offer high language stimulation. Through conscious efforts, teachers can raise the level of conversation in their groups.

The atmosphere of acceptance in a group will contribute to the confidence children show in using language to make their needs felt. If they are treated with respect, they will try to communicate. If they get answers to their questions, they will ask further questions. If they find teachers who will listen, they'll tell stories of events that are important to them.

 Talk It Over

What are your early memories of talking? Did people always understand you? Did people correct you? Were you shy about talking in a group? Discuss your positive and negative feelings related to talking.

ARTICULATION ASSISTANCE

Children may have some difficulty with language—with pronouncing certain consonants or with faltering speech. Such problems are not uncommon in young children, and most will be outgrown. Consonants, such as *s, v, t, r,* and *l,* and blends of two or three consonants, such as *cr, str,* and *bl,* are frequently difficult for children and may not be articulated clearly until children are seven or eight years old. If the child is encouraged to communicate freely, these errors will diminish. If the child does not talk at all, or only a little, a speech therapist should be consulted. A speech consultant should offer the school advice when a child has a problem. A careful routine of therapy may be suggested for the teachers to follow, with one adult assuming responsibility for helping the child and others refraining from pressuring the child.

It is important that the other adults in the center (cooks, bus drivers, custodians, or volunteers) do not add pressure to these children with language problems. It can only make problems worse if at every hand someone is making them repeat or asking what they said. If you notice a child with articulation problems be sure to discuss the plan for the child with the teacher. If there is no plan, perhaps one could be made.

OTHER LANGUAGE USAGE

Many teachers and caregivers are faced with children who do not speak the language of the teachers or caregivers. It will be important for you to simplify your English and use gestures and physical guidance, such as helping and demonstrating to enable the child to understand your words. You can make efforts toward learning to speak some words in the children's and families' language. Get one parent to make a list of key words used around your center. Perhaps post the words where you might see them and be reminded to use them.

Of course, you are not expected to become bilingual overnight, but you are showing an interest and respect for the family's language by making these efforts. There are many little songs that can be sung in various languages.

Books for individual children to use alone or with a friend are part of a rich literacy environment.

(Marshall University Child Development Laboratory)

Most immigrant families are very anxious to learn English and some may not appreciate having their child's native language reinforced. You might explain that your efforts are merely to show interest and respect for their language.

You will be amazed at how fast the children learn to speak English. Also, you will be amazed at how the children know that they can speak their home language to certain children and teachers and must, and do, use English with others—quite a complex differentiation for these youngsters.

You can encourage the parents who wish to learn to speak English to participate in certain community classes. Or, you may want to help them by organizing parent support groups where they'll learn to speak English.

For children who simply do not speak standard English, you can model the standard pronunciations for them and let them repeat rhymes and the like that help them correct the sounds and endings they have difficulty with. This works well, too, with children who are having speech problems.

Children who come from homes where the language is different from that of the teacher will have a difficult time for a while bridging this gap. The teacher's respect for them as persons will make it easier for them to learn a new language. When there are helpers in the classroom who speak their language, the children's needs may be more comfortably met. Teachers should consider the cultural shock they would feel in a foreign country and appreciate the feelings that a young child must have when first placed in a school where the language is different from that spoken in the home. Fortunately, most body language can communicate across cultures and language barriers and express love and respect. Therefore, use body language even when your verbal language isn't well understood.

PLANNING MUSIC ACTIVITIES

Singing Time

Singing time easily dovetails with storytime. A period of singing can precede the story and help with quieting the group, as mentioned in the discussion of storytime. The teacher selects, prepares, and makes a list of a wide variety of songs and musical fingerplays in order to be able to choose those that are most appropriate on a given day.

Children enjoy learning new songs. Teach a new song using a normal tempo. Sing it for several days until children catch on to it, rather than wearing out the children by making them try to learn it all in one day. You will want to jot down the words to the songs you hear the other teachers using in order to sing them with the children the same way others do. You can locate some new songs by browsing in song books, listening to records, and recalling songs you enjoyed as a child. Words to songs are a good resource to add to your file of ideas to use in teaching.

Variety is important, for all children will not enjoy the same songs equally. They may tire of certain songs, and if asked specifically, "Do you want to sing . . . ?" they may say, "No." It is usually better guidance if the teacher keeps singing time moving with new and known songs integrated in a way that keeps interest high. Giving children choices often slows down the event, and some children get bored waiting for their friends to come up with a choice, or they do not like the choice and the time is spent on that discussion. Therefore, it is usually best if teachers know the songs they want children to learn and simply sing them through at a lively tempo, taking children's choices whenever they come up quickly and incidentally. Teachers may discuss choices of songs with children during snack time, having the songs ready to sing the next singing time.

Teachers of each of the small groups can be teaching the same songs, so that if the group meets as a whole or teachers are interchanged the children will be familiar with some of the same songs.

Singing can be encouraged out of doors or during any of the various school activities. Guidance that is sung, such as, "Pickin' up toys, put them on the shelf," which is sung to the tune of *Paw-Paw Patch,* usually is quite effective.

Creative Movement

Creative movement is usually incorporated into the self-selected activity period. Small groups are easier to work with than large groups. Spontaneous response to recorded music may be encouraged. Having rhythm instruments stored conveniently on shelves nearby helps children feel free to use the instruments as the records play. Long, flowing dresses that are part of the dress-up wardrobe may also be incorporated into musical experiences as the children dress up to dance. A large mirror adds to the occasion just as it does to dramatic play.

The key to guidance in movement and rhythm experience is to allow children lots of free expression. Young children are not ready to do special steps to music, and such lessons usually leave them tense and unhappy with the experience. Children have some natural rhythms that are fun to recognize and encourage. When you see children tapping out a rhythm, be it with foot, finger, or on the rocking boat, you might call it to their attention and even tap it out on a tambourine or drum. Some of these suggestions are fun out of doors and combine with the motor-skill practice discussed in Chapter 12.

CONCLUSION

Storytime and music time can be both spontaneous and organized events in the school day. To introduce a rich variety of material to the children, the teachers will spend considerable time planning. Storytime and music time are important periods during the day to stimulate the children's learning and to give children another opportunity for creative emotional expression. Language activities are really part of the total school day. Conscious efforts are also needed on the part of adults to be sure all children participate in conversations. The closeness that children feel to the adults will be an important factor in how comfortable they feel about expressing their ideas. See Chapters 9, 11, 12, and 14 in *Introduction to Early Childhood Education* (in the reading list at the end of this chapter) for more detailed suggestions concerning language, literature, and music activities.

REVIEW AND APPLICATIONS

Five Guides to Literature Activities

1. Select books that are appropriate to the age and experience of the children.
2. Plan daily literature experiences for every child and, especially, an individual experience when a child seems unready for a group experience.
3. Use variety in literature and in storytelling techniques to attract children to this important pre-reading event.
4. Organize children in small groups, especially the youngest children, to make the literature experience most meaningful for the individual child.
5. Encourage use of the library by young children and their parents.

Five Guides to Language Activities

1. Use every opportunity to increase children's vocabulary and to encourage practice in speaking and listening.
2. Plan a variety of games that encourage both speaking and listening.
3. Encourage spontaneous, vital conversations and interactions rather than quiet, submissive behavior.
4. Appreciate the challenge that children with a different language background may be experiencing and aid those children to feel at ease and to express themselves.
5. Obtain advice from a speech therapist before attempting to correct children's speech.

Five Guides to Music Activities

1. Plan a wide variety of musical experiences including many songs.
2. Teach a new song using its normal tempo. Sing it for several days until children learn it rather than wearing out the children by making them try to learn the new song in one day.
3. Remember that the primary goal of music is enjoyment.
4. Keep any accompaniment to children's singing soft and in the background.

5. Use music throughout the school day, indoors, outdoors, as guidance, as an expression of joy, to relieve tension, and to foster concept development.

 Observations

1. Observe children interacting with each other. Record three children's conversations. Analyze each child's average sentence length.
2. Using the observations recorded in question No. 1, did each child use correct verb forms? What percent of the sentences had adjectives? Adverbs? Discuss.
3. Using the observations recorded in question No. 1, did each child articulate sounds correctly? Discuss.
4. Observe two children at storytime. Record what each does. Discuss.
5. Observe two children at singing time. Record what each does. Discuss.
6. Observe your case-study child responding to literature, language, and music experiences. Record what the child does.

Applications

1. Assist children at home or at school as they use books. What books are they using? What roles do the adults play in the children's literature experience? Report your findings.
2. Assist in a school with storytime by giving support to a teacher who is in charge or by telling a story that you have prepared. Report to the class what responses the children gave to the story.
3. Copy several poems or fingerplays on index cards. Recite them during appropriate moments with a few children. Report to the class on the outcome.
4. Visit the public library during young children's story hour. Volunteer to help the librarian. Give a report on your experience.
5. On a 1-to-5 scale rate your center using the Five Guides to Literature, Language, and Music Activities. Discuss.

ADDITIONAL RESOURCES

Suggested Film and Videotapes

Listening and Talking   VHS   1/2 in.   Color   30 minutes   1988

Thelma Harms and Debby Cryer explain how language develops as a medium for communication and thinking. Delmar Publishers, Customer Service, 2 Computer Drive West, Albany, NY 12212, 1–800-347-7707.

Learning Can Be Fun   VHS   1/2 in.   Color   57 minutes   1988

> Ella Jenkins demonstrates how she sings and uses music to promote learning. You can do it, too. NAEYC, Media, 1509 16th Street, NW, Washington, DC 20036-1426.

Reading and Young Children   VHS   1/2 in.   Color   15 minutes   1988

> Dr. Jan McCarthy tells teachers what they can say to parents who want their children to learn to read in preschool. NAEYC, Media, 1509 16th Street, N.W., Washington, DC 20036-1426.

Creative Movement for the Developing Child   16 mm   Black and White   25 minutes   no date

> A black and white film showing Clare Cherry's methods of involving children in simple, interesting, and creative movement experiences. CATEC Consultants, 2754 San Gabriel, San Bernardino, CA 90069.

FOR FURTHER READING

Barbour, Nita et al. "Sand: A Resource for the Language Arts," *Young Children,* January 1987, 42:2, 20–25.

Barclay, Kathy D. and Lynn Walwer. "Linking Lyrics and Literacy Through Song Picture Books," *Young Children,* 47:4, May 1992, 76–85.

Bayless, Kathleen M. and Marjorie E. Ramsey. *Music: A Way of Life for the Young Child.* Columbus, OH: Merrill/Macmillan, 1985.

Berk, Laura. "Why Children Talk to Themselves: Research in Review," *Young Children,* 40:5, July 1985, 46–52.

Dumtschin, Joyce U. "Recognize Language Development and Delay in Early Childhood," *Young Children,* 43:3, March 1988, 16–24.

Fields, Marjorie V., Katherine Spangler, and Darris M. Lee. *Let's Begin Reading Right: Developmentally Appropriate Beginning Literacy.* Columbus, OH: Merrill/Macmillan, 1991.

Garrard, Kay R. "Helping Young Children Develop Mature Speech Patterns," *Young Children,* 42:3, March 1987, 16–21.

Harsh, Ann. "Teach Mathematics with Children's Literature," *Young Children,* 42:6, September 1987, 24–29.

Hildebrand, Verna. *Introduction to Early Childhood Education.* New York: Macmillan Publishing Company, 1991.

Hough, Ruth A., Joanne R. Nurss, and Dolores Wood. "Tell Me a Story: Making Opportunities for Elaborated Language in Early Childhood Classrooms," *Young Children,* 43:1, November 1987, 6–12.

International Reading Association. "Literacy Development and Pre-First Grade," *Young Children,* 41:4, May 1986, 10–13.

Jalongo, Mary R. and Mitzie Collins. "Singing with Young Children!" *Young Children,* 40:2, January 1985, 17–22.

Krogh, Suzanne L. and Linda L. Lamme. "Children's Literature and Moral Development," *Young Children,* 40:4, May 1985, 48–51.

Myhre, S. "With Prop Boxes We're Always Ready for Creative Movement," *Young Children,* 46:2, January 1991, 29.

Smith, Charles A. "Nurturing Kindness Through Storytelling," *Young Children,* 41:6, September 1986, 46–51.

Wolf, Jan. "Let's Sing it Again: Creating Music with Young Children," *Young Children,* 47:2, January 1992, 56–61.

PART II

General Considerations in Child Guidance

CHAPTER 17

Knowing Children as a Basis for Guidance

Key Concepts

◆ Developmental Direction
◆ Reflexes
◆ Self-Efficacy
◆ Jean Piaget's Stages

"Do all babies eat sloppily?"
"Don't you think a two-year-old can learn to stay out of the street?"
"How do you know when to discipline a child?"
"Will you teach my son to read and write?"
"Isn't he big enough to dress himself?"

Teachers frequently are asked such questions by parents, new employees, and students who are learning about children as they work in a child development center. A basic understanding of children's growth and development is necessary for parents and teachers to make appropriate decisions about interpersonal communication and guidance and about educational goals and strategies for the particular children in their care.

Who are these children you are going to teach? They are your children and mine, your sister's children, your cousin's, or your neighbor's. They are rich children and poor, black children and white, happy children and sad. You'll be teaching children who desperately need a place to be while their parents work. You will be teaching children who have no parents or who are neglected by them. You will be teaching children whose parents have planned for them, cherish them, and want them to have a high-quality, enriching group experience.

KNOW CHILD DEVELOPMENT

Knowing children will be a major goal while working with them. The science of child development is still in its infancy relative to other sciences. As teachers and parents, you can add to the science of child development the insights and understanding gained through direct experience with children. Though there

A new baby is full of potential for the future.

(V. Hildebrand, photographer)

is much written about children, you will note that often it has a tentative quality, because scientists recognize the inadequacies of our current knowledge. There are many theories. Some have been tested in laboratories but require much more study in the field before anyone can say how much genuine insight they offer about how children grow, develop, and behave. However, you can use the theories to provide helpful points to observe in your work.

Theories give you a framework and vocabulary for discussing children with involved professionals throughout the country and in many other parts of the world. Based on present knowledge and thinking, the National Association for the Education of Young Children (NAEYC) has developed a guide for teachers and caregivers to help them understand child development and apply their knowledge in centers. These guidelines can be found in a booklet, edited by Sue Bredekamp, titled *Developmentally Appropriate Practice in Early Childhood Programs Serving Children from Birth Through Age 8.* The understanding of child development is a necessity for appropriate childrearing practices by parents and teachers, according to the association.

DEVELOPMENTAL CHANGES DURING INFANCY

Understanding children's growth and development will help you understand more fully some of the guidance techniques suggested in this book (Table

dent. Also, learning generally proceeds more quickly now than if started earlier. Summer is a good time for training because there are fewer clothes to get off and on and to get wet if accidents occur.

It should be noted that girls are usually trained earlier than boys of the same age. This is just one of a number of indications that girls mature earlier than boys, a fact that should be kept in mind when children of like ages are cared for in groups and thus might easily be compared. You should realize also that there are individual rates of maturity—ranging from weeks or sometimes months—among children. Daytime control usually occurs earlier than nighttime control for both genders.

In the early part of training, little boys may sit on the toilet to urinate just as girls do. Once they observe other boys they may prefer to stand. Standing may help somewhat when they have an erection, which is frequent when they are ready to urinate. They will often have some difficulty in their ability to hit the toilet, given the erection, the urgency accompanying the need, their inexperience with handling clothing, and so on. Therefore, caregivers are cautioned to be gentle when making demands for standards. Perhaps teaching the boys to sit on the toilet is the better approach.

The less fuss that can be made over toilet training the better. If training is attempted and negative behavior results, then it is far better to drop the training plan for a while than to arouse the resistance of the child. Punishment should never become associated with toilet training.

Social-Emotional Development

The toddler shows the beginnings of what psychologist Erik Erikson calls *autonomy*. That is, they begin making their own decisions, saying "no" to many things people ask them to do. This stage of development, when the compliant infant suddenly starts rejecting food, sleep, riding in the stroller, and everything that heretofore had pleased him or her, can be very frustrating to the uninformed parent or caregiver. It is best to use positive guidance— "Here's your bottle," rather than "Would you like your bottle?" because the latter will surely bring a "No," even if the child is hungry.

Toddlers are very self-centered or egocentric, and they cannot take the view of another person. For example, they may accidentally hit another child in the sand box and not be aware of the hurt inflicted.

Toddlers seem more aware of themselves than infants and enjoy looking at themselves in a mirror. They begin to have a sense of their own belongings. Thus, they can understand when a parent says "Bring me your socks," or "Bring me your daddy's book."

Socializing

Toddlers in a center may seem like satellites when you watch them at play. They move in their own orbits and may collide with other satellites momentarily, then move back to whatever they were doing. They exhibit what has been called *solitary play*. Toward the end of the toddler period they engage in *parallel play*. That is, two children enjoy playing alongside each other but have little interaction save perhaps a smile exchanged. They each use whatever toys they have and make no plans for integrating their play as they will when they are older. Even though a child at this stage is excited by the anticipation of visiting friends and seems to understand the possibility of a social outing, when the children get together each only plays alongside (not *with*) the other child.

Cognitive Development

Evidence of cognitive or mental development appears rapidly during the toddler period. Language gives clues to this development. The child may, at 18 months, appear to have few language skills and yet at 24 months be speaking in sentences. Once speech begins it seems to flow rapidly from single words to short sentences in a few weeks.

One toddler whose level of information seemed to be increasing rapidly replied when asked by her parent, "Where did you learn that?" responded proudly, "At my Children's Center." The toddlers in children's centers enjoy stories, science experiments, dramatic play, creative art activities, and all motor skill opportunities. By engaging in many activities, the toddlers provide evidence of some of the things they know. Toddlers need activities that are open to their natural inclination to move about as they learn, rather than any that require sitting quietly for a session of information giving. The school is the child's laboratory. Lecturing is inappropriate for this age.

The toddler is still in Piaget's *sensorimotor stage* and begins moving into the *pre-operational stage*. In either stage the child constructs his or her knowledge from the environment of the home, school, and neighborhood. Growth in these stages occurs through the child's hands-on experiences, rather than through teaching as such. The role of adults is to keep the environment enriched to allow the child many interesting activities for exploring.

Routines

Toddlers gain security from having the same people do things in the same way day after day. In early childhood groups a lot of time is spent in the routines of dressing, toileting, eating, and sleeping. The pace must be slow to match their tempo and allow them to learn to help themselves with the routines. It is a period of growth and development, and the toddlers can be very charming as they learn. They want to be independent and should be encouraged to help with the routines.

THREE-YEAR-OLDS

Having children turn three years old usually brings a sigh of relief to the teacher as it does to the parents after a busy, often turbulent, toddler period. Threes, like toddlers, are wonderful to watch and to work with if you follow

Table 17–2 *Average Weights and Heights of Young Children*

Age (years)	Average Weight (pounds)	Average Height (inches)
2	28	36
3	30	37
4	34	40
5	38	42

their developmental levels carefully. An old film called *The Terrible Twos and the Trusting Threes* depicts the general relief people feel to find the child somewhat easier to deal with. The child is becoming socialized for living with family and friends.

Physical-Motor Development

By age three the rapid growth of babyhood has ceased. Only a two-pound gain occurs between ages two and three, and four pounds between three and four (see Table 17–2). The baby fat disappears and the young child emerges leaner and lankier. The resulting decrease in appetite often causes parents to worry, but the fact is the child isn't expected to grow as fast as he or she did earlier and may need less food.

The threes are more adept at motor skills than toddlers, as one would expect. They feel secure climbing the slide, running around the yard, and throwing balls. Their method of walking is smoother than before. Children like to walk and run without having their hands held. They seem to know their own limits, and unless an older child overencourages them, threes will generally not go beyond those boundaries. When older children play on the same playground the threes should be carefully supervised to be sure they aren't climbing above their safety limits. Threes thrive on using motor skills, so even academic learning needs a motoric element to be interesting to them.

Small-motor skills are also improving. Children this age enjoy using various marking pens and paintbrushes. Their paintings and drawings begin to repeat figures showing a design element creeping in. For example, in the midst of a random scribble, a ladder-like design appeared in one child's drawing. However, to the unknowing adult, drawings may look like scribbles. Scissors are usually still difficult, with some help required, because threes do not quite understand the theory on which scissors operate. Zippers and buttons are handled quite easily, especially if they are large enough for tiny fingers to grasp. Most three-year-olds can handle their feeding tools easily. They may tip over their milk glasses unless adults help them remember to push them toward the center of the table.

Threes usually have daytime toileting under control, though they may still wet at night. Parents should be encouraged to select clothing that is easily and quickly managed in order to contribute to the three's independence.

Three-year-olds play side by side, intent on their own play but enjoying the presence of other children.
(V. Hildebrand, photographer)

Teachers plan routine toileting times to help remind children to use the toilet, though children are free to go anytime during the day.

Social-Emotional Development

Threes begin to enjoy playing with their peers and making new friends at the early childhood center. However, they are still likely to participate in *parallel play*, playing alongside other children, rather than in cooperative play. Many duplicate toys, such as small cars or trucks, are interesting to parallel players, allowing them each to zoom around the playroom floor.

Threes enjoy the housekeeping corner, again playing in the presence of others, such as feeding the doll, while another child puts a doll to bed. However, there is still more of an independent, rather than cooperative, quality to the play.

Being egocentric, the three-year-old has trouble with real sharing. In authentic sharing one child gives up a desired toy realizing another child also desires it. The threes will cooperate when adults ask them to take turns as they increasingly want to please their parents and teachers. Giving choices helps reduce negative responses.

Threes may get easily frustrated, for example, when they try to do something that they see others do and it fails to work correctly. For example, some try roller skating or riding a bigger tricycle and may get angry when they can't accomplish it. At times threes may feel lonesome or sad, requiring cuddling more like a toddler. This behavior sometimes frustrates parents who are beginning to appreciate the newer independent child. Yet satisfying the need requires only a few minutes of time.

Cognitive Development

Threes are beginning to show what they *know*, the heart of cognitive development. Their memories are growing. They match pieces of puzzles, beads, colors, and blocks. They can read the name tag board and select their own name tag and often the name tags of other children. The three is in Piaget's *pre-operational* stage needing real objects to handle and work with, rather than pictures and wordy explanations. They readily focus on one aspect of a project and cannot see another way to do it. For example, if they sort beads or blocks for color they will have trouble later sorting for shape, due to the fact that they *center* on the one characteristic and cannot yet see the object in another light. They cannot take another person's viewpoint.

Language Development

Both receptive and productive language skills are increasing rapidly. Most threes can get what they want by verbal means, especially from adults. They can understand the directions of adults, especially if adults remember to give them only one direction at a time and watch the child's response for indications of understanding. Giving threes some individual attention and plenty of time to explain their ideas fosters language development and the children's self-confidence.

Threes begin to incorporate big words into their sentences. For example, in a few minutes one three-year-old talked about a "discussion" and a bit later mentioned that something was "disgusting." She seemed to be trying out the "dis" prefix. Teachers can really enjoy this age if they tune in to children's expressions and record some samples to report to parents or to discuss in a professional setting to gain further insight into children's language.

Good literature fosters language development as well as cognitive understanding. Threes enjoy stories such as Ezra Jack Keats' *The Snowy Day*, depicting a little boy just their age. A small reading group of two or three children is desirable, allowing each to select a book, sit close to the adult on the lap or at the side, and have an opportunity to digress a moment to allow one child to talk about some idea the book suggests. *The Snowy Day* prompts children to talk about snow angels made outside in the snow. Allowing children to speak spontaneously when they have ideas helps foster language goals that are very prominent in the curriculum. These activities contribute to emerging literacy skills which are developing as children talk to and listen to others, handle books, and have books read to them.

FOURS AND FIVES

Fours are vastly different from threes. They are faster, more vocal, more independent, and more outgoing. They now crave the company of their peers. They have begun cooperative play, and though it may take a while to get organized

Four-year-olds exhibit planning skills as they work together to build structures.
(University of Illinois Child Development Laboratory)

the play can be intricate if allowed to continue for a time. Fours and fives need many new fresh ideas to work with each day. They are ready for field trips that stimulate their thinking or that serve to tie together some project for them. They enjoy larger groups and aren't as easily disturbed by continuous new faces, such as students or volunteers, as are the younger children. Fours and fives typically come to school with plans of what or with whom they are going to play. If disappointed, they can express their displeasure loudly or through aggression.

Physically they are, of course, bigger. Their motor skills are more highly developed. All body movement, throwing, and catching skills should be well developed by now. The early childhood period is a critical period for development that lays the foundation for later motor skills.[3]

Fours and fives drive their tricycles fast and dangerously at times. The fives will graduate to two-wheeled bikes at home and tell their friends, gaining new status in their eyes. (Then the fours will hide the fact that they still have the training wheels attached to their bikes at home!)

Cooperative play is the rule, with intricate role assignments taking place in the housekeeping corner, block corner, or play yard. With mature children, however, you also see a type of individual solitary activity that is different from that noted during the toddler stage. At age five they become very interested in a painting or other project and may continue working on it long after their friends have gone. This long interest span should be encouraged, as should the extension of projects that indicate a child's creativity. Often these children are

---

[3] Ibid.

secure in their social relations, feeling that they can enter the ongoing play anytime they feel like it.

Fours and fives are independent dressers if they are given boots and zippers they can manage. They handle bathroom routines with skill and rarely have an accident if they are allowed to go to the bathroom whenever they need to. They eat well if served foods they like and a minimum of between-meal snacks. They are not fond of napping, and compromises are needed to avoid an impasse over this requirement in some homes and centers. They are cooperative in clean-up routines if approached in a cooperative manner.

When fours and fives have been in school for several years, serious efforts will be required to plan a rich and varied curriculum. If a good program is lacking, these children will literally run the place in a chaotic manner. They may know the ropes better than a series of new or inexperienced teachers. Fours and fives are a decided challenge. However, many successes and satisfactions await the teacher who puts effort into a rich program of learning experiences for them.

INDIVIDUALITY—AVOIDING STEREOTYPES

Knowing children, parents, and teachers individually is basic to the developmental and humanistic approach advocated in this book. Through study and experience you will learn to recognize the wide range of individual differences that exists within ethnic, racial, gender, age, economic, and disabled groups and not accept overgeneralizations or stereotypes about characteristics of a group.

The early childhood movement, especially Head Start, has done an excellent job of fostering the development of children and parents without regard to a person's origin. There is still work to be done, and Head Start, in particular, is developing ways to integrate disabled children.

Stereotyping by gender is still a burden carried over from past traditions. In early childhood programs equal treatment must be given boys and girls, fathers and mothers, and men and women teachers. A broad range of expectations or goals allowing for individual differences can be set. It appears that the range of differences within a group of boys or within a group of girls is quite similar. We do individuals a great injustice if we follow old stereotypes, such as the notions that girls are weak—boys are strong; girls cry—boys don't; girls are quiet and submissive—boys are loud and aggressive; girls are dumb (girls generally went unschooled until the mid-nineteenth century)—boys are intelligent; and so on.

You can think of other examples of ethnic, racial, age, and economic stereotyping. Clearly, with new knowledge and new recognition of equality, it is time to outgrow irrational stereotypes that keep the world from being a more productive and happier place. As you interact with people within early childhood education you should become more humanistic in your approach.

Talk It Over

In what ways has your own early life followed a gender stereotyped path and in what ways has it followed a non-gender stereotyped path? What things would you change if you could? What activities do you plan to pursue in the future?

SPEED OF DEVELOPMENT

Maturation, motivation, and experience interact to influence the child's development. Maturation refers to the general tempo at which various biological, behavioral, and personality characteristics emerge. This tempo is largely dependent on the genetic makeup of the individual. Motivation refers to the child's incentive or desire to learn a behavior. Experience in practicing the skill can be provided by adults at strategic moments when the child shows readiness, thus enhancing development. Expert teachers are sensitive to children's readiness in many learning domains. Children seek ways to gain experience when they find a new skill fascinating. Watch them climb up and down when

Five-year-olds cooperate, discuss, and share while fitting a puzzle together.
(Savannah Public Schools)

they first learn to climb. Or listen to them practice talking once they've started speaking. It often seems as though they have an inner drive to excel. Rates of development vary among children and even within a child. The child may have rapid physical-motor development and be slower in speech development, for example.

Are fast growth and development necessarily desirable? "My five-year-old is already reading at the third grade level," proudly exclaimed a mother to the kindergarten teacher. Such comments are often coupled with a wish or even a demand that the early childhood teacher contribute to this acceleration. However, teachers should keep in mind that scientific research gives no basis for concluding that faster than normal growth is necessarily desirable or that future success is thereby assured. The reverse could be true. In fact, the child just described and many similar children may not be helped in attaining any higher adult achievement level, but may even be injured by excessive pressure to exceed more normal developmental rates. Developmental stages and sequences are more important than chronological age. Later development and achievement must be built on a firm base of early development and practice. Consequently, a wise early childhood teacher does not endeavor to pressure a four-year-old child to respond like a five, or fives to respond like sixes, and so on. Neither teachers nor parents should fall into a trap of pushing accelerated learning for which there is no adequate scientific support.

Young children, do, of course, differ in their readiness to learn certain skills. When interpreting a well-planned early childhood program to parents, it is important to stress that learning, growth, and development are taking place in all domains—physical-motor, mental, social, and emotional. A reasonable balance must be achieved to develop the happy, fully functioning child.

CONCLUSION

Besides knowing some general characteristics of infants and young children, such as those presented above, the teacher must get to know children as individuals. In only a few days you can notice the individuality of each child—his or her personality and way of doing things and behaving. These are challenges for caregivers to interpret.

Conferences with the parents, visits in the home, and participation of the parents in the center's programs are ways to get to know the children and their individual needs further. A total respect for what parents can tell and show teachers and caregivers is important. Respect is shown by sharing information, asking for advice, understanding differing points of view, responding to feelings and needs, avoiding blaming parents for things children do, and reporting happy and rewarding moments of a child's day.

Throughout the various chapters, further points are made regarding age differences and behavior. In addition, the interested reader is advised to pursue more in-depth reading of child development information in books listed in the bibliographies at the end of the chapters.

REVIEW AND APPLICATIONS

Ten Characteristics of Development

1. Children all follow the same general sequence of development.
2. Children develop according to individual timetables; thus, there is a range of time for an expected ability to develop.
3. Children develop in a head-to-toe direction.
4. Children develop from midline toward outer extremities.
5. Children develop from general motor, social, mental, and emotional characteristics to increasingly complex characteristics.
6. Rates of development vary within a child, being at times rapid in one area and slower in others.
7. Maturation, motivation, and experience interact to influence the child's development.
8. Girls mature slightly ahead of boys, but generally young boys and girls can do the same things.
9. Children's development can be affected by nutrition, rest, exercise, or illness.
10. Early development lays the foundation for later development.

 Observations

In the following observations select two children as widely separated in age as is feasible in your situation. Record each child's age.

1. Observe two children eating a meal or snack. Record their tool-grasping skills. Record conversation between the children. Record adult-child interaction. Summarize your observation. What conclusions can you draw about the age of the children related to their eating behavior?
2. Observe two children dressing to go outdoors. Record evidence of each child's motivation for the task and their small motor skills. Record evidence of the child's independence. Summarize your findings for each age child while engaged in a dressing task.
3. Observe and record the play behavior of each child. For each child (a) note the number of other children the child plays with, (b) the theme of the play, and (c) the conversation of each participant. Summarize your findings using the stages of play discussed in this chapter.
4. Observe your case-study child. Using these and notes taken previously, analyze the child's development based on children the same age.

Applications

1. Talk to two sets of parents with young children of different ages. Ask about their concerns for their children at this time. Write a description of each interview and compare the two. What are the similarities? What are the differences? How can you account for the differences and similarities between the two sets of parents?
2. Talk to a teacher of young children. Find out the teacher's views on children's development and on single-age grouping and multiple-age grouping. Write a paragraph about your interview.
3. Consider the Ten Characteristics of Development. How have you seen them applied in your center? Discuss.

ADDITIONAL RESOURCES

Suggested Film and Videotapes

Developmentally Appropriate Practice: Birth Through Age 5   VHS   1/2 in.   Color   27 minutes   1988

Shows teachers and children in developmentally appropriate programs. Shows inappropriate practices. NAEYC, Media, 1509 16th Street, NW, Washington, DC 20036-1426.

Seeing Infants with New Eyes   VHS   1/2 in.   Color   26 minutes   1988

Magda Gerber's exemplary program dramatically illustrates how adult interactions with infants can make a difference. NAEYC, Media, 1509 16th Street, NW, Washington, DC 20036-1426.

In the Beginning: The Process of Infant Development   16 mm.   Color   15 minutes   1980

Shows the important first two years of life. Dr. Bettye Caldwell traces the stages of development and accents the important role caregivers play in this process. Davidson Films, Inc., 850 O'Neill Avenue, Belmont, CA 94002.

FOR FURTHER READING

Bader, Lois and Verna Hildebrand. "An Exploratory Study of Three to Five Year Olds' Responses on the Bader Reading and Language Inventory to Determine Developmental Stages of Emerging Literacy," *Early Childhood Development and Care,* Vol. 77, August 1992, 83–95.

Berk, Laura. "Why Children Talk to Themselves," *Young Children,* 40:5, July 1985, 46–52.

Brazelton, T. Berry. *Infants and Mothers*. New York: Dell Publishing Company, 1986.

Brazelton, T. Berry. *Toddlers and Parents: A Declaration of Independence*. New York: Dell Publishing Company, 1986.

Bredekamp, Sue (ed.). *Developmentally Appropriate Practice in Early Childhood Programs Serving Children from Birth Through Age 8*. Washington, DC: NAEYC, 1987.

Elkind, David. "The Child Yesterday, Today, and Tomorrow," *Young Children*, 42:4, May 1987, 6–11.

Hale, J. E. *Black Children: Their Roots, Culture, and Learning Styles*. Provo, UT: Brigham Young University Press, 1982.

Hildebrand, Verna. *Parenting and Teaching Young Children*. New York: McGraw-Hill Book Company, 1990.

Hildebrand, Verna. *Introduction to Early Childhood Education*. New York: Macmillan Publishing Company, 1991.

Javernick, Ellen. "Johnny's Not Jumping: Can We Help Obese Children?" *Young Children*, 43:2, January 1988, 18–23.

Jones, Elizabeth and Louise Derman-Sparks, "Meeting the Challenge of Diversity," *Young Children*, 47:2, January 1992, 12–18.

Pellegrini, A. D. and Jane C. Perlmutter. "Rough-and-Tumble Play on the Elementary School Playground," *Young Children*, 43:2, January 1988, 14–17.

Seefeldt, Carol and Sallie Tinney. "Dinosaurs: The Past Is Present," *Young Children*, 40:4, May 1985, 20–24.

Spock, Benjamin and Michael B. Rothenberg. *Dr. Spock's Baby and Child Care*. New York: Pocket Books, 1992.

CHAPTER 18

Appreciating Positive Behavior

Key Concepts

◆ Meaningfulness of Behavior

◆ Examples of Positive Behavior

◆ Prosocial Behavior

Rod, a new child, and Joan were playing in the sandpile. Sharon came into the yard and said, "I'm hollering at you, Rod. I'm hollering at 'cha.'" Rod smiled at her and kept playing with Joan. Sharon left and yelled, "Hey, Rod," several times. An adult said, "Seems like someone is calling you." He just glowed and said, "I know who it is."

Rod was feeling the warmth of being accepted into a new group. Through this moment of child-child interaction, Rod's resources of self-confidence and security were enhanced. Acceptance by others contributed to Rod's sense of security.

MEANINGFULNESS OF BEHAVIOR

By becoming a careful observer of children's behavior, you can begin to learn how children are feeling and thinking. The positive or "good" behavior of children is sometimes overlooked by parents and teachers in efforts to correct or eliminate "bad" or negative behavior. By looking at children's strengths, you can often help them overcome their weaknesses. For this reason, the emphasis in this chapter will be on positive behavior in the hope that negative behavior can be placed in a better perspective. Of course, there is no clear line between positive and negative behavior; this will be determined by each person's value system. When adults feel positively about themselves, the behavior of children will seem positive to them, because warmth, understanding, and acceptance prevail in the adults' attitudes.

Infants

Babies will exhibit positive behavior if their needs are satisfied. Babies' behavior is the language by which they tell us what they need. When they are sleeping, quietly cooing, eating heartily, or kicking rhythmically, we assume they are having their needs met and aren't hungry, tired or uncomfortable in any way.

Parents and caregivers receive positive feedback when the baby's needs are met. Babies soon learn to gurgle and smile when their favorite person enters the room. They flail their arms and legs, shaking their mobiles or rattles, when someone stops by the crib or playpen to chat for a minute. Once they can crawl, they do so on all fours to meet a favorite person.

Babies thrive on attention, yet giving them the amount they need does not have to be a constant job. They are better off being given small amounts of attention throughout the day. In an infant center there probably is not a worry in the world that the baby will get "too much" attention. Caregivers typically have too many charges for that to happen. Like parents, though, it is just as important for caregivers to give babies the attention they need: the kind words and conversation during diaper changes, closeness during feedings, the pointing out of things to look for and responsiveness to the infant's attempts to communicate through babbling and cooing.

Happy babies are active babies. Once they are developmentally able, they roll over, they stand in their cribs, and they jump. It is a pleasure to watch them, for they enjoy themselves so. Out on the floor they scoot along until they learn to crawl, then before long they are pulling themselves up to chair legs and playpen sides. Life grows more perilous as they encounter dangerous things—the heater, the tablecloth, even that cupboard under the sink where the hazardous cleaning chemicals are kept. But locomotion is wonderful, and adults must organize the baby's environment so it is safe, not dangerous.

Happy babies are noisy, at least some of the time. They increasingly use their vocal cords to get attention and to express their excitement. A parent or a caregiver who wishes for silence should think of a deaf child who has never said, heard, or responded to a word. Parents of deaf children would give anything to hear them shout. For example, John, a child with a hearing disability, on his third birthday was finally fitted with a hearing aid. The therapist quietly said to the mother, "Call your child." The mother said, "John." When the child turned toward her, she wept openly. During all those infant months when John had been silent, she had thought of him as a "good baby" and didn't question his lack of response.

Happy babies are social. They like people and enjoy the games that people play with them. They don't try to control adults or test them. They give back what they get. If they are given love, they return it. Other human beings are so important to these small bundles of humanity that toys, and television, and propped-up bottles should never replace the human touch and voice in their day. To be happy and secure, they must be loved unconditionally and this is your responsibility when they are in your care.

The smile of the infant just learning to walk is a positive behavior.
(V. Hildebrand, photographer)

Happy babies are smart. They are constantly exploring their environment for the knowledge they need to understand their world. They are doing it through touching, tasting, chewing, seeing, and hearing. You often see them discovering that one action makes something else happen. For example, babies kick their crib and the bell on the mobile rings. They stop and the bell stops. They kick again, and the bell rings. A big smile covers their face, for they have learned a relationship that they didn't know existed—kicking makes the bell ring.

Happy babies practice sounds. Their cooing and babbling become more and more organized. Finally, they begin making sounds like "da-da" and "ma-ma," which, of course, is very exciting to parents. Their excitement and encouragement give the baby pleasure. Babies begin to enjoy the conversations exchanged. By the time they become toddlers they may have several words in their vocabulary.

Happy babies are sleepers. Nothing is as moving as watching infants sleep. What deep trust they must have to be so completely relaxed, telling you that all is well. Can you promise to support that trust as you help them grow?

 Talk It Over

What is the most positive behavior you have observed in an infant or young child? Why do you consider the behavior positive?

Toddlers

Happiness for toddlers is allowing them to try their wings—to achieve *autonomy*, according to psychologist Erik Erikson. One positive behavior is exploring on their own. Toddlers want to use the tricycle, though they may walk it along instead of pedaling it. They like to walk on a balance beam, a curb, or a wall, or something else a few inches from the ground, perhaps holding onto an adult's hand.

Happiness, too, is climbing up on high places that sometimes they may be worried about getting down from. They will look and feel like "king of the mountain" and cause parents to scurry to the rescue lest they tumble down.

Try visualizing yourself as a toddler to understand the pleasures of toddler life. For example, happiness is getting into things and poking your fingers into things. A cardboard carton from the grocery store makes a toy that you

The toddler bravely deciding to try the tire swing is a positive behavior.
(V. Hildebrand)

can play with for days—in and out, out and in, sitting down, rising up—a rhythm of exploration. You poke at Grandma's toe through her open-toed shoe and could just as well poke around the electric cord if someone didn't watch out for you.

Happiness is Julia picking up rocks on a walk and saying, "one for *my* daddy, one for *my* mommy, both of them."

Happiness is having people around who realize how hard it is for toddlers to change their minds. For instance, after they've decided they want to eat a peanut butter sandwich, it is really hard to have to settle for a jelly sandwich.

Happiness is singing the song *Eency Weency Spider* with your teacher, then singing it at home for mommy and daddy and being asked in amazement, "Where did you learn that?" Also, happiness is bringing home a drawing of pretty squiggles and having daddy say, "Matt, this looks like writing. Look, dear, at the writing Matt did today. Good Matt."

Happiness is eating your dinner from your pretty Peter Rabbit dish, getting your fingers and face sticky, and not having anyone care about the mess.

Happiness is being able to ask for help or for something you need, like saying, "Water. Kim, water." Or when mother says, "Do you want your coat on?" being able to say, "Coat on."

After toddlers turn two and become aware of the toilet, they like handling this alone. Sometimes for fun they sit backward on the toilet so they can hold on to the lid. They like surprising their teacher by going to the bathroom all alone without a reminder, and remembering to wash their hands afterward. They like the teacher's individual comments complimenting them for doing the task alone.

Toddlers really anticipate going outdoors. One teacher showed her charges how to put on their coats "a magic way," by laying them front side up on the floor, collars at the children's feet. The children put their arms into the sleeves and flipped the coats over their heads and "like magic" the coats were on and ready to be zipped up. "I did it!" each shouted happily one after another as they succeeded at this task.

Three- to Five-Year-Olds

Action for a three- to five-year-old is a positive behavior, the key to healthy development, the sign that the child is growing normally. Physical action means continuous running, climbing, crawling, and hopping. Perhaps no one ever appreciates all the things the normal child can do until observing a disabled child who can't do every activity. Happiness for disabled children comes from finding things they can do, emphasizing these things, and building other skills from them.

Young children sit still only if it is their decision and that is why it is preferable to let children choose their activity. They generally know best what their body needs next. If they decide to look at a book or do a painting, their concentration can be quite intense.

Pretend that you are a three- to five-year-old now. Positive behavior is laughing after recovering from the shock of having a turtle put in your face by a teasing boy. Positive behavior is taunting when your best friend tries to hit you with paperwads, "Missed me! You missed me! Now you've gotta kiss me!" Positive behavior is pretending about a big banner seen across the street— "Yeh! It's a big net and it is winding around us. It's got us! We can't get away!"—and having your friends pretend to be caught in the struggle and laugh with you.

Positive behavior is singing into the stethoscope and finding out if you can hear yourself. Positive behavior is making skis out of the hollow wooden ramps from the block corner, putting your feet in, and walking, and having your buddies laugh at the new discovery that they hadn't seen before. Positive behavior is wanting to throw a rope over a tree limb, then having your friend hold a stool for you while you get high enough to succeed. Positive behavior is hanging by your knees on the jungle gym and having your friend say, "I didn't know you could do that!"

Positive behavior is seeing the chick come out of the egg, hearing the cow "moo" and sheep "baa"—all those things you've been told about but never experienced until now. Positive behavior is playing lotto and knowing which large card has the picture that is turned up on the small card.

A group of children sharing on the playground with pleasant voices and laughter have positive behaviors to remember.
(Kadena Air Force Base Child Care Center)

Positive behavior is feeling big enough to say "Bye" to Mom and really not caring if she leaves you and goes uptown to shop. Positive behavior is being weighed and having the teacher say "You've gained two pounds." Positive behavior is wrestling with your friend in the grass and knowing you can hold your own and that your friend won't really hurt you. Positive behavior is feeling relieved that Mom finally brought you some blue jeans like the ones worn by the older boys in the school. Positive behavior is being glad when Daddy surprises you by stopping by the school to visit for a while. Positive behavior is doing your job at clean-up time and having the teacher say, "Everybody was really a great help cleaning up today."

For young children, talking is more interesting than listening. As a teacher, you will frequently hear conversations that sound like two interviews run together on the tape recorder with both children talking and neither listening.

Talking, getting ideas across and telling someone how they feel are positive behaviors, like when Jeff whispered to Jimmy, "I like Peggy," or when Junior took Kenny's clay and Kenny shouted, "No! no!" Talking is asking for information, "Teacher, do the moon guys wear helmets, in case they crash on the moon?" Or talking is telling the teacher the most important news before someone else does—"I have a new baby sister." Talking is inviting a best friend, "I'm going to take you and Charlie to the rodeo this night." Talking and having someone to listen, talk back, and not say "shut up" are positive interactions for three- to five-year-olds.

Positive behavior is Carolyn and Bradley playing house and Bradley going over to Carolyn, putting his arms around her neck, hugging her and kissing her on the cheek. Positive behavior, too, is Carolyn just laughing as they go on playing.

Positive behavior is Clair painting a picture for each of her brothers, or Melanie taking a cookie home to her brother, "Cause he doesn't have any cookies."

Positive behavior is Cindy tying Marilyn's shoes when she didn't have any of her own to tie. And Keith swinging alone chanting

Swing, swing
My swing is swinging
Swing, swing
I'm making it go.

Positive or prosocial behavior is spontaneously sharing with another child. For example, on seeing a playmate's need, handing over a favorite sand shovel, then making do by digging with a tin can. Or, it's a three-year-old hugging a new boy when he feels sad and cries because his mother left him at school. Cooperation, altruism, empathy, and sympathy toward others grow as children mature. These prosocial behaviors are fostered when children are in a warm comfortable environment where prosocial behavior is modeled for them by adults whether they are parents or teachers.

Talk It Over

Describe your memory of a positive behavior of your own as a child. Who liked what you did? How did you feel?

Behavior has meaning, and your job as parents and teachers is to search for that meaning. What do all the things children do tell you about them? You can't draw conclusions from one or two incidents but must watch children over a period of time before drawing conclusions and making decisions about them.

A five-year-old quietly working on her drawing is a positive behavior.
(University of Illinois Child Development Laboratory)

Positive behavior is children cooperating, laughing, and shrieking in the game using parachute silk and sponge balls.
(Brigham Young University Early Childhood Laboratory)

When you sit down after school each day, or at home after the children are safely tucked in, and reflect on the day's events, you should ask yourself "What positive behavior did I observe today?" Then you can analyze what you did to help or hinder what happened. These can be lessons for the future.

Of course, problems should not be ignored—even problems may be positive behavior for some children. For example, you might have children who are quiet and withdrawn who then gradually grow to trust you and themselves and begin to stretch and strain the rules. These may be problems for you, but for those children the actions signify growth. What do you do? Don't try to control their behavior and push them back into their shell, for heaven's sake! Ignore them for a while unless someone's going to get hurt because through acts of self-expression these children may be working through a problem. The teacher's goal is to tailor the guidance to children's individual needs. Within a short time, these children will likely be willing to follow the rules again.

CONCLUSION

The samples of positive behavior in the preceding sections are only a few of the types and kinds you'll find in any group of healthy children. The various kinds of positive behavior are resources, the human resources that education attempts to develop. Friendship, love, laughter, curiosity, initiative, language, energy, skill, knowledge, empathy, and sympathy are exemplified. There are more examples that you will find. These are real children, normal children, doing normal things, and growing into more competent, worthy individuals each day.

REVIEW AND APPLICATIONS

Ten Ways to Appreciate Positive Behaviors

1. Identify children who appear healthy and rested. Note any correlation with positive behaviors.
2. Identify children who seem self-confident. Note any correlation with high levels of self-esteem.
3. Note children who have a quiet happiness as well as those who are overt in their expression of happiness.
4. Record examples of true sharing.
5. Record children's techniques for handling frustration positively.
6. Listen to language of children who have well-developed social skills, especially in free-play situations.
7. Note the handling of rules or limits by children who usually exhibit positive behaviors.
8. Note the behavior of children who have internalized school schedules and the location of equipment and supplies.
9. Observe the relationship between a parent and child when the child tends to exhibit many positive behaviors.
10. Note your own feelings after observing children relate positively to each other.

 Observations

1. Observe children in routines such as dressing, eating, and toileting. Record three instances when a child appears to feel satisfied with an accomplishment.
2. Observe children playing. Which children seem to be friends? What do they seem to contribute to each other? Explain.
3. Observe your case-study child and go over notes from previous observations to analyze the child's prosocial behaviors. Give specific examples of the child's behavior.

Applications

1. Assist with young children in a home or in a school and make two two-minute diary records (an account of everything they do or say) of two young children's activities. Analyze the records by listing each bit of behavior in a positive or negative column. What kinds of behavior do you find in each column? Trade lists with one of your classmates and observe whether you and your friend agree on the behavior rating. What are your conclusions?

2. Discuss with a parent or a teacher the kinds of behavior they consider positive or good. Summarize the conversation. Do you agree with their position? Discuss with your class.

3. Record three instances in which one child appeared to give another pleasure. What were the settings in which the behavior occurred? Describe.

4. Discuss with a teacher or a parent the positive behavior you have observed in a child. Report how the adult helped you complete your view of the child.

5. On a 1-to-5 scale rate your center on the Ten Ways to Appreciate Positive Behaviors. Discuss.

ADDITIONAL RESOURCES

Suggested Videotape

Building Self-Confidence   VHS   1/2 in.   Color   30 minutes 1988

Explores how parents and caregivers can develop self-confidence and a positive self-concept in young children. Work of Thelma Harms and Debby Cryer. Delmar Publishers, Customer Service, 2 Computer Drive West, Albany, NY 12212, 1–800-347-7707.

FOR FURTHER READING

Atkins, Cammie. "Writing: Doing Something Constructive," *Young Children,* 40:1, November 1984, 3–7.

Betz, Carl. "The Happy Medium," *Young Children,* 47:3, March 1992, 34–35.

Brazelton, T. Berry and Michael Yogman. *Affective Development in Infancy.* Norwood, NJ: Ablex, 1986.

Briggs, Dorothy Corkille. *Your Child's Self-Esteem: Step-by-Step Guidelines for Raising Responsible, Productive, Happy Children.* Garden City, NY: Doubleday & Company, 1975.

Cawlfield, Mildred E. "Velcro Time: The Language Connection," *Young Children,* 47:4, May 1992, 26–30.

Colon, Alice. "Giving Mrs. Jones a Hand: Making Group Storytime More Pleasurable and Meaningful for Young Children," *Young Children,* 47:3, March 1992, 14–18.

Greathouse, Betty, et al. "Suggestions from the Sunbelt: Increasing K-3 Teachers' Joy in Teaching," *Young Children,* 47:3, March 1992, 44–46.

Greenberg, Polly. "Promoting Positive Peer Relations," *Young Children,* 47:4, May 1992, 51–55.

Hildebrand, Verna. *Parenting: Rewards and Responsibilities.* New York: Glencoe/Macmillan/McGraw-Hill, 1994.

Kostelnik, Marjorie, Alice Whiren, and Laura Stein. "Living with He-Man: Managing Superhero Fantasy Play," *Young Children,* 41:4, May 1986, 3–9.

Melson, Gail F. and Alan Fogel. "The Development of Nurturance in Young Children," *Young Children,* 43:3, March 1988, 57–65.

Phillips, Carol Brunson. "Nurturing Diversity for Today's Children and Tomorrow's Leaders," *Young Children,* 43:2, January 1988, 42–47, 59–63.

Schiamberg, Lawrence. *Child and Adolescent Development.* New York: Macmillan Publishing Company, 1988.

Werner, Emmy E. "Resilient Children," *Young Children,* 40:1, November 1984, 68–72.

CHAPTER 19

Understanding Negative Behavior

Key Concepts

◆ Limits on Children's Negative Behavior
◆ Role of Parents Regarding Children's Negative Behavior
◆ Strategies for Coping with Negative Behavior

Timmy, age four, pounded abusively on the piano. He noted the approaching adult and quit. He said, "Teacher, I can play a song." "Good," she said. "Let me hear it." She listened a while, but had to leave to take care of another child. Timmy lost interest in the piano, and walked into the room where three jack-o-lanterns were displayed on the shelves. He rolled them off in one fell swoop. An adult arrived to care for Timmy and restore order to the mess he'd made.

Just a few instances like this one can make teachers feel that Timmy's whole day is spent in mischief. Teachers may even tend to avoid dealing with him, feeling quite ineffective and hoping that others will step in and cope with him. In this instance, the teachers knew that Timmy's behavior was interfering with the work of the school. He destroyed the other children's learning environment, he hurt children, and he damaged equipment, although minimally up to this point. Sadly enough, he was beginning to be a scapegoat in the group, for if anything troublesome happened it was easy for children to blame it on Timmy. Something had to be done.

MEANINGFULNESS OF BEHAVIOR

Timmy and other children who knock things over, hit children, and pound pianos abusively are telling us something by their behavior. They are saying as clearly as they know how, "All is not right in my world. Help me."

As Timmy's teacher, you would wisely ask, "Is this just a bad day for Timmy or does he do these things with regularity?" How would you proceed so you could help Timmy and get your class to function adequately again?

Being sure that children have adequate food served when they are hungry can help prevent negative behaviors.
(Howard University Preschool)

Observation

Observation is a first step in learning about and correcting troublesome behavior. As mentioned earlier, observation frequently is helpful in appreciating positive behavior—finding the "good" or strengths in troubled children. One teacher began making notes of Timmy's activities. Where did he play? With whom did he play? What "good" things did he do? When did the blow-ups occur? How often did he really blow up or disturb the learning environment? How often did he really hit others?

In Timmy's case, the teachers observed a very bright little boy. He knew answers to questions, and he quickly concluded from clues what was going to happen next. He was much more comfortable when close to an adult, especially the head teacher. She could give him attention and attend to others' needs at the same time more effectively than any of the other adults. The other children tended to be afraid of him.

When materials and curricula are designed to zero in on "problem," "disadvantaged," or "disabled" children, individualized observation is frequently neglected. A narrow focus on the "problem" may ignore the very strengths that will help a child to correct a difficulty. Whether the difficulty is minor or severe, the child's strengths should be assessed first.

Developmentally Appropriate Behavior

You should also watch closely and note whether the alleged "problem" is really a problem. Sometimes adults simply have expectations that are unrealistic for the age of the children or expect them to know something that no one has bothered to teach them.

Frequently parents, teachers, and others label a troublesome behavior as bad or negative, whereas, if the adults understood children well and knew how to plan for them, many of their behaviors would not be considered troublesome.

Knowing the typical developmental characteristics of children of various ages helps teachers, parents and caregivers plan for and prevent or at least creatively cope with what they label as troublesome behavior. Actually, most knowing people probably would not label many of the behaviors troublesome. There are typical characteristics for each age. This book has discussed various typical characteristics throughout. Some children will come closer to being typical than others. Some typical behaviors may also be troublesome, but adults should not view these behaviors as problems or make these behaviors worse by their treatment of the child. For example, toddlers are frequently chastised for saying "no" or for their intense curiosity, which makes them want to handle every loose object in sight. Or three-year-olds are scolded for their shyness or for hiding behind their parents' legs when someone, especially a stranger, approaches them. And four-year-olds are considered problems when they act brash, talk loudly, or make up fantastic stories.

At each of these stages a careful study of developmental characteristics of the age would help adults understand that certain behaviors are typical. Then they can challenge themselves to plan strategies for making the daily plans and environmental conditions fit in with children's typical behaviors such as their desire for motor freedom. The National Association for the Education of Young Children's popular publication on appropriate developmental practice and inappropriate practice helps to focus on desirable actions for teachers to take.[1]

Parent Conferences

The head teacher made an appointment to talk to Timmy's mother, whom the teacher knew from other conferences and home visits. They talked about her job, how things were going for Timmy and the baby, and so on. The teacher learned that Timmy's father had recently joined the Army. The teacher wondered how his absence was affecting Timmy. This question allowed the mother to open up about Timmy, including a discussion on the fact that he played with matches. She reported that the children's babysitter spent the afternoon watching TV and gave Timmy very little attention.

The teacher reported that the adults at school had observed some of the same behavior and told the mother that their present emphasis was on giving him the attention he seemed to be wanting so badly. The mother was pleased with the assessment that Timmy was a bright little boy who answered ques-

---

[1] Sue Bredekamp (ed.), *Developmentally Appropriate Practice in Early Childhood Programs Serving Children from Birth Through Age 8* (Washington, DC: NAEYC, 1987).

tions that other children couldn't answer. They talked about things she might do to help with the problem.

Parent conferences will be discussed in more detail in Chapter 21. One precaution wise teachers follow is to avoid blaming parents or putting them on the defensive regarding a child's behavior.

In a very real sense the child's troublesome behavior may not be a parent's responsibility. The behavior could be a reaction to the school—to teachers, children, the schedule, curriculum, crowding—or be related to other factors. Even if the basis of the problem is in the home the parents often cannot do anything about the behavior exhibited at school per se. Lecturing the child is often ineffective. The parents might do greater damage by punishing the child who doesn't behave properly. The child may be helped if the school and parents work together, for example, by securing counseling or appropriate assistance.

Teachers' Actions

After making notes for a number of days, the teachers met to decide what action to take. They agreed that the head teacher should stay near Timmy, stopping his problem behavior firmly if needed. Primarily, the head teacher was to involve him specifically in activities, and refer to him by name frequently, giving him the attention he seemed to crave. The head teacher also planned activities he particularly enjoyed and let him know that it was done because he liked those things. If Timmy wandered away, an assistant continued the activity with the group so the head teacher could stay near Timmy. Soon Timmy began acting up less. Other children became more accepting and less fearful of him. He was now able to show off his bright observations using his keen intelligence. The problems didn't cease, but improvement was evident.

A troubled child like Timmy must be helped, or the entire group will be affected. Some would say that Timmy was getting more than his share of the teacher's time, and that's true. Strangely enough, the other children were glad to have him more relaxed and under control. They didn't vie for the teacher's time when Timmy needed attention, but willingly accepted help from the other teachers.

Three things helped the situation: (1) observation to be sure of what was actually happening; (2) conference with the mother; (3) staff planning and carrying out of the plan; and (4) sincere respect for both the child and parents.

Inappropriate responses to a child's negative behavior are:

1. punishing a child verbally or physically;
2. giving a child a negative label;
3. shaming the child;
4. creating competition or comparing the child with others; and
5. threatening the child with expulsion or with calling the child's parents or some other authority figure.

Solving a Pushing Problem

One director reports how two teachers of a group of three-year-olds came to her for advice. Jerry was pushing children backward with both hands, then laughing as they lost their balance, fell, and cried. The teachers said they had tried a number of their usual techniques, such as isolating Jerry, talking to him, and staying near him. Still, when they were away from him he frequently turned to a child and pushed him or her backward quickly without apparent provocation. His derisive laughter following the event especially bothered the teachers.

The director went to the classroom to observe. She then called the parents to arrange a conference. The morning of the conference, the father brought Jerry with him. He was shocked when he, too, saw Jerry go to a circle of children and push over a child. He told the director how much he disapproved of the behavior he had just witnessed.

The director and father talked for a time attempting to understand Jerry's behavior. The director listened for a clue as to where the child might have learned the behavior. Finally it became clear. The family lived on a college campus where the parents were the houseparents for a group of college students. The college students frequently played with Jerry. They taught him to push them and then they would fall back and laugh. It was a game that they all enjoyed. Of course you see now where Jerry was very confused. A behavior that was highly rewarded in one setting was getting him into trouble in another setting, the group of young children.

The conscientious parents immediately instructed the college students to stop their pushing game. They were encouraged to play with a foam ball and develop various games around helping Jerry gain more motor skill. At the early childhood center Jerry was helped through close adult supervision to interact more gently with his peers at school. Little by little he quit pushing children and became more accepted by them. He was still too young for a talk about proper behavior to be an effective method of dealing with the problem.

With this example you can see how easily it might have been for adults to institute a plan that was unrealistic and one that would not have gotten at the root of Jerry's problem. Conferring with the parents helped both to clarify the problem and thus solve it. Fortunately, the director had a strong policy of conferring with parents.

TROUBLESOME BEHAVIOR

Negative or troublesome behavior needs to be discussed to keep it in the proper perspective. Regardless of a teacher's strong emphasis on cooperation and helpfulness, troublesome behavior often arises when a child cannot cope with limits set on behavior. As indicated elsewhere, these limits are (1) a child may not hurt others; (2) a child may not destroy another's learning environment; and (3) a child may not destroy property. Most troublesome behavior falls within one of these groups of limits.

 Talk It Over

What types of children's behaviors really bother you? Do you feel different if the child is a boy or a girl?

Behavior of Frustrated Children

Frustration is frequently the initiator of troublesome behavior, and it takes a considerable amount of time for a child to learn to cope with it. Frustrations arise (1) when the child is stopped or thwarted in some desired activity; for example, when the child is riding a tricycle and another child builds a barrier in the road; (2) when the child fails to get something that he or she has waited for; for example, when a child wanted to hold the bunny and a quick spring shower required a shift of children and activities indoors, the child was very frustrated because the promised "turn" was delayed; (3) when there are insufficient toys and equipment and the child doesn't see anything to use as a substitute for the desired one; (4) when the child attempts or is encouraged to attempt activities that are too difficult for that child; and (5) when a change in familiar routines, people, or activities occurs.

Response to Frustration

Children's responses to frustration vary just as they do for adults. Some children who have been frustrated may hang back or withdraw for a while, seemingly unable to redirect the forward momentum they had before being frustrated. This is explained by Piaget and other psychologists whose research and experience have shown that once young children make up their minds about a choice or a right course they get "centered" and find it very difficult, if not impossible, to think of another solution or to change direction. The adult's role is to calm the child, encourage the child's thinking, and help the child discover a different course of action.

The frustrated child often cries, gets angry, and may strike out, perhaps to get whatever is desired or just to relieve tension. Anger is a common response to frustration. Angry children may hit, push, bite, cry, scream, or have temper tantrums. Helping children learn to handle frustration is part of a teacher's or caregiver's job. Teaching some problem-solving skills may help.

Being sure that children rest when tired and don't become over fatigued can help prevent negative behaviors.
(Bill Mitcham, photographer)

Overcoming frustration is a normal part of every person's life. Although early childhood centers are set up to minimize frustration, it is neither possible nor desirable to eliminate it totally.

Coping with an Angry Child

When dealing with an angry child or any troubled child, remember to stay professionally calm. Responding to the child with anger often makes the situation worse. Keep your voice low and quiet, squat down to the child's level, and look the child directly in the eyes. You can remind the child of the limits he or she has overstepped, staying near to assure that the behavior stops. However, you should make it clear you are not rejecting the child personally. You may need to remove the child from the group with an explanation like, "Bobby needs some time to think over his behavior."

When the child begins to regain control you can suggest alternative play activity—based on your knowledge of what the child likes, does well, or finds rewarding. Making observations like, "The green tricycle is waiting for someone to ride it," or "The children in the sand box are making birthday cakes," often helps redirect children's interests and helps them learn to choose appropriate alternative activities. Avoid rushing the child back into the group situation where the problem occurred, however.

Keep in mind the need to avoid positively reinforcing angry outbursts, for the extra attention gained may become rewarding to some children, especially if such outcomes occur frequently. In some cases, a favorite activity or privilege must be denied if the outburst reoccurs. Thus, the children learn that there are consequences to their behavior.

Review the principles of indirect guidance you learned in Chapter 2 and consider how those principles can be applied to angry children to help avoid problem situations.

The following direct responses to children's angry behavior may help. Encourage children to talk about their feelings by saying, "I'll listen if you want to tell me about what is bothering you." Giving children an opportunity to act out their feelings may help. For example, role playing in activities such as playing in the housekeeping area or in the play yard, or in other activities that involve using small human figures at the clay table, in the sand box, or in the sawdust box, or by using puppets or dress-up clothing may help children to transfer feelings to imaginary persons. Fingerpainting, hammering clay or lumber, or pounding the punching bag may also help relieve tensions. A number of children's picture books may also be useful in helping children identify with characters in stories who feel the same way they do.

Caring about the individual child is essential even though you are concerned with the total group of children. Recall that one goal of guidance is for the child to develop into a self-guided individual. As a troubled child gains self-control the whole group benefits. One troubled child can make life miserable for an entire group at school, just as a troubled child at home can make a family miserable.

 Talk It Over

Describe how a parent you know coped with a troublesome child. Do not use names but try to figure out how the situation developed, how the parent felt, and how the child felt. What do you think are the long-range effects of the parent's method of dealing with the problem?

COPING WITH DIFFICULT CHILDREN

At times a child may seem "difficult" in general instead of having one particular behavior problem. Help may be found from those specialists who advise parents.

A difficult child is generally one who is easily distracted, and who adapts to change very slowly. The child's temperament may be the source of difficulty. According to Stanley Turecki, a psychiatrist who advises parents on children's behavior, it is important to describe the difficult situation in terms of behavior. Parents must be able to put their own feelings aside and deal objectively with the child as an outsider might. Turecki and Leslie Tonner recommend deciding on whether a "difficult" behavior is worth reacting to and perhaps focusing instead on changing three or four specific behaviors.[2] Some of the procedures recommended by Turecki and Tonner can be useful for teachers.

Teachers must learn to avoid confrontations with the child, and to set reasonable limits on essential behaviors. Like parents, teachers can help the child become more focused and more acceptable to the school situation.

Experience also shows that children generally become less difficult as they participate in early childhood programs. This likely occurs because teachers are trained to maintain the limits on behaviors that help children overcome what parents and others may label as "difficult." Also, teachers usually understand the developmental levels of children and set appropriate expectations for the children. That is, teachers expect a two-year-old to behave like a two-year-old, not a five-year-old, and set appropriate levels of expectations for each age. Teachers set the stage for childlike behavior and should guide parents in setting their home expectations for typical child behaviors.

Aggressive Behavior Toward Others

Aggressive behavior toward others is usually considered a troublesome behavior in the child development center. Aggression should be observed carefully before the caregiver attempts to correct it. What purpose does it serve for the child? When does it occur? With whom does it occur most frequently?

Aggression isn't necessarily all bad. The successful business executive is often thought of as one who is "aggressive enough to get the accounts," or one who acts without timidity. It can also mean that others are pushed aside in the process, however.

Infants occasionally hurt others by pushing too hard or striking another child with a hard toy held in a wobbly and uncertain grasp. This action is often a form of "Hello," a way of greeting for a child short on vocabulary. The striking is seldom done with any malice but more from lack of coordination. It isn't

---

[2] Stanley Turecki and Leslie Tonner, *The Difficult Child* (New York: Bantam Books, 1985), p. 168.

sensible to scold infants for these transgressions. We need only to keep them apart or free from toys or other objects that might be harmful. They are easily distracted, and a harmful toy can be spirited away quite easily and a soft one put in the child's hands instead.

Toddlers, too, are still short on vocabulary as well as social skills. They learn to defend their place with shrieks, which may sound like they are badly hurt when that usually isn't the case. The shrill shriek serves a purpose. It causes adults to come running and to scold anyone in sight, assuming the "poor baby" was the victim. This technique is successfully used on older siblings. Once the habit is established at home, you will see it practiced at school.

Physical aggression is usually disruptive in the child development center, and you have to protect the other children. One psychologist advised a mother to take a bubble bath whenever her three children bickered. The psychologist had said, "The children are manipulating you, seeing which one you'll side with. When they fight, go take a bubble bath." Unfortunately, for teachers, the solution is seldom that simple.

Hitting and Kicking. A young child seldom hits and kicks with malice. Often these children strike out because of frustration or because of some interference or assumed interference from another child. The adults must stop the hitting or kicking by restraining the child if necessary, and saying, "Ed, I can't let you hit me, it hurts" or "I can't let you kick Jenny, it hurts her." Though it is restraining, the comforting arm on the child's shoulders also reassures that you still like him or her. Continue to attend to the child until control is restored.

On occasion, one child may act as a bully and terrorize other children when adults' backs are turned. Parents have been known to withdraw their children from a school with such a child, and for good reason—their children become fearful of attending school. Teachers should be on the lookout for such occurrences and should listen to parents' complaints. A policy of calling to follow up on reasons for drop-outs might help reveal this problem.

Some children may not know how to deal with interferences other than by striking out. They can be helped to learn better ways. Teach them to say, "Jimmy, move over" or "Mike, I'm using that bike." You can also remind them that Jimmy or Mike may not know what they want when they hit instead of using words to let their wants be known.

What are helpful clues to look for? Carefully observe the situation when a particular child strikes out. Is it on the playground where there isn't much adult guidance? If so, provide the extra guidance. Is it when others are in too close proximity and interfere with the child's play? Then arrange to prevent overcrowded play areas. Does the child use words to express feelings? If not, you can say, "Tell Todd that you are using that block."

Is there too much pressure on the child at home or at school or both? Are activities scaled too high, making the child strain to achieve expected goals? Are activities of low interest or scaled below the child's ability, leaving him bored and unchallenged? If these situations exist, work to reduce the pressures or to generate interest in something new or worthwhile both at school and out-side the school.

Does the child seem tired or hungry? Fatigue often accompanies out-bursts of aggression. The child may not be getting sufficient rest or food. There may be too many children in the group, contributing to crowding, noise, and consequent fatigue. This may also be true of the family situation. Adjustments can be made in mealtimes and planned rest and naptimes. Parents can be alerted to help with the problem. However, teachers should be sure that par-ents won't harshly discipline the child. They may need suggestions for positive responses to the problem.

What can adults do about hitting or kicking? First, stop the behavior without blame or punishment—neither of these stops negative behavior in the long run. Second, make adjustments in indirect guidance, arranging the space, schedule, routine, and so on in ways that may more readily suit the children. Third, recognize the child's strengths and good behavior and avoid making issues over transgressions of rules. In other words, give the child attention for "good" works, not for "bad." Fourth, give the child opportunities to talk about feelings. Fifth, find a diversion for energy.

One diversion for hitters is an inflated plastic clown that the child can try to knock down repeatedly as it bounces back. Or boxing gloves can be used to hit a bag. Carpentry is a good outlet for children who have aggressive feelings. The pounding may provide a good emotional release if children are allowed to hammer away before some incident triggers hostility. Of course, you can't give children tools when they are angry until they are capable of working alone awhile with adult supervision.

Teaching a child to say "I'm sorry" rarely does any good toward stopping aggressive behavior. A child can say "I'm sorry" and really have no feeling for what he or she is saying.

Biting and Spitting. Biting and spitting are actions that are often resorted to in moments of extreme frustration. A child who feels weak, as far as other forms of defense are concerned, may bite or spit or both. First, watch closely to see that no one gets hurt. Then observe the occasions when the child bites or spits. Determine whether there is something or someone particularly involved. Try to alleviate those situations. Some spitters have been helped by having them spit in the toilet until they are "through." Tell them, "When you are through spitting come out and we'll have no more spitting."

Verbal Aggression. Verbal aggression is generally preferable to physical aggression. You often hear children say, "I don't like you," "You're stupid," or "No! No! No! I told you I wasn't playing with you, I'm busy." Any of these chil-dren could have chosen to hit a companion but clobbered him verbally instead. Fortunately, these kinds of disputes generally blow over quickly, and children resume playing together.

Teachers need to listen to, but seldom need to stop, verbal aggression. In fact, they should encourage children to talk out their rage instead of striking out. Teachers can say, "John, talk instead of hit. Tell Dean you don't want him to take your blocks." In addition, you can verbally reflect the child's feeling, saying, "It makes you very *angry* when Dean takes your blocks. You *really* don't like it at all." This accepting, rather than judgmental ("You shouldn't hit Dean"), attitude helps children cope with their feelings of anger. In the meantime you also stop Dean from infringing on John's territory.

Teasing. Teasing is a form of verbal aggression that develops in the fourth and fifth years as children become more skillful with words. Older siblings often tease younger ones, a form of aggression that wouldn't guarantee punishment by parents, as hitting would. Providing other means of achieving attention usually solves the problem.

Name-Calling. Name-calling, harsh language, and swearing may also be considered aggressive behavior. It can be a habit learned at home or in the neighborhood. A double standard is often seen in adults who swear but feel it should be stopped in children. Of course, it is useful to teach the child some new words to replace swearing. However, if children hear the language at home and if it is common even in college dormitories, then teachers should attempt to determine what the language means to the child before trying to squelch it. Clearly, the words do not mean the same things to the children using them that they do to adults. Guidance offered before tempers flare is usually the best solution. Explaining, "These words are words I don't use. Can you think of words like we use at school, so I'll understand?" may help redirect the problem. It may be surprising how young children adapt to the standards of the school. One driver noted that the children in the station wagon used pretty strong language en route to and from school, but seldom were the same words heard at school. The driver had not heard anyone correct the children; they just adapted to not using the same words in school.

Destroying the Learning Environment

Acts destructive of the learning environment are disturbing to the children and to the teacher. You should arrange your rooms to help avoid accidental interference with the learning environment. Blocks arranged out of the traffic lanes, puzzles on a table, books in a quiet nook—these are the learning environments for children using those materials. Children thoroughly enjoy knocking down blocks, but it really isn't fair for anyone but the builder to do the task. Therefore, good guidance calls for redirecting wandering children who might interfere with others' projects. They usually need something to do themselves. There is really no substitute for a good, rich program that keeps children so busy with their own activities that they don't have time to interfere with others. If a child wants to be with a child who is already at work, then positive verbal guidance can be used to help him or her enter the play in an acceptable manner.

Destroying Property

Respect for property should be learned, or else there will not be toys for other days. Acts of aggression and neglect with respect to equipment should not be allowed. Of course, there is normal wear and tear on equipment. Paint gets chipped and toys get broken, for example, but reasonable concern for driving tricycles without wrecking them or driving them into the walls can be taught. Children who fail to comply with rules simply are not allowed on the tricycles until they agree to follow the rules. Rough play usually occurs in older children who are capable of understanding the rules and the consequences.

Children can develop pride in their building and playground by helping to keep it neat and clean. They can go on litter hunts to pick up the accumulation of materials that blow in or are left around. Helping children appreciate beauty may serve as a countermeasure to those who may disregard the environment and destroy it.

Attention-Seeking

Children, like Timmy in our opening anecdote, may display multiple problems. Besides striking out, Timmy was an attention-seeker.

Children who behave like Timmy may be resorting to unacceptable behavior to get attention—negative attention being better than no attention at all. They may seek help when they could do a task themselves. They may seek reassurance. Their behavior clearly says, "I want you to notice me." Using children's names frequently in working with them helps a child know you are talking to and noticing him or her. Greeting children individually each day with special little conversations about something that others don't know about, such as something the teacher learns on a home visit, helps individualize teaching. Keeping groups small so individual attention is the rule, not the exception, also helps.

Denying attention does not improve attention-seeking behavior. Children must be allowed legitimate ways to shine and increase their self-confidence in order to cast off their attention-seeking devices.

Quiet and Withdrawn Behavior

Quiet and withdrawn behavior may be the most difficult to deal with. In large groups, quiet and withdrawn children may actually move through the day almost without notice because the assertive and aggressive children receive all the teacher's time and energy. In such groups, if you were to ask a teacher for a character sketch of each child, the quiet and withdrawn children are the ones most teachers would likely "forget" or have little to say about.

One quiet child's mother said, "I'd jump for joy if my little girl would stamp her feet and yell, 'No!'" The mother truly seemed to want the child to be more of an extrovert. Perhaps that was not in the child's nature, but the teachers did notice that the child gained confidence as skills and interests grew through the year.

Another child, Mary, was frequently an observer when the other children were active. She was seen, for instance, watching the children at the carpenter's bench for over fifteen minutes. She sat nearby, watching them intently and laughing at their jokes. Some adults wanted to force her to participate, but

Being sure that children have enough personal attention can help avoid negative behaviors. (Kansas State University Early Childhood Laboratory)

she was extremely stubborn if pressed to do something she didn't want to do. Consequently, a more personal method of helping her participate was designed. There was no doubt that she was learning as she watched. Her mother cared for several babies in a mobile home, so it was easy to see why quiet behavior was approved by the parents.

Removing pressure to do certain activities and the reassuring presence of the same adult usually help the withdrawn child cope with the school situation. Protection may be necessary to keep others from approaching a withdrawn child too quickly.

Some of these children may need help from their parents in making the initial adjustment to the school. Parents may have to bring them for only short periods for several weeks or stay in the classroom with them until they adjust.

Lying and Fantastic Tales

Lying and telling fantastic tales are closely related. The young child sometimes denies doing a misdeed that at the moment of doing may not have been remembered as wrong. The adult may contribute to lying of this sort by the way questions are asked. The child's natural inclination is self-defense; therefore, when asked, "Did you dump out the puzzle?" the child may say, "No." He or she may also report that someone else did it, noting your apparent displeasure. Some "Who did it?" questions simply don't matter that much.

Young children often spin fanciful tales. Some may be designed to get attention or make the child feel powerful. Others may be wish fulfillments, as in the case of the fatherless child who told many stories in which his father played heroic roles. Sometimes it helps to remind a child "That is one of your pretend stories, isn't it?" to keep reality in check. There seems little reason to make a young child admit a story is a lie.

Tattletales

Tattletales are troublesome to some teachers. Children who tell on other children are often unpopular with their peers. Parents of a tattletale may be encouraging tattletaling by having older siblings be in charge of younger ones. There are obvious times when adults appreciate having problems pointed out to them that they may be unaware of. Hence, there is some ambivalence and resulting confusion regarding a child's telling what peers or siblings are involved in.

One response to a tattletale child is "Don't worry, I'll take care of Mary, if you take care of . . . " (using the child's own name). However, if you respond immediately by going to check on Mary, then the tattletale will be rewarded for reporting. One thing that can be said for the tattletales is that they know the rules and can verbalize them, which may indicate a higher level of conscience than some of their peers have. The adult should help these children develop more rapport with other children and to seek the teacher's attention in other ways.

Thumbsucking, Nailbiting, and Masturbating

Thumbsucking, nailbiting, and masturbating are all habits that may grow out of tension and a need for comfort. These may be devices that relax the child for sleeping. Rather than attempt to deal with the behavior, you should look for the cause of the tension in the child's life. Stopping one behavior usually results in starting another unless the pressure that is causing it is removed. Shaming or calling these behaviors naughty and the like is usually counterproductive. Some other points regarding masturbating are discussed in Chapters 1 and 8.

CONCLUSION

These are some of the kinds of problem behavior that teachers will see in classes of normal children. Behavior deviations tell us that a child needs help with a problem. Many behavior problems cannot be ignored, for they interfere with other children's safety and learning. The first step is for the teacher to observe the child over a period of time to be sure that an act is typical for that child. Through discussions with the parents, a teacher can learn whether the behavior occurs at home, what the parents are doing about it, and perhaps also whether home factors are contributing to the tension that may be part of the problem.

It is unfair to conclude immediately that the parents are at fault for the child's troublesome behavior. Erroneous conclusions can be drawn based on too little information and it is certainly unwise to make premature judgments. While deep psychological problems may be at the root, such an analysis and corrective therapy are outside the domain of most child development center teachers. However, talking with parents is essential, and teachers must learn how to counsel parents so they feel competent and willing to deal with the child's problems instead of resentful and defensive. It is very irresponsible for teachers to allow a problem to persist over a period of months without conferring with parents.

Following a careful study, the teacher will attempt to set the stage for the positive behavior the child can perform to replace negative behavior. A coordinated plan made with other staff members is desirable to avoid working at cross purposes. Helping the child to find outlets and to talk over behavior may be helpful.

In cases of extreme deviance, the teachers should get in touch with behavior advisors in a guidance or mental health clinic. Such a professional might visit the school and offer the staff advice for coping with a troubled child. Persons skilled in behavior modification might be called in with parental knowledge and consent.

An inventory of the possible assistance available in the community should be made before notifying parents. Once the strongest and most reliable source of help has been located, then referral recommendations can be made in a conference with the parents. Teachers must provide both assured and delicate guidance to the parents if the child is truly expected to get treatment from the agency. Discussing problem behavior in their children is often very difficult for parents, and taking advice from a variety of agencies does not come easily. Teachers should be very much aware of this fact.

REVIEW AND APPLICATIONS

Twelve Ways to Cope with Troublesome Behavior

1. Remember that the goal is to teach self-control.
2. Keep professionally calm using a quiet voice and manner.
3. Set and enforce fair limits consistently.
4. Stop, then redirect troublesome behavior.
5. Observe and record what, when, and with whom a child has problems.

6. Set expectations at an appropriate level for the age and experience of the child.
7. Teach the child ways to cope with frustration by using problem-solving techniques.
8. Help a child verbalize statements to use in response to frustration.
9. Plan activities that allow children to play out their feelings.
10. Check out a child's health, hunger, and fatigue and alleviate any problem.
11. Consult with parents and encourage their helpful assistance.
12. Secure outside opinions regarding troublesome behavior.

 Observations

1. Observe three children busy at play. Record instances where the adult intervenes to stop a negative behavior. What values appear to be behind the reasons for stopping the behavior?
2. Recall other observations along with the present one and report on children who appear to have sufficient negative behavior to warrant special attention. Describe the behavior. Write an essay on recommendations you would make for these children if you were responsible for them.
3. From your previous notes, analyze the negative behavior your case-study child has exhibited. Tally the number of instances of each behavior. Be sure to include any insights you have gained regarding the causes, timing, or other characteristics of these behaviors.

Applications

1. Discuss with a parent or a teacher the kinds of behavior considered negative or "bad." Summarize the conversation. Do you agree with that position?
2. Help with a group of children in a classroom or on a play yard. What are the kinds of behavior you find yourself stopping? What is your basis for deciding to stop a particular kind of behavior?
3. From your memory, recall the types of behavior that your own teachers or parents labeled as "naughty." Can you remember any feelings you had then about the way people reacted to such behavior? Explain.
4. Observe or attempt to recall instances of behavior that teachers stop. What appear to be their reasons for doing so? Discuss the matter with them if feasible.
5. Report on children who appear to have sufficient negative behavior to warrant special attention. Describe the behavior to your class. If

these children were your responsibility, what would you do to help them?

6. Using the Twelve Ways to Cope with Troublesome Behavior, rate your center on a 1-to-5 scale. Discuss.

FOR FURTHER READING

Christophersen, Edward R. *Beyond Discipline: Parenting That Lasts a Lifetime*. Kansas City, MO: Westport Publishers, Inc., 1990.

Elkind, David. *The Hurried Child*. Reading, MA: Addison-Wesley, 1981.

Elkind, David. *The Mis-education of the Preschool Child*. Reading, MA: Addison-Wesley, 1987.

Feeney, Stephanie. "The Aggressive-Child," *Young Children*, 43:2, January 1988, 48–51.

Greenberg, Polly. "Learning Self-esteem and Self-discipline Through Play." *Young Children*, 44:2, January 1989, 28–31.

Honig, Alice Sterling. "The Shy Child," *Young Children*, 42:4, May 1987, 54–64.

Honig, Alice Sterling. "Stress and Coping in Children (Part 1)," *Young Children*, 41:4, May 1986, 50–63.

Honig, Alice Sterling. "Stress and Coping in Children (Part 2)," *Young Children*, 41:4, July 1986, 47–59.

Hymes, James, Jr. *Behavior and Misbehavior*. Englewood Cliffs, NJ: Prentice-Hall, Inc., 1955.

Jacobs, Nancy L. "Unhappy Endings," *Young Children*, 47:3, March 1992, 23–27.

Marion, Marian. *Guidance of Young Children*. Columbus, OH: Merrill/Macmillan, 1991.

Meddin, Barbara J. and Anita L. Rosen. "Child Abuse and Neglect: Prevention and Reporting," *Young Children*, 41:4, May 1986, 26–30.

NAEYC. "The Difficult Child," *Young Children*, 43:5, July 1988, 60–68.

NAEYC. "Discipline: Are Tantrums Normal?" *Young Children*, 43:6, September 1988, 35–40.

Osborn, D. Keith and Janie Dyson Osborn. *Discipline and Classroom Management*. Athens, GA: Education Associates, 1978.

Schiamberg, Lawrence. *Child and Adolescent Development*. New York: Macmillan Publishing Company, 1988.

Soderman, Anne. "Dealing with Difficult Young Children," *Young Children*, 40:5, July 1985, 15–20.

Solter, Aletha, "Understanding Tears and Tantrums," *Young Children*, 47:4, May 1992, 64–68.

Turecki, Stanley, and Leslie Tonner. *The Difficult Child*. New York: Bantam Books, 1985.

CHAPTER 20

Mainstreaming Special Needs Children

Key Concepts

◆ Mainstreaming
◆ Obligations of Governments
◆ Resources for Teachers and Parents

"I'd like to ride in your wheelchair," said four-year-old Ervin.
"When can I have my turn, Joey?" asked Beverly.
"Erv," decided Joey, "you go down to the jungle gym and back, then it's Beverly's turn." Joey was in the midst of a new and popular sport in this group of four-year-olds as he allowed each one to take a ride in his wheelchair.

Integrating a special needs child into a group of children usually brings forth new perceptions to both children and adults. While a wheelchair may seem confining to some, it was a novelty to the children in the classroom above, and they wanted a ride. Children may react the same way to crutches and special chairs and tables that other disabled children require. They will want to experiment with them. Such explorations may help the child with special needs adjust.

Joey's leg had been broken and put into a bulky cast a few weeks earlier. After a few days at home he was ready to resume his normal activities. His parents consulted with the teachers and it was agreed that Joey could return to his early childhood program.

EARLY CHILDHOOD EDUCATION PROGRAMS FOR SPECIAL NEEDS CHILDREN

Thousands of people like Joey join the ranks of the disabled each year. Says one spokesperson, "Our minority is one that does not discriminate. Young or old, black or white, rich or poor, you can join up anytime. Usually joining up is based upon no decision on the part of the individual, it just happens. Most have a dysfunction in only one part of their body and are not totally disabled, that is, they simply have a few different characteristics." Joey, for example,

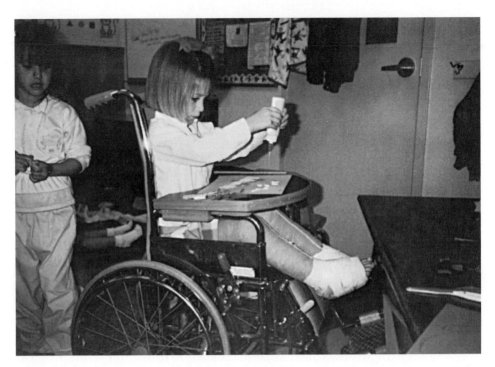

Special needs children can be served by early childhood programs when staff members understand that the children have special needs, but also that their needs are similar to all children.
(Methodist Hospital Child Care Center, Lubbock, Texas)

had his leg broken when a large object fell on it while he was helping clean a garage. Other children may be disabled from birth or a part of their body may become dysfunctional from disease. Many children with special needs are gradually being integrated into on-going classes with so-called normal children in a process called *mainstreaming*. Mainstreaming requires that a disabled child be placed in the "least restrictive environment."

The Laws

Mainstreaming was incorporated into the Head Start program in 1972. At the time, 10 percent of the Head Start spaces were made available to disabled children through the federally funded Head Start program, which was founded in 1965 to provide early childhood education for children of the poor. During the 1970s, state after state passed legislation for support of education for special needs children. Some states designated special attention for babies from birth whereas others designated special care for children three years of age and up.

In 1986, the 99th Congress passed new legislation that increased federal monetary assistance to states and local educational agencies to enable them to provide free appropriate public education to all disabled children aged 6–17. At that time 27 states were still serving disabled children starting at age three and up. Many parents and specialists felt that age three is too late to begin services for disabled youngsters. Thus, Congress also passed P.L. 99–457 to authorize new Federal assistance to states for the development and delivery of educational and related services to all disabled children from birth to school age. Additional support was given to educate the deaf in P.L. 99–371.[1]

The Americans with Disabilities Act (ADA), passed in 1990, applies to all agencies dealing with children. According to attorney John Surr, early childhood directors, teachers, and policy boards have special responsibility for applying ADA. The hope is that programs serving disabled youngsters will be improved and increased. The act also applies to employees.[2]

The Schools

Some community agencies have been overwhelmed on discovering the actual needs in their area. In November 1975 the National Association for the Education of Young Children passed a resolution calling for the association's commitment to improving programs for disabled youngsters. Since that time, NAEYC has assisted with in-service workshops, literature, and programs designed to assist teachers and parents in many aspects of mainstreaming. Although mainstreaming is successful, there are still individuals who cannot be served in a regular classroom or even by parents at home.

The National Association for the Education of Young Children (NAEYC) stipulates in its center accreditation guidelines that a lower staff-child ratio, specialized training, and special environmental arrangements and equipment may be needed for children with special needs.[3]

ADMISSION TO PREPRIMARY GROUPS

Joey's admission to the four-year-old group was fairly simple. He was already enrolled and a popular member of the class. The teachers were well acquainted with Joey's parents so they readily understood the parents' interest in getting Joey back on a routine of involvement with interesting activities and friends. "He's a bear at home," says his father. "He's bored without his friends around." With some minor adjustments by parents and staff, Joey became quite self-sufficient. As noted in the opening anecdote, Joey's friends envied him—at least momentarily—for his new mobile toy.

---

[1] Library of Congress. *Major Legislation of the Congress* (Washington, DC: Congressional Research Service, November 1986), MLC–015.

[2] John Surr, "Public Policy Report: Early Childhood Programs and the Americans with Disabilities Act (ADA)," *Young Children,* July 1992, 47:5, pp. 18–21.

[3] Sue Bredekamp, *Accreditation Criteria and Procedures of the National Academy of Early Childhood Programs.* (Washington, DC, NAEYC, 1991), p. 21.

The example of Joey makes an important point in considering the admission of disabled youngsters to preprimary programs. Many children have a dysfunction in only one part of the body, while the other body parts function well—often above par. Therefore, the stereotype of the disabled with total disabilities is often untrue.

Children with special needs may range in need from a child like Joey whose condition is temporary to one with a predictably permanent condition. There is speculation that there will be many entrants into early childhood programs requiring special attention due to the increasing numbers of mothers who used crack cocaine during pregnancy, causing prenatal damage. A researcher, Rist, offers insight into this forthcoming problem. Early identification is expected to be a key to treatment for these children. Many are abandoned by their birth mothers and reside in foster care. These children will need lots of attention, structure, and emotional support.[4]

Joey's teachers had the advantage of knowing Joey before his disability and thus were not afraid of his "hidden" problems. They knew his strengths—his drive for self-sufficiency, his brightness, friendliness, curiosity, language facility, and so on. They were sure that Joey would easily become involved in the many activities of the classroom even though he could not run and climb like the typical four-year-old. Lucky for Joey, too, the facility was easily accessible by wheelchair, making it unnecessary for adults to lift him.

Fetal Alcohol Syndrome (FAS) is a mental retardation condition that is seen with increasing frequency by early childhood teachers. The brain damage is caused by mothers' alcohol consumption during pregnancy. The book *The Broken Cord* by Michael Dorris is a source of excellent descriptions of a FAS child's behavior. Dorris, unknowingly, adopted a FAS child. He writes with sensitivity, describing a parent's search for help as he comes to recognize the child's disability. He tells of the early childhood teachers, also uninformed about FAS, who thought the child would outgrow the condition.[5]

In addition, a number of children with chronic illnesses, including AIDS (acquired immune deficiency syndrome), will require the support of specialized early childhood caregivers and teachers in the future. Potential teachers who wish to work with special children should realize that there appears to be a shortage of teachers prepared to work with these youngsters. Teaching children with special needs is recognized by the Council for Early Childhood Professional Recognition for the Child Development Associate (CDA) program. They have established caregiver/teacher's competencies for helping the CDA candidates learn about special needs children who will need their attention. Children with second language needs are also given attention.[6]

---

[4] Marilee C. Rist, "The Shadow Children: Preparing for the Arrival of Crack Babies in School," *Research Bulletin*, July 1990, pp. 1–6. Reprinted in Karen Paciorek and Joyce Munro, *Early Childhood Education 92–93* (Guilford, CT: The Duskin Publishing Group, Inc. 1992), pp. 15–19.

[5] Michael Dorris. *The Broken Cord*. New York: Harper Perennial Books, 1989.

[6] For details, see Council for Early Childhood Professional Recognition, Two volumes: *Preschool Caregivers* and *Infant/Toddler Caregivers*. Washington, DC: Author, 1992, various pages in each volume.

Being part of a group involved
with a new toy is important to a
special needs child.
(Michigan State University Child
Development Laboratory)

Individual Assessment

Knowing the individual needs of each child is essential when considering admission of a child with a disabling condition to an early childhood program. The total situation—available staff, facility, program, and ratios of adults to children—must be considered when such a child is admitted. In some states, a special consultant may be available to interpret to an early childhood staff what the child's needs will be. The consultant can help the staff identify the child's strengths and abilities so the teachers can build an appropriate program for the child.

It is important to avoid assuming that one disability means total incapacity. When admitting a child who is unknown to the staff it can generally be assumed that the child has some personal strengths and abilities that will help compensate for the disabling conditions. For example, blind children usually have extraordinary sensory acuity in hearing and touching. Deaf children may have only a hearing problem, and may make good use of their other senses. Generally each child will be able to laugh and cry, love and be loved, and many will be able to run and climb.

 Talk It Over

What experiences have you had with a disabled child? How have these experiences made you feel about the way the child is being treated and educated?

One-to-one adult guidance can encourage a child to learn.
(Michigan State University Child Development Laboratory)

Individualized Programs

Individualization of programs is a hallmark of all high-quality early childhood education programs. Teachers typically plan a wide range of activities allowing every child to choose those that suit personal tastes or respond to an "internal drummer." Being aware of the developmental ladder, early childhood teachers who find a language-delayed or a language-advanced child simply interact with and plan for that child to help move him or her to a higher rung on the developmental ladder. Certainly, rigid age standards are not followed. All early childhood educators have had experience with children whose success in one area encourages them to pursue other areas. For example, shy children may come out of their shell when they discover music or painting. Sharing and taking turns increase as children learn words to express their needs. From this routine practice early childhood teachers are generally quite skillful and sensitive as they help special needs children who join the mainstream in an ongoing group. In fact, early childhood educators often handle the disabled child so successfully that the diagnostic personnel sometimes begin to question their diagnosis. In mainstreaming, the teachers simply extend the range of "normality" as they meet individual needs of each child.

ADVANTAGES OF MAINSTREAMING

Advantages of mainstreaming are real for all children—disabled or not—as well as for teachers, parents, and the community. Usually only one or two children with special needs are incorporated into a group. In some cases a special aide is hired when special funding permits.

First, children without disabilities serve as models for special needs children to imitate. Motivation to practice the skills children learn increases as a child observes and imitates peers. For example, disabled children will want to move or move faster, to talk or talk more clearly, to try an activity when others seem to be enjoying it, rather than just watching.

Second, the classroom that contains special needs children is more like society at large—there are more people with more diversity. This enriched experience gives children preparation for functioning more effectively and fairly in the larger social system.

Third, normal children are often quick to spot the special child's strengths and to give positive responses to the child for those strengths. For example, children may recognize a good art project done by a disabled child. They may enjoy the fact that the child sings well, laughs heartily at their stories, or tells stories they enjoy. They let others know when they are pleased.

Fourth, children and adults who become well acquainted with special needs children overcome their fear and apprehension because they are different. Such familiarization can usually be expected to carry over into later contacts with disabled people making children more accepting and friendly.

Fifth, parents of special needs children can gain helpful support from sharing with other understanding parents. Many may be painfully isolated, not feeling comfortable taking their children where other parents typically take their children—to stores, churches, parks, or school events. Through the parent involvement activities of a high-quality early childhood program, parents often discuss their joys and disillusions with parenthood. Parents of a disabled child may learn that parents with normal children have their problems, too, and thus reduce some of their own guilt feelings. As the child spends some part of each day in school, all parents receive needed relief. Such help is especially important to parents of special needs children, who often have had continuous responsibility for their child over several years, perhaps without the helpfulness of relatives and neighbors that parents of normal children receive. Thus the admission of a child into the early childhood program allows parents some needed rest and much needed support. Parents who are closely involved in the school program may learn new techniques of dealing with their child if the staff explains, demonstrates, and encourages their active participation. Fathers as well as mothers benefit from this important involvement.

Sixth, teachers will gain a new area of experience when they become involved with mainstreaming. Enriching their professional lives by reading, attending workshops, and consulting specialists—psychologists, physicians, and education specialists—will broaden teachers' skills for working with all children. Many teachers confess to early attitudes of fear and prejudice that they have outgrown. Most have become devoted supporters of mainstreaming and have evolved a love for a wider group of children. Teachers say they have learned to become perceptive of the progress made by special needs children and readily rejoice with those children and their parents.

For some teachers there is a heavy emotional and physical drain as they attempt to give so much time and energy to a number of children with widely differing needs and, also, to their parents. Parents may have repeatedly been discouraged by other agencies, so it takes teachers a lot of time and painstaking effort to build their confidence. Coordinating and giving service to children and parents tax a teacher's total strength. Early education systems must realize the maximum load a teacher can handle. All young children, and especially children with special needs, require an early educational program that guides and supports the parents as well as the child if the maximum good is to be achieved. Any plan for the child must include plans for the parents. This interaction with parents requires additional time and skills on the part of the teachers.

Seventh, the community, including the country as a whole, also gains from mainstreaming. Trained and self-confident disabled children can more readily take their place in the larger society. They may move beyond city and state borders, making a case for federal funding. Trained and educated children will become self-sufficient contributing citizens—even substantial taxpayers. Disabled individuals are gradually being trained and admitted into many areas where they perform well at jobs that are of value to society. Programs for disabled youngsters are expensive, but far less so than the expense of institutionalizing children for a lifetime as was the practice only a few years back. Certainly the new approach is more humane and helps to build a more just society.

Participating in a cookie baking project is an enjoyable experience.
(Michigan State University Child Development Laboratory)

GUIDING CHILDREN IN A MAINSTREAMED CLASSROOM

Basically, all children need to be valued as individuals. They need to be given love and acceptance, to be encouraged to grow in independence, and to have worthwhile learning activities planned for them. Therefore, guiding young children with disabilities is essentially the same as guiding any other children.

Knowing the range of behaviors to expect of normal children is a basic first requirement for guiding a special child. This knowledge helps teachers set realistic standards. A skill, for example, is best organized in sequential steps rather than according to age if such children are to gain the most.

Disabling conditions are varied and wide ranging; therefore, teachers must expect to get specific information and advice from special consultants.[7] They should be able to depend on diagnostic sources for suggestions of the type of program and guidance the child needs. One teacher may learn certain behavior modification techniques, for example. Others may need to learn sign language in order to work with a deaf child. Some trained specialists are being funded through special state and federal funds and a director of early childhood programs should seek that support when becoming involved in mainstreaming.

When introducing a new child with special needs to a group of children, all the points suggested in Chapters 1, 2, and 3 apply. That is, indirect guidance, direct guidance, and suggestions for introducing a new child can all be adapted in a logical fashion to serve the child. Also, be prepared to talk over with the children the differences between themselves and the special needs child, differences that they will note immediately. Help them learn to relate to the new child constructively and quickly. Such comments as, "Yes, Barry has a brace on his leg. The brace makes his leg stronger so he can move around." Or, "Rita is blind. She learns about things by listening with her ears and feeling with her hands. You can tell her where toys are. She'll understand." Statements should be short, honest, and restated when children ask.

The early childhood classroom and play yard can be adapted with railings, ramps, and hold bars. When presenting learning materials teachers can creatively adjust these to the needs of the special child. Preparations may be more specific than open-ended until you know how the child usually responds.

---

[7] Excellent information on particular disabling conditions can be found in a 1978 series of eight publications published by the Administration of Children, Youth and Families, Department of Health, Education, and Welfare, Washington, DC 20402. They are titled *Mainstreaming Preschoolers*:

Children with Emotional Disturbance, Miriam G. Lasher et al.
Children with Health Impairments, Alfred Healy et al.
Children with Hearing Impairment, Rita Ann LaPorta et al.
Children with Learning Disabilities, Alice H. Hayden et al.
Children with Mental Retardation, Eleanor Whiteside Lynch et al.
Children with Orthopedic Handicaps, Shari Stokes Kieran et al.
Children with Speech and Language Impairments, Jacqueline Liebergott et al.
Children with Visual Handicaps, Lou Alonso et al.

Participating in a creative project is fun for special needs children. (Nazarene Child Care Center, Lansing, Michigan)

For example, you may present a simple form board puzzle and see what happens, next choose a puzzle with four or five pieces, and continue increasing the difficulty until the child is challenged. Or present one large crayon and paper for drawing, and seeing that the child can use these, add more colors and materials to be used in the art projects. Advice from parents and consultants can be helpful guides as you develop new ways to present learning materials to children.

PARENTAL SUPPORT

Admitting a disabled child to an ongoing group may call for some explanation to parents of the present enrollees. The anecdote about Joey at the beginning of this chapter could help parents handle the admission of a disabled child. You may need to reassure parents that the quality of the program will not diminish as the teachers take on this added responsibility. Perhaps teachers can report that an extra assistant or two has been added to the staff, which will actually benefit all the children.

Special efforts will be necessary to bring all parents together as a supportive group for the benefit of the total program. Such effort is discussed in Chapter 21, and it applies equally to programs which include children with special needs. Parent education is one benefit of parental involvement, but another outcome is that, when acquainted, parents can become support persons for each other and realize their mutual interests and concerns.

 Talk It Over

What additional pressures are on parents who have a special needs child compared to those with typical children? How do you think the other children in the family are affected when a sibling is disabled?

As more and more parents demand equal education for their disabled children, teachers and directors may become involved in helping them secure the public funding required to serve them in early childhood centers. Oversights have occurred; in some legislation services were mandated for children starting at birth or at age three but funds were not allotted until kindergarten age. Through negotiations some parents were able to get funds for children younger than kindergarten age. Some parents have learned to become strong advocates for children.

Frequently, a diagnostic panel meets with parents to discuss the placement of a special needs child. Early childhood teachers may be called upon to lend their professional experience to that panel, or accompany parents as a friendly supporter. Parents frequently find such a meeting extremely difficult and appreciate a familiar teacher's presence.

CONCLUSION

A new profession has begun to emerge as early childhood teachers integrate special children into their groups. Placement services are increasingly receiving requests for professionals with a combination of skills linking early childhood education and special education. Mainstreaming is working in many groups across the country and serves children, parents, and society quite effectively.

REVIEW AND APPLICATIONS

Ten Guides for Assisting Mainstreaming

1. Apply principles of child development, child guidance, and curriculum development when mainstreaming children.
2. Realize that anyone can unexpectedly join the ranks of the disabled.
3. Learn to identify a child's strengths and abilities that can be used as building blocks to growth and learning.
4. Use creativity in adapting familiar techniques to children with special needs.
5. Utilize consultants who have specific information about a particular child or information about specific disabling conditions when admitting and planning for a particular child.
6. Explain to children and parents the special ways they can help the special needs child.
7. Extend your own knowledge and ability to work with special children through reading and by participating in classes and workshops.
8. Talk over your fears and concerns about mainstreaming with an understanding person.
9. Become familiar with the local, state, and national systems of support for young special needs children in order to advise parents more effectively.
10. Unite all parents through educational and social events for the benefit of all children in your group.

 Observations

1. Visit a classroom or center that enrolls one or more children with disabling conditions. Record what you see happening. Discuss the developmental problems of the child or children. Make a report and discuss with your classmates and instructor.
2. Describe experiences your case-study child may have had with special children. Does your case-study child have any condition that might be considered disabling? Describe.

Applications

With the advice of your instructor select the applications appropriate to your community. Divide responsibilities among class members; only one person should contact a school or agency.

1. Check with the local school system to learn the procedure for admitting a disabled child into the public school. Report to your class.
2. Call or write to the Department of Education in your state capital and ask:
   a. At what age can a disabled child receive financial support for care and education?
   b. Is state assistance available for helping young disabled children in child development centers?
   c. What professional preparation is required for teaching young disabled children below age five?
   d. What professional preparation is required for teaching disabled children above age five?
3. Call or visit a local child development center to discover what experience the center has had with admitting and working with special needs children. Write a report.
4. Interview a parent of a disabled child. Record their answers to these questions:
   a. What procedures have you used to secure educational services for your child?
   b. What agencies have you found helpful to you and your child— church, school, social service department, medical service, other?
   c. Can you tell me what it is like to be a parent of a disabled child? Write a report and discuss in your class.
5. On a 1-to-5 scale rate your center on the applicable Ten Guides for Assisting Mainstreaming. Discuss.

ADDITIONAL RESOURCES

Suggested Film and Videotapes

Meeting Special Needs   VHS   1/2 in.   Color   30 minutes   1988

Focuses on the alternatives parents have for the care and education of young children with special needs. Describes home, mainstreamed, and specialized programs, along with parent and professional comments. Work of Thelma Harms and Debby Cryer. Delmar Publishers, Customer Service, 2 Computer Drive West, Albany, NY 12212, 1–800–347–7707.

LATON's Family Album   VHS or 16 mm.   Color   17 minutes   1988

LATON, this physically disabled child, is 10 years old. He got his start in Head Start. The Family Album shows how the "family has grown to include teachers, doctors, physical therapists and others who provide services." Craighead Films, Shawnee, KS 66203.

Child Check: A Practical Child-Find Program   VHS   1/2 in.   Color   24 minutes   1982

A community action program to identify all children from birth to 21 years who have any disabling condition. Stresses the significant role of the parent in noticing possible disabilities and seeking help, as well as the importance of early intervention. Lawren Productions, Inc., P.O. Box 666, Mendocino, CA 95460.

More Than Hugs and Kisses—Affective Education in a Mainstreamed Class-room   VHS   1/2 in.   Color   23 minutes   1981

In a classroom of three- to seven-year-olds, the teacher determines each child's personal psychoeducational goals. Then through intervention and activities helps the students improve their communication skills and behavior. Filmmakers Library, Inc., 133 East 58th Street, Suite 703A, New York, NY 10022.

FOR FURTHER READING

Allen, K. E. *Mainstreaming in Early Childhood Education*. Albany, N.Y.: Delmar, 1980.

Dorris, Michael. *The Broken Cord*. New York: Harper Perennial Books, 1989.

Fauvre, Mary. "Including Young Children with 'New' Chronic Illnesses in an Early Childhood Education Setting," *Young Children*, 43:6, September 1988, 71–77.

Froschl, Merle et al. *Including All of Us: An Early Childhood Curriculum About Disability*. New York: Educational Equity Concepts, Inc., 1984.

Hanline, Mary Frances. "Integrating Disabled Children," *Young Children*, 40:2, January 1985, 45–48.

Rist, Marilee C., "The Shadow Children: Preparing for the Arrival of Crack Babies in School," *Research Bulletin*, July 1990, 1–6. Reprinted in Karen Paciorek and Joyce Munro. *Early Childhood Education 92–93*, (Guilford, CT: The Duskin Publishing Group, Inc., 1992) 15–19.

Ross, Helen W. "Integrating Infants with Disabilities? Can 'Ordinary' Caregivers Do It?" *Young Children*, 47:3, March 1992, 65–71.

White, Barbara Palm and Michael A. Phair. "'I'll be a Challenge!': Managing Emotional Stress in Teaching Disabled Children," *Young Children*, 41:2, January 1986, 44–48.

A father participates in celebrating the theme, "Our Heritage." (Parent-Child Development Center, Houston)

Working parents especially may find it difficult to arrange for visits but may make a number of short observations if encouraged just to drop in.

CONFERENCES

Numerous conferences will be held over the telephone when parents feel free to call the teacher. These can be very helpful for receiving news of family activity or a crisis that may affect the child in the school. Teachers can also set the stage for calling parents when the need arises.

Many short conferences can take place as parents bring their children and pick them up each day. Appointments can be made then to tackle problems needing more time.

Longer conferences can be scheduled periodically to evaluate the program for the parent's child. The teacher should be well organized for these conferences so that they can be productive. Conferences may be most useful in getting information from parents, in contrast to giving them information.

HOME VISITS

Home visits are one of the best ways to become acquainted with children and their parents and to help them with any problems. Meeting on their home base places the focus on parents and child and their concerns. The teacher can meet the other family members and learn incidental information about the child's interests that may serve as conversation topics when they meet again in the school. Children feel more secure knowing that the teacher knows where they live. On occasion the teacher might have to take them there. Parents usually are not reluctant to have teachers visit when visits are explained as routine procedure that all parents are taking part in. Focusing the conversation primarily on the child and on topics the parents wish to discuss helps avoid any concern about the quality of furnishings. Home visits pay off later in dealing with the child at school. Children are often heard to say, "You came to my house, didn't you, teacher?" Please refer to Chapter 6 for further details.

HOME TEACHING

Parents are teachers, too. They are the children's first teachers, and they'll be there long after early childhood teachers are outgrown. We must learn to appreciate the opportunities parents have for being learning resources for their children's education. Middle-class parents have long provided their children a wealth of stimulation and experiences that encourage learning. Some researchers have demonstrated the effectiveness of lending toys and books to families and giving ideas about how to use them with their children. Other projects have shown parents how to do learning experiences with children—teaching them concepts, colors, and the like.

Many parent education programs help parents learn child development principles and apply them to their own children. Child Study Clubs, Mothers of Twins Clubs, and Parents Without Partners are examples of self-help associations. The Parent Effectiveness Training (P.E.T.) course, developed by Thomas Gordon,[5] and the STEP (Systematic Training for Effective Parenting) program, designed by Dinkmeyer and McKay, contain promising techniques for helping parents talk to and interact with their children.[6] Many such efforts help build warm personal relations between parents and children.

One example of home teaching that pays off is related to children's emerging literacy skills. In a study of three- to five-year-olds, children whose parents read to them, took them to the library, and provided ABC books, blocks and letter forms scored highest on the Bader Language Inventory.[7] Literacy appears to begin emerging earlier than age three, because many of the three-year-olds could easily do the tasks. Teachers can help parents foster emerging literacy by encouraging them to use books and do other print-related activities with their children at a young age.

[5] Thomas Gordon, *P.E.T. Parent Effectiveness Training* (New York: Peter H. Wyden, 1970).

[6] D. Dinkmeyer and G. McKay, *Systematic Training for Effective Parenting* (Minneapolis: Guidance Associates, 1980).

[7] Verna Hildebrand and Lois Bader, "An Exploratory Study of Parents' Involvement in Their Children's Emerging Literacy Skills," *Reading Improvement*, 29:3, Fall 1992, pp. 163–170.

GROUP MEETINGS

Parent meetings are one type of parent-teacher interaction. These may be held in small or large groups. Organizers often have difficulty getting working parents to participate. It is understandable that night meetings might be unpopular. When parents work all day and don't see their children, it is difficult to leave them again, perhaps with another stranger, just to attend a meeting. Most successful meetings are those organized by a committee of parents. They plan the type of meeting they desire, issue the invitations, and help with rides and babysitting.

Commenting on the value of discussion groups for parents of young children, Lawrence Balter, a practicing psychologist, writes: "In some instances the topics chosen by parents reflect age-appropriate behavior on the part of children which appear as problems to their parents. However, these behaviors may not really present a problem in the sense of being a pathological process and it is in this regard that a psychological consultant can offer a coherent frame of reference regarding child development."[8] Thus, letting parents' interests guide the selection of topics for discussion will likely increase their participation.

Open houses held at the school inviting the children and their parents to visit the classroom and meet the teacher are popular with some groups. Children enjoy decorating the room for their parents. They may bake cookies and plan a few songs to sing to their parents. Some groups plan family picnics. Such events allow teachers other opportunities to see parent-child interaction.

  Talk It Over

How do you think the parents feel they are treated in the center where you are assigned? Would you like to be a parent of a child in that center?

PARENT COOPERATIVES

Parent cooperatives are one type of early childhood program that specifically involves parents in the operation of the school. A governing board of the parent cooperative sets the policy of the school and hires the teachers. Parents take turns serving as assistants to teachers. Not only do they receive the service at reduced rates for their children, but also most parents appreciate the opportunity that participation offers them to learn to work with their child and to further influence the child's development.

---

[8] Lawrence Balter, "Psychological Consultation for Preschool Parent Groups: An Educational-Psychological Intervention to Promote Mental Health," *Children Today,* 5:1, January-February 1976, p. 21.

Full-day groups are also organized as parent cooperatives, especially among parents who have some flexibility in their schedules that allows them time to participate. In both groups parents may organize work parties on evenings or weekends to help with painting or improving the facility or equipment.

Cooperatives often sponsor parent education classes to help parents in their parenting roles. Besides providing useful information, these classes involve parents in a pleasant social group. They encourage friendships and other human resource exchanges among families, which are especially important for families who may be new to a community.

The parent cooperatives have set an excellent example of involving parents within programs. Managers and staff of many other types of programs would be well served to consult with professionals involved in parent cooperatives in order to reap the benefits of their successful programs.

COMMUNICATING WITH PARENTS

Parents need to be informed about the program of the school or center. Managers and staff may use various means to keep parents informed. Of course, telephoning a parent for urgent information-seeking or -giving is important. Parents should realize that this is a two-way system. Whoever answers the

Centers and schools supplement the care and affection provided by the child's parents.
(V. Hildebrand, photographer)

phone at the center must be helpful even when it is not feasible to call the teacher at that moment. A careful record of the parent's question and phone number should be made so the teacher can call the parent at the earliest moment.

Personal notes can be exchanged between parents and teachers as needed. Centers often have a routine of sending home information on a child's day using a check-sheet form that the parent picks up near the door while picking up the child. Additional personal notes can be added to these routine reports.

Some centers have developed newsletters that are sent home regularly— once a month or so. Others feel it is better to make shorter newsletters and hand them out more frequently. The idea here is that very busy people will read one or two pages but might put a longer publication aside. The present technology of desktop publishing via the computer makes these newsletters relatively easy to produce. Besides routine announcements of vacations or special events, certain curriculum innovations might be highlighted—the what and why of a certain event or activity, for example.

POLICYMAKING

In parent cooperatives, Head Start schools, and many parent-child centers, parents are elected to the policymaking boards. They help with selection of goals and may make decisions regarding the distribution of resources. From this experience of active participation in governing, many parents gain confidence in their ability to effect change in social institutions. They then may run for school boards or other elective offices in the community. Parental input allows the programs more accurately to reflect the needs of the children they serve.

The early childhood education center manager and teachers can often encourage parents to participate in policymaking forums or on committees in the community. Parents may feel insecure about nominating themselves, especially the first time. However, school personnel can ask parents for permission to nominate them for various committee posts in the community. Once parents gain a little experience most can easily handle the responsibility themselves.

CONCLUSION

Parenting and child care received special emphasis in the White House Conference on Families. The possibilities for the child development center to help parents with their parenting roles are many. The cooperative nursery schools and Head Start programs have had significant success in working with parents. At no time in the child's educational experience is a close relationship between home and school more important than during the early years. Teachers must work at involving parents and communicating with them. Parents have a great deal that they can offer their child, the teacher, and the school, if they are encouraged to contribute.

REVIEW AND APPLICATIONS

Ten Ways to Involve Parents

1. Make efforts to get acquainted with parents.
2. Accept parents as they are, not as objects to change.
3. Be openly hospitable to parents, inviting them to visit the school "at any time."
4. Develop ways to involve parents in the early childhood program.
5. Plan conferences with the parents of individual children.
6. Plan meetings for groups of parents of young children.
7. Make home visits to give parents and children a chance to know you on their territory and vice versa.
8. Encourage parents to broaden their children's home experiences by providing ideas, materials, and information on community resources.
9. Support parent cooperative nursery schools and other parent-oriented programs.
10. Encourage parents to become active in public policy decisions on legislation affecting children and in the political arena generally.

 Observations

1. Observe a teacher-parent interaction. Write down what you saw and heard. State what you think was accomplished.
2. Observe an organized meeting in your school or elsewhere in your community. After it is over, write down what you believe the goal of the meeting was and whether it was accomplished. Evaluate how the leader(s) treated the parents.
3. Visit the home of your case-study child if you have not yet done so.
   a. Describe the environment of the home:
      ◆ the people of the home,
      ◆ the people of the neighborhood,
      ◆ the physical surroundings, and
      ◆ indications of how the child relates to all of these while you are there.

    b. Ask the parent:
- What is most important to you about your child's early childhood program?
- What does the child tell you about the early childhood program?
- How does the child feel about going to the early childhood center?

Applications

1. Visit a parent for the purpose of learning about a child. Before doing so, prepare a list of questions that seem appropriate for learning about the child. Check the list with your instructor and get advice about making the appointment.
2. Write a summary of your visit—a "She said, I said" report. Then conclude with a summary of what you learned about the child.
3. On a 1-to-5 scale rate your center using the Ten Ways to Involve Parents. Discuss.

ADDITIONAL RESOURCES

Suggested Videotapes

Harmonizing the Worlds of Home and Child Care   VHS   1/2 in.   Color   30 minutes   1988

> Thelma Harms and Debby Cryer examine ways that parents and caregivers can deal with the demands of home and child care so that the child feels support and continuity in both settings. Explores way to reduce family stress through effective home and child care communication and cooperation. Delmar Publishers, Customer Service, 2 Computer Drive West, Albany, NY 12212, 1–800-347-7707.

Mister Rogers Talks with Parents   VHS   1/2 in.   Color   43 minutes   1988

> TV's Mr. Rogers discusses some of the pressures on children today and gives a brief visit to "The Neighborhood." NAEYC, Media, 1509 16th Street, N.W., Washington, DC 20036-1426.

FOR FURTHER READING

Berger, Eugenia Hepworth. *Parents as Partners in Education*. Columbus, OH: Merrill, 1987.

Bigner, Jerry. *Parent-Child Relations*. New York: Macmillan Publishing Company, 1985.

Bjorklund, Gail and Christine Burger. "Making Conferences Work for Parents, Teachers, and Children," *Young Children*. 40:3, March 1985, 23–27.

Boutte, Gloria S., Dannie L. Keepler, Violet S. Tyler, and Brenda Z. Terry. "Effective Techniques for Involving 'Difficult Parents,'" *Young Children*, 47:3, March 1992, 19–22.

Brooks, Jane B. *The Process of Parenting*. Mountain View, CA: Mayfield Publishing Company, 1991.

Bundy, B. F. "Fostering Communication Between Parents and Preschools, *Young Children*, 46:2, January 1991, 12–17.

Christophersen, Edward R. *Beyond Discipline: Parenting That Lasts a Lifetime*. Kansas City, MO: Westport Publishers, Inc., 1990.

Dorris, Michael. *The Broken Cord*. New York: Harper Perennial Books, 1989.

Feeney, Stephanie, Lillian Katz, and Kenneth Kipnis. "Ethics Case Studies: The Working Mother," *Young Children*, 43:2, January 1988, 48–51.

Furman, Erna. "Thinking about Fathers," *Young Children*, 47:4, May 1992, 36–37.

Galinsky, Ellen. "Parents and Teacher Caregivers: Sources of Tension, Sources of Support," *Young Children*, 43:3, March 1988, 4–12.

Galinsky, Ellen. "Why are Some Parent/Teacher Partnerships Clouded with Difficulties?" *Young Children*, 45:5, July 1990, 2–3, 38–39.

Greenberg, Polly. "Parents as Partners in Young Children's Development and Education: A New American Fad? Why Does it Matter?" *Young Children*, 44:4, May 1989, 61–75.

Halpern, Robert. "Major Social and Demographic Trends Affecting Young Families: Implications for Early Childhood Care and Education," *Young Children*, 42:6, September 1987, 34–40.

Herrera, Julia F. and Sharon L. Wooden. "Some Thoughts about Effective Parent-School Communication, *Young Children*, 43:6, September 1988, 78–81.

Hildebrand, Verna. *Introduction to Early Childhood Education*. New York: Macmillan Publishing Company, 1991.

Hildebrand, Verna. *Management of Child Development Centers*. New York: Macmillan, 1993.

Hildebrand, Verna. *Parenting and Teaching Young Children*. Macmillan/McGraw Hill, 1990.

Hildebrand, Verna. *Parenting: Rewards and Responsibilities*. Macmillan/McGraw Hill, 1994.

Hildebrand, Verna and Lois Bader. "An Exploratory Study of Parents' Involvement in Their Children's Emerging Literacy Skills," *Reading Improvement*, 29:3, Fall 1992, 163–170.

Jacobs, Nancy L. "Unhappy Endings," *Young Children*, 47:3, March 1992, 23–27.

Kamerman, Sheila B. *Parenting in an Unresponsive Society: Managing Work & Family*. New York: Free Press, 1980.

Morgan, Elizabeth. "Talking with Parents When Concerns Come Up," *Young Children,* 44:2, January 1989, 52–56.

NAEYC. "Infants and Toddlers Away from Their Mothers?" *Young Children,* 42:4, May 1987, 40–42.

Robison, Bryan E. "Vanishing Breed: Men in Child Care Programs," *Young Children,* 43:6, September 1988, 54–58.

Swick, Kevin J. *Perspectives on Understanding and Working with Families.* New York: Stipes, 1987.

Turecki, Stanley and Leslie Tonner. *The Difficult Child.* New York: Bantam Books, 1985.

CHAPTER 22

Being a Professional
Early Childhood Educator

Key Concepts

◆ Advantages of Professional Memberships
◆ Preventing Burnout
◆ Being a Significant Adult in Children's Lives

The children had just finished listening to a record about rockets. The teacher was discussing it with them. Diana moved over by the assistant teacher and snuggled up very close to her. They exchanged glances that indicated feelings of mutual love and affection.

All adults who perform services for children are significant adults in their lives. It is important to believe that the things you do, even a seemingly simple exchange of human warmth such as occurred between Diana and the teacher in this anecdote, really make a difference in the total development of the child.

BEING A PROFESSIONAL

Your professional reading and experiences throughout this and other courses are preparing you to become a professional early childhood educator. Being professional means committing yourself to work with others of similar educational and experiential backgrounds to fulfill the standards set by the profession of early childhood education and to serve the needs of children, families, teachers, and others who have concerns regarding children's programs.

The early childhood education profession has matured in recent years. The largest organization of all persons interested in early childhood education, the National Association for the Education of Young Children (NAEYC), has led efforts to set standards for preparing teachers and for accrediting early childhood programs.[1] NAEYC now includes around 80,000 members. Affiliated with NAEYC are regional, state, and local associations. Members carry out the work of the associations at the grass roots level—where the children and families actually live. These associations are all open to you for one nominal fee.

There are many other organizations for professional early childhood educators to join and work within, such as Head Start, Child Development Associate, Association for Childhood Education International, the World Association for Early Childhood, the Southern Early Childhood Association, Organization for Cooperative Nursery Schools, National Association of Early Childhood Teacher Educators, and many associations with more specialized interests. A list of the names and addresses of some of these organizations is included at the end of this chapter. The extensiveness of this list should confirm for you the depth of interest that many individuals have in young children. You might consider joining one or more to enhance your work with and for children.

In your work as an early childhood education professional you will realize early in your career the need to be in contact with other professionals beyond your place of work. These contacts can be achieved through memberships in the local branches of the national organizations mentioned earlier and through local and state committees that may be organized for a specific task for general advocacy for children over time. Local service clubs, churches, the League of Women Voters, and government groups frequently have committees focusing on children's needs. These are natural outlets for anyone professionally interested in children.

One way for you to avoid burnout, the tired, unproductive feeling on your job, is to gain stimulation and nurturing from the colleagues you'll meet in one or more of these professional associations in your community. If no such group exists, you and others can be instrumental in forming one.

Another advantage of memberships is the excellent publications that they provide members. These publications also help you, as a professional, improve your performance on the job and encourage you to keep improving and learning. NAEYC publishes the journal *Young Children*. Many members read this attractive journal the day it arrives in their home or office. Aside from articles

---

[1] The following three publications state standards that NAEYC has established for teacher education programs and for children's programs in schools and centers:

Early Childhood Teacher Education Guidelines (1982) states standards for four- and five-year programs in colleges and universities for preparing teachers to work with young children.

Guidelines for Early Childhood Education Programs in Associate Degree Granting Institutions (1985) states standards for use in community and junior colleges for preparing teachers to work with young children.

Accreditation Criteria and Procedures of the National Academy of Early Childhood Programs (1991), edited by Sue Bredekamp, states high-quality standards for children's programs in child care and early childhood schools and centers.

Each of the above publications is published by and available from NAEYC, 1509 16th Street, N.W., Washington, DC 20036–1426, 1-800-424-2460.

Conferring among staff members is an essential ingredient of high-quality programs.
(Michigan State University Child Development Laboratory)

on topics helpful to one's job, *Young Children* contains the latest information on legislation or projects of the association. NAEYC also publishes many additional worthy publications every year.

The various associations hold meetings throughout the year that can help you keep up to date on information and procedures for working with children or understanding more about children's needs. Opportunities abound for your leadership qualities to gain expression within the associations. You'll get to know the leaders around your community, state, and nation, indeed, even around the world. There are active international associations. You can contribute to meetings when you've developed some expertise you'd like to share. You'll decide you are ready for this step when you attend meetings and come out saying, "I could have made that presentation." Most presenters at meetings are members like yourself who know the needs of others and develop presentations to share. Each organization has a procedure for recruiting program volunteers that is published in their newsletter or journal. As you meet others at conferences and share information focused on children, you'll develop friendships that can become enjoyable and helpful over the years.

Many professionals and parents have found that through cooperative efforts within organizations they can make a difference for children. They may propose legislation or give advice on the pros and cons of pending legislation that affects children. Efforts can focus on local, state, or national issues. Political leaders grow to appreciate the efforts of professionals to interpret the effects of legislation and communicate with them regarding those efforts.

Group efforts help all professionals involved feel that they do make a difference for children and families. Organizations have various means for keeping members informed. Some inform members through their newsletters or journals, through committees, or telephone networks.

BEING A TEACHER INSTEAD OF A SUPERVISOR

Teaching is more than supervising. You are playing a teaching role, whether in the classroom, at home, or on the playground. This means that there are many opportunities for children to learn and for you to facilitate learning. You are there, alert, interested, and knowledgeable about the situation. Teaching calls for interacting, enriching, observing, and planning for interaction with each child in the group. It involves far more than supervising. If you were only a supervisor, you might rest at ease until trouble broke out, and you might not expect to deal with the consequences of your negligence, as a teacher must.

Being a teacher calls for a great deal of planning. When NAEYC developed the criteria for high-quality programs a requirement for paid planning time was specifically included.[2] In establishing this standard it is acknowledged that only with careful planning will the many worthy goals of early childhood programs be fulfilled for children, parents, and the community. Such careful planning requires time and should never be left to chance. In your preparation to become a teacher you should take advantage of every opportunity to learn about and participate in planning, which includes evaluation of day-to-day as well as long-range programming.

BEING A DECISION-MAKER

Social Decisions

The interaction decisions that make up the major portion of your guidance are called *social decisions*. In social decisions the alternatives are often not clear-cut. Each decision results from mediation of alternatives. That is, you may do the best you can for the moment, knowing that it is not completely satisfactory to many. There may be a conflict in values or goals. For example, a child wants to stay inside to finish a painting. The teacher and the child both value completing work started. Also, both value outdoor play. The other children are ready to go outside, and no teacher is available to stay indoors with the child. The teacher decides to take all children outdoors, then tells the child to leave the work out to finish when they return inside.

---

[2] Sue Bredekamp, *Accreditation Criteria,* p. 37. "Staff are provided paid planning time."

Sometimes a compromise must be worked out whereby individuals tolerate parts of all the conflicting factors. Such a situation arises when several children want to be leader. Choosing the one the teacher thinks asked first may be only a tolerable solution, not a happy one, for most children.

Sometimes the decision-makers behave as though the conflicting factors did not exist, which, of course, may mean that they behave in an inconsistent manner. This happens if a child's needs or feelings are ignored, perhaps when a child prefers to be active and the teacher requires listening to a story.

Educational Decisions

A teacher also makes many educational decisions. These are technical decisions related to choice of curriculum, goals, and content. They also include choice of teaching technique and choice of educational resources for achieving goals. Educational decisions should be based on knowledge, research, and experience.

Resource Decisions

Resource decisions are made when the means for achieving goals are allocated. Teachers and administrators of child development center programs are continuously allocating both human and nonhuman resources for the achievement of the program goals. These decisions should be made on a thoughtful basis when children are not present.

In making decisions or choices, the decision-maker must have enough information to recognize the alternatives. There is no opportunity for choice unless there are at least two alternatives. The consequences of classroom decisions will last a long time. Each decision may not seem earthshaking in itself, but the cumulative effect can be. Material or nonhuman resources are expendable and must be replenished. Though human resources aren't used up, the optimal time for their development and utilization may pass. An opportunity for an exchange of human resources once passed may never reoccur again in the same way—for example, when a child's enthusiasm is squelched instead of praised.

GUIDING TO FULFILL POTENTIAL

Whether you are a parent, teacher, assistant teacher, or volunteer in a home, in a family day care home, or in a child development center, you will have the opportunity to help children develop their human potential in the process of your interaction.

In making the moment-to-moment guidance decisions that help children become self-directed individuals, you will first apply your general knowledge of

children's development as discussed in Chapter 17. Second, you will use information about the individual children in your group and their very personal
needs. Third, you will find the principles of indirect and direct guidance
described in Chapters 2 and 3 very useful. Fourth, your values and goals, as
discussed in Chapter 24, will influence each decision you make.

Guiding children to help them reach their fullest potential requires the
pooling of much information on your part, then acting with warmth and personal concern for each child. Even with a great deal of experience you will be
saying, "There is so much I don't understand," so you must keep your mind
open to learning more.

There are a number of personal qualities that will help you make the
decisions and become the most effective and significant adults that you can
become. Discussion of these qualities follows.

 Talk It Over

What are the lives like of early childhood professionals you know? In what
ways has their profession contributed to their own family?

BEING KNOWLEDGEABLE ABOUT CHILDREN'S DEVELOPMENT

Your basic knowledge about how children grow and develop will serve you in
many ways as you work with them. Your study will tell you what to expect of
children at every age. With this information you can then relate your own
observations of particular children and use that information as you interact
with them and plan for them. This knowledge is derived from research in the
sciences such as child development, physiology, psychology, and sociology and
provides the basis for sound decisions by parents, teachers, and caregivers. The
more you know about how children grow and develop, the more you'll want to
know. It is good practice to keep a child development book handy for checking
information and relating observations you make. Each year scientists report
studies that help practitioners do a better job with children.

To help teachers, parents, administrators, and others understand more
fully the importance of basing early childhood planning and practice on appropriate developmental levels of children, NAEYC has published a very useful
guide. The chapters focus on infants, toddlers, three-year-olds, four- and five-
year-olds, and six- to eight-year-old youngsters. Examples of both appropriate
and inappropriate practice are included.[3]

---

[3] Sue Bredekamp (ed.), *Developmentally Appropriate Practice in Early Childhood Programs
Serving Children from Birth Through Age 8* (Washington, DC: NAEYC, 1987).

Staff members confer in a resource room established to provide teachers with the materials they need.
(Sinclair Community College Early Childhood Center, Dayton)

BEING A NURTURING PERSON

Being a nurturing person is a role that you will play as a child development center teacher. This is a nurturing role that includes providing needed emotional support—warm, interested, friendly, affectionate, comforting, and helpful personal responses—to each child. Nurturing is a basic responsibility of teachers of young children. This role is also called "mothering"; however, there is good reason to believe that male teachers who are joining the early childhood education profession are as competent in providing nurturing as women. Men may label their role "fathering," although it has become common to use the genderless term "parenting." The inclusion of men in early childhood education is a welcome change. Children benefit by having both genders represented throughout their education.

Nurturing is crucial to a child's development. Living in an environment without nurturing for three to ten hours each day, five days a week, would certainly leave a child emotionally deprived. Children's "hurts" must be comforted. They need someone to show them affection and to appreciate their accomplishments. Teachers and caregivers are not expected to supplant the love parents have for their children, only to supplement it. Teachers can often help parents become more loving and appreciative of their children by sharing with them the exciting growth of their child each day. In one infant care center caregivers keep a list on the blackboard of new skills and words each child learns. Parents regularly check the list under the child's name, and frequently a helpful dialogue with caregivers follows.

Parents may feel some guilt over leaving a child in a child care center, fearing that the child is being deprived of needed love. Parents like to be reassured that their child is special. They warm up to even a small bit of information about their child's day. However, you should not compete for the child's love and make parents feel insignificant. Occasionally a child, especially an infant or a toddler, cries when the parent arrives at the end of the day. Dr. T. Berry Brazelton, a prominent Harvard pediatrician, believes that this reaction in the young child is a cry of relief that the parent is back. Realization that the parent really exists when away isn't clear to a baby. The crying is not fear of a parent or an indication that the child likes her teachers or school better than parents. It would do the parents a grave disservice to say, "But Berniece never cries while she's in the center."

BEING A MODEL

To do your teaching and caregiving job well, you must be a model of the type of a person you'd like the children and parents to become. If you want them to be kind, then you must be kind. If you want them to be loving, then you must be loving. If you want them to be smart, then you must use your intelligence. Children imitate those around them. When you have the opportunity and responsibility to be with children on a regular basis you can expect children to pattern their behavior after yours. One teacher asked a group of children, "What do you want to be when you grow up?" "A teacher just like you," came the quick reply. The teacher's love affair with the children probably explains why the parents could think only of superlatives when describing this teacher.

As a teacher, you may also serve as a model for parents. Parents will learn attitudes and skills by watching you—even when you may be unaware of their watching. If you are relaxed, they, too, may become more relaxed in their interaction with their children.

BEING A PERCEPTIVE OBSERVER AND LISTENER

Through perceptive observing and listening to children—really seeing and hearing what they do and say—you will be able to apply your knowledge of children's growth, development, and behavior. You will become attuned to children's verbal and nonverbal language and learn to interpret their needs. You can help them become the most that they can be for the time being. Learning to understand behavior requires developing skills in listening to children, co-teachers, and parents. Their uniqueness will challenge you to learn more and more about human beings.

BEING SKILLFUL IN SELECTING AND USING GUIDANCE TECHNIQUES

Guidance techniques must be selected on the basis of individual children's needs. There is a tentativeness about all the suggestions in this text that cautions the reader to think before using. You are dealing with unique human beings who must be perceived in terms of their individuality. The challenge here is to use the techniques of guidance while remaining aware of the uniqueness of each child. Your philosophy should be child-oriented and humanistic—that is, most of all you should care about children.

BEING ABLE TO SET AND ENFORCE LIMITS

As a significant adult in children's lives, you must set limits on behavior at times. It is your responsibility to make the decisions children can't be expected to handle, while encouraging other decisions by children. For example, you may decide *when* art materials are to be used; children may then decide *what* materials they want to use. Children should not be overloaded with decision-making, but allowed to decide things they are ready to decide.

Limits must be set that (1) protect the children from each other; (2) protect the learning environment; and (3) protect the equipment and property. Firm decisions about what behaviors can and can't be allowed should be discussed in staff meetings and agreed upon, and then limits should be fairly maintained by all staff members.

Some teachers are confused about setting limits. They feel a permissive atmosphere is best. These are, of course, value positions that must be reconciled. One might say that one child's limit is another child's freedom. For example, if I can't hit you, then you are free from being hit. If I can't knock your puzzle on the floor, thereby destroying your learning environment, then you are free to learn as you put your puzzle together. If I can't knock over the highchair, breaking it and the doll, then you are free to play with the doll for days and weeks to come.

It seems that these three types of limits are fair if children are to live together in a group and if children are to be prepared for life in the larger social world. Limits can be clearly stated to children. Opportunities to knock and hit can be provided in legitimate areas of the school, thereby allowing the children to get rid of the feelings indicated by such behavior. These outlets were discussed in more detail in Chapters 3 and 17.

BEING SELF-CONFIDENT

You should be confident of yourself and your ability to cope with your responsibilities. Confidence is not developed overnight, but comes a little at a time from small challenges. In your assignments in a child development center, you will be given opportunities to develop your skill gradually. At the same time you should look for opportunities to be useful to the children and to the adults who work with you. There is always so much to be done that a helpful person, who has a sincere motivation to learn, and who does not have to be told every task to do is a real asset to a center.

Confidence grows when you find time to get down on the children's level and laugh and enjoy them. When you are warm and accepting of both children and their parents, they will be warm and accepting of you. Confidence grows when you feel you are a friend of co-workers, when you find opportunities to praise a job well done as you hope they will praise yours. Comments such as, "That was a neat painting project," or "I wish I could lead music like you can," cost nothing, but mean a great deal to the person who hears them. These are, of course, examples of human resource-exchange.

Confidence grows from knowing what is expected. Time used for getting clear directions from those in charge, or giving clear directions if you are in charge, is well spent. Posting some directions and communicating to others in staff meetings and through individual contacts are means for knowing what is expected. Being alert and keeping your mind on the situation help you know what is expected. It is your responsibility to ask, seek, and be assertive if you do not have enough information to do your job well. In the immediate environment it may mean appropriately questioning a director, head teacher, co-worker, or parent. In the larger sense it may mean reading books or attending classes or workshops.

Your confidence will grow as you feel that you measure up to the standards you set for yourself, those set by your administrator—whether director, principal, or parent board—and the standards set by the profession as a whole. The last are communicated through books such as this one and through the journals published by professional organizations. (See the list at the end of this chapter.)

BEING DEDICATED

You should be dedicated to your role of serving children, or you really should look for some other occupation. Children deserve people who like them and enjoy working around them, not people who are just working until something better comes along. If children get on your nerves, then caregiving and teaching are not for you. If you think children are out to beat you, then these roles are not for you. But if you find real satisfaction in serving children, in seeing them smile, grow, learn, walk, and run, then teaching and caregiving may be a rewarding profession.

If you are dedicated, you will try to learn as much as you can about your tasks. Being dedicated doesn't necessarily mean that you must sacrifice your life to this career, because you can play many roles in your life. You will actually be a better teacher or caregiver if you have interests outside your job that are very different from your career tasks. You can join art, music, or sports clubs instead of child-study clubs just to give your own personality an opportunity to grow in other directions at the same time that you are devoting many of your hours to learning about and working with children.

One positive outcome of the women's movement is that a woman today does not have to restrict herself to the traditionally female roles of teaching and child care unless that is her preference. Discrimination against women is slowly subsiding. Career opportunities are opening up in everything from applied mechanics to zookeeping. Therefore, the women who might formerly have been locked into careers in child care can happily look elsewhere for their mode of livelihood, service, and self-expression. Gone are the days when parents counseled all their daughters to go into teaching. Therefore, only men and women who are sincerely dedicated to the development of human potential need to find themselves pursuing an early childhood career. Of course, there are linkages between children's services and many other fields of specialization and your outside interests may help you discover some of them.

BEING CONFIDENT OF THE BASIC GOODNESS IN PEOPLE

You should have confidence in people. Try hard to believe that people are basically good. Recognize that behavior has meaning and seek ways to discover the meaning of the behavior, whether in a child or an adult. If you feel a dislike for a child, such as Timmy, the troubled child discussed in Chapter 19, then seek out more information about him or her immediately. What is the child's background? Is there a health problem? What are the child's strengths? What does the child do well? Think how you might behave if the same things had happened to you that have happened to this child. Use time in staff meetings to share, in a professional discussion, the knowledge various members have about individual children and families. "Staffing," as this sort of briefing is sometimes called, must be done in a professional manner. Information communicated as gossip can be harmful to the child, to the parents, and even to the reputation of the school. Remember that the intimate facts and feelings that parents may share with you to help you more fully understand their children should be kept in confidence.

BEING STRONG, HEALTHY, AND ENERGETIC

You need to be strong, healthy, and energetic if you are to work effectively with young children. This is not an easy job. You are up and down dozens of times a day. You are on your feet indoors and out. You lift and carry equipment and sometimes children. You need patience when all children seem to need you at once. The requirements are not superhuman, of course, but simply demand a good constitution supported by proper diet, rest, and attention to your health. Proper shoes, boots, and other comfortable attire will be important to the way you feel.

It is disconcerting to children, not to mention administrators, to have their "teacher" absent frequently for health reasons. If you find yourself even considering calling in sick on a frequent basis, then this may not be a career that you are suited for. Either you really don't have the physical stamina required, or your health is an excuse for avoiding a job that perhaps you unconsciously don't like. Mental health is, of course, as important as physical health. The ability to keep life on an even keel is very important when you deal with children on a day-to-day basis. For example, if things are going badly with you and your spouse, friend, or roommate, then the stress will eventually affect the children in your group. You may lose interest in them, fail to plan for them, or fail to respond to them with patience and understanding. People with their own problems should not attempt to deal with vulnerable people such as infants and young children.

BEING KNOWLEDGEABLE ABOUT CHILDREN'S CURRICULUM

You will need to know about the curriculum of schools for young children and realize what possibilities are available in equipment and experiences offered to the children. When children are provided a rich and varied curriculum, they keep productively busy. The author's book, *Introduction to Early Childhood Education,* listed in the bibliography at the end of the chapter, is a source of detailed information on curriculum. It can help teachers plan a rich learning environment. With the book as a guide, the creative teacher will be able to plan a program that is highly challenging to every aspect of a child's development. Knowing about curriculum, equipment, and supplies is very helpful in planning the guidance of children. Behavior problems can be dealt with effectively through expert knowledge and use of curriculum.

Be sure to take notice of the curriculum in all your practicums with experienced teachers. Start a file of the many worthwhile ideas you see them use. Supplement what you observe with reading in journals and books and by seeking out curriculum information at conferences you attend. There is a sizeable body of information on theoretical and practical aspects of curriculum development that you will want to explore.

 Talk It Over

What are some of the most interesting innovations in children's curriculum that you have observed? How do curriculum innovations spice up the lives of the teachers as well as the children?

BEING EFFECTIVE WITH YOUR VOICE

Your voice is a teaching tool. It can be effective for helping children know what to do. The firmness in your voice can give the children confidence. They will know that you expect them to comply with your directions by the way you tell them to do something. Of course, if they do not do what you ask, you will patiently lead them through the desired behavior so the next time they will know that you expect them to comply. You will speak in a normal voice directly to children rather than using a "to whom it may concern" approach. Speaking in a quiet manner is more effective than loudness. If you observe a classroom where loud or shouted guidance is being used, you can predict fearful children, unheeded guidance, or both.

BEING ALERT TO HEALTH AND SAFETY

As the responsible adult, you have to be constantly alert for children's health and safety. You will always stand or sit where you can keep an eye on the portion of the room or yard that has been designated your responsibility. You will not leave the area unless it is to advise another teacher or there is no child there. You will be conscious of cleanliness, contagion, and drafts, all of which can affect children's health.

You will become attuned to the sounds of a smoothly running school just as a mechanic knows the sounds of a smoothly running automobile. If voices are raised or crowds gather, you'll sense that something is amiss. You'll act to alleviate a problem before it becomes serious. Perhaps you'll change the schedule, add a new piece of equipment, use a personal touch of physical or verbal guidance, or whatever is called for to ease the situation.

Safety

Children's safety is of foremost concern to parents, teachers, and caregivers. Children must be protected from traffic, usually by an enclosed playground. Precautions must be taken where children enter and leave automobiles or buses. Parents and children must be encouraged to use safe procedures—which children can learn. Parking lots are especially dangerous because drivers are often backing out their cars and young children, being short, easily go unnoticed in rearview mirrors.

Falls that might prove harmful should be prevented by building ramps and railings. Being overly cautious and scaring children should be avoided. Refrain from saying, "You might fall," and "Be careful," frequently. Falls that would hurt an adult usually won't hurt children, because of the way their long bones are cushioned. Children usually take good care of themselves, not being too daring, unless friends overencourage them. Therefore, being an alert observer ready to step in with precautions when necessary is often the best adult guidance. It is wise for staffs to discuss what the necessary limits are, then follow the rules and interpret them consistently to children.

Fire safety is of primary concern when you are responsible for children. Practice safety drills for fires or severe storms are important—these can be made fun to be less alarming. Be sure the exits are *always* open. And be sure you know the plan for evacuation during children's sleeping times.

Health

The physical and mental health of children is another major concern to parents, caregivers, and teachers. Keeping infectious bacteria under control requires using sanitary practices in handling food. It also requires frequent and thorough washing of hands by both adults and children. Use of hygienic procedures when changing babies' diapers and cleanliness in the toileting situation are very important for inhibiting the spread of disease.

The threat of AIDS (Acquired Immune Deficiency Syndrome) has prompted many centers to require use of disposable plastic film gloves for anyone handling any bodily fluids. With infants being born infected with AIDS from infected mothers, it is possible for centers to have children who are infected with AIDS, prompting serious precautions. Of course, teachers and caregivers should protect themselves from the risk of AIDS by avoiding any of the risky behaviors associated with the disease.

Immunizations

All parents, caregivers, and teachers should be alert to the advantage of requiring immunization against common childhood diseases for all children. Statistics from the National Center for Disease Control indicate that many children's immunizations are being neglected, causing children to have diseases that could be avoided. Measles, mumps, rubella, smallpox, diphtheria, influenza, whooping cough, tetanus, meningitis, and polio are all readily controlled by immunizations. Numerous risks occur from contracting these diseases, including permanently crippling effects. Immunizations should be required for admission to a center. In urban areas these immunizations are given free in health clinics.

In all child development centers all adults should be concerned about the spread of colds. Policies regarding admission of children with colds must be developed with local health officials. Chickenpox is also highly contagious and is one disease that, as yet, has no vaccine. Teachers may see cases of chickenpox from time to time. They should report any outbreak to health authorities and to parents.

All adults working in centers should follow legal requirements for tuberculosis testing. Adult carriers have been known to infect young children in their care.

Detecting Child Abuse

"Ray came in with bruises over both eyes and with lips all puffed up," reported a teacher to the child care center director. The director immediately turned to the task of reporting this abused child to the agency handling such cases.

Child abuse is becoming a common problem, so common that legislatures have passed laws requiring teachers and caregivers to report any evidence of it in the children under their care. The laws give no choice about reporting, even though teachers might prefer not to become involved in cases such as this. It is important to remember that the health, safety, and perhaps the very life of the child are at stake. Be sure to check the procedures for reporting cases in your locality. Besides detecting abused children, you may at times enroll children who are placed there by authorities for the purpose of relieving the abusing parent of pressures from childrearing. If a child's placement is part of parental therapy you should ask the social worker in charge for suggestions for dealing with the child.

Child abuse is a complex problem. According to Rebecca Schmidt, a protective services specialist, "Dealing with child abuse calls for a multidisciplinary approach. It is a *medical* problem, involving treatment for the child; *psychiatric,* requiring treatment for the parents; *legal,* involving the state's right both to protect children and to prosecute the parents; *social,* cutting as it does across all socioeconomic groups although most frequently reported in the least affluent; and *family,* requiring knowledge in parenting, child development, and family relations."[4]

Neglect is also a concern. You may encounter children who wear dirty clothing and come to school without baths or are hungry. Any case of such neglect should be reported to the manager for further study and action through the parents and the authorities.

Child abuse has reared its ugly head in child care centers in recent years. The number is few, fortunately; however, managers are particularly concerned if any type of staff members' behavior could be construed as abusive. You will be advised about your interaction. Doors will be left open to make staff monitoring easier by both outside authorities and workers and parents on the inside. Any evidence of abusive behavior should be immediately reported to the director.

Another aspect of neglect is the neglect of regulations. One mother arrived at a center to pick up her son and found that no one was supervising the children in the nap room. She took several minutes to dress her son, then went in search of someone to report to that she was taking the child. After several moments of calling out, an employee came down from an upstairs room. The mother felt this was totally neglectful behavior and told the person that she was not only taking her child that afternoon but was taking him out for good. Regulations were clearly being violated that day because children are required to be supervised at all times.

BEING SUPPORTIVE OF DIVERSITY

Children and their parents come from many racial, ethnic, religious, economic, and lifestyle groups. Early childhood teachers and caregivers, too, are from many diverse groups. Each deserves to be appreciated for her or his uniqueness and treated with utmost respect. Early childhood professionals should

---

[4] Rebecca Schmidt, "What Home Economists Should Know About Child Abuse," *Focus on Services to Young Children* (Washington, DC: American Home Economics Association, 1978), pp. 39–40.

work to ease communication among various groups. Cultural groups often have special strengths that, once you are aware of, you can build on in your work with them. Families with lifestyles different from yours have a right to their uniqueness. Bias of any kind hurts children and prevents them from reaching their fullest potential. Your efforts toward developing harmonious relations among diverse individuals and groups and encouraging understanding and cooperation will be appreciated by parents, professionals, and the community.

BEING AN ADVOCATE FOR FAMILIES

You can become an advocate for families. Parents often feel that they are rearing their children all alone without much support. As the caregiver or teacher in their children's lives you may be a life-preserver. Through your early childhood school or center you will supplement, in a professional manner, the care given by parents. You will serve the needs of parents and never exploit them or their children. You can speak for their needs when occasions arise to come to parents' defense. You may serve as a parent's advocate during special needs placements, or as a confidant when needed. You'll know when confidentiality is required and learn to protect it.

BEING SCHOLARLY AND PROFESSIONAL

Your scholarship and professionalism will grow as you work in your chosen field. Take the initiative today to join at least one early childhood professional group and to work within it for the good of children and for growth for yourself and for other professionals serving children. Set your goal to become top-notch in your knowledge and skills associated with being an early childhood professional.

From your early teaching you'll be able to branch out to positions that may serve more children, more teachers, more parents, and more communities. For example, you may become a consultant to a business or corporation or to a government agency helping to open new early childhood schools for children still unserved. You may become a parent educator, perhaps helping parents support the educational opportunities that dedicated teachers are producing for their children. You may use creative avenues such as writing, speaking, or making educational videos, to get new ideas across to those wanting to serve children and families better. You'll be glad you did.

Your scholarship should go well beyond the subjects you will teach children. Your reading should help you understand the political, social, scientific, and aesthetic world that you and the children and their families live in. Knowledge of the implications of education in a democratic society is important for teachers. Your scholarship should also include reading and courses in parent education, family relationships, family sociology, and family counseling to help you work with families more effectively. And, of course, your scholarship will include study of human growth, development and behavior to help you understand and plan for the children with whom you work.

As you work and study you will evolve a professional style that is unique for you. It will be your personal way of integrating all you know and all you feel about the standards, rules, information, and creativity of your chosen profession, early childhood educator.

CONCLUSION

Being a professional early childhood educator means being a decision-maker. Being the decision-maker means you are the one who weighs alternatives and carries the choice into action. As a teacher you are assuming responsibilities for human encounter—an ongoing process that demands commitment and involvement. Your values will be tested over and over again as you work with parents to make the best possible life for their children.

All decisions should be given conscious thought. Without such thought, some decisions get made by default, and the people involved are buffeted along, much as the tide along the coast sloshes a piece of driftwood. Preferred goals are seldom achieved under such circumstances.

REVIEW AND APPLICATIONS

Eighteen Qualities of an Early Childhood Educator

1. Being knowledgeable about children's development.
2. Being a nurturing person.
3. Being a model.
4. Being a perceptive observer and listener.
5. Being skillful in selecting and using guidance techniques.
6. Being self-confident.
7. Being dedicated.
8. Being confident of the basic goodness in people.
9. Being strong, healthy, and energetic.
10. Being knowledgeable about children's curriculum.
11. Being effective with your voice.
12. Being able to set and enforce limits for children.
13. Being alert to health and safety.
14. Being a teacher instead of a supervisor.
15. Being a decision-maker.
16. Being supportive of diversity.
17. Being an advocate for families.
18. Being scholarly and professional.

Observations

1. Interview an early childhood educator. Using the chapter as your background, find out what this person feels is important. Write a summary of your interview.
2. Observe one or more teachers working with children. Make some generalizations about their approach to teaching. Write a summary of how your observation correlates with what you've read.
3. Observe your case-study child interacting with the teacher. Evaluate how the teacher fulfills some of the characteristics mentioned in the chapter.

Applications

1. Make a list of the various headings in the chapter. Observe and talk to either a parent or a teacher to learn how she or he is fulfilling the suggested aspects of being a professional early childhood educator.
2. Rate yourself on the Eighteen Qualities of an Early Childhood Educator. Make a chart or write a short narrative showing the results of your self-analysis. List the goals you hope to achieve next.
3. Explain how limits are set in a home or school setting where you can observe. What are the limits? Who sets them? Do you think they are consistent over time? How do you think the children feel about the limits?

ADDITIONAL RESOURCES

Suggested Videotapes

Celebrating Early Childhood Teachers   VHS   1/2 in.   Color   22 minutes   1988

> An upbeat view of the role of the early childhood professional with a serious side concerning the problems in retaining qualified staff. NAEYC, Media, 1509 16th Street, N.W., Washington, DC 20036-1426.

Salaries, Working Conditions, and the Teacher Shortage   VHS   1/2 in. Color 17 minutes   1988

> Marcy Whitebook and Jim Morin discuss the complex issues contributing to the crisis in recruitment and retention of qualified staff. A new advocacy tool. NAEYC, Media, 1509 16th Street, N.W., Washington, DC 20036-1426.

Professional Organizations and Their Journals

American Home Economics Association, 1555 King Street, Alexandria, VA 22314. Publishes *Journal of Home Economics*.

Association of Childhood Education International, 11141 Georgia Avenue, Suite 200, Wheaton, MD 20907. Publishes *Childhood Education*.

Council for Exceptional Children, 1920 Association Drive, Reston, VA 22091. Publishes *Exceptional Children*.

National Association of Early Childhood Teacher Educators, Dr. Anne Dorsey, Editor. Arlitt Child Development Center, University of Cincinnati, Cincinnati, OH 45221-0105. Publishes *The Journal of Early Childhood Teacher Education*.

National Association for the Education of Young Children, 1509 16th Street, N.W., Washington, DC 20036–1426. Publishes *Young Children* and *Early Childhood Research Quarterly*.

National Council on Family Relations, 1219 University Avenue, S.E., Minneapolis, MN 55432. Publishes *Family Relations*.

National Association for Gifted Children, 4175 Lovell Rd., Suite 140, Circle Pines, MN 55014. Publishes *Gifted Child Quarterly*.

Organisation Mundiale pour l'Education Pr'escolaire (OMEP), U.S. National Committee, 1341 G Street, N.W., Suite 400, Washington, DC 20005–3105. Publishes *International Journal of Early Childhood*.

Southern Early Childhood Association, Box 5403, Brady Station, Little Rock, AK 72215. Publishes *Dimensions of Early Childhood*.

Additional Journals and Magazines

Child, The New York Times Company Magazine Group, 110 Fifth Avenue, New York, NY 10011.

Child and Youth Care Quarterly, Human Sciences Press, 72 Fifth Avenue, New York, NY 10011.

Child Care Information Exchange, C 44, Redmond, Washington 98052.

Child Development, University of Chicago Press, P.O. Box 37005, Chicago, IL 60637.

Children, Rodale Press, Inc., 33 E. Minor St., Emmaus, PA 18098.

Children Today, Children's Bureau, Office of Child Development, U.S. Department of Health and Human Services, Washington, DC 20201.

Day Care and Early Education, Human Sciences Press, 72 Fifth Avenue, New York, NY 10011.

Early Child Development and Care, Roehampton Institute, Southlands College, Wimbledon Parkside, London SW19, England.

Early Education and Development, Psychology Press, Brandon, VT 05733.

Human Development, S. Karger AG, Allschwilerstrasse 10, P.O. Box CH-4009 Basel, Switzerland.

Journal of Family Issues, Sage Publications, Inc., 2111 W. Hillcrest Dr., Newbury Park, CA 91320.

Parenting, Parenting Magazine Partners, 501 Second Street, San Francisco, CA 94017.

Parents Magazine, 685 Third Avenue, New York, NY 10017.

Teaching Pre K–8, 40 Richards Avenue, Norwalk, CT 06854.

FOR FURTHER READING

Blank, Helen. "Early Childhood and the Public Schools: An Essential Partnership," *Young Children,* 40:4, May 1985, 52–55.

Bredekamp, Sue. "Composing a Profession," *Young Children,* 47:2, January 1992, 52–54.

Bredekamp, Sue and Barbara Willer. "Of Ladders and Lattices, Cores and Cones: Conceptualizing an Early Childhood Professional Development System," *Young Children,* 47:3, March 1992, 47–50.

Gunzenhauser, Nina and Bettye M. Caldwell. *Group Care for Young Children.* Skillman, NJ: Johnson & Johnson Baby Products Company, 1986.

Hendrick, Joanne. *Early Education for the Eighties.* Columbus, OH: Merrill, 1984.

Hildebrand, Verna. *Introduction to Early Childhood Education.* New York: Macmillan Publishing Company, 1991.

Hildebrand, Verna. *Management of Child Development Centers.* New York: Macmillan Publishing Company, 1993.

Kostelnik, M. J., A. P. Whiren, and A. K. Soderman. *Developmentally Appropriate Practice for Early Education: A Practical Guide.* Columbus, OH: Merrill/Macmillan, 1993.

Lombardi, Joan. "Viewpoint. Early Childhood 2001—Advocating for Comprehensive Services," *Young Children,* 47:4, May 1992, 24–25.

Mazur, Sally and Carrie Pekor. "Can Teachers Touch Children Anymore?" *Young Children,* 40:4, May 1985, 10–12.

Radomski, Mary Ann. "Professionalization of Early Childhood Educators," *Young Children,* 41:5, July 1986, 20–23.

Readdick, Christine A. "Schools for the American Nanny: Training In-Home Child Care Specialists," *Young Children,* 42:4, May 1987, 72–79.

Seefeldt, Carol and Nita Barbour. *Early Childhood Education: An Introduction.* Columbus, OH: Merrill/Macmillan, 1986.

Zigler, Edward F., and Mary E. Lang. *Child Care Choices: Balancing the Needs of Children, Families, and Society.* New York: The Free Press, 1991.

CHAPTER 23

Developing Human Resources

Key Concepts

◆ Definition of Resources
◆ Human Capital
◆ Human Resource Development
◆ Resource Exchange
◆ Inhibitors of Resource Development

"Daddy, Daddy," shouted Barbara. She was happy to see her father, who was picking her up at the child development center. "Daddy, come here and see what I can do," she called. Mr. Baker smiled and followed his little daughter to the climbing bar. Barbara said, "Watch me!" She expertly grasped the crossbar and held tight while she slipped her legs over the bar, then dropped her arms and swung by her knees. She smiled at her father from her upsidedown position. Watching closely, her father said, "That's great, Barb. I didn't know you could to that. Do it again, will you?"

Mr. Baker's human resources of interest and praise encouraged Barbara's development of motor skills. These skills became resources or means for Barbara to achieve the more difficult skills she would soon be learning, such as bike riding and roller skating.

RESOURCES

Try thinking of resources as intermediate goods required for making other goods or as means for achieving other goals. For example, you can think of steel as a resource for making automobiles, wheat as a resource for making bread, physical coordination as a resource for walking, and spelling ability as a resource for writing.

We are accustomed to thinking of common resources such as money, fuel, and food, which often make the headlines. However, people and the talents and knowledge they are developing are the most important resources. Without people's knowledge, abilities, skills, interactions, and communications, a society cannot progress. These human characteristics are often referred to as *human capital*. They are the assets available to combine with other resources to ensure the progress of a human society. Americans have generally invested heavily in schools, though at an early point in history the investment served boys more than girls.

Americans have been able to combine that investment in human capital with the capital assets of a vast and fertile country with large deposits of minerals and so on. We've become an industrial nation and the bread basket of the world. Japan, on the other hand, with a small geographical area and fewer natural resources, has, during its modern period, invested heavily in human capital to develop citizens' technical skills and know-how. Thus, by successfully developing human resources, Japan has been able to join the nations with high incomes and high exports.

HUMAN RESOURCE DEVELOPMENT—THE GOAL

Developing human resources is the goal of education from infant schools to classes for senior citizens. Through reading, study, and practice your personal competence will blossom. You'll find you have abilities that perhaps you are unaware of at this moment. These are your resources, your human bank account for the future.

What are your talents? What are your strengths? What do you know? What can you learn? Your talents, strengths, knowledge, skills, and potential to learn are your human resources. Human energy is the basis of all human resources. These resources will give you the means to achieve some goal. Money is the most familiar resource. It is a material or nonhuman resource that can be spent for some desired object or service, that is, goal. Human resources can also be "spent" and are means for achieving some desired goals. Lucky for you, though, your human resources don't become depleted like money, but will become enhanced with use. The more you use them the more you'll have.

As each goal is reached it can become a stepping-stone or resource for achieving additional goals. For example, with the development of your potential abilities for guiding young children you can become a more effective teacher or parent. Or, if you have special aptitude for music or mathematics, you might develop these resources and become a musician or a mathematician.

Two aspects to look at when you consider human resources are that they are both *utilized* and *developed* in the school and in the home. For example, writing this text has utilized energy, knowledge, and experience to help you in the development of your teaching and parenting skills. You, in turn, as a teacher or parent will sooner or later utilize your energy, knowledge, and experience to develop children's human resources—their abilities, skills and knowledge—in the best possible way.

In addition to utilizing and developing human resources, the helping professions call for the *exchange* of human resources. "Two heads are better than one" is an old adage that is at work when an individual interacts with and is helped or challenged by another person in solving a problem. That is one reason for committees and research teams. Often, too, two or more can handle a feat or project that would be impossible for one alone.

Person-to-person interaction on the educational scene can promote the exchange of human resources. The interaction can be teacher-child, child-child, parent-child, teacher-parent, or interaction with an important person, sometimes called a "significant other." Of course, interaction can have a negative impact on the involved individuals, but with skill, knowledge and a firm ethical position on the part of teachers and parents the interaction can assure positive results for children and adults.

Individuals learn from each other through interaction and communication. You can note the exchange of resources of skill, knowledge, and encouragement for the resources of friendship, respect, and love in the following: a teacher shares an idea for a bulletin board with a colleague down the hall; a farmer asks the extension agent for advice in selecting seed wheat; a grandmother pats her grandchild's head and says, "You're real pretty." In each interaction both the giver and the receiver are strengthened through the exchange. Though the resources given or received are intangible, they are valuable nonetheless.

Educators are concerned with the human resources of intellectual abilities, physical skills, creativity, and the motivation to put resources to work to achieve goals for the individual and for society at local, state, national, and global levels.

Building such human resources such as love, trust, empathy, and loyalty is important, especially in this day of stress on cognitive abilities, computer know-how, programmed learning, and concept cartridges. Person-to-person interaction and communication need to be nurtured in the home, school, and community. Humans need other humans regardless of the material comforts and gadgets they possess.

Think of Bea, a young early childhood teacher, who still vividly recalls a day many years ago when she was only four. She came running into her grandfather's little grocery, saying excitedly, "Grandfather, Grandfather, I can write my name." She remembers how his eyes lit up with interest as he tore a strip of paper from a roll of butcher paper, sat down with her by the counter, and asked her to "show me." She produced the letters bold and clear. He complimented her generously on her accomplishment and placed the little paper in his wallet. "He carries it to this day," she reports. It symbolizes to her his support, at an effective moment, for achieving an education.

As teachers and as parents, you will utilize both human and nonhuman energy resources for reaching the goals you set for individual children. Nonhuman resources include funds, facilities, equipment, supplies, and materials. Human resources include health, energy, ideas, motivation, creativity, mental and physical abilities, and the emotional support and help you freely give and accept from others. Children, siblings, parents, teachers, and other professional and lay individuals of the community all possess human resources capable of being developed, utilized, and exchanged in the process of educating young children.

All should appreciate the contributions made by the custodian, the cook, or the bus driver to the education process. The attitudes and helpfulness of secretaries, as well as the professionals, in agencies serving individuals and families can make valuable contributions to human resource development. For example, Anna, a foreign-born woman, may be seeking help in learning to speak and write English. She phones the basic education office. The answer can be courteous, communicating, and understanding, which will assure Anna's participation in appropriate classes. A single negative comment might frighten her away for a long time, thereby inhibiting her resource development.

Humans both *create* and *transform* human and nonhuman resources. Creating and transforming abilities must be preserved and strengthened in each individual. The children of today will be the leaders of the twenty-first century. They will face situations that neither their parents nor teachers can totally predict. Their success will require full use of their creative abilities to cope with new situations.

 Talk It Over

What are your personal resources? Which ones are outstanding? Which ones are you developing?

Teachers as Resources for Children

The teacher is a decision-maker, selecting goals and setting the stage for children to utilize both nonhuman and human resources. The allocation of both types of resources is part of every decision the teacher makes.

For example, a teacher who possesses resources of good mental and physical health, lots of energy, and emotional stability is able to help children in ways not possible if these resources are lacking. Teachers who possess excellent mental ability and are well informed, and those who have high motivation and are well prepared, surely achieve more goals for children than those without these resources. A teacher with the ability to relate to all children, to empathize with them, and to love them may be expected to develop more of these abilities in children. Children gain from teachers who utilize or set in motion the human resources that are available in other teachers, parents, and community members.

Teachers also need the ability to marshal nonhuman resources for the teaching and learning tasks at hand. Even as you study this course you have books, paper, classrooms, libraries, and money that have been allotted toward a goal of preparing you to guide young children. Teachers endeavor to increase human and nonhuman resources to enhance the learning experiences for students. Teachers of young children are noted for their resourcefulness in expanding resources through use of volunteers (human resources) or through "found" materials (nonhuman resources) such as scrap lumber for carpentry or odds and ends for art projects or play materials.

Children as Resources for Other Children and for Teachers

The idea of encouraging older children to help the younger ones creates in some people a nostalgia for the one-room school of the American pioneer era. The British Infant School and the Open Classroom are modern-day examples. This concept is in operation when sixth graders assist in the kindergarten. One child operates as a resource for another in any class where a child who is already skillful shows another how to do something. Children learn many of their new skills as they watch and imitate others in the child development center. If admitting ignorance were not so discomforting, demonstration and idea exchanges would operate at upper age levels more frequently and with greater ease.

Children in a family or within a school are resources for each other. This infant has two sisters who will love, console, and teach her throughout life.
(V. Hildebrand, photographer)

Teachers receive energy from children as well as give energy to them. Many teachers who have worked with children over a period of time know how much about life and learning these children have really taught them. Motivation to continue teaching depends a great deal on the positive response children give the teacher's efforts. Children really are a resource for the teacher, giving love, respect, and friendship as the teacher shares knowledge and skills with them and stimulates them to develop.

Parents as Resources for Children and Teachers

Children learn knowledge, skills, and abilities within the home and family. These qualities will serve them throughout life. Their first social interactions are learned within the family. Their language develops as they attend to verbal demands and hear expectations explained there. A reward system is learned, and it helps the child know what to do and what not to do. The family transmits its values of what "ought" to be through many of its behaviors.

Cognitive skills of reasoning, thinking, and memory are practiced. Children also learn to work within the family, helping with the production and maintenance chores required. It is within the family that the child gains a sense of self—of who he or she is—and gains a sense of the future and of what it is possible to become.

When children are enrolled in a child development center, they already have a background of learning, unless, of course, they are very young infants. Because children and others learn by relating new information or ways of doing things to their previous learning, it is very logical that the teachers and caregivers must strive to link together the home and school—the child's two places for learning. Most parents want to be a resource for their child's education. Many do an excellent job of utilizing both nonhuman and human resources to provide a stimulating educational environment in their homes. This advantage has been referred to as the "hidden curriculum" of the middle-class child. Parents may need to be guided, and sometimes reassured, as they strive to use their resources to help their children during the school years. Nowhere in the long process of education is the parent's contribution more important than in the preprimary schools. Involving parents in order that they can truly contribute must be the goal of every school program.

Mothers' energy resources have traditionally been tapped for serving on bake-sale and carnival committees, as room mothers, or as drivers on field trips. However, you need to keep in mind that traditional stereotyped roles are no longer binding for either men or women. The many talents of women are now being widely applied. Major benefits to women and to society are indeed apparent. Though some parents may have little time or interest in baking cookies, they may be helpful to the teacher in other ways.

For example, one mother who was a bus dispatcher invited the children to the bus station to see the bus being washed in the bus wash. Another mother was associated with cable television and arranged for children to appear on television and to observe themselves in action.

Parents are children's most important resource for learning—their first teacher. Parents' close alliance with the school increases the effectiveness of both the home and school. (Parent-Child Development Center, Houston)

Fathers, too, can be a valuable resource. Remember how Mr. Baker encouraged Barbara in our little story that opened this chapter. Fathers' visits and participation in the school scene should be encouraged. They can also share their vocational or avocational skills. For example, a carpenter father may supervise room renovation, or a contractor father may supervise the building of new tricycle paths. Parents with a talent such as playing a musical instrument can perform for and lead children in a musical experience. Either fathers or mothers may offer resources for field trips or special demonstrations at their place of work. Fathers can also bake cookies.

Families as Resources for Other Families

Parents or the family as a whole can become resources for other families. This exchange of resources can sometimes be facilitated through the center. The parent-cooperative centers have been particularly effective in linking families together. They may begin exchanges by sharing baby sitting. Children from one family may play together and later spend the night at one another's homes. Thus develops a support system that is especially needed when extended family systems are not available. In some cities baby-sitting co-ops

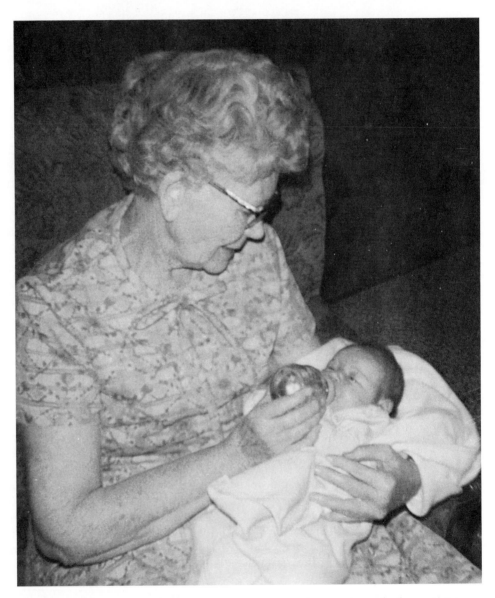

Adults are resources for children. This grandmother will be a resource for her grand-daughter for years to come.
(L. Butcher, photographer)

develop among ten to fifteen families in a church or in a workplace. The parents are given paper checks "good for one-hour of baby sitting" to exchange for baby sitting among the members. Thus, a support system is built up for extending the resources of each family. Of course, the extended family provides a traditional support system for families with young children; however, with many grandparents working or with families living far apart, this system is frequently unavailable to families. Neighbors and friends are among many families' support system. However, with the aging of the society the neighbors may be elderly people who are unable to care for children. Single-parent mothers and fathers especially need to find reliable sources of backup support.

 Talk It Over

From your experience, in what ways has another family helped (or been a resource for) your family, or your family helped another family? Was the exchange a one-time exchange or continuous reciprocity? In what ways did both families gain?

Many nonformal family-life programs have developed over the years to help families help themselves. The Cooperative Extension Program that is organized in every county in the United States, the child-study clubs, and churches of all denominations are sources of information and support for families to exchange resources. Most are voluntary, some are supported by government funds, and others are privately operated.

Teachers as Resources for Parents

The teacher's role becomes one of guiding parental resources so that they can contribute toward reaching goals. Supporting the parents' ability to help their children grow, develop, and learn is usually part of the school's parent-education program. Because the school can achieve little success without support from parents, the parent-education or parent resource-building aspects must be undertaken simultaneously with educational programs for the child. Helpful activities are conferences, meetings, and newsletters.

One way that skilled and experienced early childhood educators can link home and school is to communicate carefully about what the child does at school. They can give the family support when there is something the parents want the child to learn or do. Teachers can suggest alternatives should parents' goals seem inappropriate, especially when the parents seem to expect more from the child than he or she is developmentally capable of doing. The staff can be sympathetic toward the complexity of life for many modern parents.

Teachers can provide individual consultation to parents. They may furnish reading materials, or direct them to community services that will support needs of the child and the family. In this mobile society teachers may become advisors to the family, because they may be more interested in the child than any other individual outside the family. Refer to Chapter 21 for further suggestions.

Volunteers as Resources for Children

Volunteers of various types can be recruited to help children during and after school. Such exchanges of resources can be mutually beneficial. Programs that organize such volunteers as foster grandparents, cadet teachers, high-school or college students, and classroom aides all help put human resources to work benefiting children. For example, many students who expect to teach children do volunteer work in children's centers to gain experience in addition to that offered by their courses. They learn from children, enhancing their personal resources, while children learn from them.

Some retired men and women give their time, skill, and energy resources to children in child development centers and to children in neighborhoods as they babysit for them or respond to them as friends. Many retirees have time to give attention, help, and a warm comfortable lap to sit on. They like the feeling of being needed and appreciated that they receive in return. Some homebound senior citizens crochet or knit clutch balls for active catching or warm mittens to protect children's hands from the cold. One 90-year-old man has been playing his harmonica for children's groups for years. Like the Pied Piper, he boasts a following of happy children. Through these examples you can begin to understand how the exchange of human resources enhances the lives of both the receiver and the giver.[1]

Planning for, guiding, and rewarding volunteers are essential tasks that the teachers must attend to if this wealth of human resources is to be effectively utilized for children. Volunteers want specific directions. They want recognition for what they do. They want to feel important to the job. If volunteers leave school one day with a feeling of not being noticed or appreciated, they may never return.

INHIBITORS OF HUMAN RESOURCE DEVELOPMENT

Prejudice, discrimination, and inequality of opportunity are inhibitors that deter or prevent a child's human resources from developing to the fullest extent possible. These inhibitors may occur in the family, in the school, in the state or nation, or among nations. Individuals are denied opportunities to develop through accidents of birth—being born black or female, for example. A

---

[1] For a description of an effective program that integrates senior citizens in a child care program, see Carol Seefeldt et al., "As Children See Old Folks," *Today's Education,* 66:2, 1977, pp. 70–74. See also Lillian Phenice, *Children's Perceptions of the Elderly* (Saratoga, CA: Century Twenty One Publishing, 1981), a report on children who had senior volunteers in their child care center.

counselor once attempted to track a minority student into beauty school when she said she wanted to know about college programs. Happily this young woman had determination and persisted in her desire for a college education and eventually became one of the country's top early childhood educators. Another woman was sidetracked out of a career in mathematics, being told that "they don't hire women math teachers." It is now a U.S. government policy to provide equal opportunity and prevent discrimination on the basis of gender, race, or religion. The goal is still unachieved, but all early childhood educators should be working to be sure that these inhibitors are not at work in their centers—that each child or parent receives equal opportunity and the encouragement to develop all human resources regardless of gender, race, religion, or economic status.

CONCLUSION

Considering a broad global goal of developing the human capital for fulfilling the wants and needs of the future society helps early childhood educators view their work as very essential, not only for the child's future, but for the future of society as a whole. Helping individuals and families maximize the development of their human resources as suggested in the following Ten Ways to Foster Human Resource Development can be an important contribution of the child development center staff.

REVIEW AND APPLICATIONS

Ten Ways to Foster Human Resource Development

1. Appreciate that human capital or human resource development is essential for the world's future.
2. Value the potential in each child for developing human resources of knowledge, ability, skills, and so forth.
3. Recognize the contribution the family makes to children's human resource development. Strive to link home and school in a cooperative effort.
4. Strive to eliminate every hint of prejudice, discrimination, and inequality of opportunity that could inhibit the development of children or parents.
5. Recognize ways that teachers are resources for children.
6. Recognize ways that parents and children are resources for teachers.
7. Recognize and encourage children to become resources for other children.
8. Recognize and encourage families to become resources for other families.

9. Recognize ways that community members can become resources for children and families.
10. Develop strategies for strengthening child development services within the community, state, nation, and world.

 Observations

1. Observe and record an example of resource exchanges:
   a. A child being a resource for another child.
   b. A teacher being a resource for a child.
   c. A teacher being a resource for a parent.
   d. A parent being a resource for a child or the teacher.
   e. Summarize your conclusions.
2. Analyze your records of your case-study child taken in previous weeks for evidence of human resources the child possesses.
   a. Give examples of the child's strengths and abilities.
   b. Describe the skills the child seems to be concentrating on at the present time.
   c. Give examples of the teacher being a resource for this child.
   d. Give examples of the child's parents being a resource for the child.
   e. Give evidence of the child being a resource for other children or of their being a resource for this child.

Applications

1. Assist two children in a home or a school. Note examples of exchanges of human resources. Explain what happened. How were the children's resources helped or hindered?
2. Recall a point in your own experience when one individual used personal resources in a way that supported your human resource development. Explain what happened.
3. Analyze one of your own skills. What are the skills that this new skill is built on? At what age did you begin developing the original skill?
4. Refer to the Twelve Performance Standards for Participators in Chapter 1 or the checksheet you developed. List and discuss the human resources you have developed this term.

FOR FURTHER READING

Bader, Lois, and Verna Hildebrand. "An Exploratory Study of Three to Five Year Old's Responses on the Bader Reading and Language Inventory to

Determine Developmental Stages of Emerging Literacy," *Early Child Development and Care,* Vol. 77, August 1992, 83–95.

Elkind, David. "Readiness for Kindergarten," *Young Children,* 42:3, March 1987, 2.

NAEYC. "Good Discipline Is, in Large Part, the Result of a Fantastic Curriculum," *Young Children,* 42:3, March 1987, 49–51.

Stone, Janet I. "Early Childhood Math: Make It Manipulative!" *Young Children,* 42:6, September 1987, 16–23.

CHAPTER 24

Valuing as a Basis for Actions

Key Concepts

◆ Definition of Values
◆ Reconciling Value Differences
◆ Definition of Ethics
◆ Values and Accreditation

"Oh, there you are, Dana," Miss Stevenson said to a shy little girl who was arriving late at the child development center, after the activity was well under way. "We've been hoping you would come to help us make the applesauce." Dana smiled and went to remove her coat. Miss Stevenson spoke quietly to Dana. She understood that this shy little girl needed quiet recognition and did not want attention drawn to her from all the other children.

Individualized and personalized teaching were very high on Miss Stevenson's hierarchy of values. She felt that it was important for each child to be recognized and spoken to as he or she arrived each day. The quiet yet warm greeting assured Dana that she was very important to her teacher.

TEACHING—ART OR SCIENCE?

Teaching is often referred to as an art, and credit is sometimes given to intuitive or creative teachers for the exceptional programs they devise. However, in addition to possessing intuition and creativity, teachers should be able to process rapidly (1) knowledge of child development; (2) knowledge of individual children's needs; (3) knowledge of guidance techniques and alternatives; (4) knowledge of curriculum and materials; and (5) knowledge of their own and others' experience. With such knowledge, coupled with intuition and creativity, teachers should be able to make on-the-spot decisions and implement those decisions in a satisfactory and growth-producing manner for all concerned.

Decision-making in the child development center, in the family day care home, and in the home can be person-centered and in keeping with the human resource development ideas proposed in Chapter 23.

VALUES—BASIS OF DECISIONS

Your decisions regarding what to do with children will be based largely on the *values* you hold. Values are concepts of the desirable. They are the "oughts" or "shoulds" that guide our actions. Your values are reflected in your behavior and determine the goals you set and the actions that grow from your goals. Many values may be unconscious until you work at bringing them to the level of awareness, or search for the implicit values on which your actions or the actions of others are, in fact, based.

Where do values come from in your own scheme of things? Actually, you've been acquiring them all your life, from your family, your friends, and your community, including your schooling. Values get firmly set early in life and are difficult to change. They relate to such things as family, religion, economics, politics, work, play, health, freedom, individuality, order, and beauty. What are the "oughts" or "shoulds" related to each of these concepts that immediately come to your mind?

You, as a teacher, hold values; the parents whose children you serve also hold values (and these may be different from yours); and the children are developing their own values. These three viewpoints must be considered if you are to provide the best guidance for young children.

 Talk It Over

When do you hear yourself saying "you ought to . . . " to a friend or relative? What value does your "ought" phrase indicate?
What do your parents tell you you "ought to" do? What does this advice indicate about what your parents value?

VALUES AND THE PROFESSION

Does a commitment to the early childhood profession bring with it value positions? How are these value positions developed? Are they different from personal values?

The United States Constitution, under which all American professionals work, provides a framework for valuing and for acting. The concepts of equality, freedom, free speech, freedom of religion, and due process under the law are very strong value positions defined in the Constitution. These values must be considered paramount and inviolable in any profession.

The Constitution provides the framework for every American profession. The specific values that a profession might define must operate under all constitutional provisions. Any action of individuals working in any public service,

When you value the individual learning of children you take time to talk to children to understand what they know and how they learn.
(Savannah Public Schools)

such as an early childhood school or center, must never infringe on these fundamental constitutional rights of the parents, children, or employees.

Can personal values differ from constitutional and professional values? It may be theoretically conceivable for an individual manager or teacher to hold different personal values from the constitutional and agreed upon professional values. However, the likelihood is that personal values of individuals determine many interactions, decisions, and behaviors. Undoubtedly the individual would have many periods of discomfort and dissonance. Thus, by choosing to work in a profession one must ascribe to certain generally held values.

VALUES AND ACCREDITATION

The most important indicators of high-quality programs in early childhood schools and centers are the basis of the National Association for the Education of Young Children's (NAEYC) accreditation system. To arrive at the final list of indicators or criteria of high quality in a program, a large number of professionals, center and school managers and teachers, and parents reviewed the indicators. After several rounds of recommendations, reactions and revisions, they reached a consensus on the list that is being used that was accepted by the board of the organization. Compromises were made to get agreement between the theoreticians and the practitioners. Thus, the accreditation system brings together the widely held values of persons involved in the profession. The resulting program has created a system of recognition to which individuals within and outside the profession can turn for measures of what programs "ought" to be. Therefore, the accreditation system is based on the most widely held values of people in the profession.

When you value children's curious minds, you provide a variety of activities to engage their curiosity.
(University of New Mexico Manzanita Child Care Center)

NAEYC's decision to move toward accreditation is in itself a value position, in that the association wanted a way to recognize centers and schools that were producing excellent programs for children.[1] There was no mechanism for public recognition of excellent programs. To date over 2,500 centers nationwide have been accredited and numerous others are in the process of becoming accredited. Not only does accreditation of a center ensure children an excellent program, it brings prestige for the center. A center with NAEYC accreditation is being recognized by many parents as preferred over a nonaccredited center. In addition, teachers are choosing to work in accredited centers, because of the indicators in accreditation that make the center a good place to work. Such indicators are paid planning time, staff-child ratios, staff benefits, personnel policies, and generally more effective operating procedures than centers that are not accredited.

A concept that is used extensively in the *Accreditation Criteria* is the term *developmentally appropriate practice*. To help further define high-quality, another NAEYC effort produced the booklet that gives details of developmentally appropriate (and inappropriate) practice for several age groups.[2] Each age requires a special understanding and environment. A widely held belief is that inappropriate practice is harmful to young children.

Clearly, in both the Center Accreditation system and the statement of developmentally appropriate practice the profession has taken a strong value position. This position has been arrived at by a consensus of the researchers and practitioners in the organization. It means that professionals agree to base

---

[1] Sue Bredekamp (ed.), *Accreditation Criteria and Procedures of the National Academy of Early Childhood Programs* (Washington, DC: NAEYC, 1991).

[2] Sue Bredekamp (ed.), *Developmentally Appropriate Practice in Early Childhood Programs Serving Children from Birth Through Age 8* (Washington, DC: NAEYC, 1987).

actions and programs on information from research and practice with both children and parents.

There are those who believe child care and early childhood education are becoming too costly with the emphasis on high quality and a current emphasis on increasing the salaries of child care employees. Some argue that children of poverty will not be able to gain from such idealized programs. However, others who have worked with poor children will argue that they benefit the most from high standards. As Cartwright says, "To build a little school filled with mutual affection, humor, and cooperative learning in the midst of such a 'community' isn't easy. But it's possible. It's important. For democracy it may be imperative. And I believe that parents, teachers, and citizens who meet this challenge may be coming to grips with the very meaning of life."[3]

ETHICS IN THE PROFESSION

What is ethical behavior if you are an early childhood professional? Are professional ethics and personal ethics the same? Is our profession sufficiently mature to need to define more specifically ethical behavior?

Ethics is an academic discipline dealing with right and wrong behavior in the line of duty. Ethics goes beyond rules and laws. Ethics is an extension of a concept of values and moral behavior. All early childhood educators are confronted with ethical and value problems. These should be discussed within each center or school as they are applied to specific children, families, and employees.

The results of the NAEYC's study commission that worked on a statement of ethics for the association is titled *The National Association for the Education of Young Children Code of Ethical Conduct*. The code addresses ethical responsibilities toward children, families, colleagues, community, and society.[4]

VALUES INTO ACTION

"Do values really make that much difference?" you may be asking.

Following are nine stories about nine hypothetical teachers. These stories were developed for and are part of some research conducted by the author. Each story is designed to illustrate a particular value orientation. Can you identify and label what value orientation is predominant in each story and in the decisions the teacher is making in the class? In real life, every teacher is probably a combination of several "stories." Which one illustrates for you the

---

[3] From an insightful rebuttal to the idea that high standards won't help children of poverty, see Sally Cartwright's, "Quality Classrooms for ALL Children, Especially for Children of Poverty," *Young Children,* 47:3, March 1992, p. 2.

[4] NAEYC, *Young Children,* 45:1, November 1989, pp. 24–29.

most important focus of a teacher's decisions? Which is most like you? Least? Pick out the first- and second-ranking stories and the lowest-ranking story according to the values you think are important in teaching. Can you explain your reasons for ranking the stories the way you did? If you can discuss the stories with a few parents, you may find that their views differ from yours. Where do these differences arise? How can you mediate the differences if you have their children in your classroom? The nine stories that follow are reproduced as used in the research project. Female teachers are used in all the examples to help avoid making choices based on the gender of the teacher.

1.   Teacher A thinks it important for children to learn to get along with others. She feels children learn to get along, to help each other, and to share by having freedom to interact. Her classroom is usually a beehive of activity. She willingly puts off a science lesson if there is a spontaneous group activity in progress at that moment. Teacher A makes friends with children and parents and arranges situations so that each child will know and make friends with all the others. When difficulties arise, she prefers to let children work out the problem, intervening only as a last resort. She sometimes helps parents arrange their children's play groups during weekends or vacations.

2.   Teacher B believes that children should be well prepared for "real school." Her classroom schedule is arranged so that she gets lots of basic learning material covered each day. She avoids getting sidetracked during a class project; therefore, she is able to carry out lesson plans completely. She believes she must teach children a good deal of information, including ABCs, colors, shapes, and numbers. Her children frequently achieve above-average scores on standardized tests, which indicates to her that they are learning the material. Her talks with parents focus on children's preparation for first grade. She participates in lectures and seminars to expand her own learning whenever available.

3.   Teacher C is concerned that children develop a sense of morality and good judgment. She often discusses with them how they ought to behave.

When you value a child's motor development, you take time to play ball with him.
(S. Russell, photographer)

She tells them her own views and introduces religious stories and ideas to the children. The children are taught what is right and wrong and are expected to behave accordingly. Manners and saying "please" and "thank you" are stressed. Teacher C discusses any topic that is of interest to children, especially if she feels it will aid their character development. She encourages them to correct each other if they feel someone is doing something wrong.

4.   Teacher D keeps her classroom looking attractive at all times. She takes special care that the colors are harmonious and that various artifacts are displayed in the room. Children's art objects and paintings are carefully mounted and labeled. Creative movement and music, including works of the great composers, are a part of the program. Well-written children's literature is used regularly. Teacher D wears colorful and fashionable clothing. She helps children arrange their hair and clothing to look their best.

5.   Teacher E's schedule and activities are outlined by the school's director, and she carefully follows these guidelines. She is grateful for the leadership of her school's director and values the opinions of fellow teachers and parents. At the beginning of each year the director distributes a list of policies and regulations that give Teacher E a guide for administration in her classroom. She believes that the director is a competent administrator and knows a lot about running the class. She is pleased when the director brings in new learning programs for her to use.

6.   Teacher F likes children to have lots of fresh air and sunshine. She carefully checks to see that the children have sufficient light, correct temperature, and chairs and tables of suitable height. Each morning she checks up on their habits of good breakfast, daily bath, tooth brushing, and proper rest. She checks throats and chests for signs of contagious disease and has children taken home when they seem ill. Routines of toileting and hand washing are frequent in her schedule. Nutritious foods are always available for snacks.

7.   Teacher G feels that children should really plan their own program. She avoids thinking ahead about what children will be doing each day, but brings toys out as children arrive and indicate their interests. She may choose an activity because she particularly wants to do it that day. She tries to respond to children's needs of the moment and avoids pushing them into organized learning tasks. She emphasizes spontaneous learning, picking up on some project that the children seem interested in. Her schedule is completely flexible, and rarely do the children follow the same schedule for two days in a row.

8.   Teacher H believes that each child learns in a different way. She considers the child a person first and a student second. Her program is arranged so that each child can express his or her individuality. A supportive atmosphere prevails that allows the child to feel free to venture into new experiences, but at the same time it is not one of indulgence. Teacher H strives to plan a rich variety of experiences with fresh views of familiar scenes, excursions to new places, or walks in parks. She uses many methods of motivation and novel ways of sparking children's imaginations.

9.   Teacher I stresses protecting the school property and conserving materials. She teaches the children to use supplies such as paint, paper, and glue sparingly. She searches for "found" materials to supplement her supplies and utilizes all volunteer services available. She shows children how to use all their paper for a picture even if they paint a small spot and start to leave. Teacher I is also concerned with saving time, works at being efficient, and expects to teach children these traits. She thinks education is a way of improving one's station in life and a way of making a good living.

In these nine situations the primary value orientation in each story is

1. socialization,
2. intellect,
3. morality,
4. aesthetics,
5. authority,
6. health,
7. freedom,
8. individuality, and
9. economics.

Researcher Judy Harris Helm surveyed a panel of early childhood educators to determine how the educators thought various values in early childhood education programs would be effectively implemented by (1) the teacher's role; (2) the scheduling procedures; (3) the choice of activities and equipment; (4) the policies of the school; (5) the space allocation; and (6) the physical facilities. Over two hundred statements were agreed on by all panel members indicating what teachers and others holding the listed values would do to support those values. The following list of value areas was studied in Helm's research:

Valuing aesthetics

Valuing confidentiality and ethics

Valuing creativity

Valuing the emotional development of the child

Valuing the health and safety of the child

Valuing the intellectual development of the child

Valuing the individuality of the child

Valuing involvement of the parent in the preschool

Valuing the physical development of the child

Valuing the development of school skills

Valuing the social development of the child[4]

---

[5] Judy Harris Helm, "Indicators of Early Childhood Program Values," Ph.D. dissertation, West Virginia University, Morgantown, WV, December, 1977.

When you value a child's positive responses, you take time to enjoy moments with the child.
(C. Hildebrand, photographer)

By this time in your study of guiding young children you should be able to write a list of ways these values are implemented in your early childhood programs and another list showing what you would do to implement these values if you were in charge of the programs.

Each teacher places certain values in higher priority than others and therefore in decision-making situations chooses alternatives that reflect these values. For example, if the children have unloaded the entire shelf of blocks in the classroom, teachers who place a high value on order may be upset. However, they may be reconciled to the behavior when they notice that the blocks are being used in a creative manner, because creativity is "good" in their value system. In the moment between when the teachers almost scold the children for unloading the blocks and when they actually compliment them for their interesting structure they must weigh several value-based alternatives.

RECONCILING VALUE DIFFERENCES

When several teachers work as a team, as is typical of most early childhood classrooms, frank discussions about values must be held so that the short-term and long-term goals can be established for the group and for each child. Teachers' values are not likely to be identical, but the teachers must come to some level of agreement; otherwise, conflicts arise and children and parents will be predictably confused. If Miss Laissez-faire and Miss Highly Structured are assigned to the same classroom, results may be damaging to children unless compromises are worked out.

Conflicts over values may arise between parents and the teachers. Should teachers teach a white child to love a dark-skinned child when that is not the accepted value of the community? Should teachers teach views that parents do not agree with? Should teachers teach children to be "better" or different than their parents? A serious acceptance of each other's rights to differing views and a willingness to mediate the conflicts are essential for resolving problems.

  Talk It Over

Should a teacher tell you that you are capable of doing better or more advanced work when you have never asked for such an evaluation? How do values figure into such advice?

Given demands by parents or others to teach upper-school content or to use methods unacceptable from a personal-professional value base, the teacher's ultimate resort is to quit the teaching position, unless parents or others can be convinced that the teacher's value position has validity and are willing to compromise. Teachers must live with themselves. Working day after day in a system that defies one's values would not only damage the teacher psychologically but might also harm the children.[6]

For example, a striking value conflict arose when a new teacher, Susan, began working in a child development center. She discovered that caregivers regularly disciplined children by spanking their bare buttocks with rulers. She protested that form of discipline to the caregivers and to the director. However, failing to get the practice modified, Susan said, "I quit. I've got my own conscience to sleep with." When she left the center she picked up the rulers, took them to the social service authorities responsible for licensing, and reported the case.

State and national values are translated into laws and into policies resulting from laws. These provide guidelines for teachers to follow and may protect the teacher by defining the number of children legally permitted in a class, the minimum space requirements for the school, the training that is required before certification and so on.

---

[6] For a creative essay by a humanistic person-centered teacher who observed so many actions against children in one school where she taught that she finally gave up teaching there and relocated to another school that was compatible with her value position, see Carol Catron, "Circles of Sunshine," *Young Children,* 31:6, September 1978, pp. 449–459.

When you value a child's sense of security, you take time to provide support for that security. (University of Illinois Child Development Laboratory)

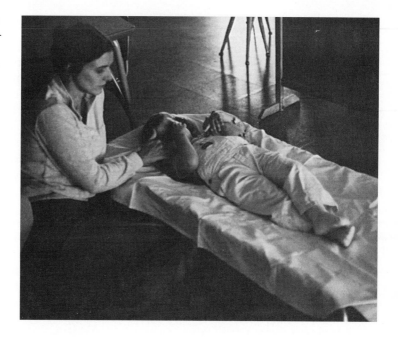

The teacher's philosophy of life, of human development, of family dynamics, and of education will be reflected in the program that is developed for children and in the interaction that takes place between and among individuals.

Teaching styles develop out of the teacher's personality, knowledge, experience, and values. "Teaching style" denotes the unique way that the teacher makes decisions and interacts with the children in the class. For wholesome development to occur, the classroom management must reflect the teacher's understanding of the child's total existence. There must be a joint endeavor between home and school. Children may spend as many as nine hours a day in a child development center, but the child spends more hours away from the center than in it, though it is to be hoped that many are bedtime hours. A teacher may plan for as many as fifteen or twenty children and several assistants, which complicates the decision-making considerably. Enough adults should be available to preserve the person-centered philosophy of the total child development program.

Value orientations are hard to change, but persons do change their values given adequate reasons and time to practice their new behavior. With increased knowledge of child development, teachers and teachers-to-be can learn to adjust their expectations to fill children's developmental levels. Given alternatives to authoritarian teaching styles, they can learn to be more democratic and person-centered. Or, given experience with a flexible schedule, disorganized persons can become comfortable when they learn to be more orderly. Most importantly, a better understanding of alternative value systems and implications for children is gained.

CONCLUSION

Values and ethical positions are part of each person's life. Values indicate what "ought" or "should" be done. When you become involved in a profession like early childhood education, which provides a service to the public, you have a special responsibility to follow the values set forth in the U.S. Constitution and those of the early childhood profession. Agreeing to join a profession obligates you to think seriously about values and ethics in your professional life.

You are reared with values. Because children are very impressionable, family values are often very influential in the behavior of an individual. These values may be expanded through socialization and education. As individuals reach an adult abstract reasoning level each can mentally reason the outcomes of various value positions. People can change values if desired, though it is usually difficult. Behaviors are based on the values individuals hold, though some may be part of the unconscious. Human beings are rational and thus are capable of changing long-standing behaviors, once they make up their mind to do it, that is, once they begin to value differently. For this reason it is important to help individuals bring values to the levels of awareness.

REVIEW AND APPLICATIONS

Ten Characteristics of Values

1. Values are defined as concepts of the desirable.
2. Values are learned throughout life through study, instruction, and example.
3. Values can be either conscious or unconscious.
4. Values can be brought to the level of awareness.
5. Values guide actions and decisions of individuals.
6. Values have been enshrined in the Constitution, laws, and regulations.
7. Values are rarely identical for two individuals.
8. Values are reflected in an early childhood program.
9. Values are the basis for regulations and standards in early childhood programs.
10. Values can be changed through the conscious effort of individuals.

Applications

1. Read the value stories in the chapter and rank the one you think is the most desirable focus of a head teacher's planning. List your second-place story. List the ninth-place story. Discuss or write an explanation of reasons for your ranking.

2. Write a description of another teacher who represents the kind of teacher you would like to be. Which values do you find you have included?
3. Discuss with a parent what he or she feels is the most desirable focus of a child development center program. Write a summary of the comments. Identify the values emphasized.

 Observations

1. Observe the teachers working with children in your center. Record ten minutes of their behavior—exactly what they do. Type the observation down the left half of a page. On the right-hand side note the possible values each behavior episode seems to imply. Summarize what you find.
2. Observe a parent interacting with his or her child. Write down the episode and then note the values the episode implies. Summarize what you find.
3. Look over all your notes regarding your case-study child. Do you have an indication of the parents' values they hold for their child? What are they? What action do they seem to be carrying out that indicates they really value this? Summarize.

ADDITIONAL RESOURCES

Suggested Videotape

What Is Quality Child Care?   VHS   1/2 in   Color   57 minutes   1988

Why isn't our society child oriented? An inspiring keynote address by Asa G. Hilliard III. NAEYC, Media, 1509 16th Street, N.W., Washington, DC 20036-1426.

FOR FURTHER READING

Feeney, Stephanie. "Ethical Case Studies for NAEYC Reader Response," *Young Children,* 42:4, May 1987, 24–25.

Gartrell, Dan. "Assertive Discipline: Unhealthy for Children and Other Living Things," *Young Children,* 42:2, January 1987, 10–11.

Haiman, Peter E. "There is More to Early Childhood Education Than Cognitive Development," *Young Children,* 40:1, November 1984, 8.

Kipnis, Kenneth. "How to Discuss Professional Ethics," *Young Children,* 42:4, May 1987, 26–30.

NAEYC. *The National Association for the Education of Young Children Code of Ethical Conduct. Young Children,* 45:1, November 1989, 24–29.

Riley, Sue Spayth. *How to Generate Values in Young Children.* Washington, DC: NAEYC, 1984.

Schweinhart, Lawrence J. and David P. Weikart. "What Do We Know So Far? A Review of the Head Start Synthesis Project," *Young Children,* 41:2, January 1987, 49–55.

Wardle, Francis. "Are You Sensitive to Interracial Children's Special Identity Needs?" *Young Children,* 42:2, January 1987, 53–59.

Willert, Mary K. and Constance Kamii. "Reading in Kindergarten: Direct vs. Indirect Teaching," *Young Children,* 40:4, May 1985, 3–9.

CHAPTER 25

Evaluating—Who Needs It?

Key Concepts

◆ Perspectives on Education
◆ Accreditation Procedures

"Watcha doing with that book?" inquired five-year-old Mandy, pointing to the little black book carried by Mr. Alonzo, the curriculum coordinator. "I may write in it some time," answered the school official. "Well! If you're not using it, why don'tcha put it away?" remarked Mandy, probably repeating lines she had heard adults use.

Mr. Alonzo's mission was evaluation. He visited all classrooms regularly to *examine* and *judge* how the school's stated objectives were being met.

The values of the parents, school, community, nation, and world will influence school programs. Often values are implicit, that is, not specifically indicated. However, better understanding of policies and programs is assured if value judgments are given explicitly, that is, clearly stated.

Values are of major significance and a source of much lively controversy. Lively controversy is a healthy sign in a democratic society and the source of much progress. However, different and changing views in the area of values create fascinating problems for Mr. Alonzo's mission of evaluation.

If there is anything that makes some people uncomfortable, it's evaluation. It's scary to have the minister visit unless the house looks just right because you think a judgment might be made about you. Perhaps you wish your mother-in-law would call before she drops in because you think she judges your housekeeping. A teacher becomes "uptight" when aware that the curriculum coordinator is in the building. Or perhaps it's the licensing officer from the department of social services who is the bogeyman for the child development center. These individuals are usually making judgments or evaluations of children's programs as it is their job to do so.

Evaluators are supposed to see if you are meeting some standard. Standards are criteria or values that society holds for children's programs. Hopefully, you know what those standards are. Should teachers fear evaluators? Actually, most good teachers are doing a far better job than the minimum licensing standards for child development centers require. So why should you fret about evaluations?

Be sure you have read your state's licensing standards and the center accreditation standards of NAEYC. Then you'll understand what you are working toward and what you'll be evaluated upon.

YOUR EVALUATION

At the close of Chapter 1, twelve Performance Standards for Participators were listed. It was suggested that you use them as summarized in the proposed checksheet (Table 1–1) to evaluate weekly your performance in the participation part of your course. At the close of the other chapters were lists of guidance methods, techniques, and principles. You were asked to rate the applicable ones for your center on a 1-to-5 scale. Undoubtedly it has been a challenge for you. Looking at something with the purpose of evaluating it is never easy. However, now you have some important experience in evaluation. It will help you as a future teacher. As you read this closing chapter you'll learn why evaluation is so important.

 Talk It Over

What were your feelings about being evaluated during the term?
Was it easier to accept positive feedback than negative feedback?
What does this tell you about evaluating children?

WHO NEEDS EVALUATION?

Managers

The managers, principals, and directors of early childhood schools and centers need to do evaluations and they need to be continuously alert to deviations from standards that they and others set. A school or center is given a mission or mandate when a school is funded. A board generally delegates to a manager-level employee the responsibility for maintaining the agreed-on levels of performance and service. Periodically the funding agency will want to know that the mandate is being carried out.

In each state there are minimum standards established by the agencies that license and monitor child care and other early childhood education programs. School systems generally have systems for evaluating programs, as the opening anecdote indicates. The curriculum coordinator was a mid-level administrator who monitored what was happening in the kindergarten.

Accreditation. Accreditation is a recent development in early childhood schools and centers. As indicated throughout this book, the National Association for the Education of Young Children (NAEYC) established the accreditation system in 1984 following an exhaustive process of establishing the criteria and procedures by contacting a cross-sectional sample of people involved in early childhood education.[1] The National Academy of Early Childhood Programs was organized as an arm of NAEYC to manage the accreditation program. The accreditation process is totally voluntary.

The system works in the following manner. The manager orders the materials for accreditation from NAEYC, paying a fee, the amount varying depending on the size of the unit. The manager and staff initiate a *self-study* using the NAEYC materials. They look at staff training, staff interaction, educational programs for the children, involvements of parents, administrative procedures, health procedures, nutritional standards, safety provisions, and other aspects. When they find conditions that do not meet the established criteria they begin efforts to improve. When finally they believe all the criteria are met they inform NAEYC that they are ready for a validation visit.

A *validation visit* is done by a professionally trained early childhood educator who is unknown to the center manager or staff. The validator spends a day or so in the center methodically checking to see if the conditions reported in the center's self-study are at a high level of excellence. The validator confers with the manager regarding the findings and then reports to the National Academy of Early Childhood Programs. Finally, a commission reviews the self-study report and the validator's report and awards or rejects the accreditation. Accreditation is valid for three years after which a compliance review is initiated.

The fact and the symbol of accreditation may be displayed in the school, used in publicity materials, and in recruiting both children and staff. There are now over 2,500 accredited centers in the United States with hundreds more in the initial self-study phase. Many children are benefitting from the enthusiasm of their teachers and managers as programs are improved to meet the high-level standards of excellence.

Teachers

Teachers should be the first to say, "Of course we need evaluation. We are evaluating all the time, every minute of the day. We make a decision, see the effects of the decision, and make adjustments, even in the immediate situation if necessary, to remedy a situation that doesn't come up to standard. That's evaluation."

Evaluation is nothing more than checking up to see how well you are meeting standards. Teachers evaluate far more often than once a year, or once a term, or once a month, or even once a day. Good teachers are constantly working to do their jobs better. "Better" means that they have some standards to which they compare their performance.

---

[1] Sue Bredekamp (ed.), *Accreditation Criteria and Procedures of the National Academy of Early Childhood Programs* (Washington, DC: NAEYC, 1991).

Where do the standards come from? They are established by the profession. They come from national, state, and local licensing and funding agencies. They come from state departments of education and state departments of social services, whichever may have licensing control. Standards come from a parent board in a parent cooperative, a school board in public schools, or a board of directors in a private agency. Typically, these are all minimum standards—the least you can get by with. However, good teachers aren't comfortable with minimum standards, and when you take a close look at some minimum standards you can understand why. Minimum standards really are minimal, and capable teachers want better programs for children.

Therefore, teachers who are real professionals set their own high standards for the children's programs. They work to improve their teaching every day, every month, every year. They look constantly for new ideas, new materials, new ways to help children. They read professional journals, which give them new ideas to try—new standards to achieve. They go to school, take courses, read, and study. When you are a true professional, it's your job to improve your profession.

As mentioned earlier, custodial child care, the type that gives only minimum physical care and little or no education, simply must not be allowed to exist in an affluent nation that knows how to do more and can afford to do more. Standards should rise for the sake of present and future generations of children. Teachers have a stake in raising those standards because it's their future, too. They are helping to raise the standards when they take stock and improve their own programs every day. They are helping raise standards when they willingly share their ideas with other teachers. They are helping raise standards when they help parents and other citizens recognize the components of high-quality child development center programs.

Around the country states are instituting testing criteria for teachers, trying to find some basis for selecting excellent teachers and for eliminating poor ones.

 Talk It Over

What efforts have you made this term to exceed the minimum standard required of you? Give examples. How does it make you feel?

Children

Children need evaluation of their child development centers. And children, too, evaluate. Children tell others by their behavior how the program is going. They tell you if you've selected equipment and material at the right level by the way they use that equipment and material. They are happy if everything is in pretty good balance; they're grouchy if it is not. You can tell, and parents

By observing a child closely on a regular basis you can record the child's progress.
(Cloud County Community College Child Development Laboratory)

can tell. Do children want to go to school, or does someone have to drag them? If they don't want to go, then something isn't quite up to standard. But if the children happily anticipate their arrival each day, you know that all is well.

Children need evaluations of their schools because their whole future is at stake. It is their human resources—skills and knowledge—that aren't being developed if they have a substandard, mediocre program day in and day out for all their early years. If their safety is in danger, then children do need someone to say, "Hey, this place is unsafe, you can't keep kids here." In one school, for example, a chest was placed next to the fire exit. The fire inspector demanded that it be moved. The standard and its enforcement protected children. Building human resources is the goal of education. Efforts are being made to measure the outcomes of education by means other than grades derived exclusively from paper-and-pencil tests. You will often hear the terms *competency-* and *performance-based criteria*. Under such a scheme you, as a teacher, may be judged by your performance in the classroom with children as well as by what you can say or write on paper about teaching children.

Attempts to define the desired outcomes of education for young children have been made for many years and are still being worked on throughout the country. When public monies are being spent there is increased concern that desired goals be met. Therefore, standards of performance are being set that apply to children, to teachers, and to some extent to parents.

There is a real hazard that some individuality and humanism may be lost in this evaluating process, and one should be on guard to prevent this. However, it is clear that human resources are not well developed in the substandard custodial-type child care found in some early childhood education programs. Substandard programs cannot be tolerated in a literate and rich country. Children are the world's greatest resource for the future; their potential must not be wasted.

Child development services, along with other human services, have become important consumer items for families and for society in general. When you buy something and pay good money for it, you want to be sure you get the quality you pay for. You can take back the jeans if the stitching rips. Public interest groups are forcing manufacturers to make higher-quality products. But in human services, such as in centers for nurturing and educating children, the outcomes are far more serious when quality control is lacking. You can't toss out the product and start over.

Testing Children. Tests are sometimes used to evaluate children's progress. Testing children has become a controversial topic in recent years. Some tests are ability tests, giving an IQ or intelligent quotient, which is supposed to indicate how hard or how easy learning tasks should be for a child and to predict a future level of performance. Other tests are achievement tests, measuring what the child has learned in school thus far.

Some people feel that tests are discriminatory, unjustly testing children from minority groups on concepts that are out of their range of experiences,

Evaluations of children may be done using tests; however, tests must be appropriate and administered and interpreted carefully. (University of Georgia McPhaul Children's Programs)

thus having no bearing on their ability to learn. Others feel that knowing the child's social and economic situation would tell you just as much as testing will. Testing is an uncertain part of the science of child development and child psychology. What do tests show? Tests are often invalid—not measuring what they purport to measure. Tests are often given by people who know very little about young children. As strangers they often are unable to get the children to respond adequately to show their maximum ability.

Many tests have very little long-range predictive value, as far as predicting now how the child will perform later as an adolescent or adult. One test should never be used alone as a definitive criterion for placement. If tests are used they should be used in conjunction with other tests and by individuals with long-standing experience in observing children. The more one knows about tests, the less one would want their own child placed in either an advanced or remedial class on the basis of one test.

As a teacher, you may be placed in the position of supporting tests or going along with the results of tests. You should avoid being overly confident regarding the meaning and significance of a single test score. Be sure you understand the tests and scores thoroughly. Skilled teachers with well-developed observational ability can often tell much more about a child than tests administered by strangers.

Parents, before allowing their child to be placed out of a class of normal children, should insist on several tests to see if there is a consistency of recommendations based on the tests. Tests can be given on various aspects of their child's development. In addition to achievement or ability tests, a thorough physical examination, sight and hearing tests, or balance and motor skill tests may give insights into a child's problem. Tests should be carried out by independent people who work for different agencies, to help rule out agency or school bias for one solution over another. For example, sometimes a school with extra funds in a special education fund may want to place additional children in special education. Parents should have sufficient information to help make such a decision.

When a young child enters elementary school and the authorities want to place the child in a special education program, basing their action on tests, parents often seek the advice of the child's early childhood teacher. Many parents find it overwhelming to be surrounded by high-powered psychologists with their testing instruments and scores and the teacher may offer to attend the meetings as the parents' advocate or consultant.

Parents often express hostility toward schools—especially when they find out later that errors were made in testing and placing their child.

Parents

Parents need evaluation of the schools for young children. And parents, too, evaluate—as they learn from Johnny or Mary what happens in school each day. They ask other parents about the school, too, when they meet them in the grocery or at a ball game. Parents judge how things are going by how happy or

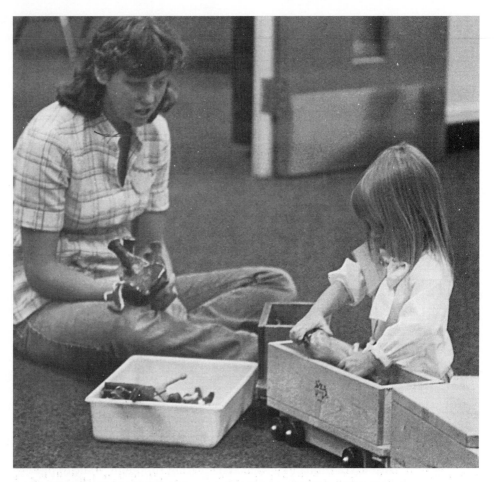

By listening to a child who is playing you can better understand their thought processes, such as how an object will fit into a space.
(South East Oakland Vocational Technical School Child Care Center)

reluctant their child is to attend. They can tell how things are going by the new ideas their children bring home, by their paintings, and by the things they see at school. Parents care about their children and are watching and listening to be sure that the school they attend has a high-quality program.

Parents need evaluation of schools for young children by outside forces because they may not understand fully what the standards ought to be. They are very trusting, sometimes believing that "you couldn't call it a school if it wasn't a good one." Parents may be misled for a while by fresh paint, bus service, and good advertising. They are sometimes desperate for a place for their child. Society should check up on the people offering child development center services and be sure that standards are being met. These, indeed, are consumer services as significant as businesses like barber shops, restaurants, and swimming pools that have been government-inspected for years.

Parents are pleased with the NAEYC Accreditation recognition. It helps them to evaluate a center and not have to rely solely on the center's own publicity for information, often given in glossy brochures that may be overstated.

Society

Society needs evaluation of child development center services. As these schools serve more and more children, their influence on future generations grows. Lots of people, professionals, researchers, philosophers, and the like, all need to keep their fingers on the early childhood school pulse. What types of people are they turning out? What values do they hold? What skills do they have? Certainly a democratic society is committed to the development of the human resources of every child. You should always remember that in a democratic society every child is expected to become an active member of the governing class. Under the democratic ideal, the responsibility for the quality of life— that is, the extent of justice, equity, general welfare, and basic human rights— rests on the shoulders of every individual. Teachers, parents, children, and society at large want child development services to be evaluated. The manager of the center is obligated to monitor quality criteria and improve on any deficiencies if standards are not met. This is called quality control. According to licensing regulations, centers that do not measure up to standard will be closed if they are not improved.

Many states, through their legislatures, have initiated tests for teachers to receive or maintain their certificates in an effort to upgrade the quality of teaching in their schools.

In using this book throughout this course, you've been given the chance to discover many of the standards of a high-quality child development center. In each chapter under the section labeled *Applications* it is suggested that you rate the center you are involved in using a 1-to-5 scale on criteria listed at the end of each chapter. If you have done these applications you have had considerable experience evaluating a center. You probably have learned that it is the little things that make a high-quality program or detract from its excellence.

In addition, you have also had an opportunity to evaluate your own performance, using the criteria listed in Chapter 1. This experience brings evaluation close to home for you. How did you feel? What did you learn? It is the type of evaluation that your instructor and future employers are obligated to perform. Society expects them to evaluate you and to be ready to verify your qualities for teaching young children. It is hoped that you have learned ways to improve and have gained confidence in your teaching ability, skills, and knowledge as a result of the evaluation process recommended throughout this book.

CONCLUSION

Evaluation is necessary for children, teachers, parents, managers, and the society to assure that high-quality educational programs are being provided for young children. As more and more young children are cared for in facilities outside the home, the government has an obligation to monitor them just as they do any consumer service.

High-quality programs for young children are services that this country can and must afford. Failure to accept the responsibility for this aspect of modern life will be far more costly. Excellent programs for young children represent investment expenditures that pay a high rate of return.

Responsibility for the future heights that the nation and the world achieve, whether humanitarian, intellectual, aesthetic, industrial, or celestial, rests squarely on the generations to come. Will even our best be good enough?

REVIEW AND APPLICATIONS

Five Characteristics of Center Evaluations

1. They show how values in the form of standards are being met.
2. They point out legal obligations of the managers of centers.
3. They are carried out by children, parents, teachers, and society.
4. They are essential if high quality is to be maintained.
5. They are nonthreatening when individuals continuously monitor their own performance.

 Observation

Complete your final draft of the case study of the one child you have been observing. Arrange an appointment with the teacher of the child to discuss your final report.

Applications

1. From the viewpoint of a child, develop a list of evaluation criteria and rate your center on a 1-to-5 scale. Discuss.
2. From the viewpoint of a parent, develop a list of evaluation criteria and rate your center on a 1-to-5 scale. Discuss.
3. From the viewpoint of a teacher, develop a list of evaluation criteria and rate your center on a 1-to-5 scale. Discuss.

4. Based on the evaluation criteria listed in Chapter 1, go over your self-evaluation with your instructor. Make constructive suggestions for your future performance. Record and reflect on suggestions your instructor makes.

ADDITIONAL RESOURCES

Suggested Film or Videotape

Head Start: How It Works   VHS or 16 mm.   Color   15 minutes 1988

The film presents evidence that Head Start produces positive, lasting effects in the lives of low-income children and their families. Provides a colorful overview of Head Start activities in seven states. Craighead Films, P.O. Box 3900, Shawnee, KS 66203.

FOR FURTHER READING

Bader, Lois. *Bader Reading and Language Inventory*. New York: Macmillan Publishing Company, 1983.

Bader, Lois and Verna Hildebrand. "An Exploratory Study of Three to Five Year Old's Responses on the Bader Reading and Language Inventory to Determine Development Stages of Emerging Literacy," *Early Childhood Development and Care*, Vol. 77, August 1992, 83–95.

Bredekamp, Sue (ed.). *Accreditation Criteria and Procedures of the National Academy of Early Childhood Programs*. Washington, DC: NAEYC, 1991.

Council for Early Childhood Professional Recognition. *Assessment System and Competency Standards: Infant/Toddler Caregivers* (Vol. 1) and *Preschool Caregivers* (Vol. 2). Washington, DC: Author, 1992.

Hildebrand, Verna. *Management of Child Development Centers*. New York: Macmillan Publishing Company, 1993.

Hildebrand, Verna. *Introduction to Early Childhood Education*. New York: Macmillan Publishing Company, 1991.

Powell, Douglas R. "Effects of Program Models and Teaching Practices," *Young Children*, 41:6, September 1986, 60–67.

Uphoff, James K. and June Gilmore. "Pupil Age at School Entrance—How Many Are Ready for Success?" *Young Children*, 41:2, January 1986, 11–16.

Zigler, Edward F. and Mary E. Lang. *Child Care Choices: Balancing the Needs of Children, Families, and Society*. New York: The Free Press, 1991.

Author Index

Subject Index

ISBN 0-02-354518-6

90000>

9 780023 545184